Undergraduates in a Second Language

Challenges and Complexities of Academic Literacy Development

Undergraduates
in a Second Language
Challenges and Complexities
of Academic Literacy Development

Ilona Leki
University of Tennessee

Lawrence Erlbaum Associates
Taylor & Francis Group

New York London

Cover design by Tomai Maridou.

Lawrence Erlbaum Associates
Taylor & Francis Group
270 Madison Avenue
New York, NY 10016

Lawrence Erlbaum Associates
Taylor & Francis Group
2 Park Square
Milton Park, Abingdon
Oxon OX14 4RN

© 2007 by Taylor & Francis Group, LLC
Lawrence Erlbaum Associates is an imprint of Taylor & Francis Group, an Informa business

Printed in the United States of America on acid-free paper
10 9 8 7 6 5 4 3 2 1

International Standard Book Number-13: 978-0-8058-5638-5 (Softcover) 978-0-8058-5637-8 (Hardcover)

Visit the Taylor & Francis Web site at
http://www.taylorandfrancis.com

and the Routledge Mental Health Web site at
http://www.routledgementalhealth.com

To my beloved and amazing Nina Leki

Contents

Preface   xi

1   Introduction   1

    Inquiry Procedures   5
    Reporting Findings   12
    Context for the Study   16

2   "You Need Really Understand":
    An Undergraduate in Engineering   19

    Background   19
    Context for Learning   24
    Professional Training:
        Engineering Education and Industry   25
    Literacy Experiences   26
    Socioacademic Relationships   47
    Special Circumstances for International Students   55
    Ideological Education   60
    Conclusion   61

3   "Don't Have Easy": Nursing in L2   63

    Background   63
    Educational Context: The Nursing Program   67
    Context Shapers   72
    The Trouble With English:
        Language and Literacy Struggles   78
    The Trouble With American Education   98
    Socioacademic Relations   102
    Special Circumstances for International Students   110

Ideological Education 115
Conclusion 119

4 "Suddenly You Get Recognized":
The Power of Community 121

Prologue to Jan 121
Background 122
Academic Portrait 123
Business School 137
Developing as a Writer 139
Socioacademic Relations 160
Special Circumstances for International/
  Immigrant Students 168
Ideological Education 172
Conclusion 174
Appendix 176

5 "Yuko Can Handle Intimidation":
Becoming a Social Worker 177

Background 177
The Social Work Major 183
Writing Development 187
The Nature and Role of Yuko's Undergraduate Writing 192
The Development of Other Social Work Skills 214
Socioacademic Relationships 216
Special Circumstances for International Students 221
Ideological Education 227
Conclusion 230

6 University Literacy 233

Writing at the University: Less Than Expected 234
Writing for General Education 237
Writing in the Major 241
Writing, Learning, and Learning to Write 248
ESL Classes 251
Writing at the University and Individual Goal Setting 255
Conclusion 257

**7 Social and Ideological Contexts
of Literacy Development**   **261**

    Social Group and Individual Identity   261
    Conclusion: Socioacademic Factors   274
    Ideological Contexts: The United States
      and the World   276
    Conclusion: Ideological Factors   280
    Conclusion   282

8 Conclusion   **283**

Appendix A: Interview Guides   **287**

**Appendix B: Main Coding Categories
for Student Interviews**   **295**

Endnotes   **299**

References   **309**

Author Index   **321**

Subject Index   **325**

Preface

This study originated in questions about my bilingual, international, and immigrant students and the English writing courses I was teaching. How useful were these courses for the students who were required to take them? What did the students carry with them from these courses to their other disciplinary courses across the curriculum? In what ways did my English as a Second Language (ESL) writing courses help second-language (L2) students even to figure out how to meet the varying literacy demands they would encounter in their undergraduate careers? What happened to my students academically once they left 1st-year ESL/writing classes? My initial goal in the 5-year-long qualitative research reported here was to answer these questions by capturing the literacy experiences of a small group of L2 students during their entire undergraduate careers. The long intensive contact with these students did answer some of my questions, provoked others, and afforded at least some understanding of their academic development as it entwined with their social experiences and identity formation and with the ideological context of studying at a U.S. university in the 1990s.

This book is written for present and future writing teachers, compositionists, writing researchers, and second-language studies professionals who share the kinds of questions I had. It is intended for both those who work with domestic students and those who teach ESL, bilingual, international, immigrant, L2, or non-native English-speaking (NNES) students. This long list of qualifiers hints at the complexities of identity inherent in the latter students' status in English-dominant countries like the United States and the difficulty of finding appropriate, adequate, and nonlimiting ways to refer to them as a group beyond their status in political terms or the stage of their English-language proficiency. The findings of this research in fact reiterate the suggestion that grouping itself is a problem.

Since the time this research project took place, the tragic events in the United States of September 11, 2001, and the disastrous U.S. response to them have intervened. Much in the world of immigrant and international students in the United States has changed. Although it would be impossible to say precisely how they would be different, I suspect the academic and personal experiences of the four students whose stories are told in these pages would not have played out in quite the same way had they taken place after 9/11. For one thing their ability to study in or immigrate to the United States may have been compromised, perhaps made impossible. By the same token, much of what seemed crucial in the 1990s, though still important now, has necessarily faded behind more insistent, far-reaching crises facing L2 studies professionals (along with many others). Events like 9/11 and its aftermath remind us, however, how vitally important it is to sympathetically know more about the world and about our students. It is my hope that this book can help contribute to the sympathy for and solidarity with those who cross multiple linguistic, cultural, and political borders.

Chapter 1 lays out methodological tactics and issues in carrying out and reporting on research of this kind. It also sets the context for the study. The next four chapters constitute the book's unique contribution to L2 and literacy studies, each chapter documenting in detail the years-long undergraduate experiences of one of the focal students. Chapter 6 returns to the questions that initiated the study, including the role and path of development of L2 literacy at the tertiary level. Chapter 7 explores some of the unanticipated findings of the study in relation to the social and the ideological context of these students' literacy development.

Portions of the data from the study reported here have been used in the following publications:

(2006) Negotiating socioacademic relations: English learners' reception by and reaction to college faculty. *Journal of English for Academic Purposes, 5*, 136–152.

(2005) Moving inside: Socioacademic relationships and institutional literacy demands in the transformation of social and literate identities. *The International Journal of Learning, 11*, 368–373.

(2003) Living through college literacy: Nursing in a second language. *Written Communication, 20*, 81–98.

(2001) "A narrow thinking system": Non-native English speaking students in group work projects across the curriculum. *TESOL Quarterly, 35*, 39–67.

(1999) "Pretty much I screwed up": Ill-served needs of a permanent resident. In L. Harklau, M. Siegal, & K. Losey (Eds.), *Generation 1.5 meets college composition: Issues in the teaching of writing to U.S.-educated learners of ESL* (pp. 17–43). Mahwah, NJ: Lawrence Erlbaum Associates.

Acknowledgments

My deepest gratitude goes to the four students who shared their lives with me for so many years, unflaggingly showed up for interviews, and patiently answered questions. My thanks as well to the faculty who willingly gave of their time to inform me of their ideas and practices and to allow me and my research assistants to attend their classes. I was extremely lucky to benefit from the talents of those research assistants over the years: Shannon Carpenter, Susan North, Jennifer Worth, and most especially my brilliant ex-student Leslie LaChance. The Department of English was most generous in supporting this research and my thanks go to Allen Carroll, Mary Papke, and John Zomchick for helping to make this work materially possible, as did a grant from the National Council of Teachers of English. It is always rewarding and a pleasure to work with Erlbaum personnel; thank you to Sondra Guideman, Lori Kelly, Erica Kica, and Joy Tatusko for their help in the final stages of this publication, and especially Naomi Silverman, who has become a professional colleague and friend to so many of us in the world of second-language writing. I deeply appreciate her calm and sensible temperament and her perceptive intelligence and am proud we have been fellow travelers. Linda Blanton, Chris Casanave, Ann John, and Stephanie Vandrick's detailed and supportive reading of and astute suggestions on earlier drafts of the manuscript have made this version more worthy of them. Thank you to my gifted and cherished friend Kirsten Benson, for her gentle, insightful commentary. And to you, my Kenny, for your endless patience in listening to me talk about this project, your excellent advice, your encouragement, and your fervent faith that some day the project would finally be finished—"Thanks, thanks, and ever thanks again."

1

Introduction

Since the early 1990s, research into second-language (L2) academic literacy has moved increasingly toward qualitative research methodologies that allow for more detailed descriptions of student writers as people and at the same time require those descriptions to be set in a broadened context of when, where, and how their writing takes place. These studies have helped us understand something of the complex, sometimes hidden, often unpredictable processes that student writers experience as they gradually develop academic literacy, that is, membership in communities of academic readers and writers. Of particular value in this body of work is the orientation beyond 1st-year writing classes toward other academic disciplines and toward acknowledgment and examination of the role college courses other than English courses play in the initiation of students into academic disciplinary communities. Although the number of such reports is relatively small, it has been growing for both native English-speaking (NES) students (Berkenkotter, Huckin, & Ackerman, 1988; Carroll, 2002; Chiseri-Strater, 1991; Faigley & Hansen, 1985; Flower et al., 1990; Haas, 1994; Herrington, 1985; Herrington & Curtis 2000; Herrington & Moran, 1992; McCarthy, 1987; J. Nelson, 1990; Sternglass, 1997; Walvoord & McCarthy, 1990; Wolcott, 1994) and non-native English-speaking (NNES) student writers (Adamson, 1993; Casanave, 1992, 1995; Currie, 1993; Fu, 1995; Harklau, 1994, 2000; Leki, 1995a, 1999, 2001, 2003a; Leki & Carson, 1994, 1997; Losey, 1997; Prior, 1991, 1998; Riazi, 1997; Spack, 1997). Many of these reports have been an inspiration, particularly in what they reveal about student literacy life at the tertiary level and, more specifically, about how these students cope with the literacy demands they encounter in their other courses across the curriculum.

The first detailed book-length study with which I became familiar was Chiseri-Strater's (1991) revealing exploration of the literacy experiences of two NES undergraduates in English and other classes. Then in Sternglass (1997), we saw L1 English and a few L2 students who were perhaps at risk of not succeeding in college because of their difficulties with reading and writing but who in fact did succeed eventually. Sternglass made the argument that students with literacy difficulties should nevertheless be given the chance and, especially, the time to develop these skills by not being denied access to college. This is an argument that is supported by Carroll's (2002) research on L1 English students who were not underprepared but whose most profound development as writers took place only *after* their 1st-year writing classes, gradually, within the context of their majors. Carroll makes the point that even after they became successful writers within their majors, those who had had difficulty writing in English-class genres continued to have that difficulty; in other words, the link between general writing courses and writing needs across the curriculum is tenuous, a point made strongly in L1 research by Russell (1991) as well. In research focused on L2 students, Spack (1997) traced the variety of sources that fueled an L2 student's literacy development, including her L1 literacy and reading of popular literature in her second language, English. In Prior (1991), we watch jointly constructed texts develop through complex diglossic interplay between the authors, their peers, and their teachers. Blanton's (2005) account documents the nearly insurmountable problems created for two L2 college writers by interrupted and stunted literacy development in L1 and later in L2.

In reading reports of this extremely valuable type of research done by writing specialists, I have nevertheless come to be struck by how constricted the view of the students and of the students' experiences has been. Even in qualitative research studies that do try to look at context, that context has often been defined rather narrowly as the context of various writing assignments (some in writing classes, some in other courses across the curriculum), the previous or current writing the students did for one course or another. Each of these studies has added tremendously to our understanding of literacy development among undergraduates, but given that they were all intended to shed light primarily on the development of writing skills, their relentless focus on writing gives the impression that between writing assignments, nothing was happening in these students' academic lives. Furthermore, the students themselves are often portrayed as though they too had these writing assignments continuously foremost in their minds and memories.

Similarly, because the initial goal of my own study was also literacy, interviews with my research participants during the 1st year of the study were devoted almost entirely to questions on the nature of the reading and writing assignments the students were dealing with. By some time during the 2nd year, however, it became clear that their literacy experiences were so embedded in personal, social, and other academic experiences that however much I would try to draw the research participants into talking about writing, their answers to questions about writing were much less engaged than their answers to questions about other aspects of their academic experiences. That is, they themselves were much more interested in other aspects of their lives than they were in their writing.

My focus in this book, however, cannot be to try to tell these students' complete life stories for the 3 to 5 years that I worked with them, first, because I did not have access to everything about their lives and, second, because it is obviously not possible to do such a thing in any case. My focus, then, has to be narrowed, as has the focus of other books of this type; but I came to realize that narrowing the focus solely to these students' struggles with academic literacy tasks greatly distorted the value the students themselves placed on those experiences—overestimating their importance in their lives at the expense of other concerns, issues, and interests. Furthermore, such a narrowing would be untrue to the very social nature of some of those literacy experiences.

So the focus during the 2nd year of the study expanded to include as much about my participants' academic experiences beyond reading and particularly beyond writing as I could manage to gather. Both the institutional nature of the students' experiences (i.e., the course and curricular requirements they had to meet) and the social nature of these students' literacy experiences (their relationships with their teachers and especially with other students) became increasingly evident and compelling. Prior's (1998) research clearly demonstrates the degree to which the texts his research participants produced were heteroglossic, that is, created with and existing as strands of thought and language reflecting the contribution of teachers and peers. The studies presented here extend the view of that heteroglossia to issues beyond text and beyond language to include a still broader frame.

By academic literacy I mean the activity of interpretation and production of academic and discipline-based texts (or as Street, 1984, puts it, "shorthand for the social practices of reading and writing," p. 1). Other kinds of literacy, such as image, sound, computer, or other literacies referenced by such researchers as the New London Group, were not particularly prominent features of these students' academic environment during the 1990s. However, literacy as used here is not limited to the technology of reading and writing, a unitary skill, or a strictly cognitive activity but, rather, includes the interpretation and production of a variety of texts often within important social contexts, such as group-work projects or writing center assistance, and variable reliance on a wealth of previous experience with text. Furthermore, the meaning of academic literacy was not uncontested by the students themselves as they sometimes resisted literacy activities or brought competing views of literacy to academic arenas in which they sometimes struggled.

My interest in L2 students' literacy development began in writing classrooms. I take seriously the concern that L2 writing courses not construct themselves as mere service courses, nothing more than staging areas before the real work of college literacy, striving only to train students to accommodate themselves to the demands of others in their courses and in this country. Nevertheless, like many other writing teachers, I also take seriously the responsibility heaved on us by the institutional demand that all undergraduate students take 1st-year writing courses. The students in these writing courses have the right to expect that their work in the writing courses will somehow contribute to their academic success (Silva, 1997).

Do the writing courses in fact do this? Certainly most writing teachers and researchers believe or assert that they do, despite the difficulty of showing a clear correlation between such complex concepts as writing improvement and writing instruction (see Leki, 2003a). Many students, on the other hand, often do not see the point of 1st-year writing courses, ubiquitous in U.S. higher education; others, perhaps especially visa or overseas students, do not feel they can afford the time. Most telling of all, some manage to circumvent regulations requiring that they take these writing courses in their 1st year—ostensibly to prepare them for writing they will do in their other courses—and avoid writing courses until later in their academic careers, often succeeding perfectly well in those other courses without the touted benefit of the writing course. If these writing courses are so beneficial in improving student writing and if writing is so crucial to academic success, why has this news not penetrated through to the student grapevine and resulted in students flocking to the courses rather than avoiding them?

Assuming that students do learn something about writing in our writing classes, the next question concerns the degree to which they can transfer that information or those skills or even those predispositions to courses across the curriculum or other writing contexts, because in the end whether students write well (however that may be defined by programs and individual teachers) for us in our English classes is irrelevant. This research, then, was originally intended to investigate just how the writing courses articulated with writing demands across the curriculum for students like mine, ones for whom English was a second or third or fourth language. It grew, however, as qualitative research projects tend to do, into a broader picture of what the academic side of college life was like for the four students in the study.

INQUIRY PROCEDURES

The research design consisted of two phases. In the first phase in fall of 1994, all new L2 undergraduates in entry-level ESL writing classes (credit bearing) were asked to respond to a survey intended in part to identify those who were concurrently enrolled in courses across the disciplines that required writing. My research assistant and I conducted qualitative interviews with all students who agreed to talk about their writing in those courses. Three sets of interviews took place in the middle of the first semester, at the end of the first semester, and at the end of the second semester of these students' studies, and focused on writing demands and experiences across the curriculum and writing requirements and instruction in the writing courses. Partial results of this phase of the research have been reported elsewhere (Leki & Carson, 1997). From among the 30 or so students who participated in this first phase, 3 first-year and 1 sophomore NNES students who expected to continue to have writing in their disciplinary courses in subsequent years expressed interest in participating in the second phase, long-term case studies to trace their academic literacy development over the following 3 years, or until they graduated.

The data collected for this second phase of the project consists primarily of the following:

- In-depth, qualitative, semistructured interviews (Denzin, 1989; Taylor & Bogdan, 1984) with each of the four students as close to every other week as possible, focusing on their perceptions of the work they were required to do in their courses across the disciplines and on the resources they had or developed in attempting to meet those requirements. The interviews lasted between half an hour and an hour, except for end-of-term interviews, which lasted somewhat longer, up to 2 hours. Interviews were conducted by either my research assistant or me, depending on whose schedule best matched the students', which varied from term to term. All interviews were then fully transcribed by either my research assistance or me. (See the Appendix for sample interview guides.)
- E-mail contact with the students as needed.
- Examination of documentation related to these four students' course work, for example, syllabuses, class texts, writing assignments, drafts of papers, copies of exams, and other kinds of course and curricular announcements.
- Nonparticipant observation (by either my research assistant or me, depending on whose schedule matched) of selected classes in which the students were enrolled, particularly those that included a substantial writing component.

- Interviews with the instructors of all courses that required evaluated writing.
- Transcribed recordings of selected writing center sessions.
- End-of-term debriefing interviews with each of my research assistants, whose identities changed more or less each year.
- Collection of weekly journal entries in which participants maintained an on-going commentary on their work during the semester and their responses to it.[1]

These varying sources of information, in addition to reviews of literature in both L1 and L2 writing research, reflect the qualitative researcher's work as *bricoleur* (Denzin & Lincoln, 1994) and are intended to ensure data source and methodological triangulation (Denzin, 1989).

Research Questions

Again, as in much qualitative research, the original primary research questions here were maximally open-ended:

1. How do NNES students experience and respond to the literacy demands of an undergraduate course of study in an English-medium university?
2. How and how well did their experiences in their English-language and writing classes help them in meeting literacy demands across the disciplines?
3. How do these students become initiated into the specific discourse of their disciplines?

Within this framework, more detailed research objectives included exploration of the following issues:

General education:

- How these students perceived the role of reading and writing within a variety of academic disciplines.
- How faculty within these academic disciplines defined the role of reading and writing.
- How writing and reading were used to initiate students into different disciplines.
- How students and faculty represented the same academic tasks.
- How much students were able to draw upon previous work in English and writing classes to accomplish literacy tasks across the disciplines.
- How the students' academic literacy developed through exposure to a variety of disciplines.

The students' majors:

- How the students were acculturated/initiated into their majors.
- How their perception of their majors changed over time.
- How reading and writing functioned in course work in their majors.
- How reading and writing functioned beyond the classroom within their major fields (i.e., among disciplinary professionals).

During the 1st year of the interviews, it soon became clear that a major feature of these students' academic lives was group-work projects of two kinds: those officially assigned in their courses and spontaneous informal group work. Interacting with these people as often as we did also created curiosity about other features of their lives, which the participants talked about freely, such as their social lives, their contacts with family, and simply their daily routines. Thus questions in all these areas were added to the regular interview guide.

Although the intention was that all the questions on the interview guide should be covered in some form at each interview, I wanted the interviews to remain as conversational as possible so that the students would bring up issues of importance to them that I could not have anticipated. For the participants there were basically four types of written interview guides:

- Beginning of the year, in which participants were asked to talk about their summer experiences and their expectations for the coming term.
- Regular interview guides covering the issues related to the research questions.
- End-of-term interview guides focusing on final exams and looking back over the semester.
- Graduation interviews, in which the students were asked to reflect on their entire academic experience.

The questions on particular guides shifted to take into account comments the participants had made in the previous interviews.

Except for minor additions and adjustments, the interview questions for faculty and for my debriefing of research assistants remained more stable over time. The faculty interviews in particular were scripted so as to make efficient use of professors' time. In all 58 faculty members were interviewed. Samples of the various interview guides appear in the Appendix.

Data Analysis

Data analysis was carried out through a form of analytic induction (Goetz & LeCompte, 1984), in keeping with qualitative research methodology, which "involves scanning the data for categories of phenomena and for relationships among such categories" (Goetz & LeCompte, 1984, p. 180), examining the data "for meaningful themes, issues, or variables, to discover how these are patterned, and to attempt to explain the patterns" (Johnson, 1992, p. 90), and reiteratively comparing data collected over time and across data types (e.g., interview data with published research data). The transcribed interviews and other sources of documentation (e.g., student papers) were thus recursively read and examined in an attempt to get at salient themes both within the boundaries of the research objectives and departing from them where appropriate (to include, e.g., information about other aspects of the participants' lives that they deemed important enough to mention in the interviews). Data analysis was intended to be "an inductive, data-led activity" (Coffey & Atkinson, 1996, p. 10) leading to "richly detailed narratives of personal experiences" (p. 145). Within this framework, three interpretive strategies were employed: "direct interpretation of the individual instance" (Stake, 1995, p. 74) (i.e., attempting to interpret single events of particular salience, "epiphanies," in Denzin's, 1994, terms); categorical aggregation (i.e., collecting instances of the same event or behavior to interpret); and formation of thematic coding categories based on the research objectives and on any other salient thematic strings that arose.

As is typical in qualitative research, although the research questions and objectives guided the data collection and analysis process, some of the research objectives shifted over the research period and the interview guide changed periodically to accommodate newly emerging themes or areas of interest as they arose from previous interviews.

Furthermore, this research was neither strictly phenomenological nor social constructivist (Denzin & Lincoln, 1994). That is, though I was interested in capturing these students' experiences on their own terms, I was specifically interested in their academic literacy experiences; therefore, in analyzing the data, rather than detailing only the research participants' emic perspectives and limiting this report to the themes that were the most salient for them, I elected to also elaborate certain themes that will be, I believe, of most use and interest to writing teacher/researchers. In other words, the themes that I saw in the data were only partly the themes that the students would have pointed to as most expressive of their experiences; other themes were ones I imposed through the interview questions and the analytic focus, and ones that I then selected to report here. This point carries special significance because, as noted earlier, in fact the student informants were often less inspired by academic literacy development issues than they were by other aspects of their experiences. For example, although always cooperative, the participants appeared to find little interest in discussing their English writing classes in the years that followed the completion of those requirements. This theme would then not be particularly salient for them. For us writing researchers and practitioners, however, I believe what they say and what they do not say about their English courses is telling. Nevertheless, in elaborating on the selected themes, I have attempted to remain as true as I knew how to be to the emic perspective of the study participants.

But I have no illusions about providing transparent access to real experience. Rather, what the students told me and my research assistants, what I learned from interviews with their professors, what I saw and noted in my field notes, what influence the professional literature exerted on me that day, or how I remembered and reacted to rereading sets of interviews from one or the other participant, all of these and many other factors served as reality filters.

A list of all the themes coded from the students' interview transcripts is included in the Appendix. From that complete list, the primary themes explored and reported on in the four case study chapters follow. The selection of these themes was based on their pertinence to the research questions, the students' experiences, and/or (what I deemed to be) the interests of academic literacy professionals:

Academic Issues:

- Professional training.
- Writing/reading.
- Written feedback.
- Writing center.
- Role of English class.

Social Issues:

- Socioacademic relationships with peers.
- Group work.
- Socioacademic relations with teachers.
- Teachers' comments on L2 students.
- Special circumstances for L2 students.

Ideological Issues:

- Ideological promotion of capitalism and U.S. values and practices.

In all, the academic, social, and other life experiences reported here offer, I believe, a rare opportunity to witness something of the academic lives of English L2 learners as they unfolded outside the English classroom within one English-medium postsecondary institution. The central concern here, as with all qualitative research, has been "to capture the complexities of the social worlds we seek to understand" (Coffey & Atkinson, 1996, p. 3). Although the social worlds of the participants in this research will be different from those of other L2 students, as indeed they were quite a bit from each other, they are provocative examples of the kinds of worlds our students live through.

Qualitative Research Issues

In the last several years, consumers and writers of research reports have called for greater public acknowledgment of the messiness of research generally, challenging both qualitative and quantitative research to own up to its constructed, and not straightforwardly reflective, nature (Block, 1995, 1998, 2000; Cox & Assis-Peterson, 1999; Freeman, 1996; Holstein & Gubrium, 1995). For this study, one aspect of this messiness arises from my decision not to include as part of the study the English classes these student participants were enrolled in at the beginning of their academic careers.[2] Although the students were questioned generally about the role of their English classes in their academic literacy development, my role as director of ESL in my department made me reluctant to learn from the student interviews about the specific practices of teachers under my direction for fear of intimidating the teachers or making them feel uncomfortable knowing that students in their classes were discussing those classes with the director of the program. Thus, although their English courses may (or may not) have been an important area of student academic development, information about specific experiences in specific English courses at this university was not solicited while the students were enrolled in those classes, though they sometimes volunteered information or opinions on their English courses. Once they completed those courses, however, we did question the focal students generally each term about their experiences both in ESL classes and in their English classes before coming to the United States but without asking about specific courses.

Each time I begin to write a report of a qualitative research study I have done, I am awed by two perceptions. The first is the overwhelming volume of data that accumulates from this type of study—crate after crate of files filled with student writing, interview transcripts from students, teachers, and research assistants, documents collected from courses the students have taken, xeroxed articles by other researchers illuminating facets of the study. The original manuscript was more than twice as long as the one which became this book. But the second is much more humbling. It is the realization that despite all the data collected, I will never have the opportunity to communicate to a reader all that I might tell of what I have seen, heard, and read in relation to the students in this study and the events that occurred in their academic lives; no reader would have the patience to take it all in.

Furthermore, I am fully and painfully aware that no matter how much I think I have seen, heard, and understood about these students, this does not represent all of their stories, which are, always and inevitably, still more complex, more interwoven with the many other factors in a human life, and more opaque to comprehension and interpretation. Nevertheless, the opportunity to see and try to understand portions of these students' academic lives has been invaluable to me, opening a window to a view of the experiences of the students I teach that I had never seen before and that now informs my every interaction with them.

That said, it is also frustrating to realize, as Lincoln and Guba (1985) remark in reference to case studies, that "by the time the case is written and produced, it is out of date" (p. 215). And perhaps even more worrisome, I realize that a highly descriptive study of the type presented here is likely to provoke contradictory responses—one (if I am lucky) perhaps referring to the richness of detail, the other irritated by features of the reporting that might seem almost novelistic. But again, as Lincoln and Guba note:

> It may read like a novel but it does so for the same reasons that novels read like novels—in order to make clear the complexities of the context and the ways these interact to form whatever it is that the case report portrays. (p. 214)

On the other hand, Newkirk (1992) expresses the opinion that case studies that "work" (i.e., that are satisfying) document transformations; they give pleasure because they activate readers' recall of some implicit cultural narrative or myth and in that sense are "profoundly conservative and conventional" (p. 136). But the case studies reported here fail in that regard; they are much more like 4 years taken out of any person's life than they are tales with beginnings, transformations, and endings. Only for one of the students, Jan, did there appear to be something approaching an actual transformation from a frightened student doing everything necessary to survive to someone with enough self-confidence to begin to depend on his own strengths and interests rather than trickery to move himself forward in a world that was finally becoming legitimate to him. The stories of the other three students were not grand narratives, and in this I think they reflect the normal lives of most people over a 4-year span, ups and downs, problems encountered and sometimes solved, sometimes waited out, and sometimes ongoing, and a gradual movement as students toward greater academic proficiency that is only to be expected. Understandings sometimes coalesced and then faded away. These people learned, but in the way suggested by Wenger (1998), where learning "is as much a part of our human nature as eating or sleeping, … inevitable" (p. 3). Learning was also, for each of these students in different ways, a fundamentally social process. The interest for readers then is not in the grand narrative but, I hope, in the details, the side alleys that here and there may serve to illuminate our understanding of the kinds of experiences L2 students may encounter in their undergraduate lives.

Research participants

The participants in the study then were four bilingual undergraduate students. They were, with their pseudonyms:

- Ben, a 22-year-old immigrant student from the People's Republic of China (PRC) majoring in engineering (Ben was the one sophomore).
- Yang, a 36-year-old visa student, a woman from the PRC majoring in nursing.
- Jan, a 19-year-old U.S. permanent resident from Poland majoring in a variety of subjects over the years of the study but finally settling on business.
- Yuko, a 26-year-old Japanese woman on a visa majoring in social work.

There were thus two permanent residents, two visa students; two males, two females; aged 19 to 36 when they first enrolled at the university; from Japan, Poland, and the PRC; studying nursing, engineering, social work, and business.[3] The participants all signed human-subject research consent forms each fall. My aim in the main body of this book has been to give the floor as much as possible to these students; the focus is substantially on their words, thoughts, and experiences.

REPORTING FINDINGS

The Case Studies

In Wolcott's (1994) terms, the "transformation" of the data (i.e., the strategy used to interpret it) in chapters 2 through 5 of the book is primarily "descriptive" or narrative, providing detailed portraits of the student participants and their academic lives during the time they participated in this study. Each of these chapters begins by setting each student in her or his own personal historical context. But the data transformation frequently shifts back and forth even in these chapters between descriptive and "analytical,"[4] between data and ideas, identifying key relationships and major events of importance in the students' lives and including data on the study's salient themes (see later discussion). Because each student had different experiences and differing academic demands, the salient themes are not necessarily the same for each student, and neither is the amount of space given to each theme.

In order to leave maximum room for these students' voices and experiences, however, I have kept to a minimum outside scholarly references in these chapters, saving most of them for the more interpretive chapters. In addition, I have tried to resist the temptation to reduce these individual students and their stories to exemplars of a small number of distinct concepts pertinent to language or literacy acquisition, immigrant or international student experiences, or any other principles. I hoped instead to maintain as far as possible the complexity, fluidity, and fuzziness inherent in people's lived experiences, expressed in the student interviews, and observed in the other data collected. As a result, it should not be possible to come away from these narratives with the idea that each case carries some single identifiable meaning or even several meanings. Although this choice makes it more difficult for readers to come away from the narratives with "the point," it helps the narratives remain somewhat truer to the students' experiences.

Literacy, Socioacademic Relationships, and Ideology

Chapters 6 and 7 expand on the selected and the recurrent themes in the students' interviews and in the class observations, centering on university literacy (chap. 6), socioacademic relationships, subject positioning/identity construction, and ideological indoctrination or issues related to the portrayal in these students' classes of the United States and capitalism (chap. 7). Breaking with traditional research report genres, I have chosen to delay discussion of the interpretive or theoretical framework that informed analysis of these themes. The reason for the anomaly is, nevertheless, in keeping with qualitative research assumptions that analysis will be a "data-led activity" (Coffey & Atkinson, 1996, p. 10). The qualitative researcher seeks to "to locate [the data] in explanatory or interpretive frameworks" (p. 156). But those frameworks in an important sense cannot be known before the data is processed descriptively and analytically. It was often *as* these themes recurred in the data, not before, that it became necessary to consider the theoretical frame that would inform interpretation (i.e., both analysis and interpretation in Wolcott's, 1994, terms) of the themes. Hence, rather than appearing before the narrative of the students' experiences, frameworks for interpretation of the experiences in focus are discussed after the data that suggested them.

Interpretation of the themes in chapters 6 and 7 attempts to connect the data to broader concerns or, as Coffey and Atkinson (1996) put it, to "enable the analyst to transcend the local settings of his or her primary data collection in order to *generalize* [italics added] to a wider range of social domains" (p. 144) because "what is characteristic of much qualitative research really calls for ways of generating new ideas" (p. 156). As Coffey and Atkinson are at pains to point out, the generalization of which they speak is not generalization to other populations, typical of quantitative inquiry, but rather generalization to "theoretical ideas about social processes and cultural forms that have relevance beyond those data themselves" (p. 163). Interpretation of the research data reported here draws on previous research data on the development of writing proficiency among undergraduates and on theoretical formulations of literacy and learning that emphasize the social relationships, identity construction, and ideological context in which learning and human interactions are embedded.

A word about social relationships: I have used the term *socioacademic relationships,* discussed in chapter 7, to refer to a category of social interaction with peers and with faculty that proved to be critical to the students' sense of satisfaction with their educational work and sometimes even to the possibility of doing that work. These relationships were not friendships because the participants did not spend off-school hours with their socioacademic relations even in the case of the closest working relationships. But for these students, having socioacademic relationships, particularly with domestic peers, meant not passing anonymously and alone through the academic world. Good socioacademic relationships facilitated the students' academic lives in a variety of ways, and the students worked diligently on the establishment and regulation of these relationships with both peers and faculty. The nature of the socioacademic relationships they developed had important implications for the subject positions that were made available to the students in their classes and within their many group-work projects.

Finally, in my field notes and other places, I coded certain events as "indoctrination." What I intended there was to capture references, usually made in classes, to a system of shared assumptions (or of comments that served to inculcate into students shared assumptions) about, in particular, the United States, its position in relation to other countries, its practices in relation to those of other countries, practices and values in the rest of the world, capitalism and its logic, and other issues of this type that would implicitly represent the ideological views of the speaker (for the most part teachers, occasionally students). These episodes were a particularly significant feature of the focal students' experiences in their classes because of their potential to implicitly privilege certain groups, those designated as "Us," with the United States as reference point and norm, and cast the non-U.S. world, of which the focal students were obviously representative, as the Other, and less valuable. Because this type of indoctrination through ideologically charged comments reproduced in the classrooms usually went unchallenged, the students were left to decide how to align themselves in relation to this Othering.

Researcher Stance

As Denzin (1994) notes, "The age of a putative value-free social science appears to be over" (p. 501). Although this study is not an ethnography, it nevertheless shares elements, I believe, with Quantz's (1992) description of the aims of critical ethnography as an attempt "to represent the 'culture,' the 'consciousness,' or the 'lived experiences' of people living in asymmetrical power relations ... [and to promote] emancipatory and democratic goals" (pp. 448–449). Similarly, in Pennycook's (2001) discussion of engaged research with a critical applied linguistics orientation, he notes four characterizing elements:

- Engaging with difference and opposing essentialism.
- Working with participants' interests, desires, and lives.
- A focus on the workings of power.
- Orientation toward transformative goals. (p. 161)

The importance of a commitment to these elements became particularly evident to me in moments when power differentials became noticeable, such as when the students' interests and desires came up against those of their institutional settings or when unexamined assumptions about U.S. practices and values were reproduced in classes. In analyzing, interpreting, and reporting on the data of the study, I hoped to be able to lay claim to operating within this growing tradition.

In keeping with that hope, I acknowledge as well my own privileged position. As Quantz (1992) puts it:

The researcher's insinuation into the social reality of a disempowered[5] group is itself an act of power/knowledge and the academic authoring of ethnographic description is wrought with contradictions that claim projections of emancipation while alienating people from their own cultural descriptions. (p. 475)

At the same time, as Sullivan and Porter (1997) argue, qualitative research can be seen as a form of advocacy, as words speaking *for* the disempowered group, not "instead of" but in support of, and in this sense may hope to achieve a measure of catalytic validity (Lather, 1991; Pennycook, 2001), a kind of emancipatory washback effect for students like these.

In addition to acknowledging a privileged position, I also claim a committed rather than neutral one. Thus, I admit to responding with emotion and without impartiality to numerous events I witnessed or heard about, as related, for example, to essentializing attitudes toward cultures and peoples. My commitment to social justice also underlies a generally negative response to capitalism as it plays out in the United States (e.g., consumerism, antilabor attitudes) and to smug self-satisfaction with regard to U.S. political, economic, and cultural hegemony. I have not tried to disguise this positionality in reporting the research here.

CONTEXT FOR THE STUDY

In research of this kind, it is important to have some understanding of the background against which events and experiences occurred. The context is of particular interest here because of the eventual significance that socioacademic relations held for the participants in the study.

The school where this study took place is a large land grant university of about 25,000 students that enrolled approximately 4% international students at the time of the study. Somewhere between 30% and 40% of the domestic students, drawn primarily from the state itself rather than from outside the state, were first-generation college attendees, many of whom had had little experience outside the region, much less in countries abroad, where they might otherwise have developed a firsthand, personal understanding of what international students and other non-native speakers cope with in foreign countries. The campus is semiurban, that is, one that is interlaced with town roads and traffic but that is still separated off sufficiently from regular town affairs to maintain something of a campus feel.

Located in the foothills of the Appalachian Mountains, the town itself, with about 380,000 inhabitants in the metropolitan area, has a rather conservative, quite racially homogeneous population mainly in service, small business, a bit of manufacturing, and public sector employment. Although the predominantly White students express pride in aspects of their heritage, many have also internalized the prevailing national negative stereotypes of and prejudices against people from the Appalachian and upper South regions, their culture, their accents, their intelligence.[6] About 12% of the town population is African American; at the time of this study, the university itself enrolled only about 5% African American students despite stated efforts by university officials to recruit more. The immigrant population in this town, though growing, is also small. This lack of diversity means first that international students stand out in the general public and second that they are likely to find little or no community outside the university. After their 1st year or so, three of the four participants in this study moved out of dorms and into apartments near campus, as do most other students. Only Yang and her family remained in university housing during her entire education, surrounded by Chinese-speaking international student neighbors.

It was in this setting then that each of the students navigated an undergraduate education in English. Their experiences began in hope and ended in success. But along the way the stories are intricate and, I believe, have a great deal to tell us about undergraduate education, the special circumstances of L2 students in academic settings, the positive and negative forces, interactions, and relationships that may confront our L2 students after they leave our ESL classes, and the challenges and complexities of academic literacy development in a second language.

2

"You Need Really Understand": An Undergraduate in Engineering

BACKGROUND

Ben was already in his sophomore year when this study began and already a declared engineering major. Although he never said so directly, he seemed to be willing to participate in and then continue with the research project over the years mainly because he liked his English teacher (who recruited him for the project) and was happy to be able to be helpful. An amiable, easygoing fellow, he was somewhat heavy-set, with a soft and slow manner enhanced by an unusual lilt in his English intonation, one that gave the impression that he was fully engaged in his conversations in a thoughtful, friendly, and forthcoming way. In his classes he was not really noticeable, sitting somewhere slightly to one side a few rows back, never asking questions, more or less lost in the crowd of students. Even as late as the end of his junior year, he felt that most of his major professors probably did not know who he was, a fact that he stated matter-of-factly, without any resentment, in his usual mild manner.

Ben had moved to the United States from the PRC at about age 17, joining his parents and younger sister, who had preceded him by a few years and had secured green cards, allowing them to become permanent U.S. residents; Ben's own immigration status was to become a significant problem during the time he participated in this study. His father was a physicist at a laboratory in New York and his mother, who had been a mathematics teacher in China but whose English was minimal, apparently did not work outside the home, consequently finding herself homesick and bored.

Academic Portrait

Language and Literacy Background.   Ben had studied English primarily in middle and high school in the PRC for 6 or 7 years, but as is often the case, when he arrived in the United States, he found oral communication so difficult that he described the experience as similar to being deaf, as conversations among hearing folk went on around him. Nevertheless, his excellent training from the PRC in math and in Chinese history drew the favorable attention of some of his U.S. high school teachers. In fact, he was asked by the history teacher to serve as his assistant. Ben described his experiences both in his English classes and in his ESL classes in high school as quite positive, allowing him to "really communicate" with his high school classmates in the English class through required journal entries that students shared with each other.

When Ben entered the university, he would have wanted to be a history or a math major, but he deemed both of these possibilities unrealistic in his new life in the United States, the first because of the great obstacle language would pose, the second because of the difficulty he perceived of finding work with a degree in math. Still, his obvious talent for and interest in these two areas continued to emerge and serve him well throughout his college career.

Ben declared an engineering major from his 1st year and entered a program with considerable reputation, particularly among international students. In fact, the School of Engineering had so many international enrollments that some years ago, the administration made a conscious decision to limit international enrollment to no more than 10% so as to assure a spot in the program for in-state students whom this land grant university is chartered to serve and who, because of less impressive records than some of the international students, perhaps were less competitive in the admissions process. Ben's area of specialization was chemical engineering, one of the more demanding programs, and included courses with heavy theoretical content such as quantum mechanics, as well as courses in higher math and physical chemistry.

As a college student, Ben sometimes did very well and sometimes did not. His grade point average (GPA) declined steadily throughout his college career. After his 1st year, he had nearly an A average, but he completed college with a GPA of about C+. He took full loads (between 15 and 18 hours) every semester, including during two summers.

As his interest in history might suggest, Ben enjoyed reading in both Chinese and English but felt much less enthusiastic about writing. He learned to write in Chinese in the traditional way, that is, first through repeated practice of writing out Chinese characters, a hundred to a page, until they were perfectly drawn. However, once this necessary preliminary groundwork had been laid, he described with quiet relish the many stories the children wrote in grade school and his classmates' reactions as the children read them aloud to each other. His were apparently often funny, and self-deprecating, sometimes autobiographical (about coming home after only a couple of hours as a little tyke at his first day in school because he happily mistook a recess for the end of the school day), sometimes fanciful (about how to keep a cat from hearing what you say by tying its ears down!).

By the time he got to college, writing had become either a necessary, though mild, evil or somewhat irrelevant. The journal in his ESL writing class, for example, became something of a burden because of the number of entries required weekly. In his other classes, writing served in general either to test his knowledge (e.g., in one of his history classes) or as the final, almost meaningless, step in engineering research projects. For Ben, the excitement occurred doing the experiments, thinking up creative solutions to the engineering problem, working with new equipment, and deciding on rationales for experimental procedures. Writing up these experiments, then, was merely a boring matter of transcribing the experience into written words. When asked whether writing ever gave him pleasure, Ben answered:

> Ben: For writing? No, I wouldn't say. I wouldn't consider myself that … I really enjoy reading more than writing. … The idea in those papers most of the time is I have to [write them]. It's not just I enjoy … . (second-term junior)

The Believing Game.   But then Ben was not one to complain. In most of what he reported during interviews in this study, Ben rarely complained about anything. He played a believing game, always seeming to look for the rationale behind whatever he was required to do in college and, once he understood it, to find it reasonable and beneficial. We get some insight into Ben's placid acceptance of various school requirements from a comment he made in response to a question about his expectations for the courses he had taken one term. He said he had had no expectations for these courses because he had not chosen any of them voluntarily. Rather, they were all required courses and, as he said:

> Ben: All these classes I had to take. ... If you have like free choice, then you wanna know what kind of class you gonna take. You expect to learn something here. If you have to take something, it's just there. (second-term junior)

Ben's ready acceptance of the specifics of his college career was perhaps in part the result of his not having chosen that career path for himself but rather having had it thrust on him as a reasonable possibility for a decent professional life, given that his first choices, history and math, were deemed improbable. Nevertheless, even in courses (and a career path) that were "just there," Ben had faith in learning. Questioned about what advice he would give to someone about writing lab reports in engineering, Ben replied in what would be his refrain throughout the interviews:

> Ben: First of all, you need really understand the procedures, and while doing the lab, you must follow the procedures because that will make your accuracy on the lab result. (first-term junior)

Central to Ben's sense of his own education was the value he placed on understanding. His purpose and intention when he did problem sets, experiments, or lab reports were to establish to his own satisfaction that he understood fully the bases for the work he was doing.

Ben's expression "really understand" seemed to faithfully echo one engineering professor's characterization of engineering education generally not as exposing students to facts but as developing "concepts" in students. As another faculty member explained:

> Professor W: We learn how to multiply ratios and so on; we probably never really need those particular things per se, but don't we put them together to solve something? And so all the things they learned before are little pieces of building blocks that allow them to do the real fancy stuff. Which, by itself, does not correspond to any particular subject matter, but you have to have understanding of them in order to know how to do the real part you're supposed to do.

Ben's sense of what was important and why in his work in engineering closely matched what faculty would say in interviews about why students were given certain assignments. In fact, whereas the other research participants' views of assignment goals were consistently far narrower than those of the faculty, Ben typically saw assignment goals equally as expansively as did faculty making the assignments. When asked what he thought teachers' goals were in setting various engineering assignments or what he thought he was supposed to get out of doing these assignments, Ben often began his answer by saying, "We are engineers," thereby working to construct this very identity for himself.

His clear sense of himself as an active learner came out in his interview responses to questions about courses other than engineering as well, particularly about his history course. Reading the transcripts of Ben's responses seemed like reading some professor's lecture on, for example, Cherokee law, their relations with the British, or British lack of understanding of Cherokee ways, complete with side comments and anecdotes. When asked a simple question like what was on the last quiz, Ben often replied with an elaborate, lengthy summary of the book the quiz was testing. When asked whether such quizzes were merely intended to make sure students read the texts, his answer was telling:

> Ben: No, ... he just want you to know that's part of history. ... you know history is good for own good. When a person know history, the events [that] happen in the past and you learn from this. ... That's why it's personal. (second-term sophomore)

Ben was very good at developing an understanding of what was going on in his classes that matched what his teachers said was going on or what they wanted to be going on. Often his comments in his interviews were almost verbatim statements of what his professors then said themselves in interviews about the course. Even when Ben's accounts did not match those of his course professors, his were certainly plausible, sometimes perhaps better explanations than the professor gave. In one of Ben's American history courses, for example, the students were asked to read nonscholarly accounts of historical events written for a popular audience. One of those books described the tragedy at Donner Pass. Ben's professor described his rationale for using this popular account:

> Professor H: I just want them to have the experience of reading something in history besides a textbook.

But Ben's explanation for why such a book was included is in fact more satisfying than that of his professor:

> Ben: Because it create the background for the people in the West and during that time the teacher teach about national expansion, about the people going west. ... that's that period of time and this just more background and how difficult it was at that time. Right now you can just drive a car to go through it [the Donner Pass], but you don't have to worry about you caught in a storm. (first-term sophomore)

So, whereas the history teacher's stated goal in assigning a popularized account of a historical incident was fairly minimalist, Ben saw the text on the Donner party's experience as a means of setting the background for the study of U.S. 19th-century expansion toward the West as discussed in the lecture and in the textbook. Ben saw the goals of the assignments in engineering in a similarly holistic way:

Interviewer: ... what's the point of doing [these experiments]?
Ben: ... the laboratory put several parts together, you learn the whole picture. (first-term junior)

Unlike for others, like Jan, for Ben school was not a series of hoops to jump through. Rather, he was actively forming himself, with the welcome aid of his educational experiences, into his image of an educated person and well-trained professional.

CONTEXT FOR LEARNING

Immigration Status

An important feature of Ben's nonacademic life was his problems with the Immigration and Naturalization Service (INS). Like many others who are forced to deal with the INS, Ben experienced intense frustration and insecurity with what appeared to be INS incompetence, or gratuitous cruelty. Because Ben's family already had green cards, he was eligible to apply for a green card as a family member as long as he was still under 21. Although he applied in plenty of time, INS lost his file, and 2 1/2 years later, when Ben was over 21, INS informed him that his application was now invalid and he was out of status, meaning he would need to leave the United States immediately. Ben spent a great deal of time during his junior year frantically dealing with INS, lawyers, and visa documents. Because INS offices are not open after 5 p.m., Ben was forced to deal with such issues during the schoolday, seriously distracting him from his classwork and resulting finally in having to drop a required Japanese course because of excessive absences. By the end of his junior year he still did not know his fate or what he would do if INS denied his stop-gap application for a student visa.

Although Ben may have been incorrect about this, he interpreted his unclear immigration status as a factor in his repeated failure to be offered an internship in an engineering company during the summers, as many of his classmates were. The subject of these internships arose in a required professional seminar in engineering:

Ben: ...   the speaker was from the career services department. ... she strongly suggest us to get an internship in summer. ...

Interviewer: So what do you think about that?

Ben: I know about that [possibility] a long time ago. I'm trying to do [get an internship], but it's kind of hard for me to find because I'm not U.S. citizen. I don't got a green card. I don't know. They never tell me what's really the reason for not getting internship. I guess the reason is when they have pretty much a lot of students for the interview [and] we have the same kind of status, same kind of degree, they get somebody else, not me. (second-term junior)

Social Life

In his social relations Ben seemed to be about as successful as he might have wanted to be. He had a group of (apparently all male) friends with whom he relaxed, on the weekends he was free, by going bowling or fishing together. In his 1st year, he selected a Guatemalan, rather than a Chinese-speaking, roommate, whose English Ben judged to be excellent, so that he could continue to work on his English at home. Not surprisingly, given his sweet, easygoing disposition, Ben's relations with his engineering classmates appeared to be generally relaxed and friendly, with one notable exception that will be discussed later. However, in the many group projects the engineering students did and in more informal study sessions, Ben often worked with other international or permanent-resident students rather than with a group of primarily domestic students. Finding these international/permanent-resident students was easy enough because they made up about 10% of the engineering student population.[7]

PROFESSIONAL TRAINING: ENGINEERING EDUCATION AND INDUSTRY

Because engineering is a professional training program, it perhaps should not be surprising that engineering departments work closely with industries that might eventually employ their graduates and see their educational efforts at least partly as training students for the profession. In their interviews, the engineering faculty indicated they often had industry needs in the back of their minds as they instructed students. They tried in the experiments or other assignments to duplicate as much as possible real problems that engineers might face outside academia. In a special program for honors students, for example, chemical companies like Dow or DuPont collaborated with departments across the country by sending faculty real, though minor, problems for the engineering students to solve that industry was confronting in their operations. At the end of the semester, the students would travel to the chemical company and present their results or solutions. In this way the company benefited from the work of students at several universities and could choose from several possible solutions to their problem.

The department saw the benefit to itself as the provision of real engineering projects for their students to work on and the opportunity to carry a project right through to its presentation phase before the very audience who might accept or reject the solutions, thus emulating what might occur as part of a practicing engineer's actual work. Individual faculty, however, also saw disadvantages to the arrangements. Because the students were only apprentices, they needed a great deal of guidance in these projects. That guidance often required certain faculty members with particular expertise but who were not part of, and not paid for participation in, the honors seminar. In other words, not only were students providing free, or very inexpensive, advice for industry, but faculty too were essentially working without pay for the company. In this type of arrangement as well as in the general atmosphere of the department, there was a frequently expressed sense that industry called the shots and that the university's role was to do what it could to accommodate industry needs.

The presence of the chemical engineering industry permeated the department at other levels as well, for example, in a mandatory professional seminar consisting mainly of videos and guest speakers from industry and in the many job fairs that took place when industry representatives came to campus to recruit students. Announcements about these fairs or about other impromptu visits of industry representatives to the department were made widely available to students. On one occasion, in the midst of a class, a member of the faculty interrupted by popping his head in the door to make one of these announcements, an interruption of class time that is not unusual for high school classes but rarely occurs in classes in a university of this type. These kinds of events, and the many announcements about job possibilities and professional organizations that covered the walls of the Engineering building, contributed to a sense of community in the department, on one hand, but also, to a sense of a kind of engineering minor-league training camp, where everyone worked hard to try eventually to develop new talent for "the show."

LITERACY EXPERIENCES

Ben's Experiences With Writing

In Table 2.1, an overview of reading and writing requirements for the courses Ben took during his 3 years with the study, courses are noted that required substantial writing assignments or unusual efforts for Ben in reading.[8]

TABLE 2.1

Ben's Academic Writing and Reading Assignments in Courses Other Than English

Term	Course	Writing	Reading
fall sophomore	Chemistry	weekly short lab reports	
	Physics	weekly short lab reports	
	Psychology		substantial and difficult
spring sophomore	Chemical Engineering	weekly 1-page reports	
	Psychology		substantial and difficult
fall junior	Chemical Engineering	6 short reports	
	Chemical Engineering	5 full group lab reports	
	History	2 essay exams	
spring junior	Chemical Engineering	6 group lab reports	
fall senior	Chemical Engineering	1 group lab report	
	Chemical Engineering	1 group project	
spring senior	Chemical Engineering	1 group project	
	Chemical Engineering	4 group lab reports	
summer senior	Microbiology	1 short lab report	

For a college career, the extent of the literacy demands seems rather minimal. Even the many lab reports were often primarily graphs, charts, and calculations. In his senior year, Ben and his group partner produced a 100-page report that included a mere 10 short paragraphs of writing. With the work split between the two partners then, Ben's chore was to write only five paragraphs.

What this literacy table does not include, however, is the hours spent doing the lab work or the elaborate, time-consuming calculations required to work problem sets. Both faculty and students in engineering were well aware of the difficulty and complexity of much of the work the students were asked to do, of the equipment the students had to become familiar with, and of the problems they were required to solve. Chemical engineering is an exacting and demanding major with an enormous body of both conceptual and procedural knowledge to acquire and to acquire well. It was completely unexceptional for groups of engineering students to stay up well past midnight, sometimes all night, regularly, not just a time or two on the night before exams, to work problems or to do labs. The engineering faculty interviewed all appeared to understand and sympathize with the students' heavy academic responsibilities. Among all these demands, however, except for one of the engineering courses in the fall of Ben's junior year (described later), reading and particularly writing were not central features in any of these courses.

In Ben's first interview, he repeatedly characterized the writing for his courses as easy, no problem, formulaic:

> Interviewer: What is hard about writing up the lab procedures?
> Ben: Not much. (first-term sophomore)
>
> Ben: For the lab report, what people care about is the result and the TA looking for to give me the grade is if I draw the right conclusion. He don't care [about the writing]. (first-term sophomore)
>
> Ben: [In writing] for lab, you just follow the procedure. You don't have to think, or maybe [just to write] the conclusion. ... when I do the lab report, you just like forced to do and just follow certain procedures. I think it's just like a robot. (first-term sophomore)

In the second semester of his sophomore year, he had even less writing:

> Ben: Even in psychology we don't have. Maybe in psychology we have optional quiz. Each time we answer one or two questions. Short answer. (second-term sophomore)

Thus, as Ben understood it, in writing for his sophomore-level physics, chemistry, and engineering classes, the task was mechanical reproduction of lab procedures and results, "just like a robot." Accuracy of results and in following directions was essential, and he focused his attention on trying "not to forget something" in the write-ups. In some lab reports, he was required to copy the same material from one section to another and even to include pages torn directly out of the lab book with filled-in blanks. The sole difficulty Ben reported in writing the weekly lab reports in physics and chemistry was in the physics lab write-ups, which required him to report procedures already described in the lab manual in step-by-step imperatives and which he had to in effect translate into prose:

> Interviewer: What do you concentrate on when writing for ... physics?
> Ben: For physics, what I concentrate on is how I can put all the sentences in the manual together. I don't have to think

about [unintelligible] maybe a little bit grammar. ...
Because the ideas, they're there. It's already in the manual.
... [I have to just find the] words to connect the ideas. (sec-
ond-term sophomore)

His difficulty was in finding synonyms for words already in the manual,
which the students were enjoined not to copy, and to employ appropriate connector words to transform the lab directions into paragraphs. It is
not surprising then that early in Ben's thinking about the links between
his writing classes and his other classes, he saw the value of the writing
classes in limited terms:

Ben: Most of the useful part is grammar and those like *because, however,* to
connect will be useful ... . (first-term sophomore)

Ben's difficulty with vocabulary, the sense of not having readily available
enough synonyms or enough connector words, was a recurrent (though
minor) theme throughout Ben's interviews right up to his description of
his relative lack of success with the English section of the Graduate
Record Exam (GRE).

Except for two essay exams that Ben wrote for one of his history
classes, and the writing he did for English classes, he was assigned no
other sustained writing in his college career except within science/tech-
nical courses. Semester after semester for course after course Ben's
answer to questions about writing for his courses was that there was little writing to do, that the point of the writing was to show what he knew,
and that once he did the real work of the experiment, the writing itself
posed few difficulties:

Interviewer: Do you have a lot of writing assignments that you have to
do [this semester]?
Ben: Not really much. ... Right now we deal with just all the
calculations, all analysis for the class, the diagram. ... I
don't expect much writing this semester. That's mostly ...
the calculations. (second-term senior)

Interviewer: Besides checking to make sure that you understand the
material, why do you think your professors assigned so
much report writing this year?
Ben: Well, I wouldn't say a lot of writing, I wouldn't say, 'cause
it's only one final report for each class. ... Not really a lot
of writings. Because you can see what they do to us is just
one or two pages. That's not considered a lot. (second-
term junior)

Ben: The writing itself is no problem. (first-term junior)

Although writing continued to be a minor feature in Ben's education life, his understanding of its function did shift. In his sophomore year, he interpreted the writing he was asked to do in his physics and chemistry classes as limited to describing an already existent reality. By his junior year, he also began to describe the writing in engineering somewhat more rhetorically, with more concern for his audience (i.e., trying to write clearly to be understood) and as a place to show what he had learned:

Interviewer: What does writing well mean for your engineering classes?
Ben: Writing well means clear understanding for the other people of what you write, what's your goal of the experiment, how you shape it, what your result is, the discussion of your result, how you want to improve it, what's the error, and you compare this experiment [with other similar published work]. So good writing will state clearly all these things and the conclusions. ... (first-term junior)

Interviewer: What's the role of writing in this [engineering] course?
Ben: Very important, very important. When you're done with experiments that's one thing, and writing will tell the other people and the professor what you learned, how, why, what, all those questions ... . It's very important. ... Otherwise what we learn is [only] in our heads. (first-term junior)

Thus Ben began to see the importance of writing, first, in its still limited role of display to professors of what he learned and, second, in a broader capacity, as a means of communicating what he learned presumably to other interested parties. However, the writing itself was not so important but the communication of findings was. Furthermore, the findings had to be accurate. In discussing how long it took him to complete the only writing assignment in a microbiology class—8 hours to write the report—Ben made it clear that, again, writing was not the issue; drawing the correct conclusion from the experiment was:

Interviewer: What are you trying hardest to do to get a good grade on this assignment?
Ben: This one [assignment] is tricky. You *could* draw the wrong conclusion. ... That's about it. (third-term senior)

What he was still missing even in his last writing assignments at the university was the engineering faculty's concern with more intangibles. The description during this same semester of what one of his professors valued in the many short reports she required in her class emphasized not display of what the writers learned but rather of how the writers were thinking about what they did:

Professor W: ... the meat of the matter has to be in the analysis of the results, not just a documentation of the observation of what happens ... mainly they have to offer an explanation why they get the observation they get by using a physical principle they learned, plus other prior knowledge they already know, or from mathematical analysis, some intuition, insight, into it. ... I reward for insight ... an analysis or insight which is beyond the call of duty, beyond what the assignment asks for ... creative thinking ... Integrating what they are learning with what they have learned before. ... a higher level of thinking.

Whereas Ben often talked about what he learned in engineering in terms of the new equipment and formulas he was becoming acquainted with, the faculty talked instead about all that learning as grounding for the more important learning, learning to be creative. Professor W in particular but other faculty as well described engineering students as good at descriptions, calculations, and graph and figure creation and as doing these readily. What they were still missing, however, was insight and creativity. Professor W told her students that the 90% of what they learned, the straight facts, was needed to enable the 10% of creativity to become possible. Professor C as well referred to the need for engineers to develop a felt "sense" of engineering problems.

Professor W's comments on writing sound quite a bit like what writing teachers claim about how writing helps students learn. The difference, however, is that Professor W, other professors, and Ben did not appear to believe that the learning happened *during* the writing, that writing caused discovery of meaning. Rather, learning happened because of the prolonged contact with the subject matter that came as the result of the requirement to write. In other words, it was pushing oneself to think longer and harder about a subject that resulted in learning; the requirement to write about something provided an occasion to think longer and harder. But then presumably so would discussion, reading, even just thinking.

Furthermore, for Ben, writing created specific perils. In discussing what was difficult about writing the report of a particular experiment, Ben pointed to a perhaps unexpected problem:

Interviewer: What's the hardest kind of thing about this kind of writing ... ?

Ben: You have to understand what to do [before you can write] and ... you really understand when you're actually doing the different things ... but even then you might forget something. (second-term junior)

He went on to explain that despite his group's thorough understanding of the experiment, they had a problem with their report because they forgot to include a required comparison. In other words, understanding predates writing, and writing can betray the writer, in this case, by not revealing accurately the group's understanding because in the write-up they forgot to include something they did, in fact, understand. So, in Ben's description, the danger in writing is its potential unreliability as a tool for communicating with a reader.

The Value of Writing.   In exploring the role of literacy in the research participants' experience, it was important to understand in what way the students felt they were benefiting from the writing assigned to them. What did writing itself, apart from what was learned doing the experiments or research in preparation for the writing, contribute to these students' education? The focal students were regularly asked what role writing played in fostering learning. After some hesitation and reflection, Ben's analysis placed writing in the context of social arrangements:

> Interviewer: Do you think writing about it [the experiment] helped you learn it at all, helped you be more certain of it?
>
> Ben: Probably, yeah, in one way it probably is. Because during the writing we supposed to help each other. So during this process maybe me and maybe somebody else have a certain area didn't [get] clearer during that whole period [of the experiment], and by writing the report during this period, we help each other, ask questions to each other, and answer to each other. That's maybe one way to put it, about writing to help [i.e., about how writing helped or made a difference]. (first-term junior)

Despite Ben's kind attempt to accommodate the interviewer by finding a benefit for the writing, it seems clear that not only did he have to search for the benefit but also that it was not the writing itself that he saw as useful but the discussion with his group mates that surrounded and was necessitated by the writing.

In one of his final interviews, however, again pressed for the point of the writing part of the work he was required to do, Ben's answer began to go quite a bit beyond his initial representation of the academic writing he did in his first 2 years at the university while nevertheless consistently characterizing it as being not the crux of the assignment, not the most demanding part of the work:

> Ben: Well, I guess I always think of the written part as not that difficult. Writing report is not difficult. The difficult part is

	that you understand the experiment. ... If you don't write a report, you still can understand the experiment, but you don't have to know how, you don't have to know why, you operate them. Just like operator, that's it. That's the point. ... By writing how, and writing the procedure, you have to know.
Interviewer:	You have to know why?
Ben:	Yeah. Yeah, that's the point. ... That's why I say you can operate it [manipulate the procedures], you don't have to understand it. (second-term senior)

Having to write the report, then, meant having to address issues that would not have to be addressed if only doing the experiment. That is, as long as there was a report to turn in, the report required the writers to consider issues they otherwise would not need to consider. In forcing themselves to understand the procedure well enough to be able to write it out clearly for a reader, the writers in Ben's description, almost incidentally, were also forced to come to a clearer understanding of it themselves. They had to understand not just the "operator's" version (what has to be done) but the rationale for each step, that is, the why.

Though Ben never mentioned the kind of creative insight that the faculty referred to as especially desirable in written reports, he nevertheless designated in this interview, one of his last, the same basic goals for writing as his professors intended in making written report assignments, to be able to understand and explain the rationale for decisions made during the experiment and to interpret the results.

Interestingly, in a postgraduation telephone interview during Ben's first semester in graduate school in engineering, he reported having a great deal of reading but no writing requirements for his courses or for the research assistant position he held at that same time, although he did anticipate eventually having to write a master's thesis and other reports.[9] In that interview, Ben held to his earliest explanations of the value of writing for him:

Interviewer:	What was the importance of writing while you were in college?
Ben:	Reinforcement of ideas, like practicing anything, music, sports. (first term graduate school)

Writing provided an opportunity for reflective reiteration of whatever had already been learned during the course of the experiment or the research and in this role served as an aid to remembering that learning.

If writing itself played a relatively minor role in Ben's education, his indifference to writing did not reflect his commitment to the work reported in the writing. When he was sure of his results, he defended them. One of his professors objected to the high cost of a project Ben's group had proposed, for example, but Ben did not back down from his group's analysis in the report they turned in:

Ben: ... $7.8 [billion], that's our final offer. We can't change that. So he is thinking [that's] high, but that's the way it is. ...

Interviewer: Is it [the professor's comment objecting to the high esti-mate of cost] helpful?

Ben: Well, it just a comment, I guess. His impression of our report. That's how I take it, the way I take it. (second-term senior)

It is possible that a discipline like engineering makes it unusually easy for students to speak with authority. Having carried out an experiment and found particular results, perhaps students are able to feel a personal com-mitment to their results, with their concrete, undeniable grounding in numbers, figures, equations, much more difficult to achieve in humani-ties/social science arenas, not to mention as 1st-year writers discussing, for example, social issues. Ben described his professors' feedback as just their opinion, matter-of-factly considering his own to carry equal weight. In other words, there may be various ways for young writers to own their work and one of them might be, as it seemed to be for Ben, to be quite certain that the content of what they write is accurate and to consider the rest nothing more than "his impression of our report." It is also possible that Ben's confidence came from the fact that the report submitted had been a collaborative effort, giving the report the increased credibility and weight in Ben's mind that might come from knowing he did not stand alone in supporting the report's positions.

Engineering Faculty's Description of Writing

In the interviews with engineering faculty, they repeatedly stressed the importance for engineers of good communication skills, and Ben's com-ments in interviews reflected these views. The department took very seriously industry's complaints about the writing of Engineering School graduates and, apparently pushed at least in part by industry demands for better writing skills, developed two courses with substantial writing, one in which students did full reports on five different experiments and one in which they worked on five different experiments and wrote up a full report of one of them. This department also put together a writing handbook for its engineering students to be used in these courses. Because this was the only document focusing directly on disciplinary writing that was uncovered during the study,[10] it bears further examination and offers an interesting glimpse into what another discipline tells its students about what is important in the writing they do for that academic field, and, perhaps here, for that profession as well.

The Manual.   Throughout Ben's engineering education, faculty assumed acquaintance with and access to the manual that guided the first writing-intensive engineering course. When asked how he knew how to write up a given report in any of his engineering classes subsequent to this one, Ben too referred to the manual as giving directions on how to set up a proper experiment report, although he mentioned it somewhat offhandedly as though knowing how to do these reports was no longer an issue after this course. About 90 pages long, the manual devoted the last 70 pages or so to specific directions for carrying out each of the five major experiments that constituted the core of the course in which the manual was first introduced and the first about 20 pages to the actual writing reference guide. The writing reference guide began with a Pre-Lab Check Sheet (a listing of what students needed to prepare before carrying out the experiment), Criteria for Grading Reports, and a Formal Report Checklist/Grading Sheet.

Most of the Pre-Lab Check Sheet referred to various data management features (e.g., "… always time tag the data"). A notable feature, however, was the second of the 14 items listed:

"2. Clear and *specific* statement of the laboratory objectives (… What does the person or company paying for your work want? Not things like understand Fourier's Law but to [*sic*] find thermal conductiv[ity] of samples.)."

Ever concerned to direct student attention away from merely academic exercises toward the real, future audience for their work, faculty positioned itself as though looking over the shoulders of the students in a kind of master-to-apprentice stance. Knowing Fourier's Law is assumed as necessary, and academic, background; what is required in a report, however, is the more utilitarian effort of finding a particular conductivity for industry ("the person or company paying for your work"), the psychologically ever present companion of training in this engineering program.

The sheet detailing grading criteria is reproduced here (with permission).

Criteria for Grading Reports

Item	Points	Grade
SUMMARY		
Is it complete and concise?	10	_____
ACCURACY OF OBSERVATIONS		
Did you observe		
and understand		
the apparatus and procedures	15	_____
CALCULATIONS		
Are they complete and correct	20	_____
INTERPRETATION OF RESULTS		
How do experiment		
and theory compare?		
What are the reasons		
for disagreement?	20	_____
CLARITY OF PRESENTATION		
Is the report easy to read		
and understand?		
In the proper format? Is it complete?	35	_____
PENALTY FOR LATENESS	5 points per day	_____
Total		_____

These grading criteria appeared to be consistent with Ben's interpretation of what was important for producing engineering reports. Most of the points were allocated for correctness of information, observation, and calculation and for various formatting issues. Even Clarity of Presentation appeared to refer as much to formatting issues as to rhetorical issues. Only the section on Interpretation of Results, worth 20 points out of 100, appeared to call for writing that did not draw on already existing realities and require the kind of invention, innovative thinking, or creative sensing of cause-and-effect links that faculty described in interviews as distinguishing work that exceeds expectations and that faculty said they hoped to encourage in students.

The main body of the manual's writing guidelines followed these few pages. Divided into about 15 short subsections, most of the neatly organized writing reference guide indicated in detail what each section of a proper report should contain, with such requirements as:

5. Experimental Method

5.1 Provide a concise overview of the experimental plan. It is often helpful to suggest why this plan and experimental method were used instead of some alternate method or methods.

5.2 Sub-headings are recommended.

5.3 Give an overview of the experimental system referring directly to the appropriate points or location on the flow sheet. Lead the reader "by the hand" through the flow sheet.

5.4 Provide detailed step by step operational procedures that you followed in the lab to carry out your tasks. Could someone else use your description to repeat your work? Even if, [*sic*] you were not there? …

5.7 Note that this section does NOT contain results.

The reference manual ended with examples of the proper setup for tables, figures, references lists, appendixes, and so forth. These descriptions, directions, and examples for the most part again coincided with Ben's assertion that the write-up of an experiment essentially reports a preexisting reality, either describing the steps taken or putting into prose what is already displayed in table or flow chart form.

More discursive sections of the manual commented more broadly on rhetorical features of writing for engineering:

… Keep in mind that the objective of any report is to effectively communicate results and ideas to a large range of readers: the casual reader, the reader very familiar with the work, or the reader only interested in results. Proper organization, clarity of thought, and good grammar are essential to meeting this end. A report that does not look professional creates a negative impression.

Many features of report writing are conventions. … While convention can be boring, it has found use in technical reports because it is an efficient way to communicate information. The time of both the reader and writer is used efficiently. …

General Requirements

The prime requirements of good technical writing are clarity and precision. Statements that are vague, qualitative, or open to dual interpretation should never appear in a technical report.

> To write a good report, the author must have a clear understanding of the material that he [*sic*] is trying to present and know how he wishes to present it. Poor English in reports often arises from faulty and unclear thinking rather than from unfamiliarity with grammatical rules. ...
>
> ... No colored inks should be used in the report. All the paper should normally be the same size.
>
> The subjective effect on the reader of a neat and well-prepared report cannot be over emphasized. ...
>
> ... The writer must recognize that writing a technical report is a highly stylized art. Individuality in style, however commendable in principle, is for the experienced writer only. Therefore, one should avoid the first person and always write in the third person, either active ("one can calculate the result by ...") or passive ("the result can be calculated by ...").

It is likely that the general writing requirements and admonitions of the type reproduced here drew the engineering students' attention less (if at all) than did the information about how calculations should be presented, if only because statements about, for example, being concise or not being vague, are themselves vague to those who do not already know how to avoid being vague. Still a number of features of these requirements draw our attention here for what they suggest about the engineering faculty's assumptions about writing. A pervasive concern is clearly the audience for this writing and the effort to create the appropriate impression on that audience through neatness and grammatical correctness. Nevertheless, it is somewhat difficult to imagine, for example, who the "casual reader" might be who would pick up a technical report like the ones these students were being trained to produce.

It is not difficult to imagine that students might be interested in writing out only the results or perhaps interpretations of results of their work and might not see the point in describing in detail experiments that their real audience (neither the future employer nor the perhaps mythical casual reader, but in fact their professors) were already quite familiar with. Taking students through their formal paces seemed to be a feature of training in writing in each of the academic programs in which the student participants studied but particularly in both engineering and nursing.

Interestingly, prohibition of first person is not ascribed to writing conventions nor to issues of epistemology in science (i.e., who/what warrants the truthfulness, accuracy, or validity of knowledge). Rather writing in first person is considered too artsy, too stylized, too individualistic or unconventional for apprentice engineers and is reserved for the experienced writer.

One professor did remark, in answer to a question about what he considered good writing in his course, that he hoped the writing would engage him. But his was an isolated mention of engagement. When the faculty spoke generally about the need for better writing or lamented the grammatical and mechanical errors produced in writing done by engineers or engineering students, they typically seconded industry's criticism and replicated its view that good writing is primarily grammatically acceptable.

Contradictory Aspects of Writing for Engineering.   Yet the faculty also revealed conflicted attitudes about writing. First, in answer to questions about how the students learned to write whatever textual material might be required in a given course, a frequent response was a reference to the writing manual. In other words, responsibility for initiating students into disciplinary writing was placed on the handbook, and the faculty appeared to feel themselves somewhat absolved from further need to deal with writing issues.

Second, in classes that did assign writing, nearly always in the form of a experiment project that would then be reported on, the role of writing was distinctly secondary. In Professor C's course, for example, the course project counted for fully 20% of the grade, yet the required writing involved in the project was a mere three to five pages. When this professor was asked what the difference was between doing this project for school and in the real world, he said the work itself was quite like real-world work except that in the real world "they probably wouldn't take the time to write it up." So what was the purpose of the write-up? The three to five pages were intended to allow the student to explain why they selected the particular solution path that they selected and to display their thinking process for the professor to evaluate. This requirement to explain rationales, like the mandate to follow conventionalized formal writing requirements, even when they were "boring," again reproduced the master–apprentice positioning that characterized much of the work in engineering, with faculty watching over the students' shoulders as they thought through their work.

Ironically, Ben appeared to do the least writing in the course designed to emphasize writing the most, the junior-year one-semester/five-experiment course. Because all these experiments were done in groups, it was not uncommon–in fact it was perhaps the norm here as it was in business courses–for one or more group members to be designated the writers and the others to be assigned other work. Ben was not one of the ones designated as writer. At least some faculty were aware of and somewhat concerned about this type of situation:

Professor B: Each group hands in something, so that's a problem.
Interviewer: Why?
Professor B: Well, who out of the three wrote it? In other words, the technical part, we have pretty good ways of checking on that. I give an oral exam. ... And I can, I give a grade for that. And by that means I try to separate those in the group who really do not know what's going on from those who do. ... The writing part, though, is very difficult to do. ... So I will ask them to write something where they'll have to write individually. ... I may ask them to write a paragraph or two of something else.

It is somewhat difficult to see what a paragraph or two would tell Professor B. Furthermore, as several of the faculty pointed out, although they might not give absolute top grades to what they considered weak writing, they would have been hard-pressed to be too strict with poorly written reports that were technically correct, particularly if the students were able to give imaginative solutions or show evidence of "higher order thinking" about the problems put to them.

Nevertheless that the faculty took seriously the idea of seeing at least some writing from each of the students independent of the main group report is clear from the various solutions to this problem worked out by individual faculty. Professor B used his paragraphs. Another professor had each group member turn in a full report in which parts of the report (the methods, the data, the calculations, e.g.) would be identical to those of the other group members and other sections (the abstract, introduction, and conclusion, e.g.) would be written individually. However, as always, although this mechanism served to identify and lower the grade of students whose writing was "weak" or "sloppy," most of the value of the final report grade rested on the accuracy and innovation of the solutions the students had worked out together. In other words, requiring individually composed sections served only to keep the gate, potentially hurting individual students' evaluations but not helping them. Even if the abstract, introduction, and conclusion were particularly well written, this quality would not raise the grade of a report that was technically flawed.

Realistic Projects.   One of the interesting features of the assignments made to Ben's cohort of engineering students was the faculty's effort to make the experiments as realistic and nonacademic as possible. In some cases the experiments were so realistic that even the professor did not know how they would turn out. As one faculty member admitted,

Professor B: I only partially understood the HDA process myself when the semester started. I learned quite a bit from the students as we went along, and, in one case, from the final report.

The professor in one of Ben's classes devised an assignment that duplicated reality in yet another way. In this course, the class, as usual, was divided into groups. As in the kind of jigsaw exercises sometimes used in language classes, each group was set a different experimental task, each group "owning" one experiment, which would require information gathered and figures calculated by the other four groups. After each owner group decided on exactly the information they would need from each of the data-gathering groups, the first writing task of the semester for each owner group was to formulate a set of directions addressed to each of the data-gathering groups instructing them on what to do to gather the necessary information or make the necessary calculations. Once the data-gathering groups collected the data requested by the owner group, each data-gathering group wrote up their findings in a report to the owner group. Thus, all five groups owned one experiment, wrote a set of directions for four data-gathering groups, received one report from each of them, in turn received four sets of instructions (one from each other owner group), and wrote a total of four subreports, one to each of the other owner groups that had set their data-gathering tasks for them.

These instructions to the other groups had to be carefully and succinctly written, as Ben explained, because the groups complained if they attempted to follow the directions and found them unsatisfactory:

> Ben: The procedure, you're supposed to write clearly because you have to show to other groups, for them to follow the procedure to do the experiment. Otherwise, if they follow the wrong procedure they calculate wrong data. It not help us. (third-term senior)

The real audience that the directions from Ben's group were aimed at gave Ben and his group the kind of authentic feedback on their writing that caused significant revision of the directions, motivating the owner group to struggle until the directions were appropriately shaped. In the end, however, it was not a struggle with the writing that resulted in more satisfactory directions; rather, it was going through each section of the experiments themselves in trial runs so that they knew clearly what their classmates would be up against that allowed Ben's group to rewrite more effective directions.

> Ben: … we work on it ourselves, to see how long, timing each process, how long does it take and what's the procedure for each step, and we write them down as well. So that's basically how we got [the revised directions]. (third-term senior)

As Ben said so often, the writing was not a problem; the problem was properly conceptualizing the procedures.

The writing assignments that Ben experienced in engineering revealed several contradictions. As in many situations in this study where professors talked about the importance of writing, engineering faculty asserted that writing was important for a particular reason, and yet they claimed never to assign writing that would allow students to write for that reason. For example, in engineering, faculty repeatedly asserted that engineers work for other people who are not engineers, so in order, for example, to have solutions to a problem put into action, the engineer has to convince someone who is not an engineer that his or her solution is worth doing. But Ben was never once asked to write a text like that. What he was asked to write was lab reports that resembled academic journal articles. Yet one faculty member asserted that, in fact, engineers rarely write academic research articles, especially not engineers that do not go on to graduate school. Furthermore, oddly enough, this professor stated that he himself, even as a university professor, did not write academic research articles. Yet these academic–research–style articles were what the students were assigned.

Of Ben's engineering professors, the one most concerned about writing was Professor W, and she required several varieties of writing tasks in her courses, feeling that writing skill develops by writing.

> Professor W: They learn by having to write a lot more often. Of course, read too. Read a lot more often, write a lot more often. But then they probably don't get that chance if they are engineers.

It is not entirely clear whether she meant that the lack of opportunity to write is endemic to engineers in general or only to engineering students. In either case, however, it seems at least odd to maintain the importance of writing for engineers while at the same time asserting that engineers do not get the chance to write, assigning writing tasks that engineers would not do, such as explaining why they chose a particular solution, and not assigning tasks that they might do, such as convincing a CEO of the importance or validity of a particular engineering solution.

Feedback.   Most of the writing assignments were submitted at the end of the term and usually not viewed again by the authors. In such cases, if the professor bothered to give written feedback on the reports, the students were not aware of what it might have been. On occasions when Ben did pick up reports he had written individually, they included little written feedback. From an interview based on one of Ben's returned assignments:

Interviewer: … do you ever feel like you can learn something from the professor's comments if the professor makes any comments?

Ben: Well, usually, most of my final reports don't have much comment in there. (second-term junior)

For example, on one 25-page report from spring of Ben's senior year (of which a total of only 8 pages were text rather than figures, tables, or calculations), the total amount of feedback consisted of the following notes:

> Need table of contents
>
> > list of figures
> > list of tables
>
> [Referring to a table] This should appear after the next page where it is cited
>
> The $7.8B cost was dominated by the cost for LLW disposal. Don't you think that should be discussed more? How could it be reduced?

In a class Ben took from Professor W, she responded to six short projects the students turned in during the semester. For the most part the responses consisted of check marks, indicating necessary material appearing correctly, and comments about grammar:

> You need to proofread to make sure grammar is correct, e.g., verb–subj person agreement
>
> Don't need ;
>
> Please read these with my changes—you will see that it flows smoother.

The last comment was written on a page with some sort of grammatical or mechanical correction on nearly every line. The only other comments on the reports were summative ("good explanation") or directive ("Explanation needs to be beefed up"), although because these short reports too were final versions, even if Ben knew how to beef them up, he would not have had the opportunity to do so.

In some ways, the most specific feedback Ben received on his writing appeared on the essay exams he wrote for one of his history courses in which the professor actually wrote out the information Ben had missed in his answer. But, of course, an exam is the quintessential "final draft" and did no more than to justify whatever grade the exam answer received.

In sum, Ben's writing development in Engineering took place in the context of both supportive and not particularly helpful features:

- A manual written by the department indicating in detail how a research report should be organized and giving tips on grammar issues that the faculty saw as typical student errors.
- Generally not much actual writing required on projects.
- Assigned writing most often produced by a group, meaning that Ben himself typically did little of the writing on any given project.
- Little feedback on the writing.
- Little interest in the feedback that did appear.
- Little opportunity for multiple drafts.
- A great deal of invaluable peer collaboration on ideas and problem solutions that preceded the writing.
- Faculty attempts to provide tasks that re-created real engineering problems (though not authentic writing tasks).
- A disjuncture between the writing genres assigned and the writing genres faculty felt were important for practicing engineers.

In the final analysis, although this engineering department wanted to address writing, their own notions of good writing and how to promote it (with the possible exception of those of Professor W) did not move the department in the direction of providing either instruction or real opportunity to learn much about writing in the writing assignments made to the students. As a result, though Ben sometimes repeated the party line about writing being important, its true importance in the program was relatively limited. This is not to say that it should have been otherwise, only to say that what the department wanted to do or thought it was doing in terms of developing students' writing was probably not as effective as they hoped or assumed it was.

The Writing Center

The university's writing center apparently played no role in this engineering department's universe. Despite the fact that faculty seemed to think superficial grammatical correctness was extremely important and despite the fact that the writing center was seen by some as an editing service, they never recommended the writing center to Ben. It appeared simply not to be a presence in that environment.

The ESL Writing Class

Ben took three English writing classes, which he mildly appreciated for their contribution to developing his grammar, vocabulary, reading, and writing.

In an interview after completion of his English course requirements, Ben mentioned that he had had trouble the previous year with organization, noting that:

> Ben: Chinese logic may be different from what is expected here. (second-term sophomore)

However, he noticed this supposed difficulty with logic only in English class, not in any other classes. Nor was he to mention this problem again in later years including when he wrote essay exams for his history class. Perhaps problems in organization are an artifact of English classes themselves, at least in Ben's case.

One of the assignments in his English class was a research paper, which he was grateful to have learned to do. Yet, Ben never again had to write a similar research paper in the course of his university studies.

Beyond developing literacy skills associated with English classes, he also appreciated the opportunity to simply improve his general language proficiency:

> Ben: Actually for English, for the English class itself, ... all the teachers speak real clearly and will help us to understand English much better. So, but here is a process to learn English. So that's also a big help. (first-term sophomore)

He felt his teachers' speaking "real clearly" allowed him to link code and meaning in ways that generally improved his English proficiency, resulting in turn in his increased ability to use that proficiency for all his language needs.

The Role of Reading

Like most academics, engineering faculty considered reading essential to their work and to their students' training, a sentiment that Ben perceived clearly.

> Ben: ... He [the professor in one of the courses] let us try to find the [information] through journals, the newspapers in the library.

That's basically the idea. He said that's the important part of the engineer. You don't have to write about it, you have to read about it, and you [have to] know how to get information. (third-term senior)

Predictably, Ben too described reading as extremely important:

Interviewer: What role did reading play in your courses ... ? Was it extremely important to your course work or somewhat important.

Ben: Oh yes, it was important. There are the materials we had to read about, lots of reading stuff in this one. (first-term junior)

But the actual role of reading in Ben's engineering courses was less obvious. Because most of the reading for engineering was related to a team project, Ben reported that the reading was split up among the group members with each group member only generally skimming the readings collected by other group members. Thus, although Ben carried stacks of readings with him, he himself was only responsible in detail for a portion of those readings.

Like writing, then, reading appeared to play a more diminished role than might be expected in a college career. In his two engineering courses in the spring of his junior year, course readings were treated as backup sources of information.

Ben: As long as you understand in the class, you can do the assignment. As long as you know what you are doing. If I really understand thing what's going on there, how to solve something, I don't have to go back to book and read again. (second-term junior)

In one course in Ben's senior year, there was no assigned reading at all, with the expectation being that if the students needed background information for the experiments they were expected to do, they knew where the library was. In another course, the only reading was the assignment sheets that explained the requirements for each experiment. In fact, over the course of 1 month in spring of his junior year, in the middle of the semester, Ben had a total of only 23 to 28 pages assigned over the four courses he was taking (excluding Japanese) and in one of the courses the four assigned pages were instructions for conducting an experiment.

Reading was still an important feature of Ben's professional education, but the central instructional role came not from reading, writing, or listening to lectures. Rather, according to Ben, he learned the most from actually doing the experiments assigned to him and his various groups:

Interviewer: What experiences were most valuable to you in learning these things? Was it doing lab work, working with teachers, working with other students, reading, writing, lectures, what was most valuable?

Ben: I would say the experiments, I guess, because the experiment itself involve, probably include, all those things you mention before. It's that you learn, because in class the lecture you learn is just in the paper, just on the book. The experiment give you actual datas and make you understand more about the things you learn before. It's not only on paper. (first-term senior)

Nor were the experiments done alone. Thus, Ben's learning came most forcefully from actually doing work with others, Ben's very definition of engineering: "to work together to operate the machine, equipment, and also to solve the questions."

SOCIOACADEMIC RELATIONSHIPS

Group Work

Ben enjoyed and learned from both spontaneous and course-sponsored group work. He relied a great deal on spontaneous group-work sessions with classmates (usually other NNESs) in a variety of courses to solve problem sets, often working into the early hours or all night to get them done to their satisfaction, particularly in a course in quantum mechanics, which they found exceptionally difficult conceptually. Ben felt he generally got along easily with others and enjoyed the camaraderie of group work. In fact, Ben's comments on group work were like textbook claims for the benefits of group work (Dunne & Bennett, 1990; Faltis, 1993; Holt, 1994; Jacob, Rottenberg, Patrick, & Wheeler, 1996):

Ben: I like it. ... people get together all the time and talk about it. It's fun. Sometimes we make joke. It's much helpful, it help you do the homework somehow, to understand. Sometimes, one way you just read it by yourself and you read and read and probably you just couldn't understand what that means. And like, you read an example in the book. Sometimes I don't know why they do that and why that formula equals zero. And if you work it out with some other people and maybe like three people together, maybe the second person don't know, but the third person may know. That means always one person know the material good. (first-term junior)

These groups would meet to solve problems but also to understand and learn the material. What characterized these problems was their closed-ended, almost riddlelike nature, and group work was particularly apt for solving the riddles. Consistent with his believing game approach to learning, Ben wanted to understand, not simply get the work done. Even though the tasks in group-work projects may have been divided up, Ben consistently expected and wanted to be involved with any parts of the project that would result in developing his understanding of the issues addressed in the project.

The course-sponsored group work that Ben experienced was mainly in engineering but his American history class also made use of an interesting and successful group approach to learning course material in the class-room. Having learned from his students that they considered history boring and focused on memorizing dates, the history professor was determined to turn their thinking around. He wanted them to experience the real work of historians, sorting through evidence and trying to understand patterns in the historical data. For this purpose, he had students read primary sources rather than only history textbooks. Coming to class on the day after a reading assignment on the Boston Massacre, for example, the students were assigned to groups that would role play various witnesses to the event based on documents produced at a hearing where these people testified. Ben played a Benjamin Burdick, one among a group of townspeople who had to report what they saw; other students played the roles of soldiers, sentinels, or other participants with different understandings of the event. In their groups, students answered a set of questions; each group of students would have different answers to the same questions depending on which point of view they were to represent. Ben commented about the class and his role:

> Ben: He give us a play just like in the theater. He give us each role we're supposed to play. He [Burdick] is civilian. It's pretty funny. You see if you can answer the question. You must play that role and you must follow … what it said in the book. (first-term sophomore)

Similar role plays took place in relation to Abraham Lincoln's administration, the trial of Ann Hutchinson, issues of slavery. This course-sponsored group work was unlike most of the group projects in this research in that the professor exercised careful and persistent oversight, and, at least for Ben, it was quite successful. He always prepared the readings carefully, felt that he was able to add to the historical voices, and thoroughly enjoyed this class.

In course-sponsored, required group-work projects in engineering, though carried out with much less supervision than in the history course, Ben had a great deal of faith, mostly justified, in the seriousness of purpose of his classmates. He frequently explained that group mates, at least as he described it, would willingly take over work initially assigned to another group member if that one found him- or herself pressed for time. Describing one such situation where he was called upon to do extra work, he commented:

> Ben: I think we did our best and pitch in, agree to the responsibility. ... I like it. Even though I didn't sleep the whole night, still OK. I'm glad to do it. ... as long as I have time to do it, I will do it. No problem. (first-term senior)

Group-Project Disaster.   A pivotal event affecting Ben's academic life, however, was a disastrous group-work experience in the fall of Ben's junior year. As noted, Ben took group work very seriously and enjoyed it. In fact, asked how Ben would describe what engineers do, he indicated group effort as the defining feature.

> Ben: Engineering is a group of people who know how to work together to operate the machine, equipment, and also to solve the questions while you're working on it. (first-term junior)

But the unfortunate misunderstanding that took place around the disastrous group-work project, perhaps at least partly as the result of cross-cultural differences, caused the normally calm and easygoing Ben a great deal of emotional upset and agitation and brought him to the unaccustomed and uncomfortable attention of the faculty.

In a course requiring groups of students to conduct and report on five major experiments, each supervised by a different professor, Ben found himself in a group consisting of himself and two domestic students, a man and a woman. The group decided early on how they would divide up the work they were to do and Ben was charged with making certain calculations for the first experiment in the series of five that the group was to do together. The woman in the group agreed to write up the report.[11]

In mid-October of that fall semester, however, easygoing Ben, who so much enjoyed working with people, mentioned in his interview that he had, in effect, been kicked out of this group. In talking about this experience, Ben's voice dropped to almost a whisper on the interview tapes. The apparent misunderstanding that caused the dissolution of his group was related to how the group work was initially divided and how communications among the group members broke down. It is difficult not to imagine that the breakdown in communication was somehow related to Ben's NNES status, though in what way is not clear.

As the due date approached for the assignment, Cathy, the woman group member, found herself unable to complete the write-up on time. Although Ben's hushed and disjointed recounting of this event in this or in his many references to it in later interviews do not make it clear why Cathy blamed Ben for her inability to complete the write-up, what is clear is that she felt Ben had not been doing his part of the project. She had discussed her dissatisfaction with Ben's work several times with the other group member and finally the two of them discussed it with the faculty member supervising this first experiment. Both students in fact threatened to drop the course if Ben was not removed from their group. But it was only at this point that Ben even became aware that a problem existed. The faculty member solved the immediate problem by assigning Ben to another group for the rest of the term, one with which Ben experienced no particular problems. Ben spent 2 hours talking to this professor, who later reported that Ben had been very emotional at their meeting. And to his great mortification, because the groups that were formed at the beginning of the semester for the first project were intended to remain together throughout the five experiments, Ben was forced to explain the entire situation to each of the other four professors in the course as well. He was quite worried that his reputation in the department had been severely damaged:

Ben:	I don't expect them to take my side of the story. Any conflict has two sides. I just want them to have complete story. ...
Interviewer:	[It wasn't] your fault.
Ben:	I would say not all my fault, but I have a part of it. Because I didn't aggressive and ask them to do more work. I just say I do what I can. ... [continues as if addressing Cathy] You don't trust me to do it [the writing, presumably] and you think you are good enough to do. I have no problem with that. I trust you. And usually, you take too many work with you and you can't finish. That's your problem. ... [Next time] I think I would be more aggressive. Keep asking what's going on, what can I do? If they can't finish, can I help? ... The nightmare is finally over. I don't think I have any problems before to deal with people. (first-term junior)

This negative interaction with his peers and its potential repercussions for his relationship with the engineering faculty came up again more than once in subsequent interviews, even with faculty. Several years after Ben's traumatic experience with his "team," one of the engineering faculty remembered the events of this time as being when Ben's team "crashed and burned."

Another faculty member involved in the crisis, however, saw a type of culture clash at the root of what he seemed to define as a problem that Asian people face in group work:

Professor R: A lot of the Oriental [*sic*] culture stresses conformity at the expense of individual expression. ... The doctrine essentially says that you think for the common good of the group and not for yourself. As a result, a lot of the Oriental culture people are quieter in a group situation, they don't speak out, assert themselves, as often as non-Oriental persons. Now I don't mean all Oriental persons. I'm an Oriental person and I'm certainly NOT quiet. What I mean is the product of Oriental culture. So as a result, when they are working in a group, these international persons may be quieter and not be assertive, and so this person may not call up the other members of the group as often to ask, how's your part coming along, how does mine fit into yours, let me take a look at what you have to see if I agree with it. ... One thing we have observed is that if your entire team is composed of international students, a lot of times they have less trouble with each other than if they are mixed.

Although Ben never ascribed any of his difficulties with the group, or with any other aspects of his academic life, to being from an "Oriental culture," because Professor R was one of the five professors directing projects for this course and Ben did repeat his advice nearly verbatim, clearly he agreed with the assessment that being more assertive than he had previously been would help his group-work interactions in the future. And he did put that plan into effect.

Implausibly, in the last semester of his senior year, Ben found himself again assigned to a group project with Cathy. This time, however, lines of allegiance had shifted and it was Cathy, not Ben, who was constructed by the other group members as a problem. In fact, it appeared that their common problem with Cathy created bonds between Ben and the other group members. When asked how he dealt with Cathy this time, Ben explained his caution:

Ben: I try to be nice to her. Every time I try to ask her which my part is, because last time she complain I didn't do anything for the experiment. So this time I just make sure, write everything down, what's her assignment is, what my assignment is, so later on we have evidence if she complain anything. But she didn't. She didn't complain anything about me. That's good. I'm glad. (second-term senior)

Again, however, Cathy offered to do the write-up of the report and again she found herself unable to complete it on time.

Ben: So the day before we supposed to hand it in, she couldn't finish. Again! Same problem, you see, with last time. She couldn't finish, so now she complain that the three of us don't do anything and give all the work to her. And we each, me and Mike, we stay with her in the library the whole night. We didn't sleep at all.

Interviewer: In order to finish the project.

Ben: To make her feel better, we just sit there. And she didn't give us any work to do. We just sit there with her. That's it!

Interviewer: You're laughing about this now.

Ben: Yeah. It's ridiculous. (second-term senior)

The original incident stood out in Ben's mind as the most significant academic event in his junior year, not his grades, not his much-appreciated history class, but the turmoil of this social interaction. In the end, Ben was vindicated in his own mind, to his classmates, and to his professors. The trauma of the original upsetting experience transformed into solidarity in adversity with the other group mates. At the end of his junior year, even before his vindication, Ben asserted the importance to him of the kind of solidarity that could come from peer interactions.

Interviewer: Thinking back over the whole term, what is something good or important or special that stands out for you in one of your courses or in all your courses?

Ben: I would say communication, coordinate. After last night [when Ben stayed up all night again studying with classmates for a final exam] I really feel group study help each other, and it helped me a lot. ... Last night when I drove back, I was thinking about it. I really enjoy about it very much. ... I meet a lot of new people, new friends. (second-term junior)

It was these academic and nonacademic social relations, good and (rarely) bad, that undergirded Ben's college experiences, even his literacy experiences. In talking about reading, for example, Ben referred to a reliance on others, if necessary, that got him through difficult reading material.

Ben: ... it doesn't matter if you understand everything or not because they [the group members] can talk about it. (first-term junior)

Similarly with writing, Ben never characterized it as anything resembling a solitary struggle with expressing meaning but rather as engaged with an outward reality that included things and actions, causes and effects, and people.

Relations With Faculty

Ben never developed a close relationship with any particular member of the faculty in engineering, although because of the way work in the engineering program was organized, he eventually had a great deal of contact with faculty, beginning especially in his junior year. He was probably right in his appraisal that he had remained fairly anonymous in the engineering program, much more so than did the other three focal students in their majors, and that most of the faculty did not know who he was, in spite of his crash-and-burn group problem. Furthermore, Ben himself seemed relatively uninterested in individual faculty members as well, never particularly critical or admiring of them, again unlike the other focal students, particularly Jan. For Ben, as sociable and at ease with people as he was, what mattered was the course material, not the personalities.

Yet in engineering, students worked more closely with faculty than in any of the other majors under study. Along with the heavy emphasis on group work in the program came close supervision of these groups by faculty, resulting in an intensely social form of study in which students spent enormous amounts of time working with each other and with faculty. In one of his courses in Ben's senior year, rather than holding class at all, the professor held lengthy weekly meetings with each project group one-on-one to check on their progress and to help them solve problems. This close working relationship may account partially for the faculty's sympathy with their students. Comments on how hard the students worked were numerous. Professor C even canceled the final exam in his course out of sympathy with the students' being overworked.

Staying up all night working was also the excuse Ben gave and faculty repeated as the explanation for the students' not being more careful in writing up reports. Once the real work of doing the experiments, the calculations, the thinking and discussing through explanations, the creation of graphs and figures, and the analysis of results were completed, writing up the project remained a more or less onerous technicality up to the last project Ben completed in engineering. Faculty seemed to find this conception of how writing fit with working unexceptionable. They did, however, complain that this attitude contributed to sloppiness and lack of attention to grammatical and mechanical (i.e., punctuation and spelling) issues.

Professor B: These are reasonably good students but I think they just threw it [the report] together. See, they work so hard, and they stay up till 4 a.m. the night before but they don't realize

... how bad an impression it makes not to write it up. They think they've got the technical part worked out and they just don't take the time on it. ... It's just that they're so harassed by the end and they're so tired ... they don't allow that extra time which is so important to the grade.

This last complaint echoes industry's complaints about the writing of engineers, finding it ungrammatical (Winsor, 1996), but speaks mainly to the sympathy faculty felt for their apprentices.

But faculty did have complaints about the engineering students. Several professors talked about these students' reluctance to go beyond reporting facts in their reports and to use their intuition, insight, and previous knowledge to interpret their results.

Interviewer: So you consider this a pretty hard assignment?

Professor C: Yeah. In that it is open-ended. They can make of it what they want to and that, that's difficult for students. They're used to having homework that says take this and this and this and use this equation and get the answer. They're very good at that. But when it says, when it's very open-ended ... [it's a problem].

It is perhaps this desire of the faculty for the students to push themselves to go beyond getting the equations right that accounts for the culture of self-reliance that the faculty promoted despite their close association with students' group projects. Although no one admitted to discouraging students from asking questions, Professor F referred to what he felt was students' desire for hand-holding.

Interviewer: Do people come to you before they are to turn something in to ask you to look at it?

Professor F: Oh, sometimes they do. They want to be led by the hand. Lots of students do. Others are pretty independent.

Interviewer: Do you have a negative reaction if they want to be led by the hand?

Professor F: Well, I try not to. I give them a lot of guidance if they catch me at the right time.

Presumably if the students did not catch him at the right time they received a message that they were to work it out themselves. This interest in developing self-reliance both coincided with and contributed to developing Ben's own interest in working things out for himself. Ben certainly got the message that students were not to bother faculty needlessly.

Ben: He [the professor] says he's the final resort. If you really can't find those things in the library or in anywhere—sometimes we have to use online or something to search those things—he said if we really can't find them, we have to ask him. (first-term senior)

This faculty attitude also corresponded with Ben's own preferences. He found trying to work out problems alone stimulating.

Ben: ... You have no idea what [certain new equipment] is for, so we had to find out by ourselves. (second-term senior)

In all then, Ben's socioacademic relationships with faculty (and peers) seemed to suit him well. He enjoyed working with others, did whatever necessary to be sure he personally learned the material, valued the semi-private meetings with faculty, but in the end, had no special craving for personal connection with any of his professors. In some ways, despite mutual cordiality, they were as anonymous to him as he was to them.

SPECIAL CIRCUMSTANCES
FOR INTERNATIONAL STUDENTS

What were the special circumstances that Ben described himself as facing as an L2 student in a U.S. university? Aside from his particular problems with his visa, for the most part, they were circumstances that many L2 students face. Time was always an issue.

Ben: [referring to chemistry lab] ... I have lab and lab is only 1 hour credit but it's always takes like 4 hours, 6 hours to finish. (second-term sophomore)

For Ben, as for many other NNES students, both the time it took to do work and the time it took to process language intake created a heavy burden. Ben was occasionally aware that he had missed important orally delivered information, particularly on details of assignments. At times he realized this only after missing deadline dates; at others he realized it even at the moment the information was being delivered.

Reading for some of his courses, like his psychology class, was trying because of what he perceived as his lack of vocabulary, although he never mentioned reading as a problem for his engineering or other science classes. In some of his classes, Ben found himself not able to listen as fast as his professors talked. He was occasionally unable to take notes, again, because of his professors' rate of information delivery, which he perceived as overly speedy. In his 1st year with this research project, Ben seemed to feel exasperated about this differential between delivery and intake.

> Ben: [referring to his psychology class] Right now, just like I'm crazy. He talk and talk and talk and talk and talk word faster and hardly give you any chance to thinking. Just write on the board and everything. (first-term sophomore).

He felt he was able to take in only about half of what was being said. But by the time he was in engineering classes in his junior year, a similar situation evoked only bemused head shaking.

> Ben: Sometimes, maybe at the first several class I wrote down [in the journal for that class] that she is going too fast and we can't keep up. Because she keep write down on the blackboard and this hand wrote down and this hand erase it. [laughs] (first-term junior)

In his relationships with his professors, Ben seemed to have neither any advantage nor disadvantage as a Chinese American although he did attribute his failure to secure summer engineering internships to his status as an international student. When asked what he might like his professors to know about him, he said that he would like to be sure they understood that he had only been writing in English and living in an English-speaking country for a few years and that he necessarily could not do the same things or do them as quickly in English as some of his classmates could, a modest and reasonable representation of his situation.

> Ben: I try to catch up, but when I read some other people's writings I can see there is a lot of difference. There's still a lot of things I need catch up. (first-term junior)

Although this may also be the case for some domestic college students, the essay exams Ben wrote for his history class were the first ones he had ever written in English. And, interestingly, the last as well, at least during the time of this research project.

Finally, moving to the United States and studying in a U.S. university no doubt opened some doors for Ben, but they also closed some doors he would have liked to walk through. With his love of reading, especially in Chinese, he would have liked to study history. Because of his apparent natural talent in math, he would have enjoyed that route also. Both of these possibilities, however, were closed off to him in his newly adopted country. Yet in his easygoing way, Ben seemed to be able and willing to make the most of whatever situation he was in and simply accepted these losses as trade-offs in life.

Faculty on International Students

Because this study focused on the experiences of international or immigrant students, all the faculty interviewed were specifically asked about these students in their courses. The engineering faculty was generally impressed with the performance of their L2 students, particularly international students, that is, students whose education had taken place for the most part outside the United States. They were regularly referred to as "bright," "hard working," "readily adaptable." Concerns never surfaced in terms of students' ability to do the required experiments, computer work, or problem sets. Faculty expressed confidence as well in their ability to do whatever reading was required in their course. Where fears for the students were expressed, they nearly always related to oral communication, either understanding the lectures or communicating ideas or questions orally to professors.

Professor F: It's always hard to tell whether they're understanding or not but they seem to. ... by the time they get to be seniors they're usually able to kind of pretty well understand the written, excuse me, the spoken English and they can read the textbooks fairly, they can read the textbooks better than they can understand what they hear. A lot of them can never express themselves well in English.

Interviewer: Does this create a problem?

Professor F: I think that creates a communication problem. ... Sometimes they ask questions and I have trouble understanding them.

One professor worried that NNES students sometimes missed out on informal, casually made remarks by either the professor or peers in the course of working on projects that, if understood, might have saved the students time or helped them be more accurate in their experiments.

Professor B: ... it's often a group of international students that, they don't fully understand exactly what it is we're doing. ... sometimes they simply miss out on things. I don't know how else to say it. Just [things that are] kind of just generally understood. Of course, the groups talk among themselves down in the computer room, like, well, if we make this [change] on this tower, we'll have a good design. But they just somehow, they don't ever hear that. And it's a kind of cultural thing, not as though they're missing any specific sentence, well, perhaps they are, but it's the context of it.

This professor felt that a good role for domestic students in relation to L2 students would be to provide that "context" in their group work together. On the other hand, at least two of the engineering faculty members interviewed felt L2 students were better off in groups made up only of L2 students, where they would not get ignored and where they might be able to get some moral support.

> Professor C: It certainly helps if they can identify with some group … to have someone that they can close the door and laugh at us with.

Occasionally faculty members volunteered that they either did or did not make adjustments in their classes to accommodate L2 students. (This was not a question specifically raised in any of the interviews). One engineering professor talked about lowering the scores of domestic students for grammatical errors in their work but not lowering those of NNESs. A chemistry professor described changing the way he wrote his word problems.

> Professor J: … some of my homework assignments that do have some sort of narrative, some of them were maybe not absolutely crystal clear for non-native speakers. And so, I tried every week to double proofread these and make sure I wasn't making use of any kind of idiomatic expression that might throw them for a loop when they were at home actually doing the homework assignment.

Most likely this kind of "double" proofreading was also helpful to NESs in the course. On the other hand, some faculty were less inclusive. One of Ben's history professors worried that the few NNESs in his course were not following his lecture but he simply did not feel he could help.

> Professor A: I can't imagine any way in which I have or should change the course to accommodate them.

He admitted that despite what he took to be their difficulties with oral communication, the few he had in his course were

> Professor A: … making an effort to participate in class discussion. It's hard enough for native Americans [sic] to have the nerve to participate.

In other words, although the L2 students appeared to be accommodating his class procedures, ones that even domestic students were finding difficult to do, he was not accommodating them despite their efforts. On the other hand, at least two of the faculty in engineering specifically mentioned that one reason they did work to accommodate L2 students was that they "are all trying hard."

Without making too much of the differences in attitude noted here, it might be worth mentioning that domestic engineering students were also perceived to be struggling with their studies, and the faculty seemed generally very sympathetic to their students and aware of how hard they worked. Seeing how hard the work was for even domestic students may have allowed the engineering faculty to sympathize even more with students facing the same difficulties and carrying the added burden of a nontransparent medium of communication. Furthermore, because engineering enrolled fairly large numbers of international students, developing strategies to help 10% of the student body seemed perhaps more feasible or more worth the effort than it might have to liberal arts faculty, who saw fewer L2 students in their classes and who were perhaps used to having more domestic students who either did not bother or did not have to struggle as hard as engineering students did. If fewer students were apparently struggling, faculty may have felt less need to help the minority that was. Finally, beyond engineering, in the politics of universities, the pervasive attitude in general-education courses, as opposed to courses in the major, might be that there is little incentive to work hard to make required courses more accessible to students; the students will be there regardless. On the other hand, alienating too many majors by failing to think in terms of accommodating their needs may result in fewer majors, not a good sign for a university program.

In any case, for faculty unaccustomed to working with bilingual students, it may be difficult to guess what would stump a NNES. For example, Ben did not understand the notation Professor A made in the margins of one of his history essay exams where the professor had taken off points for missing information and added the information himself:

Interviewer: [reading out loud the professor's addition in the margin of the exam] British encouraged rivalries.
Ben: Rivalries?
Interviewer: Like competition.
Ben: Oh yeah … (first-term sophomore)

And Ben proceeded to explain exactly the information he had failed to include in his essay, showing that he knew the information. It is certainly understandable that a professor might not imagine that an L2 student would not know the specific word *rivalries* though he did know the word *competition*. On the other hand, it is less understandable that a professor could not "imagine" some of the kinds of things that might make an

American history course difficult for an NNES. Perhaps a little sensitivity to issues in language acquisition might have helped.

In other instances, Professor A might have helped Ben, and possibly NES students, by understanding better the confusion caused by the arbitrariness and infrequency of encounter of proper names in a foreign language. One history quiz asked for the former name of San Francisco, possibly a salient enough piece of cultural trivia in the book where it appeared for domestic students to note it almost without thinking. Certainly Professor A thought so because he explained that these quizzes were intended only to verify that the students were doing the reading and that anyone who did do the reading would automatically do well on the quizzes. Ben did do the reading. Carefully. However, it would have been difficult for Ben to anticipate that some particular piece of cultural trivia might be especially interesting and so salient to domestic students and to then note it for retention for a quiz. By the same token, in discussing the Cherokee removal in an interview, Ben referred to Thomas Jefferson rather than Andrew Jackson as the culprit, a mistake perhaps less likely to be made by a domestic student because of familiarity with at least Jefferson but a mistake that is quite understandable in terms not only of cultural unfamiliarity for an L2 student but simply because of linguistic features. The names are somewhat similar. Jackson and Jefferson, as arbitrary phonetic tokens, may be as difficult for an NNES to keep distinct as Jian Shao and Jung Shiao might be for English speakers. Ben did well in and thoroughly enjoyed this history class. These are nevertheless examples of instances where the professor might well have accommodated his few game NNESs.

IDEOLOGICAL EDUCATION

Perhaps because engineering was so focused on technical details, clear incidents of unexamined ideological assumptions rarely made their way into the class observations and interview data for Ben's case. One such incident, however, demonstrated Ben's own self-reflective and critical perception despite his general believing game attitude. In his professional development seminar, the students viewed videos produced by chemical corporations that described the work they did, the products they made, and the happy workforce they employed with the optimistic and self-congratulatory tone typical of corporate-produced videos of the 1950s. To judge by the numbers of the domestic students in the class that sneaked out of the class after signing the attendance sheet or read newspapers during the showings, they were apparently bored silly. One possible reason for their lack of interest might have been that the information represented nothing new; it was already part of their background assumptions about American industry. But

Ben found these videos and lectures informative and felt he could learn something from them that would be new to him about how American industry portrayed itself. He did not, however, view these images of American industry without skepticism.

Ben: Like the last lecture the guy is talking about working around safety. I would just say, maybe talking is one thing and actually do is another. Because if you talk about safety about the environment, he said basically the people working inside of the factories are safer than the people who live around the factories. Pollution, waste. He said the one good thing is you have to work with the community around. Like he said it's up to the town to give the license to the factories, so they can operate. I don't know. I don't see that they have that much power to do that. Otherwise the Sesquash River [a notorious nuclear power plant in the area whose construction and continued use has frequently been protested by local residents] wouldn't happen.

Interviewer: So you didn't really believe what this person was saying?

Ben: Well, … I … watched several tapes and the people in the working area in those tapes are very good and safety. If I went to a Chinese factory, I probably know on the tape it's a lot cleaner [than in reality]. (second-term junior)

If Ben felt the corporate propaganda in these industry-produced videos distorted reality, nevertheless, the heavy involvement of this department with industry in general constructed corporate and industrial entities as the target bosses, the ones for whom this education in chemical engineering was taking place, as opposed to such other possible targets as the public sector or environmentally oriented organizations. The world of chemical engineering in the United States, at least in this department's discursive construction, was coterminous with these corporate/industrial worlds, their concerns, their goals, their ideology.

CONCLUSION

Although Ben's GPA declined as his undergraduate career went on and the technical difficulty and learning load of his engineering courses increased, he considered his academic life generally successful, and it was certainly successful enough for him to get into graduate school. The role of writing in his undergraduate career was minimal, though he felt in no way handicapped by that. Though Ben appreciated what he had learned in his writing classes, feeling grateful for the language practice he had engaged in there, he also found himself consciously drawing on it little.

The genres he experienced outside of his writing classes generally did not overlap with the English department genres he had been taught to use in his 1st college year, so long before. Most important, though Ben witnessed writing in his group projects, he rarely engaged in it himself. But his education proceeded smoothly without the benefit of much writing.

Ben was also satisfied with the socioacademic relationships he experienced with both faculty, whom he trusted but was not particularly close to emotionally, and domestic and L2 peers, using even his one calamitous group experience to build solidarity with other classmates later. In all then, from most points of view, Ben experienced an expanded universe and enjoyed his increased positive social contacts, the opportunities for learning he encountered, and his growing sense of himself as an intellectual and professional.

Of the four focal students, Ben's case is the most humbling to me as an L2 language/writing professional. Our interactions with him over text during his 1st year seemed increasingly irrelevant to his intellectual and professional development. He simply did not need us much, unavoidably prompting me to consider how much we overestimate our importance in the lives of any of our students, those students who are nevertheless so present to us as we teach, research, and write about them.

3

"Don't Have Easy": Nursing in L2

Interviewer: *What's been easy [about your classes]?*
Yang: *Don't have easy. ... I will have not easy. Never, never, never easy for me. Never easy for me.*

BACKGROUND

Although each person in this research presented a unique case, in many ways Yang's situation stood out as the most unusual of the four student participants and for second-language specialists perhaps the most interesting case. Coming to her aid in her studies in the United States were her maturity, giving her the advantage of life experience, a great deal of world knowledge, a clear sense of herself, and a degree of professional education in the very area she had decided to study at the university in the United States. But the achievement of her goals was also dramatically hampered by her distinct language difficulties. Her struggles with language continued until she graduated, and although my research assistants and I could honestly tell her (because she often asked) that we detected some improvement in her language abilities over the years of the study, it was not notable, and to someone unused to interacting with her, her English remained difficult to understand. In the end, however, despite the Nursing program's heavy emphasis on oral communication, one that was nearly Yang's downfall, Yang succeeded in her studies and graduated with a GPA of over 3.0 and several postings to the dean's list.

At the time we met her, Yang was a trim, attractive woman in her middle 30s. She smiled and joked readily, though she often seemed tense or agitated and spoke in a rapid, breathy, nervous-seeming style that may have made her more difficult to understand. In classes, she always sat front and center and worked before and after class to engage teacher and peers in interaction. She was a skilled conversationalist. During interviews she often turned questions back on the interviewer, asking how we would have handled a situation, what we thought of her solution, how things were going for us, what our normal practice might be in some circumstance. She was generally an engaging person, eager and able to reach out to others.

A childhood bout of meningitis had left Yang slightly hearing impaired; although her hearing loss was so slight that we were entirely unaware of it until she happened to refer to it in the last semester of our interviews, it may have had an impact on her English development. After she completed high school, Yang was sent, as was the custom at the time in the PRC, to the countryside to work. When the political climate changed, she took college qualifying exams and was admitted, not to engineering as she would have preferred, but to medical school.

The medical program consisted of 4 years of classroom work, part of the 4th year being clinical observation and rotation, similar to what Yang later did in the nursing program in the United States. During their 5th year, the medical students worked entirely at a hospital, observing and learning in a kind of apprenticeship. This year entailed no exams or other academic work but plenty of hands-on clinical experience. For their apprenticeship, Yang's group of seven medical students was sent to a small village hospital that had only three doctors. There, the medical students enjoyed a great deal of responsibility and autonomy in actually delivering health care, relying on each other and on their books for information when necessary. (It was in medical school that 23-year-old Yang met her future husband, also a medical student). Once their classroom and intern work was completed at the end of their 5 years of studies, the new doctors could count on being posted to medical practitioner positions without worrying about hunting for jobs or taking further licensing exams. After medical school, Yang worked for 7 years as a primary-care pediatrician.

Yang's study of English was minimal, a year or two in middle school and then in college for about a year, starting over again from the very beginning with an instructor who candidly admitted that his English was not very good.

Yang: My English teacher in China in college not speak better than me. (second-term senior)

Yang: I'm not fortunate. I ... got bad pronunciation teacher. He is good in grammar, he not good in pronunciation. We got big class, more than 30 student. He said, I just tell you grammar; I don't know how to translate. He don't know medicine terms. (third-term senior)

The decision to study in the United States was her husband's, with Yang joining him after about 6 months. Their daughter then joined them 3 years later, at about age 9. For 5 years as her husband studied, Yang worked at odd jobs (in a clothing factory, restaurants, a cafeteria, a veterinary clinic) with little satisfaction:

Interviewer: How has your time here been, good time, bad time?
Yang: Bad time, the changing time in my whole life. All life.
Interviewer: Difficult?
Yang: Yeah, difficult. (first-term freshman)

Academic Portrait

Yang was 36 years when she enrolled in the United States as a nursing student. Because of her previous medical education in China, she received transfer credit for many science and medicine courses, with the result that she was able to begin nursing studies at the end of 1 year and one summer rather than at the end of 2 years of general-education courses.[12] She was quite successful in her first experiences studying in English during that 1 year of general-education courses, which included courses requiring some substantive writing, such as English, sociology, and history. She ended her first semester of studies in the United States with a GPA of 4.0 out of 4 and began her nursing curriculum with a 3.85.

Although her score on her entering English placement exam was barely above the minimum required for admission to the first of three credit-bearing ESL courses, her adviser successfully petitioned for an exemption for her from one of those courses. This exemption eventually loomed as a piercing irony for Yang, given the unanticipated emphasis in nursing school on communication.

Yang did not find nursing particularly interesting. It had been at her husband's urging and for her family's sake that she embarked on the study of nursing, but for Yang herself, it was mere job training that she stuck with because she had come that far already, no matter how far that was at any given moment. As she described it, she wanted:

Yang: Like American people like to say, to face the music. (second-term junior)

In classes, Yang flicked her attention between the lecture and the notes she was writing or consulting. She was bold and confident enough to ask and answer questions in class, though not often, because she was not easy to understand and would be forced to repeat. Yang thought of herself as not a top student but as someone who valued education a great deal and was willing to work as hard as necessary to achieve her educational goals, or in the case of nursing, her professional training goals. For the most part, when asked what she had found interesting in a course, she would say either that at her age none of it was interesting or that whatever she did, she did out of necessity not pleasure. Thus, her motivation to study nursing was entirely extrinsic.

Advantages and Disadvantages of Age.

Yang was the oldest of the research participants, and her age was a clear factor in her experiences. She felt, for example, that the central cause of her struggles in nursing school was her problems in English and that the central cause of her problems in English was her age and late start in studying English seriously.

She mentioned other disadvantages associated with being in her mid-30s. For instance, she had few friends, particularly American friends because people her age, she said, did not socialize; they were:

Yang: ... busy, American people busy ... because they already over the play years. (first-term junior)

This lack of socializing meant that she had little occasion to use English socially in casual settings. She once estimated that, when she did not have classes or clinicals scheduled, days would go by without her speaking English and that even on days when she attended classes, her English might be limited to chitchatting with classmates for a total of 10 minutes.

But she also benefited from certain advantages because of her greater experience with the world. First was her medical education. The fact that she already knew a great deal about the human body, disease, medications, and so on decreased her learning load in the nursing school and no doubt contributed to the development of her English proficiency because she was able to use the support of known concepts to work out unknown language.

Interviewer: Did you have any easy classes this semester?
Yang: Not too easy but nutrition, this was easier.
Interviewer: Why was that easy?
Yang: Because the content I have done from China.
Interviewer: What do you think will be interesting [this term]?
Yang: Maybe the pathology because the teacher just tell us the mechanical, what are reasons contribute this disease, so that's familiar to me. (first-term junior)

Even in her sociology class in her freshman year, she attributed her success to her experience:

Yang: I already finish college, bachelor degree. ... Maybe ... my English is poor, but maybe I got another skill for help my class.

Interviewer: What skill?

Yang: Like sociology, this exam topic, discrimination for the Black people, for the Asian people, racism ... I know. (first-term freshman)

Yang's age created both openings and constraints for her. She drew on a great deal more experience but she was also dramatically hampered in achieving her goals by her difficulties with English and by the demand in her major for a high level of communication skill. Many, perhaps most, of the nursing faculty were quite tolerant of her English and recognized and reiterated that they knew Yang was intelligent, knowledgeable, and skilled. But in hospital clinicals, faculty obviously had a primary obligation to the patients she and they dealt with. The individual and cumulative effect of the various traumatic events in her academic life (see later discussion) was the creation and maintenance of a great deal of anxiety for Yang about language.

EDUCATIONAL CONTEXT: THE NURSING PROGRAM

Of all the participants' majors, Yang's program of study was the most tightly controlled. Typically students applied for admission to the nursing curriculum during their sophomore year and were admitted with a cohort of 100 to 120 students with whom they would continue their studies for 2 years. Studying with a cohort proved to have significant positive consequences for Yang because it allowed her to develop friendly socioacademic relations with a core of English-speaking peers. Once admitted to the nursing program, students all followed fairly precisely the same curriculum in the same order. Missing a single course meant making it up the following year when it would be offered to the subsequent cohort of students. In order to remain in the nursing program, students had to pass all courses with a C or better. If they scored below a C in one course, they were allowed to repeat it once. A second D or F, in any course, meant leaving the nursing program.

The Nursing College was located in a free–standing, modern building housing faculty offices, lecture halls, smaller meeting rooms, and its own library. The high walls of the entrance hallway were covered with group pictures of graduating classes of nursing students, in addition to announcements about nursing related opportunities, conferences, and other programs. On the ground floor, a small lounge offered drink and snack machines and couches where students gathered during breaks to talk or study.

The nursing curriculum was a professional training program, a self-characterization of which the students were repeatedly reminded as part of their socialization into this discipline. Nursing faculty insisted on the overriding importance of communication for success during school and beyond. Communication needed to be clear and accurate because an important feature of documents produced by practicing nurses is their status as legal entities, as the students were also repeatedly and insistently reminded. The central focus of the nursing program was the client, who almost invariably was suffering in one way or another from physical or social ills. Thus, a prime directive for Yang and her cohort was to develop the skills that would enable them to interact with the public efficiently and competently, often under stressful circumstances, and to document the interaction fully and accurately. Despite her initial expectations of success thanks to her medical background, Yang's persistent communication problems caused the nursing faculty to express concern, sometimes officially, about the wisdom of allowing Yang to proceed in the nursing major.

The all important nursing clinicals were very particular features of the nursing program. To maintain accreditation status, the nursing program required 90 total hours of clinicals, that is, time spent with patients usually at the hospital. The clinicals were attached to at least one, often two, courses per semester. Every clinical had to be completed successfully (with a grade of Satisfactory) for students to pass the courses they were attached to regardless of how well they did on the "didactic" part of the course, that is, the more traditional part of the course, which took place in a classroom. Because the physical safety and health of human beings was at stake, the nursing faculty remained concerned right up until her graduation that Yang could not always communicate in clinicals with patients, did not always fully understand what she was orally directed to do, and in a crisis situation, might not be able to make herself understood to patients, other nurses, and doctors. Yang herself was very nervous about her performance in clinicals and expressed the anxiety of being torn between needing to get information in order to perform properly and being afraid to ask questions that would reveal her lack of understanding. Furthermore, fear of making a mistake in clinicals was also rooted in Yang's understanding of U.S. medicine as embedded in a litigious society:

Interviewer: What is the most important thing you remember from these classes, something you'll always know about.

Yang: You need to do everything correctly ... Perfect, nursing everything perfect. ... we need to write correctly because the clinic documents they will be legal documents. (first-term junior)

Yang: America, you know, the case [law suits]. (first term junior)

Yang: You can do nothing wrong. Everything, you need to do
               perfect. But everybody not perfect. If you got [do] some-
               thing wrong, that's terrible. (second-term junior)

Academic Preparation

The clinicals all required the preparation of intricately detailed Nursing
Care Plans (NCPs) for the patients that the student nurses were assigned
to. Yang came to despise the long, taxing, repetitive NCPs, described
more fully later.

On the other hand, the nursing program also placed a strong emphasis on exams, usually three demanding exams in each course, based for
the most part on the lectures.

> Professor P: Those who flunk out of this nursing program usually don't
>   do well on exams. Doing well on exams is the hardest part
>   of the program for the students.

The majority of the exams were strictly multiple-choice, a fact that had its
advantages and drawbacks for Yang. As expected with an English learner,
this format challenged Yang's reading ability.

> Yang: Sometime that content, for the four multiple-choice, two
>   sentences very similar. American students can easier see
>   information, the difference. For me, they [are] the same thing.
>   (first-term junior)

> Yang: Make sentence just like a trick. (third-term senior)

> Yang: … four answers read, read, read. Pick it out. (first-term senior)

On the other hand, if the course lent itself to exam questions with fairly
straightforward answers (such as the pathology course), she felt these
multiple-choice exams were much easier to do than alternative means of
assessment, such as writing a paper.

An important reason that faculty gave for using multiple-choice exams
was to familiarize the students with the format of the state nursing licensing board exams. A particular feature of both the nursing program and
eventually the state board exam multiple-choice format was that the students recorded their answers into a small tabulator attached to each desk
in the nursing lecture hall. The exams were then machine graded
instantly so that students could know how well they had done before they
left the exam room.

Although faculty interviewed repeatedly claimed that the exams in their own courses did not call for straightforward memorization, it was clear that this type of learning was in fact required in most instances, if only in order to answer questions that called for application of memorized information. Furthermore, faculty often lectured in a way that allowed students to write down their words verbatim. Yang made a point of complimenting one of the lecturers for that day's class because of its clarity. In the field notes from that class, the teacher's lecturing style is described as:

> "somewhat unusual, clear, slow, with definitely marked clear emphasis, and somewhat strangely short sentences, shorter than normal, almost listing."

Yang liked this careful, slow delivery precisely because it allowed the students to take nearly verbatim notes that she was sure accurately contained all the information she needed to learn for the exams. Such an approach to learning was encouraged by the fact that the faculty felt certain information needed to be at the students' fingertips. In commenting on what students had to know for her course, one professor explained:

Professor C: Lectures give didactic material to get "down pat."
Interviewer: Students have to KNOW the material in the lectures?
Professor C: KNOW it.

When a particular faculty member's lecturing style invited participation, the importance of learning by heart was implicitly reiterated (from field notes):

TQ[13]:   What other problems [might arise]? Everyone's been to L&D now, so what can happen?
Ss answer.
Teacher: No.
Ss answer.
Teacher: No. You guys don't remember this, do you?

These kinds of exchanges, with faculty posing a question and students supplying the answer in chorus, were quite typical. Faculty worked hard to help students strengthen memory traces for the material covered in the courses, partly as a means of helping them deal with the stress and fatigue of this program.

Professional Enculturation to Nursing

The nursing program and faculty tried to communicate to students that they were in fact different from students in other majors; they had much more serious business to attend to and, for this very reason, much more work to do. For example, the Nursing School building was located directly next to the education college. Yang recounted the following observation by nursing faculty:

> Yang: … the teacher say you guys will go hospital. You know education building [next door]? Teacher say another guy [i.e., education majors] go to school, they can make joking, they can make play with small children, not like you. (first-term senior)

These were budding professionals engaged in important and serious work.

Nursing faculty also worked from the first day of class and throughout the program to instill in the nursing students an esprit de corps and a sense of themselves as special, working to develop in students a sense of in-group and out-group, a sense of both otherness from the rest of the university and togetherness with each other, exemplified even in their clothing. Very few other students on campus, only ROTC and the nurses, would be seen in disciplinary outfits, distinguishing them from other students.

The degree of pressure on the nursing students did seem extraordinary. In addition to the requirement to do satisfactory work in all clinicals and to pass all courses with a C or better, the clinicals were long and physically exhausting, sometimes for 8 hours at a time, sometimes for 12. For most of the clinicals, the students would have to spend 2 to 3 hours the day before, preparing at the hospital by studying the patient's chart and then going home to read up on the patient's problem. By 7 a.m. the next morning:

> Professor O: You have to be prepared to take care of your patient. And it's extremely demanding … because of the clinicals and then there's an inherent stress; there's an inherent stress in what they're doing anyway, going into patients' rooms, being responsible for their care, worrying about making mistakes, worried about communicating with people in crisis, it's inherently stressful.

The emphasis on professional initiation may have helped to make the students accept the sacrifices they were called upon to make, the hard work they were required to do, and the awful hours they were expected to put in, with faculty right there with them through it all.

> Professor P: Students tell me they are overwhelmed, there are many too many assignments, that the paperwork is unmanageable, and there is a lot of reading, a lot of clinical time. So they are really slammed. And I can appreciate it. I mean I'm right there when

> they are doing the clinicals and I'm grading the care plans. I'm
> slammed, too. So I can really appreciate … this.

Almost like military bootcamp training, pep talks also included references to the pain of junior year, a pain they had all gone through together and were now beyond, experiencing the pride and camaraderie that come with successfully going through a difficult experience with others.

In preclinical lectures, faculty heightened the drama by telling students to look professional ("take the ring out of your nose" before showing up) and to act professional by being intellectually, emotionally, and physically prepared for the serious experience of dealing with patients:

> Teacher: You have to be ready to take care of the patient. You need to be
> able to answer questions. You have to be *physically ready* to
> do care tomorrow.
> Teacher: Be sure you're mentally prepared.

Faculty also created a strong sense of mentoring, of apprentice and master, by sharing bond-tightening personal experiences, stories, and insider information and by constructing the licensing exam as their common foe, which they would work together to defeat.

CONTEXT SHAPERS

Language-Related Events

Language Problems Begin. But for Yang, the biggest foe proved to be English. Given her successful performance in general-education classes, Yang had every reason to expect to do well in nursing. After all, some of the material she would be covering would be familiar to her from her medical background. But her guarded hopes for herself in the nursing program very quickly suffered blows, as she noted in the journal she was keeping for this project:

> I have been in nursing program for 10 days. All the experience made me
> confused and frustrated.

Her score on the first exam in her basic nursing course was 66. After the exam, her lecturer spoke to her about it and suggested that she consider dropping two of her four nursing courses so that she would have time to work on her English.

> Yang: My teacher thinks it's language problem. The first time she like to
> have appointment with me, I very happy because … I think, oh
> she will help me. Well, she tell me you need to drop this classes

because your English poor. So I feel pressure for this class from
beginning. (first-term junior)

Then her first assignment, a health assessment of a classmate, was
returned as unacceptable, again because of her English. An excerpt from
Yang's paper follows:

> No abnormal found. No pregnant record.
>
> Blood test denies anemia.
>
> [Client] has all childhood shoots. ... Present leadership. ... growled up in
> a traditional pattern family. ... Natural born Caucasian, Christian, empha-
> sizes importance of education, hard working vulval, and friendship. ...
> believes the strength to guild people. ... Satisfy to her social environ-
> ment. ... takes high-carbohydrate and lower-fat diet, as well as, masters
> nursing professional acknowledge in order to be a complete, healthy,
> professional nurse.

The stern cover letter that accompanied the returned assignment
informed her this would be her only chance to rewrite any submitted
papers for this course:

> To: [Yang]
>
> From: X, course coordinator
>   Y, course faculty
>
> Re: [Course] Assignment
>
> After careful review of your paper, we find the writing style and gram-
> mar of the paper unacceptable. The paper fails to communicate the
> information that the document is intended to communicate.
>
> We are asking you rewrite the assignment. You have two weeks to do so.
> ... The paper will be graded without penalty. This option of rewriting and
> resubmitting will not be extended to any other assignment in this course.
> This has been discussed with [the program director] and she agrees.
>
> In the interim, we ask you to see [the program director] to investigate
> your options for improving your writing skills.

From this point on, Yang feared submitting any written work.

Machine Exams.   But the worst event in this first term of Yang's
nursing program occurred during the second exam in one of her courses.
As described earlier, most of the exams in the nursing curriculum were

multiple-choice and machine graded. During this exam, Yang had trouble deciding the correct multiple-choice answer and then switching to the machine to record the answer. She tried to compensate by handwriting her answers and then planned to copy them into the machine, but when time was called, she had not yet had the chance to transfer all her answers to the machine. The proctors, all instructors in the course, became agitated as it appeared that she was continuing to answer questions even though they had called for everyone to stop. They converged on her seat in the lecture hall and began yelling stop, stop, as Yang recounted several times. As she continued to try to record her answers, she made some sort of ah, ah, sound and, according to one of the faculty interviewed later, began hitting her head (with her hand?), an action that made the faculty worry that something was wrong with her mentally. She was mortified by this public humiliation and repeated her description of this incident several times in the following semesters. Every one of the faculty interviewed also seemed to be aware of it, and several mentioned subsequent faculty discussions of what should have been done in the situation. At least one faculty member suggested that a better response would have been to allow all the students to have extra time on the exam, but they all worried about preparing the students for the format of the state licensing board exam. Despite the advice of her teachers and the program coordinator to drop the course and improve her English first, Yang continued and completed the semester with respectable grades: A, B+, B, and C, this last in the course just described. It was, however, a nerve-wracking beginning to her nursing studies.

Mistakes and (Mis)communication.   Things went better in spring term. Her final grades were a quite impressive three As and a B and she made the dean's list, although she brushed that aside:

Yang: For me, some honor, that's nothing for me. For my age. Just find a job, that's good. Yeah. Important thing. (second-term junior)

Yang did not, as she had promised the program coordinator she would, attend English classes during the summer between her junior and senior years, but worked in a Chinese restaurant instead, saying that her brain needed the break. She attempted to work on her English at home by reading her daughter's junior high school books out loud and having her daughter correct her pronunciation. And she worried about what the next year would bring, hoping that in fact she would be able to make it through and graduate in spring.

That was not to be. Ironically, it was a pediatrics course that stopped her despite her 7 years of active hospital work as a pediatrician. During a clinical, Yang had made a mistake that was, correctly, regarded as an indication of her continuing language difficulties. She again received a letter from the course coordinator, who had also been involved with the machine-grading incident. The following is an excerpt:

To: Dr. X, Dean

Re: Clinical Performance [Yang]

I am very concerned about [Yang's] ability to safely communicate in the pediatric clinical setting.

1) ... As the clinical instructor, I have listened to consistent concerns from parents and ... staff regarding language difficulties. Staff and parents do not understand what Ms [Yang] is saying to them. ...

4) On [date], Ms [Yang] asked me what "B and O" medication was; I told her all the students ask this as it is difficult to find in the P.D.R. I told her it was "Bella Donna and Opium suppository" given for bladder spasms. We discussed type of med, effects of med and it would be given for pain. Ms [Yang] did not ask further questions.

5) Later in the clinical on [date], Ms [Yang] came to me saying she needed to give B and O medication. It is a narcotic and, with [one of the RN's] help, Ms [Yang] had appropriately signed [the suppository] out of the narcotic box. ... When I asked Ms [Yang] what she needed to give this medicine, Ms [Yang] turned to walk away. I stopped her telling her gloves were in the room. She said "But I need to get a drink." Thinking it was for herself, I said "This child is in pain. Let's give the med first." She said, "OK" and turned away again heading to the floor kitchen. I stopped her and said "What are you doing?" Ms [Yang] said, "I need to get liquid for patient to take B+O medication." I said,"This is a suppository." Ms [Yang], still confused, looked puzzled. I said, "It is a <u>rectal</u> suppository—you need gloves and K-Y lubricant." Ms [Yang], suddenly realizing her mistake, momentarily looked horrified. We paused, she said "she was very sorry."

6) Ms [Yang]'s patient was a 20 month old with a very limited low literacy family at the bedside. I am not sure they would have objected if Ms [Yang] had tried to give the suppository by mouth. ...

While I have tremendous respect for Ms [Yang], I believe her language difficulties make it impossible for her to effectively communicate with the children and staff in the hospital setting.

My recommendation at this time is for Ms [Yang] to withdraw from [this course].

Yang was asked to meet with the dean. In an interview on that day, a very upset Yang described the same events, saying we were to keep everything about this whole incident a secret until she graduated. She said that when she asked about the B and O medication, she did not understand the clinical instructor's response but she did not question her about it further because of their previous negative interactions. Yang also knew that the instructor already had a low opinion of her English abilities and wanted her to drop the course. Yang knew that if she dropped this course as her instructor wished, she would not be able to graduate on time, and she was very focused on the idea of a timely graduation. Part of the reason for the urgency was that her husband's postdoc would run out at the end of the academic year and they would most likely need to move.

Her husband was also called to the meeting with the dean. It was decided that Yang would drop the course and not graduate with her cohort. The whole episode made her increasingly nervous and worried, until she graduated, about her English, about clinicals, about pediatrics, and particularly about this clinical instructor.

Two weeks later, rattled by this whole experience, Yang did poorly on a midterm exam and received yet another letter from the nursing program. As Yang was later to say to us wryly, she had many letters from the nursing program.

Yet with all of these negative academic experiences, Yang's final grades in the two courses she continued with during that fall were C and B+. From looking at her grades alone, it would be difficult to imagine the struggles and distress she had been through. As she commented:

Yang: You look my hair. White. That's 1 year, got a lot of white hair. (first-term senior)

During all this time, in addition to anxiety about their finances and worries about whether her husband would be find a job once the postdoc was over, yet another problem plagued Yang, her daughter, Li.

Personal Issues

The Daughter.   At the end of most interviews, we asked participants how their nonacademic life was going. Yang nearly always brought up her daughter and the problems she and her husband were having with negotiating their desires for her against her growing desire to move in directions they did not understand. Yang and her husband watched Li's relentless Americanization with helpless anxiety. At the beginning of her sophomore year, when Li was 11, Yang fretted:

Yang: I have to keep an eye on her, or else she make trouble. (first-term sophomore)

Yang and her husband worried about the quality of Li's education in the United States, her loss of Chinese, her recent refusal to use a bowl and chopsticks to eat, her increasing adoption of preteen and teenage attitudes and habits that were alien to Yang and her husband, such as not seeing much value in working hard, not wanting to study, wanting to watch too much TV, demanding certain kinds of clothing acceptable to her peers.

But what worried the parents most was Li's growing interest in boys and dating.

Yang: She got bad influence from her friends. Because the girl write notes to the male. (second-term junior)

Then Yang and her husband apparently found and read their daughter's journal, which detailed some of this interest in "the male," and were shocked. The husband was unable to sleep that night; Yang was shaken, not knowing what to do. But she did know that:

Yang: [Among] our classmates [in nursing] … I found some people they are very young, they got children. They are single parents. (first-term senior)

Yang and her husband feared this ultimate calamity for their daughter.

The Baby.   A final major event in Yang's life came in spring of her senior year, when at age 39, she became pregnant with her second child. The baby was due around Christmas. Yang worried during the entire pregnancy that the baby would come early, disrupt her final semester, and perhaps even prevent her graduation after all her struggles. At the end of the second semester of her senior year, when she told us about her pregnancy, she was asked, as always during the final interview of the semester, about any negative event that stood out for her from that term. She replied:

Yang: I do not feel good I got the baby. … Because I just worry about influence my [studies] in fall. (second-term senior)

In the following fall term in fact, she reported feeling very fatigued during the long class hours and clinicals of her final semester. Li was a problem too; in summer she declared her displeasure at the thought of a new sister. Finally, Yang worried that all her worries would do some damage to the baby, and she felt guilty about that.

Yang: Maybe I'm too involved in the class, the exam, just my baby, that's too many worries. (third-term senior)

THE TROUBLE WITH ENGLISH: LANGUAGE AND LITERACY STRUGGLES

Yang continued to operate within a context of problems at school and problems at home. Among these worries, language challenges presented themselves on a variety of fronts, and Yang tried to meet them in her own particular ways.

Oral/Aural Work

Speech.   Unlike most others at the university, Yang's major placed heavy demands on the ability to manipulate *ordinary colloquial* English. Although Yang's constant refrain of needing to improve her English haunted our interviews, at first she did very little formally to improve her English. Still, over the years, her vocabulary, grasp of sentence structure, listening comprehension, and ability to manipulate academic conventions had expanded enormously. But on the clinical floor, those skills mattered little because all her language production ability had to be filtered through her difficult-to-understand pronunciation. Her frequent backchanneling with a nervous "Yeah, yeah" made her sound uncertain and agitated. Sympathetic faculty, peers, and hospital staff managed to communicate with her through a combination of speaking face-to-face, slowing down, repeating, and when necessary, even writing things out. And though it may not have been unreasonable to expect them to accommodate her, the same could not really be asked of the patients at the hospital and their distraught families, many of whom were from depressed economic backgrounds and had little experience outside their communities or with other languages or even dialects.

This problem of pronunciation was truly an intractable one for Yang. She had some control over the evaluations of her NCPs and papers, which, however much she struggled with them, she could at least massage in privacy and across time. But, in clinicals where she interacted with patients, she felt completely vulnerable.

Yang: No security. No security. I really no security. That is my feeling. (first-term senior)

Furthermore, Yang was also well aware that her difficult oral language would hamper her ability to find a job, the whole reason for putting herself through the torment of these years of nursing school.

Nevertheless, Yang's plan was to worry about language once she finished her nursing degree, despite her rueful admission that the degree would do her no good unless her language improved enough so that she could be hired to work at a hospital. If she did not enroll in English classes during academic terms, it was certainly in part because it took all her time to succeed, as she did, in the nursing courses. But in fact, there were few places to turn to for the kind of help she needed once she determined to try. The county adult education program offered several free English-conversation classes for NNESs, and Yang attended three different ones, but these focused on greetings and simple social exchanges meant to build confidence and fluency in their casual students, not systematic feedback and adjustment of pronunciation. Furthermore, with 15 to 20 students in a class, Yang rarely had much opportunity to speak, so she stopped going.

The university's speech pathology clinic focused on pronunciation through two components. One was a class that met 1 hour a week in which a retired speech professor taught NNES students the phonetic alphabet and modeled proper pronunciation of sounds and words, which the students imitated in chorus. As Yang described it, she repeated the professor's pronunciations, thinking she was accurate, but she later realized that what she had internally perceived as a good imitation of the correct pronunciation was not. This she realized from the second component, 2 hours a week of an actual speech correction clinic, such as those for children with speech defects. In the professor's class:

> Yang: He demonstration, we pronunciation. ... We think we learn from him correct, but we don't pick up correct. Like "with." I think that's easy, I already learn correct pronunciation from him, but when I go to the therapy class they found my pronunciation still wrong. (third-term senior)

Both these two options together meant only 3 hours of practice per week; the class could not offer individual attention and the clinic could not offer enough time, and so she discontinued.

Finally, she even started attending Bible classes, courses local proselytizing churches ran, offering friendship and English in exchange for an audience to push their Christianism onto. As Yang noted:

> Yang: Even we don't believe this, I still go" (third-term senior).

Although none of the venues meant to improve her English were ideal, she spent a large portion of one summer (she claimed 100-200 hours) working on English. Unfortunately, it did not show. She had made some improvements, but they were subtle. Her nemesis from the pediatrics class, upon hearing at the beginning of classes in Yang's last semester that she had become pregnant, went to her to congratulate, or at least make a friendly fuss over her as others were doing, and heard her speak. Later she remarked to me:

Professor B: I'm sick. She's no better [in her English]" (field notes).

Yang had once said, " I can't improve in one day." But, for whatever reason, she was not improving in many more days than one. And her refrain of "I need improve my English" continued unabated.

Listening Comprehension and Lecture Notes.   Oral proficiency was the language skill the least under Yang's control because of the immediacy of speech and its neurolinguistic and physiological base, which she could do little about and certainly not quickly. She had better success overcoming difficulties with listening comprehension and the problems posed by class lectures. Her best strategy was to borrow classmates' lecture notes. In fact, she auditioned the note givers, trying out sets of notes from a dozen different classmates before settling on a few she could count on.

Yang's study habits in fact came to center on her classmates' course notes. As Yang commented, these notes were very important to everyone, with domestic students as well as the English learners in the class constantly glancing over at other students' notes during lectures to make sure they had gotten down the correct, complete information.

What made for good notes for Yang was proximity to the original lecture. The more extensive and complete the notes the better. Although this was partly dependent on the teacher (good teachers delivered lectures such that students could write down verbatim what they said), good note takers, as she experienced it, could produce 18 to 20 pages of notes in a typical 3-hour nursing lecture; she expected at least 10 pages from a 2-hour lecture; and she was disappointed when her classmates came up with only 4 to 5 pages.[14] Faculty also cooperated in helping her get a complete and accurate set of notes by even lending her their actual lecture notes.

Yang then took all the notes home and combined them into a master set and examined them to see where they referred to something she did not understand. When that happened, she went to dictionaries (her notes were filled with translations into Chinese and phonetic transcriptions of English) and to the course textbook to look up the pertinent sections, which she then added to the notes. Yang used these notes to orient her readings, allowing her to avoid sections of the massive course books that did not come up in the notes.

When she found material in the notes that contradicted other information, she consulted with faculty. As Professor G noted, whenever Yang came to see her with a question, it was a pointed, narrowly focused, well-thought-through question, not merely a generalized complaint that she didn't understand anything, which this faculty member claimed was the typical practice of most domestic students who came to see her for help.

A comparison of Yang's notes from one of her classes in her senior year to those of her classmate written simultaneously showed that although Yang copied everything down from the board, she missed important and potentially very useful material that would ease her understanding of the lecture. For example, in this case the lecturer referred to the creation of "superbugs" as a result of antibiotic overprescription and resulting microbe resistance. Yang's domestic classmate had this notation:

"[antibiotic overprescription] merely slows bugs and creates superbugs."

Yang had:

"mear slow bugs and creat s ...."

Like other English learners (and some domestic students), Yang did not at all appreciate students' questions during lectures. In addition to having trouble understanding the questions, she did not want the instructor to fail to get to all the material she planned to cover because even if essential information was not covered in lecture, the instructor would inform the students that they were still responsible for the material and require them to locate and learn it from the massive course textbook.

Vocabulary.   Naturally, anyone studying in a second language can assume they will face a steep vocabulary-learning curve, and medicine has a particularly noted reputation for maintaining strong in-group and out-group boundaries through technical language use. As a subcategory of medicine, nursing requires familiarity with medical jargon, and the nursing faculty often commented on how difficult it was for students to familiarize themselves with not only, for example, so many parts of the human body or types of diseases or medicines but also with the technical terms for all of these. In addition, nursing made a great deal of use of technical abbreviations, which also had to be learned.

Though Yang knew the names of such things as the arteries and veins or the muscles in Chinese, she would now have to relearn them in English. But Yang had the added disadvantage of not knowing the common names of body parts or diseases. Because at the same time as language in the medical professions was exclusionary, in their objectives of establishing and sustaining rapport with patients, nurses had to also be able to use nonmedical language. For an English learner, the quantity of material to learn is in effect doubled because, whereas "measles" meant something to her domestic classmates, it rang no more bells for Yang than did rubella, leaving her to learn twice the vocabulary her peers had to learn: varicella as well as chicken pox, both pertussis and "hooping off" (as Yang wrote in her notes). Yang had to learn both terms of each pair as individual but linked vocabulary items, recording in her notes the correct English pronunciations in phonetic symbols and their translations into Chinese.

By the end of this research project, Yang had been in an English-dominant country for about 9 years, studying at an English-medium university for almost 4 years. Common vocabulary items nevertheless confused her. In a discussion of a returned class paper in her last semester, the following exchange took place:

Interviewer:	On this one, she [the professor] said this is well done. ... what makes it well done, why does the teacher say this is good? What's good about it?
Yang:	That's plenty. Well done, that's meaning.
Interviewer:	It means it's good, you did a good job.
Yang:	I still have a problem with very simple words together. ... So I said "well done," I just, "it's enough," because I learn some food, "well done."
Interviewer:	Oh, interesting, like to have meat well done means to have it really cooked and so when she says "well done" you feel like it means that you have enough.
Yang:	So that's what it really mean? "Well done," that's enough? (third-term senior)

Yang was manipulating terms like "terminate the pregnancy," "focal stimuli," and "multiple stressors" and had missed the meaning of the words "well done." Such a mixture of facility with technical terminology and confusion about everyday words is certainly not uncommon with English learners at an English-dominant university, and is poignant, perhaps even charming in some way (see Severino, 1994), but it also points to the enormous task that these students undertake in studying in a second language and to the challenge of trying to create useful English courses to help them in that undertaking. Such anomalies must have also taken the nursing faculty and staff by surprise and made them wonder about exactly how much they could presume in Yang's case. When her difficulties with language are examined, Yang's comment, "English is a major obstacle for me," seems like an understatement.

Writing Challenges

It is ironic in the case of students like Yang that universities offer, if not require of, undergraduates one to four semesters of course work in writing and usually none in reading, note taking, speaking, pronunciation, working in groups, making presentations, negotiating relations with faculty and peers, specific-purposes writing, and the host of other language-related topics that might make university studies easier. The logic of university administrators and faculty is that their graduates *should* be able to write (i.e., the institutions look bad if they do not) and *will have to* be able to write (i.e., the university's job is to train them for future employers). Because these beliefs are generally unquestioned, universities and colleges in principle offer students help in achieving those goals through course work and tutoring in writing centers, and Yang was duly enrolled in writing classes.

Considering Yang's lack of interest in English and meager exposure to it in China, she did remarkably well in writing (except for the returned nursing report her junior year). The first paper she wrote in her U.S. English class was only the third piece of writing she had ever done in English beyond single words and short sentences, the first being for the TOEFL (Test of English as a Foreign Language), the second for this university's placement exam. In interviews about the usefulness of her English writing classes, Yang invariably answered that English required grammar and these classes provided grammar. This was good and she was grateful. She felt that the English class had taken her from no ability to write at all to being able to write paragraphs, for which she was also appreciative.

Early on in the interviews, Yang expressed her sense of the importance of writing for medical practitioners: Everything needed to be carefully and thoroughly documented, and the documents had legal status. This had been true in China as well. In addition, as part of the basic requirements for promotions and pay increases in her job in China, Yang had published two papers dealing with medical topics. Though she understood and had no issue with the type of documentation required in medical settings, she felt that the other types of writing required in her nursing program were a waste of time, except to the extent that they allowed her to practice English. In response to the repeated question of whether she felt writing was important, her affirmative answer deflected the question and was always the same: Writing was important in the sense that if she could write English easily, her studies would be much less stressful. She would be able to handle the writing tasks she had with the speed and ease of her domestic peers, who she envied as able to complete assignments quickly and (as she assumed) with no trouble. Writing ability would be a good tool to have.

> Yang: If you got good writing, you will spend little time. For me ... I
> spend a lot of time. (second-term junior)

The types of writing Yang experienced in college fell into three categories: major academic papers, (the burdensome) NCPs and other formulaic nursing documents, and a grab bag of short written assignments like journals, summaries of movies, short reports, annotated bibliographies, and so on. Table 3.1 lists Yang's major and some minor academic writing assignments, excluding NCPs; major work is highlighted.

The NCP assignments are not included in the table in part because the number of such plans required in a given course was based on the number of different patients the student nurses were assigned and so would not be specified beforehand on the syllabus. Also, they had no specific weight in the calculation of the student's grade; rather, they had to be done over and over until they were satisfactory to the clinical instructor. Once satisfactory, they contributed to a satisfactory performance in general in clinical but not to a separate evaluation.

Like speech, writing potentially left Yang vulnerable to criticisms of her language ability. But she came to realize that in non-nursing classes her career was not at stake, and so she was not unduly concerned about exposure to criticism of her language. Her main concern became the time the non-nursing assignments took away from more threatening kinds of writing. The fear of being exposed by her writing emerged with the rejection of her first written assignment in nursing and the menacing letter criticizing her language. Thereafter, she worried about and worked hard on the language in all her nursing writing. When, once, envious of her classmates' lesser efforts, she attempted to relax her language guard and turn in one assignment without repeated revisions, as she observed her peers doing consistently, that NCP received the only "Needs Improvement" (i.e., unacceptable) response of the semester from her teacher, and Yang immediately reverted to her focus on repeated revisions to achieve correctness.

Academic Papers.   Yang considered nearly all academic writing a massive waste of time. But as she repeatedly said:

Yang: Maybe American system, no choice. (first-term senior)

Outside of the NCPs, Yang had five major pieces of written work for nursing, highlighted in the table. Only one of these was a traditional academic paper, in which writers select a topic of interest, collect information on the topic through library research, and make (at least some) choices about the organization of the information. Yang's writing process was heroic. Because she knew it was the tradition to assign this paper during the spring of the nursing students' senior year, Yang had researched and written most of the paper ahead of time during the semester break between terms. Once she had a draft, she asked her professor to see whether she was on the right track in terms of content. After this, she revised it and brought it to the writing center. After revising that version, she again brought it to her professor, who again made a few written alterations to the first couple

TABLE 3.1

Yang's Academic Writing Assignments in Courses Other Than English

Term	Course	Type	Prescribed or Actual Length	Weight in Course Grade
fall first year	Sociology	essay exams		unknown
		4 short papers	1 page each	unknown
spring first year	History	short-answer exams		probably 50%
		book summary	5 pages	probably 50%; in lieu of final exam
	Nutrition	diet plan	1 page	unknown
summer	History			unknown
fall junior	Nursing	**health assessment**[a]	23	35%
		health history[a]	10	10%
	Ethics	2 ethics cases	8 pages each	50% together
spring junior	Nursing	group project report	15; Yang's contribution = 8 pages, reduced to 2 pages	10%[b]
	Nursing	3 article summaries	1 page each	10%[b]
		short essay	2 pages	5%
first fall senior	Nursing	**term paper**	8	10%
	Nursing	journal + paper	4-6	25%
spring senior	Nursing	**case study**	19	25%
	Nursing	**term paper**	12	20%
	Nursing	meeting report	1 paragraph	0%
		paper	2-3 pages	0%
second fall senior	Nursing	journal	not specified	0
	Nursing	report forms	not specified but about 1 page for longest	0

[a] Basically long forms to fill out.
[b] For whole project including final oral presentation.

of pages. She gave that version to her husband to mark up fairly extensively in another color, and then she herself once again noted places to revise.

The comments appended to the submitted paper and written interlinearly provide an interesting view into what the nursing faculty deemed important in this academic paper. (The first percentage listed is Yang's score and the percentage within parentheses is the maximum possible. The italicized sections were handwritten by the evaluator):

> *40%* Content (40%)
> - *Focus of paper is an issue*
> - *Issue is clearly stated*
> - *Significance, history of issue given*
> - *Both sides adequately discussed*
> - *Nursing implications given*
> - *Personal opinion included*
>
> *20%* Organization and Clarity (20%)
> - *Paper well organized overall*
> - *Writing style clear and easy to read*
>
> *23%* Documentation (25%)
> - *References current, adequate in number*
> - *Occasional needed documentation omitted*
> - *Some disagreement between citations and reference*
>
> *11%* Format (15%)
> - *Paper typed, neat in appearance*
> - *Several errors in grammar, 0 spelling errors*
> - *Occasional error in citing references*
>
> *Grade 94*
> Comments:
> - *Nice paper*

The nursing faculty was specifically enjoined from correcting language errors on a student's paper (small wonder given the number of students they had) and had together decided on what the paper graders were to look for in the papers. However, the students were not informed of what those features were.

> Professor R: Now we don't give this to the students because obviously we'd be giving a REAL road map to them, but we literally divide it down into one point, two points, etc.

The features handwritten on the evaluation form were those agreed on by the faculty.

What is especially noteworthy in this entire process, besides the large amounts of time that a variety of people spent in the production and evaluation of the paper, is the very academic, in the worst sense, focus of the faculty's feedback. Of the 20 notations in the body of the paper, 14 focused on citations, only 1 on content. Although 40% of the summative evaluation focused on the content of the paper, 60% focused essentially on issues of academic convention. Within the content, in the evaluation of the six features addressed, arguably only two of them are central to content: that both sides be adequately discussed and that nursing implications be given. The others, though typical of academic genres and aimed at developing students' academic writing proficiency, seem less pertinent to the stated content-related aim:

> Professor O: They think they think one thing, they get into studying the issue, reading about it, they find there's at least a bit more gray area than they thought and that's part of the whole idea of getting them into it.

Yang felt the paper had been of value to her in more mundane ways: First she again had the opportunity to use writing to practice and improve her English through the feedback she received and, second, because she had explored this topic in depth, she did not have to worry about studying it for the exam; she already knew a great deal about it. Beyond this, she persisted in her strongly held opinion that the whole effort was a waste of time.

As for English practice, it simply is not possible to ascertain what effect an academic assignment like this might have had on Yang's English proficiency; it perhaps helped Yang to develop and access vocabulary more quickly, and it may have promoted grammatical flexibility. There is no way to determine this. Yet the feature of her English that was bringing her to negative light in her studies was not writing but pronunciation, and it is doubtful that writing papers did much to clarify her speech.

Medical Documentation.   Aside from the academic paper and the NCPs, the other major writing that Yang did in the nursing program, sometimes called term papers or case studies, was in fact a form of medical documentation. These assignments were intended to help students internalize the "nursing process" by drawing their attention to aspects of a medical situation pertinent to nurses. The most massive of the documentation projects focused on client cases in the community, often families, that had come to the attention of the county board of health as being in need of public support for health care. The student nurses were to go in pairs to the clients' homes, assess an array of aspects of their living situation, determine some way they might help, provide the help, and then document everything for official county records. Almost miraculously in this ethnically homogeneous community, Yang and her one Chinese classmate identified two Chinese families to work with.

The work involved in dealing with the family was satisfying to Yang because, communicating clearly and effectively, she knew her interventions and suggestions were fully understood, and Yang's Chinese family was cooperative and grateful. As a result, Yang felt that she had made a material, positive difference in their life. These people would certainly not have been as well served by a monolingual English speaker; for once in her nursing program, Yang's Chinese was an asset to her. The situation also afforded Yang the opportunity to show her competence to her course professor, who attended at least one of the home visits, and found herself, by her own description, standing sheepishly aside uncomprehending as Yang interacted expertly in Chinese with the clients. This professor, who had been a supporter of Yang during her several trials, was glad for her.

Two features of this experience stand out in terms of writing. First, for the paper documenting this case students were asked to apply a particular nursing model, going from close, excruciatingly detailed directed observation to the development of a nursing intervention plan consisting primarily of client education. The following is from the beginning of the highly specified writing guidelines:

1. Title page; no abstract

2. Introduction (what is community health and what is the purpose of this family study paper, why is this family being followed, etc.)

3. Assessment:

    Environmental assessment (community & external home) Multidimensional family assessment (including internal environment of home, family structure, people in home, medical home, educational levels, economics, developmental levels, culture, spirituality, etc.)

    Describe each family member (general physical condition) and his/her individual needs as identified through your data collection. Include family group needs if present. Assess the family's coping abilities utilizing tools presented in class and clinical conference.

A total of 10 items in the guidelines gave further detailed directions for the rest of the paper. This paper went through six separate draft/revise cycles with feedback from the professor, husband, and writing center, as well as Yang's own self-initiated corrections and alterations.

The required introductory material of the first page came fairly directly from published sources and would have been about the same in all the students' papers. The following is an extract from the second page of the fourth revision:

> The family lived at the [university's] married student housing which was a 14 floor brick building with a big entrance and a dumper tank [dumpster] close. The building was located on the northern side of [the university's] campus and ½ mile to downtown area of [the town]. About ¾ of land of the community were [university] campus and residential area, and the other ¼ is commercial area. The students and [university] staff, most of the population, consisted of the white, the black, the yellow, and the brown people. ... The community was encompassed by interstate highway XX, the highway XX, [Name] Drive, and [Name] Street which was paved 2 or more lane road with sidewalks. ...

This painstaking, if not also painful, level of detail went on for about three more pages and was followed by a similarly detailed physical description of the inside of the apartment and then of the general circumstances of the family (financial, e.g.), a physical, historical, emotional, spiritual description of each member of the family, a description of their health and health history, and so on. Details to be touched on (e.g., pollution or agricultural hazards, number of lanes of roads, bus lines, etc.) were all specified by the professor.

Though Yang could in principle see the legitimacy of learning the nursing process through reporting of this kind, it still irked her:

Interviewer: What did you get out of writing this paper?
Yang: This paper, I just spend a lot of time. I hate this paper. (second-term junior)

The second writing issue that arose with this case study was that every meeting with these clients had to be officially filed with the county. The professor felt somewhat conflicted about how to handle Yang's documentation:

Interviewer: Are you also looking for writing issues in those papers?
Professor C: In the sense that when they transfer that to the official record at the Health Department, somebody has to know

> what they're talking about. ... So yeah, I'm looking for,
> does this make sense. ... We ARE looking for some English
> things there. ... [With Yang and her Chinese classmate] I let
> it go on the records at the Health Department this time,
> simply because I didn't know how to actually have them
> write it any better; I think they wrote it as best they could.
> And I decided that when the person who reads it gets to
> the end and sees a name that's not Sue Smith, that would
> explain some of the English because some of the sentences
> are grammatically wrong. But if you know the student is
> Chinese or Spanish, it makes more sense. And I didn't
> know what to do, I just let it go this time.

This professor was willing not to make an issue of Yang's writing, essentially saying, she is obviously not an NES; it's quite natural that her phrasing might be unusual.

Nursing Care Plans.   Yang was not happy to do any of the writing required in the nursing program but what she came to despise was by far the most taxing of the written work she did, the long NCPs required as part of the clinicals. These assignments were not displayed in Table 3.1 because they were in effect forms to fill in rather than writing with traditionally recognizable rhetorical features like introductions and conclusions. They called for using specific medical terminology and abbreviations noting, among other items of information, patients' conditions, medications they were receiving, and recommendations for care. The NCPs necessitated considerable research, and they were long, between 5 and 15 pages, requiring a great deal of work and time to complete. Table 3.2 is a typical short segment, for example, from a 15-page document Yang submitted.

The briefness of the entries belies the work required to find correct and complete information to include in these plans. Retrieving that information necessitated recourse to a variety of medical sources and many hours' work. Because the plans for care stipulated in the NCPs often had to be ready to guide someone else's interactions with the patients the next day, Yang sometimes spent the whole night after a day in clinicals on a single care plan, and as many as nine might be required in one semester. If the students' NCPs were not ready each morning, the students could be barred from the clinical, potentially leading to an unsatisfactory clinical, meaning course failure. As Yang commented in the journal she kept for this research:

TABLE 3.2
Sample Nursing Care Plan Notations

Condition	Medication	Recommendation
Neurologic & mental status	Alert, oriented X4	Encourage diversional activity
occasional nervous and insomnia for 2 weeks	Ativan 1mg iv for nervous and Ambien 5mg po for insomnia	Encourage discussion with family about cancer
Immune status: Chronic bronchitis for 10 years	On high dose Methylprednisolone. NC, IV line, chest tubes	Avoid contact with infect persons and crowds. Evaluate understanding of s/s of infx & fever. Need to check on organism in sputum

> Yang: Clinical rotation is over. I try hard to get pass and felt exhausted every clinical day. All 15 days of clinical rotation I spend all my time to write care plan; sometime I sit up all night. It's painful and strenuous for me; the part of my English is poor, writing and speaking. (second-term junior)

Aside from the enormous strain the NCPs put on her, Yang came to deeply resent them for two additional reasons. First, as her peers became increasingly accustomed to preparing these documents, the amount of time they needed to complete them decreased considerably, to the point where they were able, as Yang noted, to sit in a corner at the hospital and produce a complete NCP in an hour or two.

> Yang: But American students they just fill in, they just go. I saw one male student, he maybe very smart, he just go to the clinical, find a corner, just write care plan, just hand in. (third-term senior)

Yet through to the end of her program, Yang slaved multiple hours over her NCPs, repeatedly revising them for language correctness for fear that a failure to do so would again bring her to the negative attention of faculty.

Why were her classmates able to reduce the amount of time required to produce these NCPs? As material they encountered in reference texts repeated from one case to the next, her peers were able eventually to learn the core of the information and paraphrase it, cutting their writing time. Yang was afraid to attempt this writing move and in fact did not feel she had enough English to do so. Instead she continued to laboriously copy out the necessary information from the course texts.

In addition, as noted by both Yang and her professors, part of domestic students' advantage also appeared to reside in issues of cultural knowledge and sociolinguistic expectations. The most onerous part of the NCPs for Yang were those calling for psychosocial and behavioral evaluations of the patients and their families. She felt she simply could not make determinations about whether behavior she witnessed was normal; was it normal for a wife to comment about her husband, who was being treated for lung cancer, that she knew how to handle a dying person? What were the appropriate comforting words for suffering people? How should she respond to someone who refused to follow medical advice? Certainly such responses were difficult for all the nursing students but to Yang, her peers' greater familiarity both with U.S. customs and society and with writing in English explained their ability to eventually spend less time on these aspects of the NCPs.

Yang's second reason for resentment about NCPs originated in her experience doing volunteer work at the hospital during the summer before her last senior semester. Here she was able to observe that *real* NCPs were completed in minutes and came nowhere near the level of detail and complication that the Nursing students were required to produce:[15]

Yang:	I have been a volunteer in [the hospital]. I know the daily routine. Just notes, write down notes. Have strong knowledge about patient situation, about medical. Because nurse need medical idea, medical opinion about her patient, I think, not a care plan.
Interviewer:	When you worked as a volunteer, did the nurses write NCPs?
Yang:	Just three or two lines. Care plan just for safety, just a few words. ... Not the way we write down.
Interviewer:	So how is the NCP that you do different? What do you write in your NCP that makes it different from what you saw at [the hospital]?
Yang:	They totally different. Maybe 99% different. Not useful. (second-term senior)

This incongruity between nursing education and real nursing practice reinforced Yang's sense that the NCPs were busy work and a waste of precious time that could be better spent learning medicine.

What Yang failed to recognize was the educational role the elaborate NCPs were intended to play. Faculty entirely recognized that the NCPs were immensely time-consuming; they were time-consuming for the faculty too, who painstakingly reviewed every word, every abbreviation, on each of the 120 students' many NCPs. But the NCPs were a way of guiding students' through a process of thinking that was expected to eventually become so second nature to them that they would automatically engage in the nursing process, quickly and efficiently assessing their patients and planning for care without the need to lumber through each step individually, as the nursing students were being required to do. If the faculty ever attempted to explain their intentions for the NCPs, Yang either never got that message or did not accept it.

Perhaps most ironic in her struggle to crank out these NCPs was the nature of the material she needed to fill in the charts. It was often technical material from nursing and other medical texts that could be inserted verbatim, copied directly into the NCPs. In addition, because at least some of the patients she saw shared needs, Yang found herself copying the same passages over and over into the care plans. Yang did not dare to paraphrase that material, as her peers did, for fear of creating incomprehensible or at least unacceptable text.

> Yang: If you change, you are wrong. ... If I copy correctly, there is no error. (first-term senior)

But this also led to tedium:

> Yang: Repeat, repeat, repeat. (third-term senior)

Yang's many hours spent hunting down and copying out information for the NCPs seemed pointless to her. Furthermore, published NCP books existed that the faculty were familiar with as well. They had no particular problem with students using published NCPs in their own work provided their NCPs deviated enough from the published ones to reflect the precise situation of their patient. That is, the issue was not one of plagiarizing someone else's words or ideas but of being sure to adapt those ideas as necessary to their patient.

> Interviewer: I noticed at [the local] bookstore that they actually even sell NCPs.
> Professor M: Yeah, so why wouldn't you use it? Because it doesn't apply in every situation. ... I ask them to individualize for this patient. They can go into their textbook and find a little master plan, so to speak. (second-term senior)

That such copying was not only acceptable to the faculty but even tacitly encouraged once again underscores the complexities of discussions of plagiarism, particularly among English learners. The words in published sources were there for Yang to use and she used them. She had correctly understood that in the nursing program the issue of plagiarism took a form somewhat different from that in other disciplines. In fact, as Yang was also aware, hospitals were increasingly turning to a new approach called "critical pathways," including computerized NCPs. Yang felt there was little point in slaving over NCPs, copying sections from books and repeating them from patient to patient, when all of this would eventually be replaced by computerized NCPs.

Yang also argued that her classmates were wasting time writing NCPs instead of learning medical procedures. As she maintained, she herself already had the *clinical* knowledge to do these reports (if not the experience with English to communicate that knowledge transparently) and so learned nothing substantive from writing them out whereas, as she saw it, her nonphysician classmates did not know medicine and should have been spending their time learning course content, medical information, instead of wasting their time filling in lengthy forms. Instead of *doing,* they were, she felt, just writing:

> Yang: Our job was just to write the paper. ... I don't agree this way teaching. (first-term senior)

Throughout the interviews, Yang consistently expressed the view that the writing she was doing was of no real value beyond allowing her to "practice English." At the same time, she recognized clearly that it was her inability to communicate (both orally and to a lesser degree in writing) that had created most of her problems in the nursing curriculum.

> Yang: I lack ability to demonstrate my ability. (second-term junior).

> Yang: I have more knowledge about this, but ... the teacher just say I cannot clearly demonstrate my meaning. (second-term senior)

Although the Nursing faculty worried mostly about her oral/aural skills, Yang was forced by circumstances of the curriculum to spend time on developing a certain disciplinary literacy embodied in the NCPs, a high-stakes, unrelenting obstacle. Writing, by its very nature, created that permanent record, reviewed away from the presence of the writer, that Yang feared left her vulnerable and exposed to the faculty's critical scrutiny, betraying her every unidiomatic phrase and stealing her precious time. Her view was that the written work could fail her if it was bad but could not save her if other parts of her clinicals were unsatisfactory. Thus, writing had very little redeeming value for her.

Journals and Self-Analysis.   As for the other kinds of writing assigned in her courses, particularly the journals and self-analytical writing, Yang had no use for them. Questioning what she could learn simply from the act of writing down what she already knew, Yang also felt that journal writing, far from being true self-exploration, was mere flattery for the course instructors, as she and her peers falsely (Yang thought) claimed to find various experiences interesting, useful, or satisfying. As for revealing her own feelings, she found it embarrassing for a person her age to be asked to reveal herself to the journal reader.

Yang: You know for our age, we [are being expected to] talk just like young people. (first-term senior)

Yang: The worst thing I do just write the journal. ... if you write the journal, [and then] hand it to somebody for your age, ... I just feel funny. (first-term senior)

Yang was a reflective enough person to see the value in self-analysis but did not feel the need to share everything she felt with others. Yang again saw these assignments as mere busy work.

Writing and Language Proficiency

The main value to Yang of any written work was practice with writing in English. In fact part of the reason she continued to resist the idea of dropping nursing classes in order to take language classes was that she felt she needed the pressure from the nursing classes to improve her language. With nothing at stake, she would not take the time to correct and revise as she felt was necessary in order to survive in the nursing program, and, consequently, she would not improve her language skills. But increased writing proficiency seemed to have little effect on her oral language. She was caught in an untenable situation. If having to spend time on writing took away from the time she could spend on the content of her discipline, she resented it, but if writing were eliminated from her program, engaging in writing would no longer be compelling enough to result in whatever language improvement she felt it occasioned. Still, the kind of writing that the NCPs required was alien, quite unlike normal written or spoken English. It seems unlikely that it could have done more than allowed her to repeatedly access certain technical vocabulary necessary to nursing, but not grammatical or rhetorical or conversational structures necessary to English.

Nursing Faculty on Writing

The nursing faculty's evaluation of assigned writing tasks was generally lenient for "didactic" or more academic papers but stringent for writing, especially NCPs, intended as a means of professional incorporation. Like many faculty across the curriculum, the nursing faculty wanted their students to write without errors in standard academic style but felt that teaching such skills was the job of the English department and hoped students came into nursing already equipped.

One issue the faculty struggled with was how to evaluate language issues (especially in the more technical writing) for someone like Yang, particularly in light of the fact that, as one professor suggested, many of the domestic students in the class could have been regarded as non-native speakers and writers of the academic dialect.

> Professor L: ... it's a struggle for me to know how to fairly grade them [English learners], because I have a large number of students, the whole university does, that come from backgrounds where standard English is not what they've heard and I sure don't cut them any slack.

Poorly done professional communication would reflect badly on the institution, but more important, nursing faculty felt the need to be less forgiving in medical/technical writing because it might not communicate accurately, the central goal of the NCPs.

> Professor P: When a nurse leaves a job in the afternoon, somebody has to know what went on. ... She needs to be able to communicate that clearly ... in order to pass that information along to somebody else who's going to assume responsibility for that patient.

In addition to communicating accurately, the proficiency in professional writing that faculty hoped their students would develop was intended to combine critical thinking with the ability to synthesize information. The program's version of critical thinking appeared to mean something like deep or careful analysis or creative, reflective thinking, and writing served as the occasion for and demonstration of what the nursing staff called the "critical thinking piece."[16]

Synthesizing outside sources had an extremely significant role for writing in the nursing curriculum. More than merely serving to support ideas or arguments as might be the case in many kinds of academic papers, outside sources held the specific information students needed to fulfill writing tasks, and students were sent to these sources to gather and learn that information. Thus, the synthesis the nursing faculty sought as part of the critical-thinking piece meant primarily having students apply information from their source texts to specific clients or patients.

Professor C: [We want] them to go back to their textbooks and for instance if they're going to be talking about culture, they need to have gone to their textbooks and found something out about that culture and put that in their paper ... and tie that in to why this family is or is not coping.

Critical thinking in the nursing program meant a diagnostic investigation using all physical, textual, and contextual sources available.

The Role of Reading

For Yang, and for all the nursing students, reading posed a problem, if they did it. Yang eventually stopped doing any assigned textbook readings because the textbook and the passages in them to read were simply too long to manage. She did not exaggerate when she complained that the nursing texts were 1,000 and 2,000 pages long; they were. In some courses, there were additional articles to read. But Yang managed to cut her reading down to manageable size through judicious focused attention. If the lecturer mentioned a word or concept that seemed important because she spent a great deal of time on it, repeated it several times, or mentioned a page number in relation to it, Yang would read that portion of the book.

Faculty were aware that the course texts posed problems, and not only because of their length. Part of Yang's frustration was that these long texts would soon not even be useful as references. As one faculty member noted:

Professor C: We test strongly from our lectures and we tell them that, because every textbook is out of date and medicine just goes too fast.

In Yang's terms:

Yang: ... in 3 year, this book will probably go to garbage because we got a new book.

But the texts served as crucial source material in writing. The admonition that might turn up on a paper in humanities that the student was relying too heavily on a single source was simply not an issue in nursing. If the text was the source with the information, then it was appropriate to use it as heavily as needed. In accepting chunks of already published texts copied into the NCPs, the nursing faculty was not condoning plagiarism. They were recognizing that the students had tasks to do that they could not accomplish alone and so they turned to already published texts to support them, in a kind of textual zone of proximal development (ZPD). Clearly, what intellectual property means and how it is handled differs across disciplines as well as cultures.

THE TROUBLE WITH AMERICAN EDUCATION

Yang's frustration with the perceived inappropriateness of her course text was not her only criticism of the nursing curriculum. Also affecting Yang's language and literacy experiences were her reactions to and opinions about the education she was undergoing. She was no passive receiver of her education and had no trouble engaging in the kind of critical thinking that goes beyond mere analysis. She formed and expressed many opinions about U.S. education. Her most immediate and potent impressions were that students in nursing were overworked, with too many exams and irrelevant required activities, that education was insufficiently focus led, that her domestic peers suffered from acquired dependence on their teachers to tell them how and what to study, and that textbooks were bloated with useless information.

Frenzied Busyness

Yang found it strange, for example, that at the university level students should have to waste time with general-education courses and felt that even the professional education she was experiencing was far too diffuse, over full with "activities" like journal writing, group work, and presentations instead of concentrating on building disciplinary, that is, science/medical knowledge.

> Yang: Everybody busy. Maybe I run [for] this presentation, for two exam run, for another group need to hand in paper .... (second-term junior)

> Yang: ... beside the class, beside the exam, we have clinical. Lot of work and lot of assignments. I hate this. ... I just feel it interferes with my study. (first-term senior)

> Yang: ... Asking too many things that we have to do. ... My brain! (first-term junior).

All these activities created the enormous sense of strain, pressure, stress that she reported feeling, always, and worked against building medical knowledge.

> Yang: The problem is not that you don't understanding. The problem is that you do not have time to remember. (second-term senior)

Though she had worked hard as a student in China, the work was focused. She felt that U.S. education would be better off if students were not forced to scatter their attention on nonessentials.

Yang's criticism of U.S. education went beyond the special pressures she experienced. She felt lucky to have been trained in an educational system in China that promoted certain ways of thinking that proved valuable in the two-semester pathology course where her two final grades of A were mentioned by several faculty as an impressive achievement, one of her few real successes in the nursing program about which Yang could be proud.

Yang: Nobody do both A's in here. (first-term senior)

The pathology class was the bane of the nursing students; more of them failed this class than any other in the nursing program. Yang felt that her U.S. classmates had a hard time with the pathology course because the nursing education system did too much spoon feeding of the students, telling them what the important items were that they had to learn because these would be on exams and thus preventing them, and her, from taking a more active, adult, real-student-like role in their own educations. As a result her peers, she felt, did not know how to go to a book, for example, and determine what the important information was, as she remembered having to do in China.

Yang: American student ... just follow teacher. You want to get good grade, just follow teacher. So a lot of students don't got how to study. ... Not like a really student. (second-term junior)

The pathology professor herself also felt that her students' impulse to simply memorize without understanding was a product of American education:

Professor F: ... a lot of people have been encouraged by the university system, and even secondary schools, to memorize, to regurgitate.

Thus, both Yang's and this professor's discursive construction of American education as promoting memorization and excessive reliance on teacher guidance rather than on intellectual independence reverses the usual discourse poles in U.S. discussions of U.S. and Asian education, where U.S. students are constructed as inquisitive and creative and Asians as passive receptacles of authoritative wisdom. (See also Kubota, 2001.)

Yang also saw the system of constant evaluation through quizzes and exams as debilitating and adding to students' dependence on teachers.

> Yang: Teacher say next week we have this exam, we just [drop] every-
>   thing. ... Just focus this class. If this class over, next week I'll have
>   another exam, just focus on this exam, so we don't have a per-
>   sonal plan. (second-term junior)
>
> Yang: We don't have time to organize by ourself" (second-term junior).

The teacher's or the program's schedule of exams took priority away from deeper understanding of course material and autonomy away from the students. Yang found this kind of paternalism crippling. Tight supervision over all aspects of students' program of study created another conflict as well. It became difficult to get help from instructors in clinical because they too were overly busy with advising, teaching, supervising, and coordinating programs.

Textbooks

Yang's criticism of her nursing textbooks extended beyond their short-lived usefulness to their immense size and resultant diffuseness. She complained that only 5% to 10% of the text was used for class and that it was impossible to determine which information was definitive because of the many references to other authors.

> Yang: This author say, another author say, but book author never say her
>   opinion, just said another author said, another author. So student
>   after finish reading don't know what is correct. (first-term senior)
>
> Yang: Sometimes don't have her opinion, just copy other. This article
>   say 1994, 1997, you see. ... some chapters maybe good informa-
>   tion. Some chapters read through [and still] no clear picture.
>   What does author say? [with frustrated tone] Does not have his or
>   her opinion. Just copy another. (first-term senior)

What is particularly fascinating in Yang's characterization of nursing textbooks is that the accusation of excessive reliance on the published literature without committing to an opinion is the very type of accusation made of student writing. Her listing of the dates "1994, 1997" reads like a parody of a lockstep response to the terror of plagiarism. The defense of U.S.-style textbooks, as Yang characterizes them, is presumably that they give students access to a range of opinions. But in the kind of eye-opening cross-cultural perspective on the purpose of textbooks that might be humbling to those in the dominant culture who would care to listen, Yang called this "just copy another."

Like the perceived hand holding, overly planned curriculum, and overly full courses, Yang felt bloated textbooks had a serious disempowering effect on nursing students; it made them excessively dependent on lecturers and lecture notes, illustrated by a striking feature of the nursing classes. A surprising number of students waited after lectures to get clarifications from the professor. Although the nursing students' orientation toward the professor may have had other causes (the famed approachabililty of U.S. professors, e.g.), Yang saw this orientation as the predictable result of having bad textbooks. Without decent, manageable, reasonable-size textbooks from which to study that would have allowed them to self-direct their studies by learning how to pick out and master the essential material, the students never learned to how to learn from books. With the books useless, the students had no choice but to turn to the teachers' lecture notes.[17]

Intractable Problem of Time

Yang's frustration with nursing school in the United States stemmed from a variety of sources, some of which were not under the control of the nursing school, but Yang was very critical of the need to juggle the many responsibilities related to course work. She felt that she was not getting what she might out of clinicals, for example, because instead of spending time thinking through what was occurring in those settings, she had to rush home and study for exams. And she could not always prepare for exams as much as she would have liked because she had NCPs or course papers to write.

The pressure and stress Yang experienced were in part related to time use, and in fact the problem of lack of time seems to be a central reality in U.S. universities, especially for international students. These students are expected, and expect themselves, to be able to do the same amount of work as the domestic students in the same amount of time. They are driven, some by financial need, to complete their degrees within some arbitrarily set period. Immigration also requires them to carry at least 12 hours each term, usually four classes. But it may take students like Yang three to four times as long to do reading and writing assignments, they do not have the kind of cultural savvy that domestic students do, and they do not have the kinds of social nets that may (and sometimes maybe not) make student life easier on domestic students. These universities are set up to accommodate average domestic students. The burden for internationals is immensely heavier. And often they themselves would refuse to reduce the burden even if they were allowed to; some are also fixed on the idea that they have to get their degrees and get back home as quickly as possible.

This attitude is particularly counterproductive in that there is no real way to speed up language development, which takes time. But students, including Yang, programs, and immigration appear to think that adult language learners can bulldoze their way through, just by force of will and relentless hard work. When the nursing program tried to make it easier on Yang by having her take fewer classes, she saw this as paternalistic. She was furious when they would not let her make her own decision to over-work herself. No one would ask another person not to sleep night after night in order to get work done but that was what she wanted to do, wanted to take on, in order to get this degree in as fast a time as possible. Time ends up being the focal point of several strands of competing needs and desires.

Faculty was of course aware of this problem of overworked students and sympathized.

> Professor L: You get real busy and real stressed, and their schedules are awful. … it's extremely tiring. We do the clinical instruc-tion, … and I'm not stressed by it because I know what I'm doing when I go in there, and they don't. It's a new envi-ronment for them and they're scared they're going to make mistakes. They have to prepare at a different level than I do and I still find it tiring.

But they felt their hands were tied. One of the programmatic needs the nurs-ing school faced was meeting accreditation standards that specified precisely numbers and types of courses and clinical experiences required. No one interviewed for this study was unaware of the difficulty of being in clinicals for 12 hours. Why was 12 hours the magically appropriate number of hours a clinical should be? What kind of care could patients get from nursing stu-dents in the 12th hour of a clinical? What kind of attention could students give to NCPs that had to be written up in the night following the 12-hour day? Yet, the option of spreading course and clinical requirements out over longer than the current 2 years would most likely have met with disfavor, cer-tainly from Yang. Although all students are affected by curricular decisions that lead to high-pressure conditions, L2 students are disproportionately affected for obvious reasons, and for Yang, having been a medical doctor in China offered no emollient; 12 hours is 12 hours.

SOCIOACADEMIC RELATIONS

Relations With Peers

As noted earlier, Yang came into the nursing program as part of a cohort of students. Although the nursing program was "never easy" for Yang, her work became more satisfying and perhaps even became possible at all when she realized that contrary to her assumptions, expectations, and experiences during her first year and a half of university study in the United States, once she got to know her nursing classmates, they were an enormous source of material aid, especially in the form of the lecture notes they lent her, and of emotional support.

Even in her 1st year at the university Yang relied on classmates for notes in history class. Yet early in her first semester in the nursing program, she formed, or had reinforced for her, the opinion that her domestic peers did not know how to help a classmate like her, did not want to share their knowledge:

Interviewer: Do you ask any classmate or do you have special friends you ask?

Yang: No, I just ask some student who sit close to me. Sometime nice, sometime don't nice. Because American don't have idea how to help classmate. Maybe they think everybody do class by herself. Not help [others] know something. (first-term junior)

At that time Yang's plan for improving her work in the nursing program began with a vow to cultivate friendships with her peers:

Interviewer: So you must be thinking about how to improve [work in nursing]. Do you have a plan?

Yang: Yeah, just keep good friendship with classmates, get good notes. (first-term junior)

That first semester in nursing was particularly trying. Yang was also isolated and afraid. She noted that of the 150 students who had been admitted to a previous class of nurses, only 100 of them had their pictures included in the portraits of program graduates. She asked:

Yang: I saw the graduation, the picture, only 100. Fifty people, where is 50 people? (first-term junior)

By about a month into the second semester, however, she began talking about her classmates in a much more familiar way.

Yang: Everybody is very friendly to help me so I feel easier. (second-term junior)

She also found a way to study with her classmates for exams without slowing them down with her language struggles and a way to cultivate friendly relations by reciprocating their help:

> Interviewer: Do you have a study partner when you study for exams or
> for class?
> Yang: I just study by myself. But I know some group [is] in the library. I
> know where they are. If I have a question, just go ahead and ask
> them. If I don't have a question, I just study from my own. (sec-
> ond-term junior)

Although Yang was unable to help directly in the study group, she made
an effort to participate in the study group economy by making whatever
contribution she could to her classmates in other areas.

> Yang: If I have some good material, I don't need somebody [to] ask me. I
> just bring [to] class. I ask, who wants copy? So maybe, that's a little
> help me a lot. I just do little thing, so student know we can help each
> other. (second-term junior)

By the spring of her junior year, her classmates were helpful and friendly
and she had friends among them. Part of the reason for this change was
group-work assignments.

Group work was assigned in nursing classes, according to the faculty
interviews, in part on the assumption that nurses rarely work alone.
Although most course-sponsored group-work projects were riddled with
problems, the faculty generally did not have much sense of what took
place behind the scenes and in any case remained committed to assigning
group projects in part because group presentations, which were often the
product of the group project, served to break up long class hours (all the
academic courses were 3 hours long).

Yang was lucky in one of the two projects during her junior year to find
herself with a group that not only functioned well as a group in working
together to complete their assignment but also became very fond of each
other. This group in a health practices class was so welcoming to Yang in
part as a result of the way it was formed. Yang credited her professor for
the clever idea. She instructed Yang to put her name down first on the
sign-up list for a particular topic. That meant that, because Yang was by
then identifiable to her classmates by name, anyone signing their name
below hers would know that they would be working with her, thus avoiding the possibility of group mates that might have perhaps resented her
presence in the group. (For a detailed description of Yang's experience in
this group, see Leki, 2001.)

Unfortunately, most of her experiences with group work were not satisfying. In one case, Yang's group was assigned to discuss hospital pricing
structures. Her public role consisted of holding up the syringes or ban-
dages that her NES classmates discussed as examples of variable-cost
items. She expressed mixed feelings about all this, on one hand grateful

to be allowed to contribute at all and on the other embarrassed at not contributing more because of her difficulties with oral English.

> Yang: I just hate myself, I can't get good English. So a lot of times the work my classmates do, I can do just little thing. ... I can't do presentation ... if I give presentation, give bad result. ... So I just do little job because of my poor English. (second-term junior)

Most of Yang's group-work experiences were either demeaning or frustrating. Often the problem was that members of various dysfunctional groups failed to do their share of the work. In one of the latter, one student even tried to urge the others on by using Yang as an example and saying, as Yang reported:

> Yang: If Yang can do this, everyone can. (second-term junior)

Nevertheless, being well aware of the challenges that many aspects of the nursing program posed for her, and, realizing how much easier her peers could make life for her, she was determined to do what she could to continue to cultivate friendships and support from her classmates in any way she could.

> Yang: I try to help to everybody. ... Because I know I need everybody help ... for the care plan, for the rotation I need everybody. Because for the doctor, the nurse [hand]writing, I can't recognize. I need everybody help me. Oh, help me, what is word, what it means? Because sometime I can't recognize. ... When ... we got good relationship, that's easier. (second-term junior)

And her friendships grew. When classes began again in the fall of her 1st senior year and students coalesced into their clinical-rotation groups, Yang was invited by a group that had already formed to join them. Yang's comment:

> Yang: I feel warm. (first-term senior)

It was obvious from class observations, as well, that Yang was accepted and well liked. When she appeared in class with a new haircut, for example, peers would comment. When she announced her pregnancy, her classmates were happy for her. During breaks, she interacted freely with them. Field notes from spring of her senior year, for example, capture a glimpse of the friendliness of her peers and also of her awareness of the help they gave her:

> At break Yang introduces me to an American student Kari, who she copies notes from.

Yang: I give her trouble; sometimes her husband is waiting for her. (field-notes, spring senior year)

Kari: You don't give me trouble!

Yang was very at ease and friendly with these students.

On one occasion when Yang made a presentation, her classmates applauded her, though she insisted this was merely an attempt to encourage her, not to reward her for a job well done.

Contributions of Classmates

The socioacademic relationships that Yang developed with her peers were critical to her success in her studies, first and foremost, as she came to feel she could not learn from the course textbooks and her reliance on her classmates' course notes grew. But notes were not all. She felt she could learn much from these classmates, and what Yang claimed to have learned was not insignificant: She had no idea how to construct a questionnaire required in one project; she did not know the name of the local health department; she had never heard of food stamps. All this type of common cultural knowledge came from her classmates.

Another important aspect of the socioacademic relations Yang developed with the other students was the opportunity to compare herself to them in important ways that made her life easier because they gave her benchmark data, allowed her to see how near or how far she was from what others were doing. She compared herself to them:

- To see how long it took her peers to complete assignments.
- To see how careful they were in their work.
- To see the quality of the work they turned in.
- To see what kind of grades they were getting (to gauge what kind of grade she could expect).
- To verify and support her contentions of too much work ("even Americans say this"; "a lot of students confused").
- To learn how others reacted to the nursing program ("I want to get out").

Having good relationships with peers allowed Yang to perceive herself as a part of a larger group. She could compare herself to see how she was different or to what degree she measured up but also where she and her classmates shared the same opinions, problems, annoyances, grievances, and to know for certain that she was not alone in her difficulties. Her willingness to quote her classmates' acerbic comments about the major grew as time went on.

Yang: The American students, they even make some good grades, and they just say, I want to get out of here" (first-term senior).

Such comments vindicated her own frustrations with her studies.

These socioacademic relationships allowed Yang entrance into a social context that provided for reciprocal generosity, and even if the class-sponsored group work Yang was involved with was less than satisfactory, the development of these socioacademic relations let her know she was not alone and allowed her to feel confident in her reactions to her experiences: Yes, there was too much work in nursing; yes, the paperwork was a waste of time. In the face of all the reminders of the focal students' difference from everyone else, these socioacademic contacts provided a measure of their similarity to others and a feeling of happy belonging that Yang sometimes desperately needed. As she said about her group experience in the health practices class:

Yang: So I got a lot of fun from American students. (second-term junior)

Relations With Nursing Faculty

As Teachers.   In addition to relations with her peers, the second important piece of the focal students' socioacademic relations was with faculty. Yang felt that her university teachers were generally kind and understanding. In her core education courses, every professor she mentioned had been happy to allow her extra time to do exams and, in grading her written work, had made allowances for her English. Willingness to make minor exceptions for Yang was part of what permitted her to do as well as she did in her 1st year and formed part of Yang's portrait of a good teacher.

Yang consulted freely with faculty in both general-education and nursing courses, before or after classes and in their offices. Her most common comment about faculty was that he or she was very nice.

Yang: The teacher very good. He's nice. He offer every condition to help me. (second-term freshman)

Yang clearly saw teachers as occupying a caretaking role; a good teacher did everything she could to make difficult studies easy on students, including what she termed "letting" students pass.

When Yang complained about an instructor, although often the complaint was preceded by noting how nice the instructor was, the complaint was usually that her lectures were too chatty and informal, and therefore disorganized, or the teacher sometimes spoke too fast, and so did not allow for good lecture notes, a failing she thought was particular to U.S. professors.

> Yang: Notes very difficult, very important for foreign students. Lot of American teachers don't like make notes, I think. Just talking. (second-term freshman)

> Yang: Because the American teacher not write down in a board. … just go to lecture just talking, talking. (first-term junior)

Personal

Yang worked very hard, and consciously, at cultivating good relationships with faculty as well as students in the nursing program, feeling that they were an important path to her hoped-for success in the program. She was certainly known to the faculty, particularly after her very visible problem with the exam during her first semester in the program, and for the most part she was respected for her obvious knowledge and intelligence.

Her charm and friendliness also won her friends. Faculty joined students in making a point of coming to her to hug her when it was learned that she was pregnant. And Yang was not shy about interacting with faculty. After one lecture, for example, she walked up to the professor and complimented her.

> Yang: Very good lecture, very clear. (field notes, second-term senior year)

Nevertheless, Yang eventually became convinced that two of the instructors had it in for her. They had been involved in the disastrous public clash during the exam in her first semester, in the rejection of Yang's first nursing report in her junior year, in pressuring her to drop that first nursing course, and then again in her eventual removal from the pediatrics course in her senior year, causing the delay in her graduation. What she felt was their pursuit of her colored her ability to feel at home in the program, putting pressure on her from the very first course; the repercussions of this perceived pursuit continued until her last semester when she alone was asked to meet the unusual requirement of getting specific permission to register for the final nursing clinical, a course that everyone else was allowed to register for with no such prerequisite. Yang commented more than once:

> Yang: [tearfully] I don't understand why the teacher treat me this way, to be so difficult to me. Why? (first-term junior)

> Yang: I do not do anything wrong, but she just try to find something wrong. (first-term senior)

At one point when Yang referred to American students crying when they got poor grades, she commented that she only cried when she felt treated unfairly. Yang described her nemeses as wanting her to fail:

Yang: They just want to keep misunderstanding. They do not try to understand me. ... the question is if they wanted to know [my true ability]. (first-term senior)

But Yang also believed that she herself was in part to blame for the problems of her senior year because of her failure to detach herself sufficiently from the situation during her junior year to better manipulate it to her advantage:

Yang: My husband tell me if I deal [had dealt] with the director smoothly, I do not get into trouble, so many trouble ... maybe she don't feel so upset. ... so I learn from this, I don't argue. (second-term senior)

In the end, however, as Yang said in her final comment about this faculty member:

Yang: Maybe we just go too far for the conflict. (second-term senior)

But other faculty worked actively to make life easier for Yang by defending her and emphasizing what she *was* able to do. One faculty member, for example, told me that she made a specific effort to smooth the way for Yang in clinicals by talking to the clinical staff about her:

Professor M: She understands everything. If you don't understand her, tell her to slow down or repeat. (field notes)

Both her confidence and comfort grew as Yang sensed the support around her. This was especially important in the last semester of her senior year because her cohort had graduated the previous spring, and she lost their warm, positive influence. But their acceptance of her was replaced by the support she eventually felt from the faculty, clinical instructors, and nursing staff.

Interviewer: How are you feeling about your major now?
Yang: Maybe I feel a little better about now. One reason is the clinical instructor give us, maybe give me more support, give me positive feedback, so I feel not so bad as before I feel. ... Maybe I have hope. ... I feel not so nervous. ... Not like before, I feel so horrible. ... I just fear. ... For now not fear anymore. (third-term senior)

In good measure, this change came from feeling that the people around her were not refusing to understand her English:

Interviewer: Did you feel comfortable talking to [your professor]?
Yang: At the beginning I just feel nervous, but when we talk [now], I can understand, so I didn't worry anymore. Because if you talk somebody, they don't understand you, I get more nervous. If we can talk very easy, maybe I don't get anything to worry about. She can understand me. That's very good. More confidence. (third-term senior)

SPECIAL CIRCUMSTANCES FOR INTERNATIONAL STUDENTS

Although Yang had a variety of problems during her studies, most of them she seemed to feel she could address in some way. Aside from the language issues Yang faced, probably her most difficult challenge related to cross-cultural expectations. She appeared to give up hope of making much progress in understanding the psychosocial aspects of behavior she studied in nursing, for example. This dimension of nursing was an important one but required employing reasoning based on the kinds of psychosocial knowledge that was at least partly cultural and implicit. It was often unclear to Yang what appropriate behavior was in various contexts and so when she was required to note behavior or special social circumstances in her NCPs, she was not always sure what to include. On exams, for example,

Yang: I am at a disadvantage here. ... The teacher gave five questions. ... the one teenager pregnant woman, she doesn't have good relationship with her newborn. They ask, what do you think, the bonding good or not good? I can remember definition. I know what the clear, the content from book, but I cannot answer the question. ... I just can't get it right. (second-term senior)

She was willing to change her "standpoint," as she said, but was not able to determine the appropriate American responses in such circumstances. Though her domestic peers also struggled with exams in nursing, Yang's constant refrain was that because all of this focused on their native culture and was in their native language, it was far easier for the domestic students.

Adding to the frustration of trying to address a patient's psychosocial issues through appropriate communication was Yang's sense of the motivation for this focus. She eventually came to interpret the emphasis on communicative understanding as driven not so much by medical goals as by financial ones, part of the on-going competition to attract patient/customers in a capitalist economy.

Yang: ...May be the customer is the center for the service. The hospital may be want to be more patients. So they use every method to

> appeal to the customer. So, maybe they emphasize the interaction, the attitude to serve the patient. (first fall senior year)

Often what facilitated the work of domestic students increased the burden for Yang. In one class, the students were assigned a series of movies to watch, like *Ordinary People,* to ease them into understanding the broader psychological and social issues surrounding mental illness. The videos did have this effect for the domestic students. But for Yang, rather than easing her into the study of psychological illness, the movies themselves were difficult to penetrate:

> Yang: Because some sentence, I do not truly understand, but the American student tell me, this is what it means. For example, for maybe this guy, a boy, he is in a major depression. ... he wants to go to suicide. When another patient asked him why he want to go to suicide, "I just feel I'm in a hole; I cannot get through." Just this kind of sentence is very, very simple, but I do not understand it. I asked American student to tell me. (second-term senior)

What were intended as relatively enjoyable and easy assignments for the domestic students were always a challenge for Yang:

> Yang: I will have not easy. Never, never, never easy for me. Never easy for me. (first-term senior)

In commenting on what was and was not possible as an international student, Yang pointed out the difficulties of adjusting to a new educational environment; she had just received a good score on a paper she had written:

> Yang: ... for my situation, for another foreign student, we want just pass. We don't have another choice. We can't truly understand and truly master ... American style. We don't have time to do this. We just take some technique useful for us, for pass the course.

Yang's refrain that everything was easier for her domestic peers was wistful. The expectation, reasonable when made of domestic students, that she would develop a sophisticated knowledge of patients' psychosocial circumstances was simply impossible to meet in a few months of nursing classes. In Yang's situation, the entire psychosocial segment of nursing had to be given up as a loss as she focused more intensely on the possible.

Faculty on International Students and English Learners

The nursing faculty seemed torn between wanting in principle to be welcoming to international students as a part of their commitment to tolerance of difference and worrying about their language problems, for those internationals who had such problems. Although the nursing faculty interviewed, like the faculty in all the majors involved in this study, felt writing was important, they appeared more concerned about oral skills and more generalized literacy skills, such as vocabulary or reading knowledge, than in their students' more traditional writing.

Of all the faculty in the nursing program interviewed, only one was willing to express frankly the worries about Yang's English that others on the faculty also felt. She recognized that international students' levels of comprehension were probably better than their oral proficiency, believed these students were "bright," and understood that idioms and euphemisms were bound to cause language problems. Nevertheless, certain slips shocked and worried her for what they suggested about possible misunderstandings:

> Professor R: Even sometimes in normal communication, we can't understand their questions, so it's hard to assist them and answer their questions. ... Certainly, slang and our euphemisms are different ... I remember when a student put down that the baby was shot. [She meant that] the baby had all their shots, all their immunizations. So those kinds of things are critical.

Professor D noted that clinical faculty had complained about Yang and worried in particular about her presence in the hospital during clinicals. At the same time Professor D worried about the issue of bias against NNES nursing students and just how far the nursing program could legitimately, ethically go in insisting on improved oral communication before they became perceived as discriminating against internationals.

> Professor D: ... you are taking care of English-speaking clients, predominantly. ... you hate to penalize somebody, but yet, that's one of the requirements, and it's a challenge for faculty. We have talked about it many times. ... You want to be helpful, to lay that out on the table, but then they'll think that maybe you're biased. It's very sensitive.

Looming over the students and faculty both, however, were the state licensing exams.

Board Exams

According to one professor, 9 out of 10 NNESs failed on the first round of the state board exams and sometimes on the second as well. Aside from the personal problems that failing the board exam posed for students, the nursing program they graduated from suffered as well. Nursing programs were evaluated in part on how well their graduates did on their first attempts.

> Professor D: ... so the more international students that you take, the higher risk that you are, that you won't get the same percentage passing, and the higher risk that is going to look bad for your program and the whole works.

Furthermore, without success on these exams and despite their diplomas, the candidates would not be licensed to practice nursing, a situation that posed an ethical dilemma for the faculty as well:

> Professor S: I have concerns for our non-native English-speaking students; where will they be when they do graduate? Will they get a job? I don't know how to answer those questions. Should we test them some other way?

Although there were very few international students in the nursing program during Yang's studies, it was clear that Yang's difficulties called attention to their general situation and posed unresolved dilemmas for the nursing faculty. Her language tool use in nursing was densely embedded in a network of concerns reaching far beyond the personal or course level to departmental, institutional, and even broader disciplinary issues. Yet Yang's academic success in general-education courses and then in nursing courses illustrates that her language proficiency was not unidimensional but had a differential impact on her studies and her success or failure depending on what kind of an activity system they were employed in.

Prejudice

Despite the nursing faculty's commitment to tolerance and desire to remain unbiased, Yang voiced suspicions of differential treatment of domestic and NNES students. What was Yang's evidence? In her senior year, she began to refer to special requirements made of her that were not being made of the other students. First, she was required to make a draft of her nursing notes before putting them onto her patient's chart whereas all the other students charted directly:

> Yang: The American students, they can jot down the notes on the chart, directly. For me, I need to [write them out on] another paper [for] the teacher check and then put it down. ... Because that document is a legal document. (first-term senior)

Her comments here were rather noncommittal but became more pointed as she referred to other circumstances she noticed or heard of. After she was forced to drop the pediatrics class, she seemed to stop seeing these events as primarily the result of her English problems. And she began gathering evidence:

> Yang: I don't know what is wrong here. Because the Chinese girl, one Chinese girl tell me when she [one of the faculty] saw her, she let [made] her drop the class. ... And I heard one, a student one year before me, she's Chinese, she tell me, that Russian girl drop the class, too. ... I, I try to figure out what's wrong here. I don't know. (first-term senior)

By the end of the first semester of her senior year, Yang was beginning to wonder where breakdowns in communication were really originating, on her side or on the side of certain instructors:

> Yang: I have ... knowledge about the disease, but I, the teacher just say I cannot clear demonstration my meaning. ... My knowledge, my ability not like they ... say, at this [low] level. They just want to keep misunderstanding. They do not try to understand me. ...
>
> Interviewer: How could you let them know your ability, [what] your true ability is?
>
> Yang: I think the question is if they wanted to know. (first-term senior)

After several incidents of what she considered unwarranted differential treatment of domestic students and herself, Yang began to reinterpret past events in light of these new suspicions. Talking about her traumatic junior-year exam experience, she doubted the events would have played out the same way for a domestic student:

> Yang: I think if American students do this, I think teacher, I'm not sure if teacher will do the same thing. (second-term senior)

Yang had other evidence she used as well in her private case of bias against international students. Referring to an incident where a domestic student had given a patient the wrong medication and yet was allowed to pass the clinical, she made the point that when the clinical instructor became upset with this student, the student complained to the course coordinator that she had been spoken to in an unprofessional manner. Yang noted the difference in her own situation after the exam incident and this one. The domestic student not only was bold enough to complain about what she saw as unfair treatment, she also had enough language at her command to do so. Yet despite the fact that she had committed what surely was a much more serious mistake than merely taking too long on an exam, not only did the student have the opportunity to defend herself, she was not penalized in any way; she passed the clinical and graduated, whereas Yang's graduation was being delayed.

Yang: Difference. We need very careful everything. Very different. She graduate. She very nice to me. But I know the difference. ... But not only me, another foreign student. They can feel some instructor different to American student and to us. ... Some student you know they have very good ability in speaking, nobody can give them trouble. Sometimes they give teacher trouble.

Interviewer: So you say that there is a difference between the way instructors treat American students and the way they treat international students?

Yang: Not all instructor, just some instructor. For this term, just keep secret, though, before I graduate. (third-term senior)

A domestic student could give a teacher trouble. A foreign student could not afford to.

Yang: So I learn from this, I don't argue" (second-term senior).

Yang felt she could not defend herself as vigorously as her peer had because a malicious teacher could easily fail her in a clinical based on her language problems, and because measurement of degree of language problems was entirely arbitrary, Yang felt constantly vulnerable. At any moment, an instructor could decide that Yang's language was too weak. How weak was too weak? That depended on who was responding to the question. Yang felt that reaching her goal of graduating with a nursing degree meant that she had to be cautious not to ruffle feathers and so wanted to keep these suspicions quiet until she was safely out of the program. Nevertheless, her early plaintive comment, "I lack ability to demonstrate my ability," had now entirely changed in character:

Yang: ... that instructor tried to prove my problem as big as she imagination. (third-term senior)

IDEOLOGICAL EDUCATION

Did Yang experience differential treatment based on prejudice? Though it is difficult to answer that question, what came out in lectures more clearly was a set of deep-seated ideological assumptions that Yang and her classmates were exposed to. Because Yang was so focused on getting information from course lectures that would be covered in exams, it was not clear how much attention she paid to comments in lectures that served to indoctrinate students and reinforce their prejudices about U.S. culture and the relationship between the United States and U.S. practices and the vaguely existing rest of the world.

U.S. medical practices were assumed as the standard. During a lecture on communicable diseases, for example, the instructor made repeated reference to inferior standards of cleanliness internationally as compared with the United States and to the current safe status of the United States in terms of infectious diseases compared to other parts of the world. On Yang's handout with her handwritten notes elaborating the outline based on the lecture, she had:

> Who is at high risk for infection?
> immuno compromised
> elderly
> children
> poverty
> chronic diseases
> organ transplants
> unimmunized population come from other country

The message seemed to be, on one hand, that unimmunized populations existed only in other countries and, on the other, that it was necessary to be especially cautious with those other populations; other parts of the world were scary.

Yang knew about health practices in China and had her own ideas about how these practices differed from those in the United States and which ones were better. In a rare instance in the data, however, the two sets of practices were directly compared in a clinical.

> Yang: For some, some clinical I ask my teacher a lot because I feel confused. Some principles, in labor and delivery and baby care and newborn care are different over here from China. ... I feel the different, I asked my instructor. ... Teacher explain to me. Teacher said way Americans do this is because the other way, that's bad. This is]better way. (second-term senior)

Although Yang's discussion of this incident in the interview continued, it never became clear exactly why the American way was better than the other, only that the superiority was to be accepted as true.

Despite the fact that the medical associations in the United States would accept a medical degree like Yang's, provided the applicant pass the medical board exams, officials in the nursing program were not impressed by her degree, comparing it to a chiropractor's license. One of the faculty members interviewed remarked on how little resemblance Yang's degree had to medical training in the United States:

Professor R: It's kind of like taking a nursing degree from Africa and putting it here: What standards and courses?

Africa here seemed to be the exemplar of the anomaly of medical training outside the United States, somewhere at the ends of the earth.

Yet even remaining within the borders of the United States, in some of the classes observed, lecturers set themselves up as cultural arbiters in the name of health education, passing judgments on behaviors and activities either based on what they assumed were shared values or working to indoctrinate the students into sharing those values. One teacher asserted the dangers, for example, of exposing children to the gay life styles.

Teacher: You need to be able to tell parents to pay attention to TV. [Goes on to refer to *Ellen* on TV, who was coming out as gay.] Parents should know that even a show that seems innocent might talk about things the parent doesn't want the kids to hear.

counterculture practices,

Teacher: It's important as a health educator; you need to let parents know. A safety pin through the lip is body mutilation. Are they imitating the drug culture? [This is] a reason to think about this more.

and teen fashion:

Teacher: [showing a picture of her son with a shaved head]:
What's the big deal? We weren't talking purple hair here. They weren't doing mohawks. (field notes, first term, senior year)

Mohawks and purple hair apparently indexed lifestyles that this lecturer considered off the scale, whereas the shaved head of her son—offensive as its neo-Nazi connotations might be to others—was entirely within bounds.

In another class, the lecturer drew a clear line around the U.S. middle class as an in-group. Referring to how health-related problems can turn up anywhere, she cited the apparently astonishing findings of a research study of suburban children who had emotional trouble and commented:

Teacher: It was solid America. It was *us*. They were protected Americans, part of America. (field notes)

The idea that children from "solid America," "us," experienced emotional problems was notable; apparently among those not "part of America," it would be less remarkable.

Other assumptions of this type were perhaps less obvious and so more insidious:

Teacher: When we were conquering the West, these A.D.D. children were great Pony Express riders. (field notes)

The uncomplicated, untroubled use of "we" and of "conquering the West" betrayed a cozy sense of pride and belonging that would have excluded the experiences of Yang, not to mention those of the people in the West being conquered.

Thus, I wondered just what Yang was learning about U.S. biases and U.S. culture. If she was hearing this in class and no one was disputing any of it (which was the case) and if she had little reason to hear anything about these topics outside of class (which was the case), she might assume that people in the United States would be afraid of exposing children to gay television characters who were not being mocked for being gay, or would feel that aspects of teen culture like body piercing might index drug use, or believed that shaved heads were fine but mohawks were suspicious. When we asked her about what she got out of those lectures, she responded that she knew it would not be on the exam so she essentially ignored this kind of information. But her classmates likely paid greater heed.

Finally, not only cultural issues but also professional issues were sometimes treated in a way that served to indoctrinate students into a stance that ultimately supported existing power relations to the detriment of the interests of these nursing professionals and their students. A course on leadership, for example, admonished nursing students to embrace change instead of being laggards and resisting it. The changes the course materials were referring to were changes in the health care industry, many of which had serious detrimental effects on nurses' employment, in particular asking them to do much more in shorter amounts of time than ever before. Also, because of insurance companies' control of health care, patients stayed shorter amounts of time in medical units, with a resulting decrease in the number of nursing positions available and with nurses being let go. These were certainly changes, and the nursing students were urged to embrace change. Given all the emphasis in this program on critical thinking in nursing and on nurses' struggles to be seen as professionals, it was surprising that these issues had escaped a critical eye and that the nursing faculty were potentially to become victims without protest of some of their own colleagues' ideological stances.

CONCLUSION

The participants in Duff, Wong, and Early's (2000) study of prospective nursing aides faced problems similar to those that challenged Yang:

- Despite years of living in Canada, they had few Canadian friends and little opportunity to speak English.
- In addition to the difficulty of technical medical language, they had to learn colloquial, children's, and polite terms for a variety of medical conditions and bodily functions.
- Not only verbal but also body language was important with patients.
- Medical texts were long and linguistically dense.
- Classroom discourse mixed registers freely including anecdotes, rapid and colloquial speech, videos, and professional jargon.

The only linguistic feature of these aides' experience that differed significantly from Yang's was the multilingual population they would deal with. In the setting of Yang's studies, the population was nearly uniformly Anglo or African American, and many patients spoke a dialect that Yang was likely not to have heard before.

Yang had many opinions about her experiences as a U.S. university student. Her reflections and conclusions about U.S. education, U.S. students, and the nursing profession she was now prepared to enter reveal internal contradictions and so challenge preconceived ideas on these subjects within this U.S. culture. However, access to those thoughts and opinions present the kinds of worthwhile challenges that any border crossings do, the opportunity to rethink and reinterpret the invisible ideological frames that occlude some perceptions and enhance others.

Finishing college for Yang was like escaping prison. The nursing major was a somewhat coerced choice. Although she tried her best, it was a struggle till the end for her. The relationships she established were warm and significant but not enduring friendships. She had a new baby and would soon move to a new town, carrying her unhappy teenage daughter along. She seemed to always be sacrificing herself to another cause. Would she find a nursing job that suited her skills and limitations? Would she find a job at all? Had it been worth it? Unclear.

Despite Yang's varied attempts to improve her pronunciation during her last summer as a nursing student, and her previous more desultory efforts, it is difficult not to suspect that Yang's commitment to this goal was conflicted. No doubt she *was* tired of study-related efforts and did need to take a break from schooling during the summers, and it is also true that finding the appropriate resources to improve her English proved to be a chore. Certainly, Yang frequently lamented that life would be much easier for her if her English were better. Yet there also always lurked the sense that Yang resisted the need for additional language work, justifying that resistance to the nursing faculty by saying that she would work on English after she completed her degree. But as Norton (2000) points out, learners have multiple desires and parcel out their investment in learning the target language in relation to the expected return in cultural capital and "access to hitherto unattainable resources" (p. 10). For Yang at this point the resources were not unattainable without better English. She was succeeding without investing further in English. In addition, she believed that what was of utmost importance in working in a medical field was science education; the emphasis on communication was an American quirk related to the need to attract customers to hospitals within a capitalist economy. Furthermore, she may have experienced the constant pressure from the nursing school to improve her English as an infringement on her own ability to decide, an ability she cherished and felt defined her as a competent, intelligent adult. Finally, Yang was being pushed, at least somewhat against her will, to shift her identity from pediatrician to nurse. In all, Yang's language was a site of conflicting desires and motivations as well as, possibly, emblematic of her bid for control of her own fate, control denied her by the educational system in China that made her a doctor instead of an engineer, by her husband's decision to move to the United States, again by her husband's preference for her pursuit of nursing as a career, and finally by the various bids for control of her life she experienced in the nursing program. In light of all the other issues she dealt with, the importance of academic writing, once again, if for different reasons, seems thrown into question.

4

"Suddenly You Get Recognized":
The Power of Community

In spite of curriculum, discipline, and exhortation, the learning that is most personally transformative turns out to be the learning that involves membership in ... communities of practice.

—Wenger (1998, p. 6)

PROLOGUE TO JAN

Jan's story is partially one of late adolescence, a narrative of initial expectations followed by a series of forced adjustments, which, taken together, helped to produce an individual with a very particular but not very heartening perspective on the academic world.

Jan was the youngest of the four research participants. Perhaps for this reason, his adjustment to high school and then university life in the United States was the most difficult, despite his European background and American stepfather, which might have, in principle, helped to make that adjustment easier. Jan had the best language skills of the group, was the most familiar with U.S. customs and procedures, in many ways could have been said to be the most integrated into U.S. culture, yet only Yang's difficulties came close to Jan's in intensity. Yang's battles resulted almost entirely from problems with language and had fewer deeply threatening implications for her sense of self. Jan struggled to occupy a subject position that he could inhabit comfortably, without self-consciousness, and with dignity.

Perhaps in my telling, Jan will not come off as charming. He was. His outrageous, low-key sarcastic comments made me laugh out loud (and still do as I reread the transcripts). But he was capable of holding shocking opinions, some of them apparently expressed for effect, some of them sincere. And then maybe he was joking. A complication with Jan was the question of the reliability of his statements, which often contradicted each other. This is not to say that he tried to fool me or give patently false information. I am convinced that he lived his contradictions. For example, though his attitude toward his education was usually dismissive and utilitarian, he was in many ways quite responsible about course requirements, as he was about this research project, never failing to keep a scheduled interview appointment, always arriving on time, answering e-mail or phone messages immediately. At the end of each term, he would hand us his notebook, 4 inches thick and filled with his classwork and extensive course notes. At the same time, maneuvering around rules as necessary, Jan was a survivor.

BACKGROUND

Jan immigrated from Poland when he was 17. Tall, thin, pleasant-looking, he was very sociable, often attempting to engage classmates in friendly and joking chatting before and after classes. His oral skills in English and his command of idiomatic language and teenage slang were clearly not well reflected in his relatively low 527 TOEFL score, only 2 points above minimum for admission to this university. The prosody of his accent was very nearly native, and though individual phonemes may have been somewhat non-native sounding, overall his pronunciation matched his fluency and never blurred understanding of what he said, although he often spoke very rapidly and repeated segments of phrases. (For more detailed discussion, see Leki, 1999.)

High School in the United States

Three days after his arrival in the United States with his mother, stepfather, and baby sister, Jan began high school as a junior with no English at all. He attended ESL classes while simultaneously taking such classes as junior and, later, senior English. While still in high school, he got a full-time job at Burger King, where he worked for several months and where, he pointedly claimed, he learned English. (See Norton's 2000 description of immigrants' experiences in fast-food jobs.)

Jan described the classes in his American high school as being gratifyingly behind where he had been in his Polish high school.

Jan: I hated school [in Poland]. School system is awesome over here. ... It couldn't get easier than it is. ... I would have to do three times more in Europe to have the same effect as here" (second term, 5th year)

Among the bottom 20% at his school in Poland, in the United States, despite not knowing English, as he said, he was making As, relying partly on his academic background from Poland and partly on the low level of intellectual demands made on him in his U.S. high school. Uncjhallenging multiple-choice exams allowed him to guess at obvious answers. In order to get a U.S. high school diploma, Jan took a jumble of English courses in an illogical sequence to earn credits for material he already knew before taking the courses in order to fulfill a bureaucratic requirement. His ESL classes were, as he said, "baby stuff," a situation described in other accounts of high school and college ESL classes as well (Harklau, 1994; Leki, 1995a; Leki & Carson, 1997).

Although other students in the ESL classes were friendly, he craved the friendship of American students, who showed no interest in him. As he explained it,

Jan: People are very unfriendly if you don't speak pretty good English. I don't have any friends because [they say] you are foreign, you're on the side, you know. ... [They say] oh, your English sucks, OK, bye, go away. (first-term sophomore)

In high school, Jan made no domestic friends.

The salient themes that came out of Jan's brief U.S. high school experience were:

- The work in American schools was easy and required little effort.
- The American school system was bureaucratic, requiring jumping through hoops in order to get what you want.
- His American classmates were competitive and uninterested in foreigners.

These themes threaded their way through his years at the university, coloring his outlook and behaviors.

ACADEMIC PORTRAIT

The First University Year

Unfortunately, Jan's first semester at the university was a disaster, preceded by a series of unhappy accidents. He was admitted late because, he said, the school had lost his SAT and TOEFL scores. Arriving on campus only 3 days before classes began, he missed the careful orientation the office for international students conducted for new visa and permanent-resident students. This meant he met none of the new international students who might have become friends or at least served as sources of information. It meant that he was not assigned to a dorm that housed many of the new international students, and he found himself in a dorm with 1st-year American students with whom he ended up having no relationship. And it meant that he came too late to be advised about the courses he hoped to take in fall. He was essentially operating blind, alone, fairly cocky about his academic strengths, based on his experience in high school, and somewhat wary and bruised in regard to relationships with domestic students.

In his first semester, declaring a difficult premed major, he took chemistry, math, English, psychology, a two-credit pass/fail study skills course (a total of 17 hours), and held a full-time, 40-hour-a-week job. No one advised him of the folly of such a heavy first-semester load nor of school policies that would have allowed him to drop courses if he registered for too many or found them too difficult. To exacerbate the situation were his mistaken notions about the difficulty of university study.

> Jan: Big difference between college and high school … I didn't know it was gonna be that big difference. … Like in high school they put all the stuff on the board and just get it from the board. And over here the teacher is talking and you gotta make the notes and I can't make the notes. Like you know, he's talking and I can make half the sentences, I'm losing some. I leave spaces. After, I don't understand the notes. When I try to study something after in my dorm … I don't know what I wrote. … (second-term freshman)

One avenue of aid that might have saved him did not open up to him, connections to peers. He knew no international students. Having made no American friends in high school, he could not turn to them at the university. When asked if he ever had group work to do in his classes, he replied:

> Jan: Pretty much I do all my job by myself. Because nobody wants to [work] with me pretty much. (first-term sophomore)

Although his ability to communicate informally in English by now was excellent, his informal English was not what he needed to deal with the demands of university study. As he said,

> Jan: And the exams … short essays now, like you've got a few sentences, you gotta express something. You know what's asked for, but you can't express. (first-term sophomore)

TABLE 4.1
Questionnaire

4.   What else has been difficult for you in your courses (not your English class) this
semester? Check as many as apply to you.

Jan		*Yang*	
__x___	amount of reading	_____	amount of reading
__x___	understanding the reading	_X___	understanding the reading
_____	amount of writing	_____	amount of writing
_____	type of writing assignment	_____	type of writing assignment
__x___	understanding lectures	_____	understanding lectures
__x___	asking questions in class	_____	asking questions in class
__x___	getting help from your teachers	_____	getting help from your teachers
__x___	getting help from your classmates	_____	getting help from your classmates
__x___	essay exams	_____	essay exams
__x___	multiple-choice exams	_____	multiple-choice exams
__x___	short-answer exams	_____	short-answer exams
__x___	figuring out what your teacher expects	_____	figuring out what your teacher expects
_____	using the library	_X___	using the library
_____	other	_____	other

Jan failed his first ESL writing class, viewing his teachers' calls for development of ideas in his papers to be requirements to "b.s.," which he
repeatedly said he hated and which he increasingly came to see as the perfect expression to sum up everything required of him in college. It was all
a game. He played, the professors played, the institution played.

What kinds of problems was he having? In his responses to the survey
identifying possible participants for this research that was administered
about a month into the students' first semester at the university, Jan
claimed to be having problems with almost everything. Given the kinds of
difficulties they both later faced, a comparison of Jan's and Yang's
responses to this item is surprising (see Table 4.1).

Because Jan had almost no writing assignments, he was not yet finding
them difficult. Nor did he find using the library a problem; but this was
because, as he noted in several interviews, he was not using the library

and had no idea how to do so. In Yang's case, the problems she would eventually face in nursing had not surfaced by the time of the survey, whereas it is astonishing how many tasks already posed a problem for Jan. Of particular interest was his perception of difficulty in getting help both from his peers and from his teachers.

Willing, even eager, to talk about his academic experiences, in his very first interview, Jan initiated several themes that were to continue at least through his first 2 undergraduate years:

- Professors tricked students in various ways, such as constructing exams and quizzes that were unrelated to lectures, and so attending classes or studying was pointless.
- Multiple-choice questions were long, complex, and arbitrary so that the choices could be summed up as "abcdefgh."
- Guessing (not working harder, which was pointless) was the only reasonable response possible to arbitrary exam questions.
- Classes typically enrolled "600 students."
- Domestic students had no interest in working with him.
- He studied for 2 to 4 straight days just before exams but not before that point.
- Various classes, teachers, and other aspects of school "sucked."
- The best way to approach assignments was to get them out of the way as soon as possible.

By the end of his first semester at the university, Jan's GPA was 0.65. This sad beginning was to haunt him for at least the next 2 years and perhaps partially accounts for his relentless focus on the GPA and on grades, scores, and the percentage that any given class activity was worth in calculating final course evaluations. Numerous interview exchanges in the first 2½ years gave the impression that you might awake him from a deep sleep in the middle of the night, and he would be able to instantly recalculate not only his current GPA but also what it *would* be if he got this or that grade on some assignment in any of his courses.

Jan's subsequent experiences at the university did little to discourage his focus on grades. His comments after being admitted to his newly chosen international business major would be characterized by panicky-sounding repetitions and verbal calculations, as in this example:

Jan: I gotta make the 3.0 GPA so to let me major, I gotta make 3.0 GPA, to sign up for the major. In order to major in International Business [with Russian as the required foreign language], I gotta have 3.0 GPA and I can't make lower grades than B in the Russian classes. (second-term sophomore)

Although in each semester after the first he managed to come very close to meeting the minimum GPA, his initial 0.65 was not overcome despite his struggles until the end of the first semester of his junior year.

By that time, however, clear patterns had been established. Jan was in a war to beat the system and achieve his goal, to get a degree so that he could get a job where he would sit at a desk and "dress nice, wear a tie."

Creating Masks

Although in class he invariably presented the very model of the diligent, industrious international student who has to work twice as hard as domestic students to do well at the university, Jan mainly worked hard and in a variety of inventive ways at his goal of beating the system. Many of his schemes failed. In his geography labs, Jan organized an elaborate (and illegal) work exchange system whereby each student (all NNESs) in the conspiracy did only one page of the lab work and then they all copied each other's pages. This system backfired when questions about the lab turned up on an exam, and Jan was unable to answer them, not having done any more than his one page of the lab work.

But other schemes did not fail:

- In his accounting class, he, amazingly, uncovered at the library a copy of the teacher's manual for the course text, complete with detailed answers to all the exercises. When the professor called on students in class to give answers to the exercises, Jan was the first to volunteer and of course his answers were always correct.
- To complete a course requirement of an interview with a business leader, Jan acquired the business card of a friend of his mother's, stapled it to his "interview report," and made up nearly all the information in the report except the name of the company. He got full credit.
- In another accounting class, he knew the accounting teacher checked only that the students did the homework problems assigned but didn't check the actual homework; he turned in the very same assignment over and over.

But probably the most blatant disparity between his public persona of the good student and his behind-the-scenes work as a shrewd manipulator came in Jan's descriptions of a course he was required to take as part of an application process to become a resident assistant (RA) in the university dormitories. He wanted this job because he could not afford to live alone and yet had had bad luck in roommates. As he described it:

> Jan: Every 6 months a new one. Every one bad, next one was worse"
> (first-term junior).

In Jan's tale, the first was a drug addict; the second smoked marijuana; the third, a woman, partied till dawn; the last was a smelly, dirty drunk and a "loser." RAs got private rooms at the dorm, with bathtubs, Jan pointed out with enthusiasm.

The RA course consisted of the leaders setting up hypothetical situations that might happen at a dorm and having participants explain how they would respond to these crises. Such a setup fairly begged for hypocrisy. And it was forthcoming. For example, one paper for this course required students to respond to a hypothetical situation in which dorm residents drink at a party off campus. The question was, What should the RA do? Jan piously wrote, "I would tell my residents to stay off-campus tonight and do not come back on campus, because they will break university's policies." The tone in an interview discussing this paper was quite different:

> Interviewer: So what did they ask you to talk about?
> Jan: If you would, like, turning in those people to the hall director because they're drinking off campus. I was like, Who cares? Do whatever you want to do. (second-term junior)

Jan's cynicism was fed by what he took to be the mealy-mouthed, stereotyped comments the course leaders made on his written responses to the hypothetical dorm problems.

> Interviewer: When you write the response papers ... what kind of things do they say?
> Jan: "Good idea"; "I don't think so"; "I'm sure"; "Think about it."[18] (second-term junior)

The hypothetical nature of the situations and the requirement to play (and be rewarded for playing) a holier-than-thou role were attempts to socialize the students into accepting a policing role, enforcer of university policy, in return for economic benefits. Though it is painful to see the unsuspecting course leaders duped, there was a sense in which it was deserved. It was difficult to find Jan's response so much more unsavory than the situation he was responding to.

Despite his good act, Jan did not get the RA job at the end of the course. He interpreted this in a sinister way:

> Jan: They don't like foreign people. ... Eleven got the job, and 2 international students, me and one guy from Korea, we didn't get the job, so I think they were kind of discriminating. (second-term junior)

Games and Mazes

In the elaborate game of higher education, Jan had become stubbornly convinced that professors and TAs played as well, or at least that is the understanding he articulated over and over, as shown in these typical interview questions and responses:

Interviewer:	Why were you asked to do this assignment?
Jan:	To give TAs something to do. (first-term sophomore)

Interviewer:	Why do you think the geography teacher is showing the class movies?
Jan:	It's more easy for her, probably, than to lecture. She's tired of them [lectures]. (second-term sophomore)

Interviewer:	What is the purpose of this assignment?
Jan:	To keep us busy. (second-term sophomore)

As he struggled to survive his first years in college, Jan constructed himself as battling blindfolded against impossible odds such that his failures were beyond his control. If he was having a hard time in math, it was because of the teacher:

Jan: He's not speaking English. (first-term sophomore)

Reported testimonials from his peers supported him:

Jan: No one had any idea how to do this. (second-term freshman)

Jan: No one knows what she's [the professor's] talking about. (first-term junior)

Jan: Even the TA said she didn't understand, no one can understand. (second-term sophomore)

Jan: No one finished. (second-term sophomore)

When he did not do well on an exam, which was fairly often, Jan frequently claimed to have been tricked in some way:

Jan: There were definitions on the math exam; I didn't think there was going to be definitions on math exam. (second-term freshman)

Or "there's no way to study" this material. About an exam in his management class, he said:

Jan: It's just like give you random phone numbers. You have the numbers; there's no way you gonna remember them. You remember five of them but 95% of them you're not gonna remember" (second-term sophomore).

Cheating?

Jan was accused of cheating more than once and he did bend rules. (See the section on Faculty Relations for further description of how relationships with faculty intersected both Jan's luck and his willingness to get around rules.) His academic integrity occupied a gray area. But some of these instances of cheating or almost cheating bear closer examination for what they suggest about the context of the cheating, about the accuracy of Jan's perception that many of the stipulations of the university consisted of hoop jumping, and about the difference between plagiarizing and learning.

The first example was the accounting classes already mentioned with the weekly problems to turn in that were apparently never reviewed by the instructor. Second, in another course, groups of four students were assigned a series of problems to work. Instead of working on all the problems together, members of the group each took only one to do to turn in for the whole group. Finally, when questioned about how he used information he had found in his stepfather's religion book in an important essay for his religions course, Jan replied:

Jan:	I just copied down, kind of plagiarized, [away from microphone] I'm sorry, I just changed the words a little bit around, kind of used the main ideas. I mean who's gonna know a book from 20 years ago?
Interviewer:	Do you think that most of what you wrote on the paper was taken from that reading?
Jan:	I found, one was my idea: He [Buddha] didn't like the caste system. So I wrote by myself without using any books. He didn't believe in the life after life I got from the book, that book [his stepfather's] because it was really nice described; and the second one, there's no soul, I got from the class book. So there's pretty much, each part was from one book, one book, and my ideas. (second-term junior)

In each of these cases, Jan could be said to have been cheating but from another perspective, none of the cases was straightforward. In the first example, it might be argued that the course instructor was cheating—cheating the students out of a response to their homework problem. In the second example, even though these problems were not appropriate as group work, as the instructor explained, all business courses were required to include group work (see section on Group Work), and this was what he had come up with. So the students' method for getting the work done by simply dividing it up hardly seems less ethical than foisting on students an assignment that had not been well thought through. And in the last example, Jan was able during his interview to recite the aspects of Buddhism that he had mentioned in his paper. If the purpose of this assignment was for students to learn something about Buddhism, Jan had learned it. Was his learning less legitimate because he had copied phrases out of a book?

Surviving

Anyone who has ever gone back into the undergraduate classroom as an observer cannot help but sympathize with the task facing undergraduates (and their teachers). Many introductory courses do enroll hundreds of students who sit sleepily or indifferently taking notes in what seems like interminable lectures often focusing on the minutiae of the discipline. Jan's course notes were filled with definitions, for example, as were many of his exams.

This focus on disciplinary vocabulary and ground-zero concepts encouraged Jan's odd study habits, particularly in his first few years. In order to survive exams, he crammed. But the cramming took an unusual form. Jan's goal was to memorize material, and he did this by recopying it on different sheets of paper over and over by hand until it had become etched on his memory. This memorizing, however, had no particular implications for understanding the material:

> Jan: I saw this in my notes; I think this is the right answer. I don't under-
> stand what it is, but I think it was in my notes, so I think that's the
> right answer. It's kind of guessing, guessing game. I have no idea
> what I'm doing, just guessing.[19] (second-term sophomore)

Nearly all the tests he took in his first 3 years of university were multiple-choice. But as the years went on, he began increasingly to express a preference for essay exams in which he could, as he often said, either b.s., write in garble so that the professor might give him the benefit of the doubt (particularly when he would open by announcing himself as a non-native speaker of English and express the sincere hope that he would be understood), or simply write illegibly:

> Jan: You can write so bad some professor can't read your writing, and if
> it's close enough they give you credit for it. It works. It works. (first-
> term junior)

In the second half of his junior year, Jan finally came to multiple-choice questions that required more than memorizing, that asked for sophisticated understanding and reasoning, not just definitions. He had asserted earlier that in his U.S. high school, any answers to multiple-choice questions that couldn't simply be memorized could be reasoned through logically by anyone who wasn't "stupid." It took until his junior year in college to experience a counterexample.[20]

Will the Real Jan ... ?

Rarely was Jan able to see beyond the test. When he did admit to finding material in a geography course useful to him beyond the test, he was flip:

> Interviewer: Is there anything in this class that strikes you as being important for your education?
>
> Jan: Oh yeah! Weather Channel. I understand whatever, everything they say, high fronts, low fronts, why it's cold, and all this stuff. I can understand when I watch the Weather Channel. I see those maps moving, all this stuff; I understand that stuff. When I watch the Weather Channel, I know exactly what's going on. [grinning] (second-term freshman)

This impressive knowledge, however, was not enough to seduce Jan into pursuing any further what seemed to be the only discipline in which he had expressed any intellectual interest. When asked what geographers do, he said:

> Jan: Something to South America, making big holes all around the ground. I mean he [the professor] was showing us picture all the time, you know, of this geographer going to South America, digging holes, and taking samples. I think this is what they do, and yeah, be professor, teaching, you know, students, or just go to South America, digging holes. ... On those slides he's showing us in class. "There's Harry," you know, digging holes, catching snakes, and stuff like that. I was like, "Okay, whatever." (second-term freshman)

Jan went through many courses searching for his place. Desperation to stay in school caused him to fixate on grades during his first years of college, and he consistently highlighted his shrewdness and cleverness over his efforts and academic abilities. An institutional focus on GPA fed into his insecurity. His pragmatism, framed in an interest in making money and wearing a nice suit and tie to work, short-circuited his brief admission that it might be interesting to major in geography.

Turning Points

But forays into a more committed perspective began to increase perceptibly in Jan's junior year. At about that time, a few critical events changed his circumstances:

- He was offered the RA position.
- He was assigned a series of papers in a religions course that he began to take unusually seriously.
- He was admitted to the business curriculum.

Despite Jan's suspicions of prejudice against international students and his dismissal of the RA training course, when he was eventually offered the RA position, he was thrilled to accept it:

Jan: I love it, I love to be around people. (first-term senior)

He quickly became quite popular with the freshman students on his floor:

Jan: There's lots of people coming to my room all the time, wanting something, want to play basketball in my room or watch TV. (first-term senior)

Once he became an RA, with it came the role of wise elder statesman, slightly disdainful of the silly freshmen under his guidance, who, he noted indulgently, were still wild and did not care about studying. Getting the RA position provided Jan with an important step toward social integration. (See section on Socioacademic Relations.)

About the same time, during his junior year, Jan began to occasionally express different ideas about education. He regretted that universities had grades and wished for classes that were all pass/fail:

Jan: It's always about grades. Always. So, it's not for knowledge, just for grades. ... The system is fucked up. ... Would be pass/fail, I probably would do it for the knowledge, because I don't [wouldn't] worry about the grades. (second-term junior)

In commenting on the course on religions that he was taking at the time, he remarked that educated people should know something about religions:

Interviewer: What are you getting from these assignments?
Jan: I understand more religions kind of, getting my own point of view, something to talk about if someone ask me a question.

> I'm not gonna [say], duhh. I'm gonna have my point of
> view. ... like if somebody ask you about Buddhism, you say
> duhh, Buddha, he was a fat guy, or stuff like that. You can
> talk about, making conversation. It's gonna be useful.
> (second-term junior)

Thus Jan's junior year and 2 years as a senior marked the increasing presence of a newfound, or newly emerging, interest in learning. These lapses
into appearing to really care about his academic work found their most
intense expression in the work he did for six short essays assigned in the
religions class, a class he deeply disliked, finding the lectures overly
dense, philosophical, impractical. But he took considerable time to consult about these essays with tutors at the writing center, which he had
developed the habit of visiting to assure himself that he would not lose
points on his writing because of language-related problems. For these
essays, although he as usual downplayed his seriousness of purpose, his
actions and comments went beyond the superficial. Jan related his session
at the writing center for one of the essays:

> Jan: We had like a big conversation, like an hour pretty much. We talk
> about, he's like more getting into content. You gotta make discussion
> ... before he corrects it. He wants to know your point of view, so it's
> kind of interesting. So pretty much, you gotta like, pretty much, like,
> it's like an interview. He's asking like all these questions. You gotta
> like explain. Later, like he corrects the paper. So it's kind of, I mean it
> was good, I mean. ... I mean it was interesting. You had to fight for
> your ideas on the paper. (second-term junior)

He took the paper home, worked on it, and returned the next day to
fight again.

And even Jan's image as stubbornly focused on making money was
morphing. Although he had been extremely successful selling cars during
the summer between his sophomore and junior years and had made
enough money so that for the first time since he came to the United States
he did not have to take yet another 40-hour-a-week job in the fall, he
dreaded going back to the car dealership, finding the other salesmen
"stupid," crude, racist.

When Jan was accepted as a business major in his junior year, the gradual shift toward a more satisfying and successful undergraduate experience
got under way in earnest. The atmosphere of the Business School and its
influence on Jan is discussed in the section on the Business School but two
of its salient features help put Jan's last 2 undergraduate years into perspective. First, almost every business course that Jan took included some
kind of group work. Second, Jan's was an odd major in the small role that

reading appeared to play. Jan studied his lecture notes and the course packets that nearly all the courses provided but either never bought the course books or sold them immediately after the course began, without even removing the shrink wrap. The books were expensive, enormous, and flashy, but also apparently fairly useless. Several faculty members interviewed also downplayed the importance of the course readings, of textbooks in particular. Thus, this major tended to push people together into group work rather than into the kind of isolated individual study that a heavy reading load would require.

Last 2 Years

There was a side of Jan that did not want to seem ignorant of religions or even weather functions, that did not want to be "stupid" like the car salesmen. He was maturing, and Jan's last 2 years in college, his 4th and 5th, showed many signs of a change in the direction of becoming the good student he had tried so hard to appear to be.

His academic life had also become easier because knowledge requirements in upper division courses could be met, if necessary, by supplementation from knowledge acquired in previous courses:

Jan:	It seems the higher class you take, the easier it gets kind of thing.
Interviewer:	Is it the content itself or do you think that you're a better learner than you were when you first got here?
Jan:	I think learner a little bit, but I think all the materials are based on the material learned in the previous classes. (first term, 5th year)

Jan began to express increased interest in and responsibility for his courses. For example, during his 4th year, he took a business law class required for his degree. Despite his usual flip claims of enjoying the course because he was learning how he could sue people, in fact, he took the course very seriously, was proud of the Bs he was getting, and waited after class regularly to ask the instructor further questions. He enjoyed reading and manipulating the rudiments of legal language. The professor in the course had noted his interest and encouraged it, calling him "astute" and speaking admiringly of the work he had been doing; this notice of him was especially notable because, as was the case in so many business courses, this class did in fact enroll some 300 students.

Various factors must have led to Jan's incipient change. Simple maturing must have been a factor. Increased self-confidence replaced the fear of failure that had dogged him. His work as an RA gave him the experience of a social group to support him emotionally and also placed him in a leadership role with responsibilities that, crucially, he *was able to meet*. Having been accepted into a major and taking classes with the same group of students, he was no longer anonymous. The learning curve in his course work had also decreased. The work was no longer overwhelming; perhaps what changed him was being able to succeed, with some effort so that it was not meaningless success, at something that had some value for him, for example, the material in the business law class.

His thinking had also become more realistic as seen in his comments on whether a technical writing course in his last semester might be useful to him one day:

Jan:	I'm sure. I don't think I'll have a secretary.
Interviewer:	You don't think?
Jan:	If I become CEO, probably yeah, but at the first I'm going to have to rely on my skills.
Interviewer:	That's interesting, because before you used to say that you were just skipping over to CEO.
Jan:	Yeah, I was skipping to CEO, but then reality hit me.
Interviewer:	When did reality hit you?
Jan:	I'm just looking for a job right now, and they don't offer any CEO positions, so. (second term, 5th year)[21]

At least some of the contradictions that continued to appear in Jan's interviews, in the same sentence even, began to seem as though they might in fact be superficial. In talking about a film course he took during his 5th year, for example, Jan said:

Jan: I mean, you get a different point of view on the movies right now, you're like analyzing every movie, and it's kind of stupid, kind of weird, you don't enjoy the movie as much, you just analyze how they done and stuff (slight smile), so it's kind of interesting. (first term, 5th year)

Perhaps "stupid" and "weird" meant something like "kind of interesting"? At the beginning of the following semester, I had this e-mail from Jan:

Last semester end up perfectly. I end up with 3.5 GPA and I got some cum……….. something (dean's list thing for GPA) so I am very happy. One more semester like this and I will have a 3.0 on final GPA. (second term, 5th year)

Jan graduated from undergraduate school with an overall GPA of 3.02, successfully meeting his goal of 3.0. Within a month of undergraduate graduation, he started the MBA program in a new city. He was very generous about not only keeping in touch with me during the following year but also sending me his written work. He appeared to be working hard, doing well, and enjoying the friendly and casual, collegial relationship with both faculty and other students; he felt part of a community.

Just before he completed his MBA, he interviewed for a position with a company doing business in Poland. He did not get the job but did get a free trip to Poland and was able to visit there for the first time since he was a teen. When he finally did get a job, he was sent on business to Russia, where he met a woman he brought to the United States and married about a year after getting his MBA.[22]

BUSINESS SCHOOL

The academic and social context in which much of Jan's growth occurred was the Business School. The program occupied two structures: an older campus building where relatively smaller classes were held in rooms accommodating 50 to about 250 students and a modern multistory office building with a windowless auditorium in the basement that could accommodate about 500 and where several of Jan's larger classes were held. There was no real sense of a center of student life or activities associated with the major the way there was with the other three majors in the study. Had there been such an automatic mechanism for getting students together, given Jan's craving for social contact, his story might have been quite different.

Business was a very popular major. During the time of this study, the *New York Times* published a report on serious changes in 1st-year student values in the nation's colleges and universities. They found essentially that materialism was on the rise; social activism was of less and less interest; training for high-paying jobs was desired; education for personal transformation was less valued. These findings seemed to fit Jan and his classmates very well.

In nearly every business class we observed, on the 1st day the professor, and even TAs, established their credibility by introducing themselves in terms of their experience in the business world. References to these classes being focused on "real world" issues abounded both in the field notes and in faculty interviews; it was very important to be perceived as in touch with the "real world," the world of commerce, and to use the "real world," usually the world of advertising, in course examples. In fact, some course lectures sounded like dinner conversation, pointing out what was fascinating about the latest Fritos ad.

Lectures also drew a great deal on student experience, in fact much more so than was typical in Jan's liberal arts general-education classes. Students participated actively in these classes and seemed to have a great deal of confidence in the appropriateness and validity of their opinions on commercials and advertisements, appearing to view themselves as authentic experts, sometimes even more expert than the instructor. This may have come from the students' sense that the "real world" reflected popular culture, with which they felt in tune, and that this real world aimed its products at this affluent middle class of young adults, so that they were positioned to evaluate the success of beer ads better than their instructors were. Students and faculty seemed to operate on an equal footing when the entire business school stopped dead to gaze at and then for the next week to chatter excitedly in class about Super Bowl commercials.

The business school emphasized an odd blend of individualism and at the same time teamwork. On one hand, students were constantly encouraged to stand out in the crowd, to sell themselves, particularly to prospective employers. This was a value Jan readily adopted.

> Jan: [You have to know] how to advertise yourself. How to sell yourself to potential customer. (second-term senior).

> Jan: Smile, make a good impression. (second-term senior).

On the other hand, the individual was also submerged, first, in the strong emphasis on the collective, on working cooperatively in a group, which was considered a business essential:

> Every individual must pull his/her share of the load for the team. As in business, you may find yourself in a group with people you do not know or like. You must learn to work together—like professionals. (syllabus in marketing)

A majority of the courses Jan took as a business major included group work. Unfortunately, the major upshot of offering group-work opportunities in the business school was to make him hate group work, and he was not alone. (See section on Group Work.)

The individual also disappeared behind a variety of manifestations of forms, structures, packaging, and façades. Submitted course work, for example, had to look good and include accepted formulas.

> Jan: ... You can't make mistakes. ... The way you present yourself, ... you make grammar, spelling mistakes on their presentation, I would be fired. ... presentation counts. You make grammar or spelling mistakes in your resume, you're not gonna get the job probably. (second-term senior)

A refrain that arose at every class meeting we attended in one of Jan's marketing courses was "perception is reality." In group presentations, for example, professional behavior meant dress fairly formally and prepare flashy PowerPoint slides. (See Dias, Freedman, Medway, & Pare, 1999, and

Freedman, Adam, & Smart,1994, on the differences between school and real-world business.) This perception-is-reality refrain again fit well with Jan's worldview, speaking to surfaces, masks, and façades.

Jan's assessment of the content of the business courses in general was that it was "common sense":

Jan: … it's common sense kind of thing. … [like] you gotta use bright colors [in ads]. (first-term senior)

It was this kind of material that one of my research assistants observing these classes described as "silly knowledge."

But lack of challenging content was not a problem for Jan, who believed firmly that the purpose of getting a degree in business was to provide baseline quality assurance for employers that the person they hired was not a moron. After that, Jan believed that employers sent employees to training programs to teach them how it would be done in their company. Thus, school and course work were essentially irrelevant:

Interviewer: Your grades and your GPA have been really important to you. You mention that a lot. … Are the grades more important to you than actually learning something?
Jan: Oh yes. … GPA is going to stay with me all my life. The knowledge will be gone anyway after one semester. … Anyway, if you get a job you got to relearn all stuff anyway, pretty much I don't care about knowledge. (second-term senior)

For the most part, Jan fit well into the Business curriculum. Attitudes about grades and exams in the business courses, for example, reflected Jan's fairly closely. Jump through certain hoops, prepare the right smile, manipulate the variables cleverly, and you succeed.

DEVELOPING AS A WRITER

Overview

Jan came to believe that his eventual success and confidence in writing in English developed as a result of a great deal of practice writing. At first glance, this belief seemed odd in that most of his courses either assigned no writing or made writing assignments as a part of group projects, and Jan rarely participated in any actual group-project writing. (See Socioacademic Relationships.) But Jan's trajectory toward the development of writing skills encompassed many drafts of few assignments and was deeply intertwined with visits to the writing center. It was also highly uneven. Initial difficulties were instrumental in pushing him to haunt the writing center, where his writing development was dramatically moved along. The required assignments for the religions course gave him confidence that he could succeed in writing. By his senior year, work on an elaborate marketing project made him think of himself as a successful writer, despite the fact that he did almost no writing on that project. But, needing to complete general-education requirements in his last year brought him back to the kinds of confrontations with writing problems he had experienced in his 1st year and threw him back to reliance on long-abandoned crutches.

Table 4.2 displays Jan's writing assignments over three pages long, plus the pivotal series from his religions class. Counting only final drafts of individually written papers, Jan produced about 60 pages in his 5-year undergraduate career. However, even the shortest assignments typically underwent several drafts.

The Writing Center.   In his sophomore year, still enrolled in English courses, Jan discovered the writing center, a resource he was to use for nearly all the individual writing he faced until he graduated. He came to think of the perceived grammar focus of his first English class as a waste of time because, as he now saw it,

Jan: That's what the writing center's for. Make all the corrections. (second-term junior)

Jan: They check the grammar, they check the content, and what I should change. (second-term sophomore)

But he wasn't merely looking for indications of what to change at the sentence level. He needed both grammar lessons *in context* and attention to content, which not just any tutor could deliver. He attributed his success in learning to write to a "perfect" tutor at the writing center and contrasted this "perfect" one with another tutor, about whom he complained:

Jan: … she doesn't give you any ideas. She doesn't correct anything. Pretty much, she doesn't help you at all. … I can just show my roommate, and my roommate can tell me the same stuff. [The "perfect" tutor] can help you like how to put, where you made mistake, how to change those mistakes to get it corrected. (second-term sophomore)

This particular student at this point in his writing development appreciated and apparently needed the very directive approach of the "perfect" tutor, not the more hands-off help prescribed by some versions of writing center and composition theory.

Jan signed up for hours upon hours of tutoring at the writing center, to the point where writing center supervisors had to restrict his access because other students were being blocked from getting tutoring help. In the first term of his sophomore year, he proclaimed that he had learned to write:

TABLE 4.2
Jan's Sustained Writing Assignments in Courses Other Than English

Term	Course	Type	Prescribed in Actual Length	Weight in Final Grade
fall junior	Accounting	group project[a]	??	??
spring junior	Religions	6 essays	2–3 pages each	sole criteria for final grade but professor refused to specify
	Music	30 journal entries[b]	5 minutes of writing	25% but not evaluated for quality
fall senior	Marketing	group project[a]	12–14 pages	30% including presentation
spring senior	Marketing	group project[a]	??	35% including presentation
	Advertising	group project[a]		15%
fall 5th year	Film	2 papers	about 5 pages each	40%
	Marketing	case analysis	not exceed 10–12 pages	30%
	Marketing	group project[a]	6–12 pages	15%
	Marketing	group project[c]	67 pages maximum text (came to 250 pages with figures, appendixes, etc.)	65%
spring 5th year	Ethics	2 essays	about 9–10 pages each	50%
	Logistics	group report	??	about 30%

[a]On these group projects Jan did none of the writing and usually did not read or even see the paper before it was turned in. [b]I include this course because it was designated a writing-intensive course although the individual assignments do not match my definition here of sustained writing. Jan's entries were generally two or three sentences. [c]Although Jan participated fully in the work on this project, he actually wrote only one page.

Jan: The writing center, every time I write I see effects. I get much better every time I do a paper. (first-term sophomore)

Jan: I don't have any more problems [writing papers]. It's kind of easy for me right now. (first-term sophomore

Jan calculated, like Yang, that each writing center–sponsored revision drove up his score on that particular writing assignment. But he also claimed that the verbal challenges and interactions with tutors allowed him to internalize where he needed to do more to clarify what he had written as he developed a sense of audience.

Interviewer: ... what specifically did they help you with?
Jan: Just look for the stuff like, didn't understand, or tell me where I should talk more, kind of external point of view. ... you walk into the center and they'll [say] you tell me more about this one [thing], so pretty much later on you already know where to look for it. (second term, 5th year).

Furthermore, like Yuko (discussed in the next chapter), Jan knew what he wanted from writing center tutors and rejected feedback that he did not feel helped him. In his senior year, for example, he worked on a paper with one tutor whose advice did not seem useful. Rather than wasting his time working on the revisions she suggested, he waited a few hours until her duties were over at the writing center, and he returned to work on the paper with another tutor.

English/Writing Class.   Unlike the other focal students, who got As and Bs in their ESL classes, Jan failed his first ESL writing class at the university. Like the other students in this study, initial difficulties with English writing revolved around length of time required to produce text and inability to produce the volume of text expected.

Jan: Pretty much when I finish my paper it's pretty much like five lines long. I can't express for longer. You know, like write about blah, blah, blah, blah. I write short. (second-term freshman)

His "perfect" tutor at the writing center had, in fact, been one of his ESL classroom teachers, but it was only in the writing center, with its individualized focus, that she was able to give him the guidance, practice, and confidence he needed.

Yet despite having "learned how to do papers" in the writing center, Jan filled in gaps in this knowledge with his own survival strategies. For the research paper in his last English course in his sophomore year, he proposed to his instructor, and was discouraged from, doing a history of computers. He did it anyway. In discussing this paper, he attributed his failure to heed his instructor's directions to a mistake:

Jan: I screwed up because it's supposed to be research paper and pretty much I did like history. ... so it's quotations, quotations, quotations. So it doesn't work well. I don't think I'm going to get anything good. (second-term sophomore)

But this was no mistake. He had already clearly described the directions to us in interviews; he simply ignored them. Although he knew the difference between a research paper that made an argument and a descriptive history, what Jan could not yet do was to figure out how to go to sources to support a research paper on a topic he wanted to explore, computers. So he did what was within his grasp, spending time and energy revising to avoid the plagiarism he knew he appeared to be engaging in because he had relied heavily on a single source text, *Collier's Encyclopedia.*

Jan:	Oh, resources, minimum three sources, and minimum three quotations. I had like 50 quotations.
Interviewer:	How many sources?
Jan:	Actually, one. I just put a bunch of them in the folder so it looks better, but actually I used just one source. ... Oh, it's good. It's too good. She will figure out it's not my ideas. So I had to avoid plagiarism, put in quotations, you know change a little bit around. ... So I was trying to change, for the past week, I was changing all the time to make not plagiarism. ... I have like seven or eight drafts. Try to change stuff. (second-term sophomore)

Uninterested in the admissible topics and unable to turn a topic of interest into an admissible topic, he created multiple drafts to accomplish something he *could* accomplish, massage the piece until it could not be easily accused of being an example of the plagiarism he felt it would be taken for. The final outcome was a great deal of time spent manipulating a text, arguably leading to greater facility and experience with revising, paraphrasing, and editing—perhaps for a questionable reason but with a useful by-product. The road to the development of writing proficiency for this student was both twisted and highly individual.

Writing in the 3rd and 4th Year

Initially describing English classes as a waste of time, a mere requirement, where he learned nothing, Jan later credited those writing classes with teaching him such elements of essay structure as introduction, thesis statement, body, and conclusion. He attempted with varying success to put this knowledge into practice in humanities courses in his junior year and then again in his final term as an undergraduate.

In between these moments, however, during his 3rd and 4th years, this knowledge of essay structure was of limited use in his major courses for several reasons. First, most of the writing in business courses came as part of group-work assignments and Jan's role in these projects rarely included creating text. Second, the very few individual written assignments were, with one exception, relatively informal, not essays. Finally, the genres used in more careful writing in the business classes were not similar enough to essay genres to allow crossover. (See Carroll, 2002 for similar experiences of domestic students.)

Other major differences for Jan between writing for humanities courses and writing for business courses included:

- Humanities courses tended to push students to write more, setting lower limits for number of pages required, whereas business courses tended to push students to write less, often setting upper limits for number of pages allowed.
- Business courses generally provided more extensive guidelines for writing assignments, both for group work and for the few individual assignments made, whereas writing guidelines in general-education courses were typically far less directive (than Jan needed).
- Jan had more difficulty construing the purpose of writing assignments in the humanities than in business classes.
- Jan's knowledge of marketing issues and formats increased from course to course whereas for the required humanities courses he took, each time he was starting from disciplinary scratch.

In the spring of his junior year, Jan's perceptions of the purpose of writing assignments, and indeed most of the education he was undertaking, were still naive and entirely grounded in the need to fulfill requirements external to his own motivations. But a pivotal moment in his writing development came as he encountered his first occasion to bring to bear on writing assignments both the information from his English courses and the personal writing habits and processes he was developing through the writing center.

Moving Forward: Writing in the Religions Course.   Jan felt that writing assignments in classes like the religions course were made for the same reason they were made in high school, that is, so that the professor could learn what the students thought about the issues discussed in class. In other words, the assignments were made for the benefit of the teacher, not for the benefit of the students.

Jan: He wanna see our point of view. … He just enjoy it, he got probably too much time. (second-term junior)

This was how Jan construed the purpose of all assignments whose practical value he could not fathom.

Nevertheless, in writing the six short papers for this course, Jan appeared to be developing a certain literate perspective that he had not exhibited before, even expressing some enjoyment of the course content:

Jan: Deep thinking. ... Switch my major to English. I kinda like it. You don't have to study much. Just write papers. I kinda like it. (second-term junior)

The first assignment in the religions course seemed fairly straightforward: The students were to describe a time when they learned something. Jan was able to put to work several of his favorite ploys for this assignment and to develop new ones. As with the computer history, Jan adjusted the assigned topic to one that suited him better and responded with his life story and the moral that he had taken from his experiences, that is, to depend on himself. He also engaged the essay-structuring skills he had learned in his English class, made ingratiatingly pious remarks about the plight of poor immigrants such as himself, and employed a new technique he was to use in much of his subsequent writing, which was to begin by personalizing his response to the prompt. The following represents about a third of the first page of the two-page document:

Exercise One

A time I learned something.

I founded the topic "A time I learned something" to be a very hard one. I think that the most important thing I learned in my life is to believe in myself. I will divide the process of learning in three stages of my life. The first stage will be the time I was still in Poland, the second when I came to the United States, and third which is the present time.

Since I remember life in Poland was very hard for my mom. My dad died when I was very young. Since that my mom had always financial problems. Because of the financial problems, we had to move from place to place. We moved so often that I never spent more than two years in the same place or school. During that time I never made any friends, and I was always a below average student. I always though that my life will stay like this, and I accepted. ... I turned eighteen and I moved to a different high school. While doing my senior year, my mom got an opportunity to emigrate to the United States.

The life story goes on, with the topic "A time I learned something" never particularly evident.

In other assignments, Jan's writing was more opaque. The following is the prompt for the third written assignment:

> Question: John Smith suggests that every religion is structured be [*sic*] an Ideal, a Need, a Deliverer or Means of Deliverance. How would Hinduism define the basic need that faces all human beings? Describe three ways in which that Hinduism states human beings can be delivered from this need.

Jan wrote, beginning with his newfound disclaimer technique:

> The above topic I found to be very confusing to me. I will try to interpret it the best way I can. I think that the basic need of all human beings is ultimate being—Atman. The three ways in which Hinduism states human beings can be delivered from this need are: Ideal, Need, and Deliverer.
>
> First we need to find the Ideal—Mythos, to believe. I think the best way to find it is by understanding Hinduism, by understanding the tradition, and by describing it. After we accomplish that, we have to be able to interpret the religion and at the end criticize, to see strengths, contrast strengths and ideas.
>
> After we find the Ideal we need to find the Need within us. I think that we can accomplish this by what the human needs, what we unconsciously want, insight. It can be accomplished by: Being, Knowledge and Joy. Every human being wants to have ultimate life.
>
> "Everyone wants to be rather than not be: normally, no one wants to die." (*The World's Religions,* 20). Second, we want to know, we want to have answers to our questions …
>
> The last thing we need to get to the Ideal is the Deliverer. I think that the best way to experience the Ideal is by meditation, which includes four yogas, four ways, or disciplines to experience the Ideal.
>
> A yoga is a yoga or pate [illegible].

The one teacher comment on this page came at the end of the second paragraph: "Good." (See section on Feedback.) Jan's own typically dismissive comment on this paper was that although he himself did not understand what he had written, the professor had and liked it. Because the course grade was determined solely on the basis of these out-of-class papers, Jan was willing to put in the time required to get the Bs and B+s that the professor admitted in an interview (though not to his students) were in fact the baseline grades for the tasks.

But these writing assignments marked a turning point because, except for the first one, they required the integration of outside reading into the text, there were several of them, they were short, they were prompted by a specific question to answer, and Jan realized from the grades he got that success was possible and under his control.

Developing Authorial Voice.   Jan's discovery of the personalized explanatory, even exculpatory, message-to-the-instructor began in his religions class and remained a feature of his individual written documents. In one of the papers in the religions class, he was careful to suggest that if he had done the assignment incorrectly, the mistake was probably attributable to his "stupid language problem." Similarly, in a marketing paper, he explained,

> "I apologize for any spelling or grammar mistakes. English is not my first language and I didn't have time to go to the writing center."

The personalized commentaries marked the emergence of a very strong authorial presence in Jan's more formal writing and served several purposes. The directions for an assignment in a senior-year marketing class specified three typed pages, using "relevant concepts from each chapter in your discussion to demonstrate knowledge of the material." Jan had four pages answering this question:

> "How do reference groups, family, and social class influence consumer behavior? Discuss implications for marketing strategy with examples."

Jan chose one of his favorite topics, cars, to investigate in answering the question. His answer began:

> From the time I started working on this paper, it took me a really long time to find out what I wanted to write about. After researching on the Internet for over a day I decided to write this essay on one company. I will try to show how Saturn influences consumer behavior using reference groups, family, and social class to sell Saturn cars. Some may ask why Saturn? The reason I found Saturn to be very interesting is that Saturn began in the early nineties and from the beginning caught customers with new marketing strategies which were and are a big success. I started my research by trying to find anything I could find about Saturn on the Internet. The only place I found was the Saturn homepage. Unsatisfied with the information from the Internet I started my research in magazines. What

> surprised me was that I couldn't find very much. The only thing I found was a small ad in one of the car magazines. Still not finding much I decided to go to Saturn of Xtown, to experience the feeling of visiting a Saturn dealership, which is rated number one place in customer satisfaction in the car business, and find some answers I was looking for.

The rest of the paper did in fact answer the question quite directly but this narrative of his efforts that prefaced the paper, in addition to giving Jan a precious extra page of text (always an issue for him), also cast him as a serious, inquiring, almost wide-eyed, persistent seeker of information, sincerely exerting effort to engage and respond to the task.

Clarifying the Role of Writing.   Before his senior year, Jan did very little writing in his major and of the five courses he took in fall of his first senior year, only two had any writing at all: African American studies (with two essay exams) and marketing, which was the first in his major to require individual writing assignments. The weekly short writes (one page, sometimes at the end of class) were intended to get the students involved with the reading by, for example, posing a question on the upcoming reading. These were good for Jan primarily because they caused him to keep up with the reading that term. When asked how the writing contributed to his learning, he noted that this writing helped him understand course material because to do the writing he had to do the reading and doing the reading made him understand the course material. So a major role of writing was as regulator of time spent on work for this class.

But Jan's comments on the importance of writing to him varied. As times he asserted benefits:

Jan: When you are writing … , you're thinking, you memorize more, so it stays in my head pretty much. Long, long, long time. (second-term senior)

At others he denied any benefits:

Interviewer: So all your other classes, those writing assignments didn't really help you learn the material?
Jan: Not at all. (second term, 5th year)

Furthermore, in his Saturn assignment, he claimed that all the information from the Internet and the brochures from the local Saturn dealership amounted to three lines and he had to fill up the rest of the two pages with b.s.:

Jan: Just b.s.ing. ... Big time. I had three lines from the Internet I
         expand to over a page. (second-term senior)

What he was consistently pleased with, however, was his developing
facility and confidence in his writing:

Interviewer: How about writing? Has writing gotten any easier for you?
Jan: Oh yeah. ... I learn how to b.s. I b.s. for pages. ... now I
               can express my ideas, just b.s.b.s.b.s.b.s., like the number
               of pages we need. (second-term senior)

By the end of his 1st senior year, he felt had mastered the skill sufficiently
for his purposes, that is, to meet course demands. But that perception
was challenged in his last year.

The 5th Year

Jan's 5th year as an undergraduate was particularly eventful in terms
of his writing development. The professor in one of his marketing
classes assigned the only piece of sustained individual disciplinary writing of Jan's education and for another marketing class, although this
was a group project, Jan's group produced a 250-page document. But
he was also back in humanities classes (film, ethics, and business writing), amassing general-education credits required for graduation. A C-
on his first paper for his film class made him angry, an emotion he
almost never expressed in relation to course work. But by this time, he
had become used to getting good grades and to seeing himself as a
competent writer.

Fall: Marketing Paper Successes.   The only long individual writing assignment in Jan's business curriculum was a case analysis, which
Jan regarded as requiring the kind of thinking he might want to do
some day in marketing and so he found the work fairly interesting, particularly because he could research a topic he enjoyed, car manufacturing. The course professor made this an individual assignment quite
specifically in order to address the general lack of individual writing
assignments in the business curriculum:

Professor I: Having worked in the business world for a while, there are
               a lot of assignments that are given to you that you have to
               do individually, so you have to do the research, prepare the
               write-up, and so forth. And often what I've seen in team
               activities is people play to their strengths to cover up their

> weaknesses. So ... unfortunately I think their strengths get
> reinforced, but their weaknesses don't get addressed.

The professor's assessment that students used group work to cover up their weaknesses was certainly the way Jan perceived it as well, and used to his advantage.

The professor's preferred writing style matched Jan's preferred style, what Jan had called "to the point" and what was perceived by his liberal arts teachers as lack of development. In the business school, however, his style fit right in:

> Professor N: I think a lot of business communications are quite terse and direct and to the point. ... people are inundated with information, that's one of the problems, you need to cut through all that and make your point.

Jan felt that his writing style did just that. The research methodology that Jan typically employed also fit this professor's idea of how he hoped his students would go about doing this paper:

> Professor I: Well, the first thing I would hope is that they would read the case in its entirety carefully, then probably get on the Internet and look for something about that company.

This practice of Internet researching had been the hallmark of Jan's approach for years. In all, Jan considered working on this case analysis in marketing to be the most positive event in his academic experience that term.[23]

His other marketing class that term called for the lengthy group project (described later). Jan was justifiably impressed with the immense document he and his group produced for that class; none of the interviews included in the document had even been fabricated, he bragged.

Spring: Back to Humanities.   After his two confidence-building successes in business writing, Jan's experiences in liberal arts courses the following spring were an academic and intellectual setback. Once again he talked about these courses in his interviews the way he had during his sophomore year, although with a great deal less panic. He was not doing any of the reading, asserting that the reason his instructors were making assignments at all was to have something to grade the students on and relying on his old survival strategies to get him through material he saw no purpose for.

The ethics class was required for business majors although it did not focus on business ethics. Perhaps for this reason, as the professor noted:

Professor T: [Students] put it off as long as possible because they see absolutely no use in it.

For the writing assignment in the course, Jan was back to struggling to fill up pages in his writing, "playing with fonts" again in order to stretch his 7- or 8-page case analysis on physician-assisted suicide into the required 10 pages, finding himself back in the realm of required minimum numbers of pages after having spent 2 years in courses that set maximum numbers of pages and urged students to be brief and "straight to the point" since

Jan: Nobody wants to read a 10-page memo. (second term, 5th year)

His topic, physician-assisted suicide, was hardly an area that Jan had well-considered ideas about, yet he was being asked to write 10 pages, so he looked for filler:

Jan: There's not much I can say, so pretty much my paper will be just quotes. ... I'd like to finish with two quotes. ... It's an extra page because I was really struggling with pages. ... So it gives me an extra page. ... And I like the words "ad hoc committee" from Harvard Medical School. (second term, 5th year)

Furthermore, as was typical in his liberal arts courses, the paper-writing guidance was somewhat vague and minimalist. (See Guidelines section.)

Jan: ... I can write about anything pretty much. That's the problem. He didn't assign a topic. If I got assigned a topic, pretty much I know what to look for. ... I read an article, and I couldn't find anything else, so I wrote about that. (second term, 5th year)

The guidelines for the essay directed students to include four elements: a description of the case they were examining (not to extend beyond about one page); the ethical questions at issue; an analysis of the ethical issues; and recommendations. Sample papers were also available. Thus, the guidance was not unreasonably sparse; it simply was not enough for a student like Jan.

Jan: ... what forms are expected, he didn't say anything. ... I said, what do I have to do to get the paper done? (second term, 5th year)

Jan also came to realize that "case analyses" were different from one discipline to the next:

Jan: I tried to work on the basic format, I mean, we also did a case analysis in marketing X. That kind of format, but it doesn't work on this one. (second term, 5th year)

The ethics professor himself seemed well aware that the issues plaguing Jan on this paper were the very ones that plagued most of his students:

Interviewer: What kind of difficulties do students have, or do you seem to see that they have?

Professor T: They say, "I can't find anything to write about." I say, "You can pick any topic in the universe, and somehow write an ethics paper on it." And they say 10 pages is too much to write.

But the assignment stood. So Jan was being asked to write on a topic he knew little about, based on a few readings, with little sense of how to select, develop, or arrange the information in a disciplinary area he had no previous experience with. What was the point of this assignment for Jan? Back to sophomore understandings of academic work:

Jan: Maybe he wants to read it. Probably he's interested ... So if he just wants to see our point of view, what we think. (second term, 5th year)

Although Jan expressed interest in the topic of physician-assisted suicide, it was the kind of incidental interest that readers of Sunday magazines might have, and certainly he had no particular insight into or experience with the topic, making him forced to draw on information from outside sources alone. It might be argued that these kinds of assignments set students up to rely too heavily on sources, to plagiarize, particularly in the absence of guidelines. He had an A on this paper, which had the consequence that for the second paper in the course, he felt he did not have to try very hard and ended up writing a rather infantile essay arguing that Slobodan Milosevic was another Adolf Hitler. Still, there was no reason to expect that he could write well on that topic either.

Jan noted that he would have preferred to have a conversation about the topic than to write about it because then he might have been able to learn what someone else thought about his ideas instead of writing them up in isolation.

Jan: Seeing the point of views of someone else and my point of view is just better than writing about your own views. I mean, I know my own views, so why write about it on 10 pages? (second term, 5th year)

In his junior year, Jan had been stimulated by the challenges to his ideas that writing center tutors had put. Dialogue functioned as heuristic and feedback. In the ethics class, he was isolated again and unable to use any of the written feedback on his first paper to help him on his second paper, first, because he mostly ignored it (as was usual when he scored well) but, second, because the only feedback he claimed to remember conflicted with his primary goal in the first paper, to churn out 10 pages:

Interviewer: Did he make any comments on that paper?

Jan: Just that my quotes were supposed to be single-spaced instead of double-spaced, because I tried to make up some pages by having everything double-spaced. … He wrote at the end that I tried to talk about too many things at the same time, I mean, just focus on two things, but I had to make up 10 pages, so I had to talk about everything to make it those 10 pages. (second term, 5th year).

No doubt the freedom to pick any topic and the lack of formats or guidelines that marked these humanities courses, such as the ethics course, were intended to encourage students to explore their points of view. Perhaps, as Russell (2001) notes, all disciplines behave as though their writing forms were universal, but the humanities seem to suffer from this delusion more than other disciplines. Yet being vague about what was expected in an assignment could not guarantee that students would think more deeply about it. In fact, Jan spent most of his time thinking not about the ethics of the topic but about how to stretch 8 pages into 10.

Guidance and Instructions

Despite the relapses of his 5th year, Jan made a great deal of progress during his undergraduate years in his ability to write and his confidence in that ability. The role his course instructors played in his writing development revolved around two main activities, providing instructions for writing assignments and giving feedback. Whereas the writing guidelines for the ethics course provided only a general framework, the guidelines from Jan's marketing courses were far more specific. From one of the marketing courses in his 5th year:

Case Analysis Guidelines

1. Section One:

The first section of the written case analysis should present a statement of the primary problem that is facing the firm. It is crucial to be specific and detailed in this explanation. Discuss any secondary problems that might also currently plague the organization that warrant discussion. Be sure to differentiate between the primary problem and the secondary ones.

Use Phase III questions and information to help you structure this section. [See later in form.]

Allow approximately 5% of your paper to adequately cover the primary/secondary problem issue.

2. Section Two:

The second section of the written case analysis should first present an in-depth investigation of the environment surrounding the firm (industry, competitors and customers). Last, it should present an in-depth examination of the firm itself. ...

Use Phase I and II [questions] to structure this section [See later in form.]

Allow approximately 35% of your paper to adequately cover the environment and the firm, the background to your analysis.

[Guidelines continue in this way through Section Five.]

Phase I Questions

Environment (industry, competitors, customers)

Questions to ask:

What is the general economic climate? Political and legal? Cultural? Social? Technological?

Who are the competitors and what are their strengths and weaknesses?

[Phase questions continue under three additional headings.]

Jan's paper in response to this assignment began:

On January 17, 1934 the new German Reich government received a design proposal for a people's car, a "Volkswagen," from a man called Ferdinand Porsche. Shortly thereafter, the Reichsverband der Automobilindustrie, the German motor industry association, and Porsche signed a contract (VW History). Since then, Volkswagen became one of the world's largest motor vehicle manufactures. Because of Volkswagen's big success in Europe, they decided to explore international market. One of their choices was a place in Asia where no outside car manufacture tried to do business before—China.

China had a very interesting political, cultural, social, and technological climate when Volkswagen AG entered their market. At the time of entrance, China was a communist country with Soviet influence. Also there were no private car owners. All cars were produced for government and state owned businesses, like taxi companies (Jain 164). In 1978 the Chinese government adopted "Deng's open

> and reform policy." Since then, some regions of the country became wealthy, and some people like movie stars and owners of private businesses were able to afford to buy a car (Jain 165). In 1980's a person owning a car meant symbol of privilege and luxury in People's Republic of China. Car prices were still extremely high for most of the Chinese people and auto industry was based on Russian technology from decades ago (Jain 165).
>
> At the time of entrance of Volkswagen AG into Chinese market there was very little competition. According to mechanical engineer, Liu Xianzeng there are "Three Big" and"Little Three" companies. ...

Jan's paper followed fairly closely, but certainly not in lockstep, at least some of the rubrics outlined in the Phase I guide questions: political, cultural, social, and technological climate, customers, competitors. Like all Jan's work, this paper too underwent several visits to the writing center, was of course researched on the Internet alone (with many printed out Internet pages), and was, according to the course professor, one of the best papers in the class. Guidelines for his other marketing courses were similarly detailed.

Arguably Jan's preceding paper for the marketing course was better written than were his papers for his humanities courses. (See the Appendix to this chapter for an example of a paper written for his film course during the same period.) His voice is less personal in the business writing but also more authoritative and less naïve and childish sounding. This difference was no doubt in part the result of Jan's greater familiarity with business school vocabulary and genres, after having spent several semesters in business courses, than with liberal arts or English department–style writing. However, Jan certainly had familiarity with liberal arts style–writing, having been exposed to it in several courses, including four semesters focused specifically on writing. Furthermore, because writing in business courses was typically assigned to groups, Jan had little occasion to practice business genres. Thus, although greater familiarity with the general topic, genre, and discipline contributed to the superior, or at least easier, writing in the business paper, another factor in this improved writing may well have been the more specific and detailed scaffolding provided by business faculty. (See Carroll, 2002, for treatment of the relationship between writing development in the major among English L1 students vs. development of writing skills required for 1st-year writing courses.) It might be argued that teaching writing by scaffolding its processes worked better, at least for a student like Jan, than did the attempt to teach writing through feedback to product or through freeing students to find their own way, as was more common in the humanities.

Feedback

If the oral interaction at the writing center helped Jan both revise his current drafts and, in the process, learn to anticipate how he might approach subsequent papers, written feedback functioned less successfully. Jan claimed the written feedback he received was sparse and generalized, on one hand, and on the other, he ignored it in any case.

Nevertheless, he felt resentful of minimalist feedback when he himself had put time into his paper. For the first essay in his religions course, Jan complained about how long it had taken him to come up with an idea for this essay and to find ways to stretch that idea out to two pages, always the goal in the humanities classes, and remarked:

> Jan: The only comment I got was "Thanks." ... That was big comment. (second-term junior)

In Jan's classes, one reason for the lack of feedback was the high numbers of students enrolled. In his music class, for example, there were more than 400. Yet there were also principled explanations for assigning work and not responding to it; it was hoped this would encourage writers to take ownership of their ideas free from evaluation. As the music instructor noted:

> Professor R: I stress that with them that ... we're not evaluating them ... so it really does become a dialogue with themselves in a way for them to personalize the material that's going on in the class and focus in.

Despite feeling that he had a right to feedback and that he was being cheated when he got little, like many students, Jan also disregarded the written feedback he did get. Perhaps his experiences over the years with minimalist or zero feedback trained his dismissive response to it.

> Interviewer: How carefully did you read them, the comments [on returned papers]?
> Jan: I never did. (second-term senior)

Jan's reason for not bothering with reading the feedback he got on his papers was that if his grade was fine, he would just continue doing what he had been doing. The feedback might have helped him improve, but he felt no internal motivation or need to work beyond a satisfactory grade. But focused feedback played a significant role in the lengthy, multidraft group writing assignment in his senior marketing class (described later), as it did on interim drafts for Yuko (see chap. 5).

Business Faculty on Writing

The business school generally expressed commitment to the idea that its graduates needed to learn to write clearly and concisely. Of the programs examined in this research study, only the business school required a writing course of its graduates beyond 1st-year composition, in part because, with most of the business classes full to capacity and beyond, assigning writing in courses was felt to be unrealistic except in group projects. As one professor urged students on the 1st day of class:

> Professor B: No writing in this class but writing is a skill you should continue to work on.

Business faculty interviewed defined good writing to a large extent as related to superficial features of text, and several asserted that they did not feel it was their job to attend to those superficial issues, like grammar and spelling (see Zhu, 2001), although they urged their students to do so because otherwise the paper might give a bad impression. But teaching writing was not their job.

> Professor C: The main part of that [assignment] is the content of the assignment itself. ... But I'm also interested in them being able to put together a professional report, one that is written well.
> Interviewer: How do they know how to do what they need to do to put together that report?
> Professor C: That's a good question. You guys teach them, right?

Furthermore, most business faculty believed that work groups should divide up their work so that group members could contribute whatever each one had to offer based on their personal, individual strengths. If that meant that one group member was assigned to write up a project alone, that was acceptable because the prime directive was to create a clear, concise, neat written product, no matter how that was accomplished. For the most part, it was taken for granted that not everyone would participate in the writing. Jan recounted the reaction of an accounting instructor to work submitted by his group, which exemplified her acceptance of a division of writing labor.

> Jan: ... in the first two projects we done, she gave us zero like right away. She's like, Grammar sucks ... big time. I said, We're like a group of foreign people. [She said] OK, Who is American in this group? You. You. You. You check the others' work. So it's like those two [American] guys are checking all of it. (first-term sophomore)

The emphasis that the course put on traditional writing skills was stipulated in the guidelines:

> Be sure to use complete sentences with standard English grammar and proper spelling. A portion of the grading of each written assignment is gestalt; that is, the reader's gut response to the appearance of the document. Does the professional appearance of the document instill confidence in the content? Do the misspelled words and poor grammar automatically make the content suspect?

Not only were superficial features of grammar important but the even more superficial physical appearance of the document was taken to directly validate, or not, its content.[24]

Like the writing manual created by the engineering school for its students, a three-page document distributed to students in this accounting class spelled out what good writing meant in a business course, emphasizing six points: coherence, conciseness, clarity, use of standard English, following directions, and audience awareness. The document continued with a list of do's and don't's, blending traditional prescriptive language conventions with a collection of business-genre features:

> 1. Don't use "this" or "it" unless the reference is clear. ...
> 12. Avoid "There are" or "There is" at the beginning of sentences.
> 13. Use "it" not "they" in reference to a company, unless you are referring to actual people, such as managers, stockholders, or employees. ...
> 15. Use ratios, fractions, and percentages correctly: $8/100 = 8\%$ or $\$12,000/\$10,000 = 1.20$ or 120%.

Whether or not students did or knew how to heed such advice, this is what they were meant to absorb.

Purpose of Writing Assignments.   The reasons given by business faculty for assigning writing fell into three categories:

- To verify ability to apply (and sometimes learn) content.
- To verify writing/communication skills.
- To stimulate discussion (in only one course).

In the first two categories, which included the writing assigned in all the courses but one, writing was described essentially as a form of testing. In fact, however, what the faculty seemed most interested in was giving their students practice in communication skills, though not necessarily writing skill.

The longest and most involved writing project Jan experienced took place in his 5th year in a capstone type of course. It was the 250-page opus Jan's group produced following extensive guidelines coming to 10 pages of instructions including outlines of what should appear in each section, almost each paragraph, and how much each was worth.

The project was assigned and submitted in three stages. The work from the first two segments of the project was to be added to the final report; an evaluation sheet with differentially weighted sections accompanied the returned stages of the report and included the professor's extensive summative remarks along with the grade. Feedback appeared on nearly every page of the immense document the students submitted, making recommendations, pointing out missing pieces, correcting information, applauding good work. The first two sections of the report were, then, in effect, drafts to be included in the final segment.

This was a monumental undertaking, both for the students and for this faculty member, and a reminder of how much effort must go into a course with a major writing assignment. Yet, when asked what the students would have missed if they had done all the research required for the project but did not have to produce a written document, the professor 's response seemed astonishing.

> Professor S: I, in fact, wanted ... that they had to get up and do a presentation. Time just hasn't allowed. ... You could do this same thing, you would have to gather the facts and build data tables ... and then stand up and persuade the audience with your presentation and with your facts. And then be able to field questions and answer. I think that is as strong a learning tool as [writing up the] project.

In other words, the main benefit of doing this immense piece of writing, as this professor saw it, could have been achieved through oral presentations had there been enough class time. Although writing had a role to play, its contribution to student development was not viewed as unique. The business school kept the final drafts of these documents but students could make copies of them once the term was over; no one in Jan's eight-member group besides Jan bothered to make a copy.

The Role of Reading

Despite the enormous, and expensive, textbooks required in the business courses, Jan was lucky that they were not considered essential reading because his tendency in response to a work overload was to shut down.

This tendency was clear in his handling of the heavier reading demands in liberal arts classes. His notes in the margins, highlights, or underlines in those texts typically stopped after the first few chapters, the remaining chapters appearing to be left unread, as he explained:

Jan: At the beginning … I read the chapters. But I kind of quit reading … I stopped when the pace [got too much]. … There were some confusing readings in the book.
Interviewer: So what did you do about that?
Jan: Stop reading. … Stop wasting time. (second term, 5th year)

Jan complained of failure to comprehend when the load was too great. On the other hand, he also reported that for readings that he could handle, he still had to read them twice to understand them. As a bilingual student, even an English user as fluent as Jan, he often had the extra burden of having to read even straightforward material twice to understand it.

SOCIOACADEMIC RELATIONS

Relations With Peers

As noted previously, Jan's undergraduate life, including his academic life and his attitude toward it, took a decided turn for the better about the end of his junior year. Aside from his writing practice in the religions course, the two main events that coincided with the improvement were being accepted into the business major and becoming an RA, both resulting in greatly increased positive experiences with domestic students.

Lonely Socializer

Until these alterations in his conditions occurred, Jan's main social contacts were among other international students, though even there, by his own account, the "foreign people" in his classes found him too Americanized, too quick to think of everything as "b.s." He regularly described his social life as being his computer ("I socialize with computer") or his TV, where he watched, as he said, *Baywatch, Heidi,* or *Robocop,* anything that appeared.

Yet he craved social contact, subscribing, for example, to a Polish paper by e-mail, as he said:

Jan: Just to get more e-mail. I was, oh, I got a e-mail. It's nothing impor-
       tant but at least an e-mail. (first-term sophomore)

During this time he worked as the driver of the university escort van, but
he developed no social relations there either:

Interviewer: Do you ever talk to the people [you pick up in the escort van]?
Jan: Yeah, but it's mostly like, I waited for 20 minutes! Where
               you been? (first-term sophomore)

He claimed to be unable to make social contacts even among peers in his
group projects:

Interviewer: Who are the other people in this group? You've never told
               me who they are.
Jan: I have no idea.
Interviewer: Do you talk to them?
Jan: No. I just sit, look around. (second-term junior)

But in fact he continued to try, nearly always striking up conversations
with students sitting around him in classes, working at being friendly,
interesting, and appealing, teasing and chatting animatedly with domestic classmates. The tactic of engaging classmates around him in conversation began to pay off when he was finally admitted to the business
program, started taking courses in his major in classes of 50 to 60 instead
of 300, and began to see the same students across several classes, that is,
when he became less anonymous. When asked about the best experience
he had from his classes in his senior year, it was his social life that Jan (like
Ben) pointed to:

Interviewer: Good things from classes?
Jan: Met some people in classes. That's kind of nice. Suddenly
               you get recognized on the street. (second-term senior)

The RA Job.   But those relationships were primarily on the academic
side of socioacademic. The RA job, which he began in the middle of his
junior year, plunged him into a frenzy of social activities. He prepared social
programs for his dorm floor and had to be available to students even in the
middle of the night when they forgot a room key. This was a whole community, sometimes with real community problems. Jan told of having to handle
drunken residents passed out in the elevator and of another resident being
picked up for drugs. Tragically, one terrible event that Jan had to deal with
was the death of one of his floor residents in an elevator accident at the
dorm. Jan was interviewed by both police and press on this occasion.

Despite the work, it was clear that he enjoyed the social life provided not only by the young students on his floor but also by the other RAs, with whom he could commiserate about work and school and who were thrown together regularly for RA meetings. Ironically, what he had sought with the RA job was a room to himself, further isolation. What he got along with that room to himself, however, was a group of people constantly seeking him out.

In his last semester of college, although by then he claimed to be tired of the RA work and aggravated by the constant commotion of the residents in his charge, Jan talked about the pivotal role becoming an RA had been in the development of a social life for him:

Jan:	I opened up more, because I was closed to myself, not talking to anybody, not having any friends, just sitting in my room, my 10 by 10 room, and just doing my own thing. Right now, I'm talking to people and stuff like that. I'm more open to them.
Interviewer:	You socially exploded.
Jan:	From where it was, yeah. (second term, 5th year)

Group-Work Overview. Part of Jan's social interaction with domestic students was in group projects. In his last 3 undergraduate years, Jan had 12 group-work projects, which seemed quite a heavy burden even considering only the difficult logistics of finding times when the whole group could meet. Jan mentioned several times he might have enjoyed doing some of these projects as individual assignments, but generally he did not enjoy the group work. Out of 12 group projects, only the one resulting in the 250-page paper could probably be called successful. The rest underwent collapse following one of four patterns:

- *Pattern 1—Delay and absence:* In this very typical pattern, the group would delay getting together to begin work and could usually count on one or more of the group members to be absent. This pattern caused Jan great frustration because he always hoped to get course assignments over with as quickly and as early as possible.
- *Pattern 2—Give it to the A student:* Jan often claimed that one member of the group was an A student and would do anything to secure an A on the project. As a result, sometimes after an initial delay getting started, the group simply assumed the A student would take over and get the work done.
- *Pattern 3—Pulling whose weight?* In some projects, the efforts of the group members varied widely. In one marketing group, Jan as usual did the legwork and one of the women in the group did the write-up. The other two members did little or nothing. But the two workers did not exercise their right to complain about other two

slackers because they knew they would all be in classes together again next term. Because getting the grades lowered for the other two would not raise their own grades, there was no benefit to the two workers to complain about the two slackers.

- *Pattern 4—How to rise to the challenge, or successfully avoid it:*   In an example of the fourth type of team experience Jan had, the group was required to create a questionnaire, do telephone surveys on the issue they were researching, and organize a focus-group discussion of the topic. The report Jan's group wrote up and presented in class was entirely fabricated. Instead of doing the research, the group simply polled themselves and extrapolated their own responses to a larger population.[25] For Jan, and apparently his group mates, this course requirement was perceived as perhaps many entire courses themselves are, at least to some students:

Jan: Just another class without reason (second-term senior)

The Look of Success in Group Work.   What seemed the single successful group-work project of Jan's undergraduate years, the 250-page marketing project, was carefully overseen by the professor (recalling in this Ben's successful history class group work). For the first time in Jan's experience in 5 years of school and many group projects, this group actually did the work together.

As mentioned earlier, the professor in this course provided elaborate guidelines for the write-up of the project. When the students got together, they worked at three or four computers, combining their gathered information and, a first in Jan's group-work experience, each reading everyone's contribution, making suggestions for changes and corrections. These efforts may well have been due to the unusual oversight mechanism the professor built into the project. Other business faculty regularly asked for peer evaluations of group member contributions but, as noted, for their own reasons, the students Jan worked with sometimes did not criticize another student's failure to contribute. This marketing professor, however, had the groups keep a log of all the group meetings, and each group member was required to sign the log verifying its accuracy. The following is an excerpt:

Friday, Nov X
Carrie and Jan present
12:05–4:05 pm (Alice and Mickey arrived at 12:30 pm)
Pam and Sandra arrived at 1:20 pm
Alice left at 1:45 pm
Mickey left at 2:45 pm

Sandra left at 3:30 pm

Agenda: Worked on paper

Sunday, Nov X

Pam, Alice, Jan, Sara, and Mickey present

9:30 am–12:00 pm

Agenda: Marketing Mix Objectives

This summary of the work went on for three pages. Certainly the students could have fabricated the information, and Jan would most certainly have reported that in the interviews, but they did not. Rather, the group functioned as a group, all the members contributing and feeling responsibility for the project.

Although even for this project Jan disliked not being in control of the rate at which the work would take place and the enormous commitment of time it required, he was generally pleased with the teamwork aspect of the project. However, he also mentioned that if he had been able to work alone, he would have learned more because when groups did these projects, he himself usually became fairly knowledgeable about his own small segment but could not know what the others had done with the same depth or intensity as if he had done the work himself. Jan also asserted that he was unaware of having learned anything in particular from interactions with his classmates. In this way, Jan's experience with group work differed considerably from both Ben's and Yang's. On the other hand, he had been specifically asked to join this group by its members, who he considered particularly good students. All this greatly pleased him.

Faculty Views on Group Work. The faculty ascribed the emphasis on group work in the business courses to the purported demand in the business world for graduates who could work in teams. Though all the faculty I interviewed believed that learning to function in a group on a joint project was very important, only a few recognized the problem created by the business school's insistence on so many group projects. If nothing else, students were tired of them, as one professor commented:

> Professor G: ... feedback from students is almost universal, in that almost all students would rather do more individual work and less group work.

It would seem counterproductive after a certain point to attempt to build teamwork skills when the students had come universally to dislike group projects. Further group work could only make them dislike it more.

Finally, two faculty members articulated what I had been discovering about students' preparation for the amount of group work they were sent out to do. There was none:

Interviewer: How did they, I'm curious about how they learn interpersonal skills that they need in order to learn in a group?

Professor B: Unfortunately, we're not doing much of that at the undergraduate level ... we just kind of put them in teams and tell them they need to work together.

In fact, the whole enterprise of simulating business world group work in undergraduate classes seemed increasingly unrealistic because of the dramatic difference between school and job even in simple physical circumstances. (See Freedman, Adam, & Smart, 1994, for further examples of these differences.) For students, the assignment of a group project immediately presented them with the very difficult task of first negotiating the logistics of finding a time and place to work on the project. Everyone knew this, students, instructors. Yet instructors persisted in demanding that students work out these problems because this was what had to be done in the "real world." But in fact, these initial, foundational logistics precisely do not have to be addressed by employees who simply see each other every day at work.

Furthermore, evaluations of the students' work in the group projects were, in effect, criterion referenced and as such quite unlike those in the business world. The whole class might well get As on their group-work projects. But in business, evaluations are made of individuals essentially at the expense of other individuals; not everyone can be promoted.

Finally, as one faculty member pointed out in explaining the importance of group work:

Professor G: Companies pay big money to go through these team exercises. They go out and go through exercise courses, climbing over ladders and things like that.

If the professionals in real life "pay big money" to do this, how could undergraduates without any training at all figure out by themselves how to become and work as a team? These basic contradictions, though present in the group work assigned in the other majors represented in this study, were less obvious there perhaps in part because the other majors did not make such strong claims about preparing their students for this "real world."

In fact, many if not most of the projects assigned did not actually require a group to complete them, except when the project was large. But when the only factor in a project that encouraged group work was its size, the students divided the project up and each took a portion of it to do separately, a logical strategy but not one particularly conducive to building teamwork skills. Thus, despite the emphasis on group work, the group projects in the business classes never seemed as successful as those in engineering. Perhaps the relative lack of success primarily reflected the different attitudes of Ben and Jan reporting on them. Or perhaps the reason lay in the fact that group work in engineering took place under the supervision of faculty because it involved expensive engineering equipment. Or perhaps the main difference was in the different nature of the group tasks in the two fields, with less testable and more nebulous results in business. In other words, the engineering groups had more closed-ended problems to deal with that had solutions that worked or did not whereas the business projects were ill-defined problems with open-ended solutions or series of possible solutions. In any case, nothing was done to train the business students to work together, and although faculty were aware of the contradictions, they felt that their courses had other important matters to cover that precluded instruction in group dynamics.

Relations With Faculty

If you're funny, you're magic. (Marketing professor)

Perhaps because Jan felt courses were little more than hoops and often discounted course material, the course professors became all important, and Jan's responses to them were visceral and relatively independent of how well he actually did in the course.

Jan: All depends on the teacher. ... Professor change everything.
(first-term junior)

He always sought out courses taught by professors who had received high ratings in a university publication compiling student course evaluations. He adored professors who were funny and who learned their students' names. But his biting sarcasm was merciless in his comments on teachers he disliked or disapproved of. One was "mentally screwed up," another a psychopath. He fantasized a grim future for another:

Jan: Maybe she should get a job where she's making macros for some kind of corporation, closed in a small room 6 × 6 and let her sit over there all day long. (first-term junior)

Other professors used their power to prevent students from succeeding through deception and withholding vital information:

Interviewer: What do you think you had to do well, or what do you think you had to show your teacher to do well on this?

Jan: I don't know. Maybe call psychic hotline, you know, before exam. (first-term junior)

Although Yang had specific problems with specific instructors over the very substantive issue of her ability to communicate in the nursing clinicals, her problems were quite limited in scope compared to Jan's repeated run-ins with some of his instructors. The number of times he came to the negative attention of his teachers is astonishing for a college student who generally sat quietly in the front row, looking like the model student. In the fall of his sophomore year, he was called into his world business professor's office and lectured on proper classroom behavior:

Jan: I got in a bunch of trouble; she called me in the office. ... she was, There's no excuse, blah, blah, blah, blah, blah, blah. And I was like, Yeah, yeah, yeah, you're right, yeah, yeah, yeah.

Interviewer: Sounds like a real meeting of the minds.

Jan: Yeah, I was just sitting there saying "yes" for 30 minutes, Yes, ma'am, you're right, yeah, yeah. (first-term sophomore)

In the spring of that year, he was accused (falsely) of cheating on the final exam in economics. In the fall of his junior year, he found two mistakes on the management exam; his confrontation with the course instructor led, he said, to her never speaking to or looking at him again during the term.[26] He was once evicted from the computer lab for breaking the rule not to bring computer games and play them on these computers.

His visceral responses and tumultuous run-ins with his teachers were a measure of Jan's intense desire for a relationship with faculty. He lamented, for example, auditorium courses with large numbers of students.

Jan: I hate these big classes. We got 600 people in these classes. It's ridiculous. ... No connection with the professor. ... Seated like in a movie theater pretty much. (first-term junior)

He found the anonymity of these courses intolerable and felt that he learned best when his teachers knew him. He appeared to want and need personal attention from his teachers, and got it often even if it was at times negative. He wanted to be seen by faculty as intelligent and hard working, even when he was not, but mostly, he wanted to be *seen* by faculty.

Jan: Just be in class, be nice and act smart. (first-term junior)

Jan: I sit like in the first row next to her. ... You got to pay attention, you know. Look smart, you know. (first-term junior)

Whenever possible Jan worked to establish easy, friendly relationships with his professors. In one of his marketing classes, on the page following the take-home final exam's cover sheet, Jan included a computer picture of himself in line for football tickets; this appeared to follow up on some kind of inside joke between himself and the course instructor. He frequently made a point of interacting with his professors through comments and notations on his papers like joking requests for extra-credit points, smiley faces, or other friendly nonverbal reaching out. These notes had the rhetorical effect of personalizing the writer and establishing a direct human contact with the reader. He counted on establishing these more personal, social relationships with his professors, figuring that going to the professor with questions, for example, made him stand out. He reported that when some professors heard his accent (and saw his name), they realized he was a "foreigner" and made a point of engaging him in friendly conversation. For a slightly outcast student like Jan, establishing a personal connection made an important difference.[27]

SPECIAL CIRCUMSTANCES FOR INTERNATIONAL/IMMIGRANT STUDENTS

Language and Identity

Being an international student and/or an English learner had an impact on the lives of the focal students in various ways. For Ben, problems with immigration were distracting. Language difficulties caused a cascade of other problems for Yang. For Jan, the impact of being a permanent-resident immigrant seemed more subtle, initially making itself felt primarily in his struggles to build all-important social relationships. His status as a bilingual had both positive and negative sides.

The Language Card—Two Sides.   Social relations aside, Jan freely made use of the language card to his advantage. As noted earlier, at a certain point he began to preface his essays with statements like: "I think that I had a problem to understand the exercise. ... Probably it was just my stupid language problem" (second-term junior). In planning to request permission to drop a course after the drop deadline, he remarked:

> Jan: I got to find a good reason for withdrawing. ... [I'll tell them] I don't speak any English. (second-term junior)

If Jan gained certain advantages by playing the language card, the advantages were offset by other disadvantages, forcing students like Jan into struggles domestic students were less likely to face. Jan felt, for example, that, particularly in groups with students who did not know him well, he would initially have to fight for positions he took or points he wanted to make because the points tended to be dismissed:

> Jan: They always tell the foreigners to sit on the side, but sometimes you have to scream out and prove that they are incorrect. ... They didn't always listen to you, like if you were saying something, they said "Yeah, Yeah, Yeah, whatever." (second term, 5th year)

As J. Miller (1999) notes, "Part of the struggle for linguistic minorities entails the move towards being heard as an 'insider' in a particular context" (p. 152), a struggle Jan faced repeatedly.

Speaking in Class.   Jan described his discomfort in speaking in class, feeling that as soon as his accent was heard, heads raised and eyes stared at him:

> Jan: People really pay attention when I speak up, raise heads and like what's going on? ... Maybe because I'm different.
> Interviewer: Because of your accent?
> Jan: Yeah. Kinda. I get really nervous sometimes. I don't mind asking questions from a sitting position. ... Especially in the front row they can't see my face. When I'm standing, I see all their eyes staring at me and I'm like oh shit, I'm scared.
> Interviewer: You feel like when you talk you're noticed more because of ...
> Jan: My language change. My voice change.
> Interviewer: Do you think your accent ... ?
> Jan: Gets worse. It's bad. ... It's pure Polish accent. It really change. My voice change. I have a crying voice, my hand shakes. (second-term senior)

Thus he rarely spoke up in class, and then only when he sat in the front so that his comments could be directed at the instructor and not necessarily heard by the other students. Nevertheless, in most of his classes participation was required and evaluated as part of the final grade. This kind of requirement, of course, puts burdens on bilingual English speakers that domestic students usually do not face in the same way.

Who Is an International Student?   Jan felt himself to be living between the two worlds of domestic and international/immigrant student. In his effort to position himself in relation to his adopted cultural and linguistic surroundings, he seemed to hover between integration (i.e., valuing both his home culture and the new culture he was experiencing) and assimilation (i.e., rejecting his home culture in favor of the new, target culture) (Berry, 1997).

In one course, for example, the professor asked on the 1st day of class whether there were any international students in the class; Jan did not raise his hand. On the other hand, in another business class, the professor had learned that Jan was from Poland and persisted in positioning him as such:

> Jan: I'm the expert of the East Europe, the way he calls me.
> Interviewer: Are you able to answer his questions [in class]?
> Jan: I'm guessing, I don't have no idea. ... He always look at me, and you know it's like, yeah, yeah, yeah, just wave my head [hand?] like I know something. (first term, 5th year)

But he hoped that this ambiguous status might work to his advantage in his applications to graduate school. He reckoned that because all his undergraduate and some of his high school education had been in the United States, he would not be regarded by any of the dozens of schools he applied to as an international student, thereby circumventing the kind of language scrutiny international students undergo. But he planned to have this information come out in the application essay, which he described as:

> Jan: ... talking how ... mother had to stand in line for toilet paper. [The readers] probably said, oh, this poor guy from the third world, let him in. (first term, 5th year)

In a similar, if not ruse, then use of resources to his best advantage, Jan made a point of obtaining a copy of the final 250-page report from his huge group marketing project. Jan called it his senior thesis (even though virtually none of the writing was his) and wanted a copy with the professor's corrections and notations so that he could show it if necessary to potential graduate schools or employers; they would be able to see, he said, that he was not perfect, but trying.

Subtractive Bilingualism.   Jan had arrived in the United States with no English background whatsoever, having studied Russian and German in high school, not English. As the years progressed and as his use of English increased, Jan noted the rusting of his heritage language, finding it increasingly difficult to retrieve words in Polish. By his last year in undergraduate school, his use of Polish had decreased to little more than weekly phone conversations with his mother.

> Jan: I don't read in Polish. ... my vocabulary is gone, so my mom is like, "What are you trying to say about this word, it doesn't exist." (second term, 5th year)

Much more disturbing, however, and unlike all the other focal students, Jan was clearly undergoing some kind of emotional shift in relation to Polish as a result of his interactions with English speakers in the United States:

> Jan: ... when I listen to Polish people I think, "You've got a weird accent." I just can't stand Polish accent anymore. ... It sounds so fake and, I don't know, it's just like, we've got a really different accent, the Polish accent we've got over here, like, everybody says "Oh, you've got a weird accent." (second term, 5th year)

Apparently enough repetitions of "you've got a weird accent" was making that accent seem weird, and obviously embarrassing, to Jan as well. Pavlenko and Blackledge (2004) cite work by Clement that concludes that "members of linguistic minority communities identify either with the first or the second language community but rarely with both" (p. 5). Jan seemed to conform to this pattern by appearing to invest primarily in this second community at the expense of the first.

Faculty on International/Bilingual Students

Like the other focal students in this study, Jan generally found that his instructors were sympathetic to English learners in their classes and sensitive to the extra difficulties involved in studying in an L2. In some cases Jan found instructors more willing to make excuses for him than he was himself. About one of his geography classes, for example:

> Jan: He thinks I screwed up because I didn't have enough time, because I'm foreign. I know I just didn't study enough ... I think he wants to help the foreign people. (first-term sophomore)

As for the business faculty, although some made a distinction between students coming from Europe and those coming from Asia, in general their remarks about international students and other English learners in their classes revealed perceptions of both disadvantages and advantages.

Disadvantages:

- Cannot/do not participate as much in class (but no accommodation was made in any of the classes for them to participate more; they were left to sink or swim).
- May have a hard time following lecture because of language/speed of delivery (but no one mentioned making any accommodation).

- May have a hard time understanding U.S. cultural assumptions and references to U.S. life.
- May have a hard time with everyday vocabulary in lectures.

Advantages:

- Have a strong work ethic.
- Come from a different perspective and so can escape local prejudices or can see other options (but often cannot or will not share that perspective because of problems participating).

Two of Jan's professors exemplified different responses to the realization that some of the students were being left behind in their classes. Both of these instructors delivered fast-paced, energetic lectures infused with a great deal of off-the-cuff humor, and they were among Jan's favorites. In both cases, they expressed awareness of the difficulty some students had with culture-bound references or vocabulary and noted that they were not able to anticipate what those references or vocabulary items might be beforehand. One of them, however, concluded that:

> Professor L: It hurts their grades and ... maybe they should be more comfortable with Bs instead of As simply because they have a real problem there. Things that I say and go right on by, other people understand and non-native speakers do not. (second-term junior)

The other one was the only faculty member I spoke to in the business school who made any systematic accommodation to these students in the all-important area of exams, shortening them by five questions, apparently solving a problem for the bilingual students and, as she noted, also helping domestic students who were slow readers. Though very few faculty went out of their way to accommodate the students much, still the faculty that Jan encountered in his undergraduate years were at least in principle welcoming and sympathetic to students like him.

IDEOLOGICAL EDUCATION

Particular to the business classes was the (for me) alien culture of business and the way that culture was transmitted and played out in the classroom. Given that the business school almost by definition would be filled with people who took a fairly uncritical view of capitalism, it was not surprising to hear course instructors reinforcing capitalist tenets and values to their students. Nevertheless, comments of indoctrination into the culture of capitalist business were painful to hear:

Professor S: An accountant's job is to fire people.

Professor S: If we make [the accounting] complicated, they'll pay us more.

> From a textbook:
> Soft-drink companies would prefer that consumers received their morning "jolt" of caffeine from one of their products, rather than from coffee. Because most Americans do not consider soda a suitable breakfast beverage, the real challenge for soft-drink companies is to overcome culture, not competition. ... (from Jan's textbook in marketing fall senior year, sections highlighted by Jan)

> On a transparency in a marketing course:
> Right thinking about the Consumer
> The consumer is sovereign
> The consumer can be understood through research
> Consumer behavior can be influenced

The business students, including Jan, appeared to share many of the values of the business/consumer culture. In a marketing class, for example, the professor asked the students how many felt that companies and marketers knew too much about them. Only 3 people of about 40 in class raised their hands. In fact, in all the interviews, field notes, and printed course materials from all the classes in the business school that came to my attention, in all the interviews with business faculty—and there are more of them than of any other faculty because Jan was in school 5 years—the word *critical* as in "critical thinking" appeared once.

Perhaps some of the most upsetting unquestioned assumptions in these classes were that U.S. advertisers were faced with a "dumb" public in other countries that had to be educated to understand the advertising appropriately. The students learned, for example, that the famous Chevy Nova blunder of trying to sell a car called "no va" (that is, "it doesn't go") in Spanish-speaking countries was an urban legend. In fact, it was indicated in these classes that problems in communication across cultures and languages were usually created not by blunders on the part of the advertisers but by the ignorance of the foreign public. Emblematic of the need to educate the public abroad were images and stories of some of these consumers. In a marketing class, students saw a picture of Uncle Sam trying to communicate with a perplexed-looking Asian man in a business suit, with buck teeth and thick eyeglasses covering slanty slit eyes, like the image popular during World War II. In another class, students were told that Gerber food did not sell well in Africa because the picture of the baby on the label made the "Africans" assume there was ground-up baby inside. This information prompted head shaking and amazed chuckles. Stories circulated in classes about other misunderstandings: the Chinese man who came home with a can of what he thought was potted chicken because of the chicken depicted on the label only to find Crisco inside the can; how Proctor and Gamble made sure, in developing countries, to package its clothes-washing detergent with extra lathering agents so that people would see the suds and believe they were really getting their clothes clean.

The most ludicrous moments for me came when the entire business school appeared to go into mental paroxysms around the time of the Super Bowl football games, when advertisers paid fortunes to trot out their new ads for Coke, Crest, Budweiser, Chryslers. Perhaps I have an insufficiently embodied understanding of the Bakhtinian carnavalesque. In an interesting juxtaposition, in one marketing class, the professor spent one whole class period on the Super Bowl ads, and shortly after that, one whole class period with a guest speaker, the head of the business library, who presented a video on how it could assist them. The professor asked the students whether the time spent with the business librarian had been worth it; he never asked whether the time spent talking about the television commercials had been worth it.

In class after class, the professors reiterated that in this class they would be dealing with "real world problems," like financing a car, inheriting money, getting a raise. Perhaps we do not all agree on what "real world problems" might be, but Jan and his classmates were certainly seeing what the business school of a university considered "real world problems."

CONCLUSION

As I have said elsewhere (Leki, 1999), Jan's was a complex and confusing story. It was not always easy to admire or approve of him, as it was with the other participants in this study. Unlike the others, instead of working harder to meet difficult challenges, he tended to shut down his own efforts and to blame others for his problems, especially in his early undergraduate years. On the other hand, he was very young and he had been hurt and perhaps pushed beyond what he could handle by the move to the United States, without any English whatsoever, directly into the "social and academic minefield" (Lee, 2001, p. 516) of a U.S. high school. The role models he had among the domestic students in high school and college but also in the business major he pursued were not always admirable either, and institutional barriers were often incomprehensible and illogical and may have seemed surmountable only by subterfuge.

How did Jan manage to have his less-than-admirable behaviors and attitudes pass unnoticed by his teachers (although, admittedly, some teachers did notice)? In a study of teacher attitude toward "atypical" ESL immigrant students (Vollmer, 2000), the high school teachers interviewed described certain immigrant students like Russians (Russian in this study included other Eastern Europeans) as standing out as individuals, as active, feisty, academically well prepared, eager to assimilate into U.S. culture, and successful at doing so. Vollmer suggests, as have many educational researchers, that certain immigrant groups who are expected to succeed are then seen as succeeding even when they do not. Perhaps Jan too benefited from this unspoken expectation of success and as a result was easily able to dissimulate his less than admirable activities and attitudes.

The contradictions in Jan's story point to the hazards in presuming to prescribe, perhaps even to determine, global solutions to the difficulties faced by immigrant students. These are not always the dramatic and very apparent difficulties of poverty or ethnic and racial prejudice (Valdes, 2000, 2001) but sometimes the more subtle and unpredictable difficulties created by basing courses of action on misperceptions and misreadings of alien circumstances. Decisions are made that cannot be adequately guided by the grounded experience of life in a familiar culture but rather depend on apprehensions of life circumstances filtered through an imperfectly mastered language, little familiarity with the new culture, and none with the new educational system.

Jan's frustratingly isolated and too easily successful start in his U.S. high school helped set the stage for a very shaky, and also isolated, beginning in college. It took about 3 years for Jan to begin to get his bearings and establish an identity he could be comfortable with. Before he could proceed to stop being so worried about surviving and to succeed academically, it appeared that he had to be grounded in positive socioacademic networks where he could construct himself not as someone on the outside looking in, but as a legitimate player with a degree of power and influence, and with comfortable relationships with peers (and faculty). In Bourdieu's (1977) terms, Jan began to be able to "impose reception." Although he worked at his socioacademic relationships very hard, establishing relationships proved more difficult for Jan than for any of the other focal students, who had the structural advantage of entering their majors with a cohort of students.

It would be difficult to argue, based on the documents in Jan's case, that writing played a particularly significant role in creating an advantageous subject position for him, but his changed attitude about getting help in the writing center for his work did exhibit initial signs of the identity shift he was brokering. Rather than investing (Norton, 1995, 2000) in an identity that scrambled against incomprehensible and unreasonable power structures, he could invest in his work—once he had the support of a social network in which he could find respect and admiration. As

Norton and Toohey (2001) note, success in an L2 (and perhaps in anything) is in part the result of individual agency but only in a dialectical relationship with social and institutional structures that make available to the learner advantageous subject positions to occupy.

In his last years, Jan began fronting an image of competence and contentment with himself and his accomplishments that included self-confidence and seriousness of purpose in his business education. For the most part, Jan fit well into the business curriculum.[28] Although he had often been hypercritical of his classes, his teachers, his bosses, his educational experiences generally, his sense of how the world should operate seemed to coincide with the values of the business world he was being prepared for—no room here for criticism or sarcasm about the tactics of Bill Gates or General Motors or RJ Reynolds. Jan initially presented us as educators with the dilemma of how to interpret, if not accept, his sometimes apparently unethical behaviors and unsavory attitudes; a later question becomes how to respond to the questionable values inherent in the business education within a capitalist system that Jan absorbed.

APPENDIX

Following is an excerpt from a sample of 5th-year writing in Jan's film class:

> Growing up in Poland, the only American movies I watched were the black and white American classics. ... That is why I chose *Modern Times* directed and played in by Charlie Chaplin. *Modern Times* evokes two emotional effects on me; it makes me laugh and makes me feel an emotion of sympathetic pity toward the main character at the same time. Because of the focus only on primary emotional effect, I will talk only about the comedy aspect of the movie. First, I will talk a little about the movie, and after that, I will discuss a few parts of the movie that made me laugh the most and how two elements of *mise-en-scene* contributed to evoke this emotion in me. The two elements of *mise-en-scene* I will use are: Sets and Props, and Figure Expression and Movement. ...

> [paragraph 3] The first time *Modern Times* made me laugh is at the beginning of the movie. In this scene, Charlie is working on the production line holding two wrenches in both hands tightening nuts to steel plates carried on the conveyor belt moving faster and faster. ...

> [last paragraph] *Modern Times* is a very different type of comedy. It makes me laugh and feel sorry for Charlie Chaplin at the same time. Sets and props play an extremely important role in every part of the funny scenes. Without props (like two wrenches ...) ... the movie would not have an effect like it did.

5

"Yuko Can Handle Intimidation": Becoming a Social Worker

BACKGROUND

Yuko was the type of student who almost seemed an idealization. Intelligent, extraordinarily focused, motivated, determined, sensitive to her own needs and those of others, Yuko was on the dean's list all eight semesters of her undergraduate career. My own last vision of her was as she climbed the stage of the Social Work graduation ceremony, where she ended her undergraduate career receiving the Social Work School's award for top graduate in her class. During the 4 years of interviews with her, my research assistants and I were repeatedly surprised to learn that she had taken on yet another extracurricular activity, taking flute lessons or becoming treasurer of the student social work organization. She mentioned these events off-handedly, as though nothing could disturb the orderliness and smooth regularity of her life. She was also always very modest, dismissing her successes with comments like:

Yuko: I was lucky enough to get A on [an exam]. (first-term sophomore)

Yuko: Somehow I got the highest grade. (second-term junior)

She was also bold. A faculty member in social work commented about her placement in a particularly challenging field assignment:

Professor F: Yuko can handle intimidation.

Even at a young age, Yuko was a very determined, directed person who weighed her options carefully. Yuko and her younger brother had been raised by their single-parent mother, who supported the family by working as a nurse's aide during Yuko's childhood and beyond. Yuko's father had abandoned the family when she was quite young and she never saw him again. Throughout most of her childhood, her little family lived in a kind of assisted-living complex in Japan with other single-parent families, a situation that prompted her to develop a high degree of independence. Yuko felt that from junior high school on, she was the one who made the decisions about her life and found the means to act on them.

Yuko's eventual interest in social work stemmed at least in part from her experiences as a recipient of social welfare and from a desire to contribute to society as a way of repaying a social debt for the help her mother had received but also to act as an advocate for people like her mother. Yuko's mother, at 24, with two children, little education, and no support, financial or otherwise, from Yuko's father or her own family, had had to struggle on her own to find out how to get government aid. As a young witness to those struggles, Yuko learned not only to be grateful for the help but also to take a critical perspective on Japan's public welfare system.

Yuko: ... she had a conflict with like city hall personnel because they check. It's amazing. They check if we have color TV or not. They check. If we have, they not gonna give us the money. So I pretty much learn from those things. (second-term senior)

After her graduation from high school in a science track, she completed an associate's degree in English at a Christian junior college in Japan (though she was not Christian) and went to work first in a financial investment firm selling stocks and mutual funds and then with home health care equipment.[29] Surprised at finding herself doing those "small things" rather than the more professionally oriented work she had imagined for herself, Yuko decided to take advantage of the presence of relatives in the United States and lived with her uncle for 8 months in a small, somewhat isolated town in the U.S. upper South until he moved away, leaving Yuko to live alone in the house, knowing essentially no one and very little about how things functioned in the United States, including how to withdraw money from the bank. But she got herself enrolled in an English-language institute, then a junior college, and eventually as a freshman social work major at the university, some 3 years after her junior college graduation in Japan. She agreed to participate in this research study out of a general willingness to be helpful and ended up staying with the project because she found the interview conversations a good opportunity for reflecting on her experiences.

Yuko exhibited a clear sense of direction and a strong will to succeed. Yet she nearly always gave the appearance of being relaxed, organized, and on top of things. She laughed easily and in her social work classes she very quickly developed a group of friends that would constitute a crucial social support system for the rest of her university career. She usually sat near the front of her classrooms, often casually cross-legged on her chair, and although she did not typically volunteer contributions in her classes, she clearly was highly attentive and engaged readily in casual exchanges with classmates with ease and familiarity. Although she was not shy, she described herself as "easy to be hidden by someone's shade," and so, with her usual self-confidence and purposeful determination, consciously worked at being outgoing even in more threatening, more formal contexts like during classes or social work field practice experiences. As she explained it:

> Yuko: Maybe ... if I don't talk, I don't get anything from society. (first-term freshman)

Language and Literacy Background

Yuko described herself as an avid reader throughout her youth, always getting books as gifts for birthdays and holidays and reading as many as two books a day as a teen, "fluff" for young girls, as she said. She very much enjoyed writing the journals, book reports, and poetry assigned and encouraged in primary school, describing the writing instruction there as focused on stylistic issues, on achieving elegance and beauty ("the most beautiful part of Japanese sentences"). But she quickly lost interest in the drudgery of high school writing, which tended to focus mainly on preparing students for exams and so emphasized formal features of written structure and the use of Chinese characters.

Her literacy experiences studying English at the 2-year college in Japan reflected the disappointing approach taken in high school. Although students read a fair amount in English (books about baptism and "what the monks' life is"), class treatment of the readings was limited to reading a paragraph at a time and translating. The relative ineffectiveness for her of such an approach perhaps helps to account for her 493 TOEFL score at the start of her intensive English studies in the United States.

Academic Portrait

Few students take charge of their own education as extensively and consciously as Yuko. Unlike Yang and Jan, she rarely referred to or thought of courses that she took as merely graduation requirements. Instead, she attempted as far as she could to shape her course selections to benefit her social work education. In selecting to take a course on American Sign Language (ASL), for example, her purpose was partly because she knew there was a possibility that she might later need to deal with this "population." The same held true for courses she took in aging, AIDS, local studies, and biological psychology. Even when they did not easily yield up material that meshed with social work concerns, she did what she could to salvage course material that she *could* use through careful selection of topics for her course papers.

Yuko was also unusually careful about accommodating her professors' directions, often consulting with them to understand exactly what they intended, trusting that they had a clear educational purpose for requiring whatever they required. Even her social work classmates came to realize that Yuko (the only L2 student in her cohort) would always know what the professor wanted them to do and thus would consult her for direction on how to approach a paper.

A telling example of her enlightened willingness to accommodate faculty, and one that again sets Yuko apart from her peers in her major, occurred in her senior year. Yuko had become accustomed to gathering As on her assignments, exams, and final grades in her social work courses. Although many of the faculty interviewed described their exams as requiring students to go beyond mere regurgitation and to apply, for example, theory to a particular situation, in fact, most of the exams in her courses, whether multiple-choice, short-answer, or essay, requested fairly straightforward answers—definitions, lists of characteristics, or explanations of how something worked. For example, from a course on AIDS:

"Name 3 factors that can contribute to the stigmatization of a person with AIDS and discuss why this occurs."

These types of questions required clear-cut, if thoughtful, answers that could more or less be prepared through a review of lecture notes and readings.

In her senior year, however, Yuko and her classmates were confronted with exams in one of the senior courses that presented a real challenge, calling for complex manipulation of several concepts within specific frameworks. The types of questions asked were qualitatively more difficult, requiring students to hold in their minds several abstract concepts at once and track their interactions over time. For example, one question on one exam asked:

"Discuss important ways in which power is commonly expressed over time in typical treatment groups as this relates to establishing norms and accomplishing goals."

Discussing how power is expressed over time is relatively easily thought through. But the added complication here required students to hold this issue (how power is expressed) in mind while also conjuring up information or speculation on how norms are established within a group *and* how goals are accomplished. These kinds of questions were clearly more cognitively demanding, and this blending of abstractions had never been the focus of course lectures, which tended instead to tease abstractions apart and discuss their elements separately. Furthermore, this was one of nine such questions on the exam.

The students in Yuko's cohort were astonishingly assertive in their courses and did not hesitate to complain long and loud when they felt they had a grievance. This exam was perceived as a definite cause for grievance, and in the class session after the exam, the students, very upset, commandeered the class. Several students' angry complaints to the professor were recorded in field notes:

Student:	I put everything I knew on everything and you took off on every question. I don't understand what you want us to do!
Student:	It seemed like the questions were vague.
Student:	We've never been asked to do this … so when I saw the questions, I was overwhelmed.

Yuko too was very distressed. In an interview just after she got the exam back, she reported, "While I'm taking this test, I was almost cry." Although the professor had told the class "nobody fails my class," she told us she thought "I the first." But whereas the other students complained bitterly about being treated unfairly, Yuko responded differently:

Yuko:	The differences between I and them is, I thought I need to change my study style. … I think, like if we go to graduate school, we may have this kind of test more. … Then I said, how can I change?
Interviewer:	So you asked Phil (the professer) that?
Yuko:	Yeah.
Interviewer:	What did you ask him exactly, how can you change?
Yuko:	I thought I need to change my study style. I don't complain about how he did, how he state the question, but I want to have some idea how I can study to prepare for this test. I think that was my question. … everybody complain about test style, but I said I'm not complain about test style, but I think I need to change *my* style. (first-term senior)

Yuko was not afraid to confront or challenge her professors, as described later, so the issue in the case of this exam was not some sort of culturally based reluctance to challenge authority. Instead, Yuko recognized that what this professor was requiring was a deeper, more complex, more sophisticated way to consider the material she was studying, and she intended to master that way of understanding because she felt it would enhance her education, her success in graduate school, and her abilities as a social worker. Thus her accommodations were a form of academic self-interest (doing well in this class, doing well later in graduate school).

Yuko constantly challenged herself in her profound quest to be a certain type of person, a professional who would be able to understand other people's situations. For example, she commented in an interview that she was not particularly interested in doing social work for people who appeared to have problems stemming from their own inability to control themselves or to discipline themselves to do what was necessary to live better. Having stated this conservative point of view, however, she commented that she nevertheless understood that she needed to learn to feel more empathy for such people

> Yuko: I thought I need to think more about this issue, when I have time. … This … make me aware of my weakness, which I need to work with. (first-term senior)

Yuko also related what she studied to her personal life. When her family studies class read about and discussed divorce and single-parent families, she communicated what she learned to her mother, who, according to Yuko's new information had done exactly what textbooks said was necessary to hold the family together successfully.

> Yuko: And that was really good for making my self-esteem and building up my self-esteem and … my brother's. (first-term junior)

Thus a part of Yuko's sense of her own education was that she should change as a person and use her increasing disciplinary knowledge to inform her reflections on her personal life so that she would move in the direction of becoming more understanding, including of her own self.

In typical Yuko fashion, she had decided on this major after finding out as much as she could about the profession before leaving Japan. Her decisions were deliberate, based on gathered information and careful reflection, all leading to a sense of control over her own life. Yuko was in fact the only one of the focal students who seemed able to exert such control.

Reflective, astute, a keen observer of human nature, all traits specifically nurtured in the social work curriculum, Yuko was an exceptionally successful student. After graduating in social work, Yuko was accepted into graduate school in social work at Michigan, Washington University in St. Louis, and Hawaii. Typical of Yuko, by the time she was accepted, she had already found and contacted a Japanese social work student at the school of her choice, a contact she made through one of her many extracurricular activities.

THE SOCIAL WORK MAJOR

Context for Studies

The Social Work building was a friendly, old brick building, with odd little romanesque vaulted doorways and windows, surrounded and shaded by huge trees. All faculty offices and administrative offices, such as the dean's office, and most social work classes were located there, giving the place a nurturing, community feeling. A lounge for students had a refrigerator, a dining table and chairs, a sofa, mailboxes even for undergraduates, and bulletin boards.

The faculty too appeared to try to create community in a variety of ways. Several of the senior faculty had students call them by their first names, and in their interactions with students many of the faculty seemed to put into practice the kinds of values they tried to develop in the students, of acceptance of others, openness, availability, kindness, willingness even eagerness to be helpful, and desire to understand others on their terms and sympathize with them. This faculty knew their undergraduate students individually and as a cohort, being sensitive to group dynamics as well as individual needs. Yuko took excellent advantage of the faculty's willingness to work individually with students and spent hours (sometimes over an hour at a sitting) getting help with writing assignments from them. An example of the kind of atmosphere that this program tried to create was the weekly Breakfast with the Head. Every Tuesday, the head of the undergraduate program would appear in one of the student cafeterias at 7 a.m. to have breakfast with any undergraduate social work students who cared to show up and chat with him on any topic they had the urge to address. Yuko took advantage of this opportunity more than once.

The majority of Yuko's cohort of students were women, many of them returning students. Many had had experience with social workers as clients themselves. The students in this major were somewhat more diverse than in other majors on campus, with a fair representation of African Americans, several students in wheelchairs, and more students than usual who clearly appeared to be struggling financially and in managing their lives. Single mothers were not unusual, neither was the presence of someone's child during classes when the city schools were closed for snow or such.

Two additional factors would prove to be highly significant in Yuko's experience in this major. First, like many professional training programs, the social work curriculum was for upper-division students, juniors and seniors, but in order to provide students with a taste of what social work and the study of social work would be like, potential applicants were encouraged to take two introductory social work courses during the sophomore year. On the 1st day of this course, students from the social work students' organization were present to welcome and talk to these potential colleagues. The course instructor, Sam, who was to become Yuko's adviser, began the class with an ice-breaker activity that within minutes had the group of perhaps 40 new students laughing and chatting with each other and with the representatives from the student organization. Yuko was instantly a part of things, talking freely to other students who were clearly taking an interest in her and what she had to say, a very warm, friendly, and encouraging beginning. During this year, Yuko began her academic friendship with two of the three students she would work with and remain close to until graduation—Linda, a middle-aged European American single mother, and Wayne, a married African American man with children. A third member of this group, Maggie, also a middle-aged European American woman, would join the group later.

The second factor was less pleasant. Some students were admitted into the major after the two introductory social work courses. But transfer students who completed their first 2 years of college in the local community college were also admitted. As a result, in the junior-level courses, and subsequently, there was a group of students that had already been taking classes together for a year in the university and another new group coming in from the outside, who were believed, by at least some of the university students, to be less qualified than those who had taken the two introductory courses. During the 2 years that these two groups "worked together," there were repeated conflicts and some verbal confrontations that at times seriously disrupted class and created anxiety for Yuko, who came to feel that the tussling students were getting in the way of her education as they took class time to argue about personal issues. (See the section on Socioacademic Relations.)

Professional Language.   A substantial amount of classroom talk in social work revolved around what the role of the professional was and what it meant to be a professional, to behave professionally.

Professionalization included building certain kinds of vocabulary. Despite students' complaints about the excessively academic tone of one professor's language, she refused to lower her spoken register and used vocabulary in class that the students said they were unfamiliar with, could not understand, and considered too dressed up, like *milieu* (a word with some pertinence in social work, it would seem). She responded to their complaints by telling them that the only way they would learn this language was by hearing it used, so she continued using it. Sam and Phil both annotated Yuko's written work to push her in the direction of using professional jargon. She told us that in writing as a social worker, it was important to use formal language:

> Yuko: He [Sam] talks about social work job. We have a lot of paperwork, and we need to describe something in formal language. That's why he tried to [make us] accustomed to do it. (second-term sophomore)

More specific social work terminology, particularly counseling or therapeutic terminology, was constantly employed by faculty and readily absorbed by students partly because it could so easily be inserted into everyday life, much more so than the vocabulary of engineering, nursing, or even business. In class, instructors referred not to discussing a video but to "processing that experience"; rather than talking about personal experiences, faculty and students referred to engaging in "self-disclosure," a mental habit that teachers in the social work curriculum encouraged students to develop, urging them to acknowledge and express their feelings. Students, Yuko among them, quickly took up the discourse of the need for client confidentiality and social work ethical behavior. Echoes of classroom uses filtered increasingly over the years into Yuko's writing and, more strikingly, into her speech during interviews, in phrases like:

confidentiality issues
suicidal ideation
anxiety level
denial phase
stress level
the affect of schizophrenia

Being able to use this kind of vocabulary made Yuko's speech seem unusually sophisticated.

Professional Values.   Professional social work values included a willingness to accept a range of human behavior. This attitude may account for the often chaotic nature of social work classes. From my field notes from one class observation:

> Class begins late, as T predicted it would [to me before class]. She did-n't seem pressed and took it in stride that they would come late. ... The plan for today was to show two films that Ss were supposed to be bring-ing. ... Three women arrive together late, one of them being the one who's supposed to show the film. She doesn't have it with her and says the three of them will go to get it and be back in 5–10 minutes ... Class begins at least 10–15 minutes late. Doesn't matter because nobody else is on time either. ... Ss trickle in. ...

> Eventually 14–15 Ss show up. ... One African American woman is braid-ing the hair of a Euro-Am woman sitting in front of her. The S with the film finally shows up. T says she should introduce it. She says she does-n't know anything about it. ... All she can say about the film is, "I got it from [the field site]; I don't know why they had it. It's about homeless or old people or something."

The theme of acceptance of others' behavior modeled in this class as one facet of professional attitudes might be juxtaposed against the emphasis on ethics and respect for others' rights in another class. In that class, one day the professor passed around and was instructing students to read and sign a statement of professional ethics. The impetus for this move came as the result of one of the many class disputes between the two factions in this cohort of students, as described earlier. From field notes:

> T expresses concerns about ethics. This section of the class takes maybe 15 minutes. She comments on inappropriate class conduct. ... Says that some Ss in class feel like they can't express their opinions in presence of certain other people. Ss now falling silent [from their usual constant chattering]. T makes appeal for respect and courtesy toward each other. ... Some students refuse to sign ethics statement (!).

Even in classroom management issues, such as arguing about an exam, students were reminded that everything they did was part of shaping them into professionals. In one class after complaints about an exam, one professor remarked:

Teacher: Don't attack me, my credibility, or my standards. You can ask how I reached your grade. In social work you'll be working with people you don't like, so you have to develop attitudes of social workers. You have to approach

it in a professional and grown-up manner if you expect to
discuss discrepancies between my and your evaluation of
your test.

Students were thus constantly reminded of the ethical substrate of behavior.

Professional and Personal Self-Awareness. Many assignments in
social work classes were intended to help develop another major feature
of the social worker's psychology, self-awareness. Yuko was not only
aware of the need to develop this characteristic but exercised and
expressed her self-awareness repeatedly. She did not want, for example, a
home health care field placement because she did not want to create
stress for herself and her client as a consequence of her Japanese accent.
On another occasion, she debated about accepting a field placement that
would put her into an emotionally charged health care setting and
decided against it after a self-evaluation:

Yuko: And personally, I'm not ready to talk [with] like people crying
        and [saying] maybe I'm gonna die. (first-term senior)

Aware of other personal limitations and preferences, she sometimes
felt she needed to transform herself, as noted previously, and at other
times, to understand and accept her preferences, even when they did not
conform to social work ideals of acceptance of others:

Yuko: I'm not really good at talking to people who are really aggressive
        to me, and I don't want to stick my nose in the family situation.
        Personally, I think it's their problem; they can solve it by them-
        selves. Not my problem, not society's problem. (first-term senior)

Like Ben, Yuko also regarded part of her professional training as internalizing and making her own the motives of her professors in assigning
work. It seems probable that internalizing these purposes for assigned
work promoted her ability to benefit from those activities and from her
disciplinary initiation as she rapidly took on the characteristics of the
professionalized social work student both she and the program desired.

WRITING DEVELOPMENT

Of the four students, Yuko had the most intense and varied experiences
with writing across the curriculum and in her major and seemed the most
forthcoming in talking about writing. She also made the best use of writing as a means of furthering her development as a social worker, selecting

writing topics in non–social work classes whenever she could that matched her social work interests.

ESL Writing Classes

In her most salient early writing experiences after arriving in the United States, Yuko expressed surprise, if not frustration, at the type of assignments she had in her ESL classes, writing not from a source text but rather from her own experiences. Initially she assumed this would be easier than writing from a source text. The topics of the first three or four papers in these initial writing classes focused on people the students knew:

> Yuko: How do we think about relationship father and son, mother and daughter, the most impressive person to me. Like that subject, I can't read anything.
>
> Interviewer: Which type is easier?
>
> Yuko: First I thought writing about who I know, but later I thought research and I write is much easier because I can write about two kind of paper, the first I said about detail [about what the source text says] and then I can say my opinion, so I can write longer. Make longer and paragraph make longer is very difficult for me. (first-term freshman)

But in her final interview, Yuko looked back on those writing courses as helpful and appropriately staged.

> Yuko: Writing class was really good. We got the topic and we did many short writing, like imagine like you are in the room, describe the room. Start from that kind of thing, description, to more kind of summary type of assignment. (second-term senior)

During our interviews with all the focal students, we regularly asked what they remembered getting from English classes that helped them in their current work or that helped them become better writers. In early interviews, Yuko touched on three themes common to English learners' writing experiences:

- Difficulty of producing the required length of text.
- Lack of vocabulary.
- Length of time required to create text.

By her senior year, however, she experienced an opposite problem, attempting to squeeze her expanding knowledge into limited numbers of pages.

Intersection of Writing Instruction With Writing in the First 2 Years

In the early years of college in the United States, Yuko felt her ESL writing classes had influenced her in the following areas:

- Documentation: At the end of her sophomore year, Yuko reported that learning how to create a bibliography had been useful to her. Subsequently, in her social work classes she was required to learn American Psychological Association (APA) style, not the documenting style she had learned in her English class. Interestingly, she would later complain that the APA bibliographies were a mystery to writing center tutors as well, all English majors steeped in MLA style.
- Invention techniques: Because of her difficulty generating enough text to fill the requirements of her assignments in the early years, Yuko reported at the end of her freshman year finding invention techniques very helpful. What is interesting about this assertion is that it was never mentioned in later interviews, suggesting that "invention" per se was only an issue when she was asked to write on topics where she did not control enough content to write without inventing. Equipped with a great number of ideas, as she came to be later in her career, she no longer experienced the need to invent something to say, but rather to manage the great deal she had to say by organizing it.
- Writing what you know: In her English classes Yuko had been encouraged to write about what she knew. This advice represented the crux of her difficulties in writing letters to the editor in her political science class. From a journal entry:

In English classes, I learned we needed knowledge of a topic to write an essay. Now, I experience the lesson when I write assignments for Political Science class. ... they seem easy assignments. However, they are very difficult because of my lack of knowledge.

Like invention techniques, the advice to "write what you know" may function best in English classes and is possibly less applicable in courses intended to develop new knowledge bases rather than skills.

- Paraphrases: A very important technique Yuko learned in English class was paraphrasing. In biology lab reports and other assignments, she needed to, as she said: "Rephrase, rephrase, rephrase." As noted in the literature on issues in L2 student writing across the curriculum (see, e.g., Currie, 1998; Leki & Carson, 1997; Silva, 1997), this is no small task for L2 students. Yuko's experiences were especially difficult when she was asked to paraphrase abstracts. The task was not only to understand a text well enough to repeat the gist of the text but in addition to access language parallel to the source text but different enough to constitute her own words. What was intended as a fairly straightforward means (the paraphrasing) by which accomplishment of the chore (understanding) was to be displayed became itself the chore.

- Clear versus sophisticated writing: Yuko recalled that she had been admonished both in ESL writing classes and by writing center tutors to write shorter sentences for increased clarity. She was being asked for writing that was less poetic, less metaphorical, less concerned with the beauty of language. Yuko did attempt to comply, albeit with regret in part because she felt these shorter, less aesthetically focused sentences were causing her to lose her grip on writing in Japanese, which she felt she had once been good at. At the same time Yuko felt that it was not only in Japanese that longer sentences were appreciated and favored. Several times in her upper-class years she regretted her lack of ability to write what she called sophisticated sentences in English:

Yuko: ... I was told one time when I was taking [one of the English courses], one instructor at the writing center [said] you know, I understand, you are an international student, you can write this way [with short sentences] but if you can write in sophisticated way, you should change it [to] that way. So I want to learn not like for the international, but sophisticated way to writing. Like how to use like, "I am the student who is ... ," usage of this, who, that, in which. I don't think I learn enough to be sophisticated on writing in that way [i.e., using sentence structure tricks].

Interviewer: It sounds like you mean more subordinate clauses or complex sentences or things like that.

Yuko: Because, I don't know, most of Asian students are not accustomed to writing that way. ... Then once we know, we always want to use that expression ... other way to express, not just one way to express. (second-term senior)

Her desire to write longer sentences, then, was part of a desire to write with greater variety. Ostensibly good advice from writing instructors to write short sentences inadvertently created limitations for Yuko. Although the advice no doubt had the positive effect of improving the readability of her writing during her college years, it also worked against her interest in stretching her writing abilities in English, in somewhat the same way as the advice to write what you know (i.e., to write from already established knowledge) may, by definition, not be helpful when writing about what you do not know.

Intersection of Writing Instruction with Writing in the Major

Once Yuko started studying in her major, whenever we asked her about the benefits of her English classes, we consistently got the following responses:

1. In her English class she learned what she called "exact essay style." This provided her with a clear, perceptible contrast with what she felt was the usual Japanese rhetorical style. She said, at first

Yuko: I didn't understand why we need thesis statement at the front like in the introduction, because [that is not necessary in] the Japanese ... structure. We have conclusion, then why we need to state twice? Conclusion and introduction, sometimes same thing. (second-term freshman)

This organizational style eventually became second nature to her as a framework for her writing. In fact, she found it awkward to write paragraphs as required in certain social work tasks without an essay structure overlay:

Interviewer: Did ... anything you learned in English help you in this one?
Yuko: Actually, it just make me difficult to write this paper. Because I kind of accustomed to write really essay type, or, you know, I always really care about flow of sentences. But you know, I don't need any transition for this [social work task]. I just describe about it, so ... . (second-term junior)

In other words, at times her English class training in writing essays actually made writing certain types of social work texts more, not less, difficult, as when strict page limitations were enforced. Writing, as she said, "without the assistance of the introduction" to orient both herself and the reader came to be perceived as a burden. She missed the scaffolding that the introduction, thesis, and other organizational tricks had come to provide for her.

2. She had learned in one of her ESL writing classes an approach to writing answers to essay exam questions that she used regularly and that she came to see as having given her an advantage not shared by her peers. She learned to analyze the essay question and to answer concisely only the question that was asked. As she said, it was important to

Yuko: answer accurately what the question wants, not to go beyond the question. Many of my friends, American friends, do in that way, talking about more. Then they came to be away from the topic and even though they wrote five or six pages and [I] just was three pages, but I could get more points. ... I realize the American student, the social work class, they are saying I don't know how to answer the essay question. I say, you didn't learn in your English class?! And they say no. (second-term junior)

Yuko found her experiences in her ESL writing classes and skills she developed there pertinent to her college writing. But of course most of the progress Yuko made in writing in English was the result of time spent with text, reading and writing in her major and other courses. As she noted:

Interviewer: What made your work get better?
Yuko: Time. (second-term senior)

Yuko's major required somewhat more of the generic structure taught in her English classes than did the majors of the other students in this study. Thus, she owed her ability to get something out of the ESL writing courses partly to her own talents but also partly to this confluence of focuses in the writing courses and in her major.

THE NATURE AND ROLE OF YUKO'S UNDERGRADUATE WRITING

What were the dimensions of the writing Yuko faced across the curriculum? Looking back on her academic life in her final interview in this study, Yuko perceived the writing in the general-education courses to have been minimal and the writing in the social work curriculum to have been central to the development of writing skills, skills she was told, and came to feel, she would need as a social work professional. Table 5.1 sums up the writing tasks Yuko was assigned.

The following sections discuss the assignments listed in the table.

Writing in General-Education Courses

In her first 2 years of college, Yuko was assigned approximately 30 pages of writing in courses excluding her three ESL writing classes. In her last 2 years in college, she was assigned approximately 130 pages of writing, excluding the documents required for admission to and graduation from the social work program (the academic portfolio). Although the writing required for her general-education courses was relatively meager (if considerably more than experienced by the other focal students), the series of many short assignments in several different general-education classes left Yuko at times beleaguered, nickled and dimed to distraction.

TABLE 5.1
Yuko's writing assignments in courses other than English

Term	Course	Type	Prescribed or Actual Length	Weight in Course Grade
fall freshman				
spring freshman	Psychology	4 papers	short	unknown
	Sociology	essay exam		10% of total exam
fall sophomore	History	3 essay exams	2 questions each	25%, 25%, 30%
		5 quizzes	short answer	20% included in participation
	Biology	lab report	3/4 page of prose	25/500 points
		research paper	1 page	20/500 points
	Intro to social work	article summary & reaction	2 pages	15%
		interview report	3 pages	25%
		1 essay question on each of 3 exams		whole exam = 20% of course grade
spring sophomore	Social welfare	term paper	8 pages	30%
		1 essay question on both exams		whole exam = 30%
	Political science	4 letters to editor	1–2 pages each	40/500 points
		1 essay question on each of 3 exams		45/500 points
		summary of State of the Union address	1 page	extra credit
	Sign language	book report	3 pages	100/1050 points
		activity report	1–2 pages	150/1050 points
summer sophomore		Initial Social Work progression	300 words	none--required to enter major

(Continued)

Table 5.1 (Continued)

Term	Course	Type	Prescribed or Actual Length	Weight in Course Grade
fall junior	Child & family	6 short assignments	1 paragraph each	150/600
		take home final	5 questions, 1–2 pages each	100/600
	Social Work practice	term paper	10 pages	30%
		journal entries	1–2 paragraphs	part of participation grade
	Human environment	eco-map	6–8 pages	33% of grade
	AIDS	research paper	6–8 pages	25%
	Aging	2 essay exams		unknown
spring junior	Social work research	Intro and RQ		subsumed into proposal
		lit review		subsumed into proposal
		article critique		20%
		proposal		20%
	Social work practice	term paper	24 pages	20%
	Role play lab	role play reflections	half page	1 point each week
	Field seminar	process recording	4 pages	10%
		self-reflection	5–8 pages	10%
		journal		no grade
	Local studies	research paper	7 pages	20%
		book abstract		5%
		final essay exam		15%

(Continued)

Table 5.1 (Continued)

Term	Course	Type	Prescribed or Actual Length	Weight in Course Grade
fall senior	Group dynamics	2 short reports	1 page each	10% included in participation
		term paper	8–10 pages	25%
		3 essay exams		20%, 25%, 20%
	Policy	interview	1–1/2 page	10%
		policy	2 page	15%
		policy analysis	9–10 pages	35% (group)
	Field seminar	ethics paper	3–5 pages	10%
		agency description	1 page	10%
		journal		no grade
spring senior	Integrative seminar	resume		5%
		6 item annotated bibliography		10% including oral presentation
		final portfolio		85%

Yuko was the only one of the four participants in this study to display a marked change in her attitude toward writing assignments over the course of her undergraduate career, moving gradually away from a notion of writing as something she did for teachers and closer to a notion of writing as something she did if not *for* herself then at least with an awareness of the personal and professional benefits it offered to her.

Yuko: So if I compare to other semester I feel I've done more professionalized work. ... Not in writing the paper for the theme of the professor but what I want to write. (second-term junior)

In that move, her feelings about the role of writing in her education became increasingly congruent with those of her major professors. But initially and in her general-education courses, her main concerns with writing appeared to center on attempting to follow her instructors' directions and to clearly determine their purposes. Also, although she experienced difficulty with assignments requiring her to express personal opinions, the reason for this difficulty was not grounded in reticence but rather in the lack of a knowledge base and the appropriate language necessary to do so.

Following Directions. Like many other undergraduates (see Leki, 1995b; Leki & Carson, 1997), Yuko felt that the key to doing well in writing was to obey professors' instructions as fully as possible, although this was often difficult when directions were vague, as they typically were in the writing required for humanities general education courses. This difficulty led Yuko to consult with her instructors regularly in an attempt to clarify and verify instructions, usually after class or during office hours (and later, in her social work classes, to have her instructors nearly always look over her first drafts or outlines). In her general-education classes, only once, for a biology lab report, did an instructor offer to look at students' first drafts.

Determining Purpose. Yuko's interest in following directions appeared also to have led Yuko to consider what the instructor's purpose was in making a writing assignment.[30] For her general-education courses, Yuko's speculations on her instructors' purposes fell into four categories, listed here in order of frequency: (a) to verify the completion of some other activity, (b) for the benefit of the instructor (i.e., the same answer Jan gave), (c) purpose unclear, and (d) for students' educational development. For comparison, the faculty's stated purposes for assigning writing are also noted:

1. According to faculty interviews, the desire to verify that students had done or would do something else was a frequent motivation for making writing assignments. In other words, the writing assignment was actually a form of policing, a form that Yuko at least sometimes found unnecessary because she never failed to do the activity the writing of the paper was intended to verify.
2. The idea that a writing assignment would benefit the professor was rarely named by faculty as a task goal. But like Jan, in her first 2 years, Yuko felt that her instructors genuinely wanted to know what she thought or what she understood about the readings, the lectures, or some other class-related experience, as though instructors were gauging their own effectiveness or the effectiveness/interest of their assignments. In Yuko's descriptions at this stage, the assignment was a form of instructor survey, evaluating their own work rather than evaluating the students'.
3. Faculty of course never felt that the purpose of a writing assignment was unclear.

4. Faculty frequently cited the students' education as the purpose of writing. As Yuko also understood:

Interviewer: What do you think is the purpose of the activity reports in sign class?

Yuko: Maybe she want [us] to know not just about the sign language, what we find about the words. She wants us to know what deaf people think, or what the deaf community is. (second-term sophomore)

Yuko also imagined more central purposes for writing.

Yuko: Maybe, I think if we don't write, ... we just read about book, and we don't have to think about them. (second-term junior)

Because writing about a topic required spending time thinking about the topic, Yuko came to see writing as at least one means of promoting learning.

Eventually, as she discussed the writing she did in her major, the second category, writing for the benefit of the instructor, vanished from Yuko's comments about the purpose of her writing assignments. The first category, writing as a form of policing, and the third, being unsure, became quite rare. The fourth, writing for the sake of her own educational and professional advancement, became most prominent, as Yuko came to see and to be able to articulate these benefits. Still, the use of writing in the general-education courses, where even a model student like Yuko considered many assignments confusing, pointless, directed at policing student activities, or benefiting the instructors, is discouraging. That Jan would express such understandings, with his jaded take on his educational experience, is not surprising but when even the best and most cooperative students respond this way, it becomes more difficult to see the writing assignments as a good use of student and faculty time.[31]

Following directions and determining purpose overlapped with responding to the demand for grammatically polished papers. This requirement varied by course and produced a revealing observation on Yuko's part about the resulting effect on her work. From Yuko's journal:

Last semester, I had [lists her writing assignments in all her classes]. ... I needed to revise my social work writing assignments many times because my instructor counted grammatical errors on the paper grade.

Contrary, in this semester I have [lists her writing assignments in her classes that semester]. Nevertheless, I don't feel stress as much as I felt in last semester. The reason is that I don't have to worry about grammer in those papers. Both classes assignments require me to describe my reactions for topics. Thus, I spend much more time to determine what I will talk about in those assignments than to revise grammatical mistakes.

These comments point to an interesting conundrum: By demanding error-free writing, course instructors are more likely to get it from conscientious students like Yuko but it comes at the cost of time and energy spent on those features of writing rather than on content.

Yuko's experience with feedback on papers in general-education courses was like that of most students. Because revising and resubmitting a paper was not offered as an option, whatever feedback she received on these papers could never be incorporated into a next draft. When papers were assigned to be turned in on the last day of class, as was quite common, she never even saw feedback.

Expressing Opinions.   Finally, one theme that arose in Yuko's comments about her writing experiences in both her general-education courses and to a much lesser degree in her social work courses related to expressing opinion. In her letters to the editor, she sensed a conflict between expressing her opinion/feelings, which she considered an informal, intimate, and personal form of communication, and writing a paper, which was formal, objective.

> Yuko: That topic [letters to the editor] is very formal, but [nevertheless] I need to say about my opinions. ... I don't want to make like immature composition on the paper, first of all, because we are talking about politics. ... I don't want to do [i.e., write] "I want" or "I think." (first-term junior)

Because she considered using those expressions immature and informal, but had as yet no substitute terms in a more academic register, she was at a loss about how to blend what she assumed was the expected informality of personal opinion and the formality required by the writing context and so found expressing her opinion in writing difficult as long as she did not have the linguistic means to do so.

A second reason Yuko gave for finding it difficult to express an opinion on other occasions was what she considered her lack of sufficient familiarity with the subject matter to have a reasonable opinion she was willing to express. In this way, as noted, Yuko's reluctance to express an opinion cannot be seen as the result of not being accustomed to having or expressing an opinion. Rather, her reluctance was language and knowledge based.

By the same token, because she believed that writing an appropriate paper required background information on these general-education subjects that she did not have, she felt more comfortable with being directly tested on material that had been specifically covered in these courses. Although she always worked hard on them, Yuko seemed to feel that the papers she wrote for general-education classes typically neither advanced her own knowledge nor constituted a suitable means of evaluating her knowledge.

Writing in Social Work Courses

Writing was prominently featured, even central in some respects, in social work courses, and not perfunctory (business) or beside the main point (nursing, engineering) as in the other majors examined here. Social work had the clearest reason to focus on students' writing because, as the faculty reiterated in interviews, practicing social workers were required to produce full reports recording and documenting interactions with clients for a variety of agencies and organizations. Sometimes these reports were also legal documents with specific legal standing that could help decide the social fate of clients, whether or not they would get food stamps, whether a child would be removed from an abusive home, and so forth. However, although in their field practice, students witnessed these documents being created, and in fact sometimes added to them themselves on site, they had no occasion in their course work to do this particular kind of writing. Instead the written work in their courses was primarily academically oriented, although the assignments were also used to focus students on some of the non-literacy-oriented skills and the attitudes and values they were expected to develop as BSSWs, as they were referred to, that is, Bachelor of Science in Social Work.

Although Yuko began her social work studies believing that as a practical field social work would require little writing, her experience both in class and in field placements convinced her otherwise. By her final interview, Yuko asserted the importance of writing to her academic career.

Interviewer: How central has writing been in your academic work in social work?
Yuko: Totally. Major, really major. (second-term senior)

Unlike the writing assignments in Yuko's general-education courses, so many of which seemed to exist primarily to police the completion of other activities, in social work the goals of writing assignments were usually described as allowing students to integrate what they had learned from different sources (including field placements) and to give students enough time/space to reflect deeply on some issue.[32]

For Yuko, the most important themes related to writing in social work were:

- The importance of following directions in order to understand the point of assignments and do well on them.
- An increasing commitment to the content and form of her writing along with a sense of ownership of her written work.
- Writing as a process of professionalization.

Following Directions, Again. At times, the guidelines for writing in social work were quite detailed (though never as detailed as in Jan's business courses). Although Yuko was later to criticize this hand-holding tendency of the social work curriculum, early in her career, she found it useful and was frustrated when instructors were unable to give her a good sense of what to do.

> Yuko: Everybody talking about it's really difficult to find out what [this instructor] expect for us. Her direction is very widely and vague. So, to picking up her mind is the primary issue when we thinking about our exams and papers. … Maybe … she trying to give me the freedom, but it's really difficult for me. I think maybe, you know, like student in masters course, you know, who really have the idea about what they, about what their learning is. But this is the first course we look at human behavior in depth. (first-term junior)

On rare occasions when Yuko failed to include some requirement, it seemed always to be a conscious, weighed decision. For example, in the write-up of an interview during her field assignment in her junior year, she had points taken off, as she anticipated, for not including her own feelings during the interview, as directed and as demonstrated in the model the teacher provided. In this report of an interview with an Alzheimer's patient, she said she knew she hadn't followed the directions but that this failure was because, as she said, her feelings about this patient were complicated and uncertain and she simply could not yet talk about them.

Claiming Authorship. Like many students, when asked what the interest or importance or usefulness of a writing assignment was to her, Yuko often replied something like "Assignment is assignment for student." Nevertheless, well before the last semester of her senior year, the semester of the portfolio described below, Yuko had already showed signs of an increasing sense of ownership of her texts. In her sophomore year, as she prepared her personal statement for admission to the social work program, both Sam and a peer whom she asked to look at a draft discouraged her from including some material on Japan. Yuko took the advice but commented later

Yuko: "So my feeling was I skipped something, in history. (second-term sophomore).

Her commitment to her own version gave her the sense that her readers' version did not quite represent what she wanted to say.

Culturally grounded assumptions also brought Yuko's writing into conflict with her reader's expectations. An assignment in her group dynamics class was to analyze her membership in a particular minority group, an assignment that she said made her think of herself in that role for the first time. She chose to talk about being a Japanese person in the United States, and so part of a minority in the United States rather than part of the majority, as she had been in Japan. She wrote:

I grew up as a member of a dominant ethnic group in Japan in which people believe they are racially homogeneous. (first-term senior)

The instructor crossed out the part of her statement underlined in the preceding quotation and in his written comment in the margin noted:

I don't think this part adds anything, does it?

Asked, in discussing this paper in an interview, whether the instructor's comment made sense to her, Yuko replied

Yuko: I think it's [the section crossed out] not necessary for this paper, just I want to say that. (first-term senior)

What the instructor probably failed to understand was that her comment was in fact relevant to the question of minority groups within majority cultures because it formed part of the story Japanese people tell themselves about who they are, which is why it seemed important to Yuko to repeat. (See Kubota, 1997, 1999.) Furthermore, it does not seem coincidental that these references to Japan were read by Yuko's U.S. readers, embedded as they were in their own cultures, as irrelevant, though her desire to "say that" bespoke her own claim to them.

The Senior Portfolio.   The themes of following directions and claiming ownership come to a head in Yuko's work on the senior portfolio, the culminating project for graduating social work students. This portfolio was to document their competency in 10 designated domains,[33] and constituted 85% of the grade in one final-semester social work course. It was discussed by teachers beginning even in the sophomore courses, so much so that Yuko wrote in the journal she kept for this project:

"A PORTFOLIO! It will make me crazy, some day."

The directions for the portfolio included lists of repetitious guide questions for each of the 10 competencies and for the introductions and conclusions. Because the portfolio loomed so large for the social work students in their last semester, the detailed directions took on a kind of folk life of their own among the students, who appeared to work hard at interpreting them to focus on superficial features of decorative presentation and on sheer bulk resulting from responding to every one of the guide questions.

In frustration at the ratcheting up of the requirements that her peers engaged in, in terms of decoration and bulk, not substance, Yuko eventually went to the library to look at the copies of previously done portfolios the social work program kept on file as models. There she saw that previous, model portfolios did not engage in decoration or superficial padding. With that information, she adjusted the guidelines to what seemed more logical to her, including only answering the guiding questions that seemed appropriate to her rather than slavishly following directions. So for Yuko following directions was a prime strategy for success—unless she deemed the directions to make no sense. Rewriting the directions was then one way of claiming ownership.

Another was in working out her own sense of the purpose of the portfolio. Reminded that social work faculty considered this assignment to be a stimulus of the students' critical-thinking skills,[34] Yuko's response came readily and exhibited the very "critical thinking" that the faculty appeared to be aiming for. She dismissed that motivation. Yuko did not accept the creation of the portfolio as a legitimate testimony to students' competence or critical thinking but saw it rather as a way to make the program look good to accreditation agencies.

But doing the portfolio did cause Yuko to look back over the writing she had done during her career as a social work student, and she noted her own progress over the years:

> Interviewer: Last time you said that when you look over your old written work, you see how bad it was. ... In what way do you see your work from earlier in college as not as good as what you do now?
>
> Yuko: Maybe, I feel now like sometimes overstated. (second-term senior)

This remarkable student, writing in a second language, was able to hit the nail on the head, to pinpoint quite exactly one of the major differences between novice and more experienced writers and disciplinary learners:

an awareness of the relativity of knowledge and of the rhetorical means of signaling that awareness through mitigation and hedging.

In the end, Yuko's portfolio was selected as a model to be placed in the library. In typical modest fashion, Yuko told us that, despite asking, she could not figure out why hers was chosen except possibly just to show that there were a variety of ways that the portfolio could be done.

Social Work Writing as Professional Enculturation

The most important role of writing in the social work curriculum both to Yuko and to her instructors was in its professionalizing effect. Writing promoted disciplinary initiation into:

- Procedures (learn how to do something).
- Writing (learn how to write something that social workers write).
- Content (develop disciplinary content knowledge).
- Affect (self-examine).
- Language (use social work jargon).

Procedures. Although a few of the papers Yuko wrote were more or less ordinary research papers, in several instances in the social work program, students were asked to write papers that would first entail doing or at least thinking through on paper some activity social workers needed to know how to perform. In these cases, the argument might be made that, as was the case in Ben's description of much of his written work, the learning took place in preparing for the writing; the writing was a kind of add-on after the fact to display to the teacher that the work of learning had occurred. Several cases from Yuko's assignments exemplified this type of professional training. In one course, students were asked to do a "process recording," that is, do an interview with a patient, transcribe the interview exactly, and then intersperse throughout the transcript what was going through their mind at given moments, in effect, to do a kind of think-aloud recall. Students were expected to gain both metacognitive and cognitive benefits from the assignment: to reflect on their own thoughts and feelings during the process and to learn how to do this type of interview.[35]

For the major assignment in her group dynamics class, Yuko wrote up an extensive plan for a support group for breast cancer survivors. The value of this assignment for Yuko lay in simulating the real support group experience. It was a substitute for action:

Professor P: ... the other way to [get support group experience] would be to go do a group ... , which we actually can't do.

The write-up allowed a social work student to think through what a social worker would in practice do: The writing was a substitute for the doing, a simulation of doing, and Yuko found the writing itself less essential than the preparation for writing.

> Yuko: I like information gathering. I don't want to quit it.
> Interviewer: Would you rather just do that and never have to write [this paper]?
> Yuko: Yeah. (first-term senior)

Nevertheless, the process recording and support group plan assignments were among those that allowed Yuko to practice simulated social work procedures.

   Practicing Social Work Genres.   In those two assignments, the writing played one kind of professionalizing role; another was giving students the opportunity to practice a type of writing social workers did, providing dress rehearsal.

> Yuko: Most of the time when we want to start some group, we need to propose first, so I think the skill to write our plan, it's really important as a social worker, especially BSSW, we don't have much power, so. (second-term junior)

Presumably Yuko felt that being able to forcefully and clearly present a plan of action, such as the one for the support group, would help to compensate for the lack of power inherent in the status of social work by convincing the sponsoring agency or institute to initiate or fund the plan.

   Another writing need that Yuko identified as essential to social workers and that she felt she was getting practice in as a student was reporting skill. This involved writing records with three goals in mind: Keep them short, change the focus to suit the audience (funding agency, internal report, etc.), and keep that focus to one topic. In an effort to get students to keep records short, instructors often imposed fairly stringent report length restrictions. Although these short papers were intended partly to train students in record preparation, Yuko also felt that these restrictions cut into her ability to articulate what she knew, express certain subtleties, and integrate her knowledge. Asked if she would get more out of these assignments if she didn't have to limit herself to a certain number of pages, she answered yes.

> Yuko: While I write the paper I think I pay attention more to make shorter paragraph or shorter sentence rather than ... making

careful consideration to my feeling or my thought. (first-term junior)

Again, as was the case in courses that required error-free writing, a strong focus on a more superficial feature of writing, page length here, took Yuko's attention away from a more academic, cognitive, or reflective emphasis on the work. Thus, although Yuko was glad to practice social work genres, she also reported not learning much from doing the actual writing.

> Yuko: Even though I write this or not, I learn already in the lecture what I put in this paper. (second-term junior)

Writing to Learn Content.   Yuko mentioned the relative use*less*ness of writing (writing as just an assignment) more often than she did its use-*ful*ness in terms of developing understanding, increasing knowledge, or learning course content and described writing as a mechanism to facilitate or provide occasion for the development of other skills, sometimes improve her academic style, sometimes her social worker style, sometimes her recording abilities. But on a few occasions, Yuko experienced distinct benefits associated with writing assignments. In one case, the writing assignment prompted and documented an interview with Yuko's field supervisor about policies that affected her work.

> Interviewer: What did you learn from doing the interview assignment?
> Yuko: When I talk to my supervisor … she has many levels of policy, like agency and community level. And depend on that, even though she make contact with the client, and she did her job for the client, that client cannot have any services because of outside agency policy. *So I can see these dynamics* [italics added]. The social worker's job, the practice of social work is not always the solution of the client's problem. (second-term senior)

What Yuko learned came from having the opportunity to do the interview and to reflect on it. These were the most important functions of this assignment. Writing up the interview allowed her to practice writing in a social work genre, but it had also served as the prompt for what was essential: gathering the information the supervisor gave her and appropriately adjusting her understanding of the limitations of social work practice.

She also recognized the positive educational effect of the time and concentration required to produce academic papers.

> Interviewer: Did writing down the stuff you learned about policy in your paper help you learn?
>
> Yuko: I think so. ... You know like eating food stuff. We just eat, it's OK, but when we digest, I think this is the writing process. (first-term senior)

Yuko appeared to sense a unique benefit of writing in terms of pushed output not only for language growth but for growth in disciplinary knowledge as well. But in the end, Yuko reported that the main aids in helping her learn the body of knowledge and the skills important for her social work education were not writing assignments but rather previous knowledge, previous training, lectures and readings, effort, and peers. Nevertheless, by her final interview, Yuko expressed her sense of writing as intimately intertwined in her professional development:

> Interviewer: How central has writing been in your development as a professional social worker?
>
> Yuko: I think writing paper was process of whole learning social work theory first of all. The development of professional writing skills comes with my assessment skill as a social worker. ... It comes together for me. Not just comes one. (second-term senior)

Thus, learning the social work field and writing within the discipline became intertwined and inseparable for her, each scaffolding the development of the other.

Self-Reflecting. A vital feature of the social work education Yuko received was the focus on self-examination, self-reflection, self-observation. This focus was built into nearly every class, it was modeled by the faculty in their interactions with students, and it was taken very seriously by Yuko and her particular group of friends. And it was the center of many writing assignments. The process recording mentioned previously specifically asked students to record their feelings about the interview as it proceeded.

> Yuko: Not just what they're saying. Maybe we need to reflect what we felt and what we feel during. (first-term senior)

Other assignments asked her to "analyze the feelings," "see myself objectively," or

> Yuko: ... find out my strength and weakness, to look at myself, so which part I can look at more easily and which part is more difficult to express. (first-term junior)

But the role of writing, particularly writing in English, was not a straight-forward means of expressing her own feelings or describing patients.

> Yuko: ... I can say what I think. I cannot say what I feel. (first-term junior)

> Yuko: I have a really small vocabulary to describe emotional state of the patient. (first-term junior)

> Yuko: ... before writing I need to think about [my feelings]; at that time I really get hard time. While writing I don't feel like it's actually my feeling, but I can't find another way to express among those sentences. (second-term junior)

So Yuko experienced the problem of attempting to translate a felt sense of her own emotions or those of a client and coming away with an acute awareness of the inadequacy of the language available to her for these purposes.

Taking on Social Work Language.   As noted earlier, it was fascinating, and also impressive, to watch Yuko's language change and become professionalized over the 4 years of our interviews with her. The gradual incorporation of professional jargon into speech was especially interesting to see in an L2 learner because, as a social work initiate whose main language input was academic, Yuko had some trouble knowing whether a term of jargon was one in broader academic use as well or was really restricted to the discipline, or perhaps restricted in terms of its special meaning within the discipline. Yuko became aware of this herself as she attempted to get help on a writing project from the writing center. She came to realize that her own disciplinary use of "assessment" simply did not resonate with tutors at the writing center.

> Yuko: ... maybe it's different assessment from general thought so maybe it's safe I go to social work teachers [rather than to the writing center for help]. (first-term senior)

Several social work professors gave her feedback on her writing that helped to enculturate her into the jargon of social work by substituting specialized terms used in social work for her more general vocabulary. Yuko took up these terms, which then began gradually showing up in her interview transcripts, including what became her preferred way to phrase refusals: "I'm not comfortable with that."

In her junior year, she received rewrites of her original phrasings in the report of an interview she had conducted:

The professor's changes might elicit at least the following observations:

1. Some of his changes were essentially arbitrary: which/that; Ms M … , writer/author.
2. Some of the changes represented his ideas and not Yuko's: entire last section.

Original	Alterations in italics
the writer asked M …	the writer asked *Ms* M …
She emphasized the importance of knowledge about those insurance policies such as eligibility and benefits.	She emphasized the importance of *not only knowing* about insurance policies *in general but having a clear understanding of* eligibility *requirements* and benefits *that are available*.
M … expressed a strong feeling toward the money issues which are behind these policies.	M … expressed a strong feeling toward the *monetary* issues *that* are *often* behind these policies.
She said, "Social welfare policy is not a pleasant issue for people to deal with."	She said, "Social welfare policy is not a pleasant issue for people." [i.e., changes made to quoted interview material!]
The writer	The *author* ["writer" not changed before[36]]
The writer concluded there are ways of utilizing social welfare policy in her future practice. As a first step, the writer will begin by obtaining knowledge about social welfare policies associate with her field practicum setting (i.e. health care).	The writer concluded *we are always using policies. The issue is knowing about policies, analyzing these policies and often trying to change policies. Being active in the policy-making process assists social workers in meeting their mission.*

3. The professor was rewriting this for Yuko with the portfolio in mind and so making the points more generalized and less specific to her current field setting.
4. Yuko knew and understood exactly what he was doing. She called it "making as more professionalize paper."

Yuko was perfectly aware that her professor had changed the meaning of some of her sentences and she had no real intention of using his version. But she felt he tried to make her phrasings more academic, was generally pleased at her increasing ability to manipulate social work jargon and at what she considered sophisticated, academic phrasings, and appeared to try to incorporate such phrasings into her regular speech.

> Yuko: In the syllabus, he describe, I mean, indicate, how we approach the essay. (first-term senior)

She was also aware that using these terms would make her life easier as a social work student and as a prospective graduate student or employee.

> Yuko: So in that way may be good because even other schools or job interviews, they like us to say, "I have strengths in my assessment," you know. … They like it rather than I'm just saying, "Well, I like people." (second-term senior)

In discussing how her writing had improved during her undergraduate years, Yuko focused on the issue of what she saw as academic vocabulary.

> Yuko: My paper became more like academic type. Maybe vocabulary is more. I don't use "I think." Maybe I use "consider" or something like that. That's different because I knew the meaning of "consider," but I was not accustomed to use those words. So that's big thing, I think. Maybe because I read so many literature from social work, I'm writing like what they do. (second-term senior)

Yuko used her way of carefully noting and following (or not) directions for assignments and of extending her own authorship claims onto the purposes for these assignments as a way of using the writing she did to become increasingly professionalized. The responses she got to her writing and her active pursuit of feedback also moved her in the same direction.

Written Response to Writing

Aside from grammar corrections, Yuko experienced two kinds of feedback on her writing: unsolicited written commentary on papers or exams she turned in and solicited feedback on initial drafts or outlines. The first kind was essentially the only kind in her first 2 years and was the least useful; the second form she made excellent use of mainly during her junior and senior years, mainly in her major. Like Jan, she also judiciously and strategically sought feedback throughout her college career from the writing center.

Unsolicited Feedback.   Yuko generally did little with the standard marginal or terminal feedback on papers or exams, reading it, sometimes not understanding it or how it was connected to her grade on that paper. In a few cases, the feedback consisted solely of an unexplained, even inexplicable, score. In the aging class, on one assignment she had 90, on another 89, with no other markings whatsoever, no explanation of the basis for these scores. The most useful feedback provided missing information. On an exam asking for the names of two members of the Supreme Court, Yuko's political science teacher wrote in all nine for her.

Many of her professors ignored issues of language on exams and papers or addressed them incidentally, noncommittally, noting that:

Professor J: Some of the ways the sentences read were the way she talks. ... I have no problem with that.

In other cases editing was heavy, as several faculty members considered grammar feedback an important service and aid. Yuko accepted the corrections somewhat impassively, typically neither upset nor intent on focusing on their changes when they came on final drafts, though she carefully incorporated suggestions made on outlines and initial drafts. As for final drafts,

Yuko: ... I rarely look at. (second-term junior)

Solicited Feedback.   Yuko was very adept at getting help she needed or wanted with her work, regularly soliciting feedback on initial drafts or outlines from the writing center and from her social work professors, particularly Phil and Sam, who were extraordinarily generous with their time. On one writing task, Yuko worked with Sam for close to 5 hours over the course of 2 days.

For the major course paper in Phil's class on the cancer support group, he offered to look at an outline or a first draft turned in at least 2 weeks before the paper was due. She worked very hard on it and brought him a six - page outline. They spent between 30 and 60 minutes working on that outline together, and she then left it with him. He returned it to her box with extensive annotations and suggestions on content, organization, and phrasing. She found that feedback on her outline helpful:

Yuko: It was good because he put me comment which I need, what he want, or some suggestion, so it was good to make me think where I need to put more and what I can omit. (first-term senior)

Social work faculty felt that feedback played a role not just in justifying the grades they gave but, more important, in pointing students in the right direction, providing them with correct or additional information, and sometimes suggesting stylistic adjustment. Attempting to achieve these goals through feedback on final drafts seems doomed, however, if someone as conscientious as Yuko basically ignored final-draft feedback. On the other hand, written feedback when it came before or between drafts played an important role in Yuko's development as a student, social worker, and writer of English.

The Writing Center.   Yuko made extensive and flexible use of the writing center during her undergraduate career. But the key to Yuko's successful use of feedback from the writing center was in understanding where they could and could not help her. Initially she had gone for feedback on the grammar and structure of her papers and for more and different ways of expressing her meanings, "some idioms which I never use before." She also consulted writing center tutors when she was blocked on a project, such as her personal statement for admission to graduate school.

But she realized early on that one limitation of feedback from the writing center was the tutors' lack of familiarity with disciplinary conventions. As mentioned earlier, one tutor she worked with had never heard of APA referencing style, not even of the acronym. Others misinterpreted her specialized use of social work vocabulary (as in the earlier example above of the specific social work meaning of *assessment*) and attempted inappropriate interventions in her phrasing. Once she realized this, Yuko turned to faculty and other social work students for feedback related specifically to social work.

Peer Feedback.   Of all the students in this research project, only Yuko regularly asked her peers to look at substantial chunks of her work for content and/or organization rather than strictly language-related issues, although she never felt obliged to make the changes her strong network of both Japanese and American friends suggested. For example, she had two friends read her application for admission to the social work major, but she was unsatisfied with her peers' suggestions and went beyond them to consult with the program director about revisions. In another instance, Yuko suspected that, in assuring her that her draft was fine, her NES friend was reluctant to criticize her paper. But Yuko persisted, finally drawing from the friend an admission that what Yuko had written, though good, was most likely not what the teacher expected. The success of Yuko's hard work on this paper would have been threatened had she not been able to pressure her friend into a more negative evaluation of her draft.

Reliance on peer critique typically worked well for Yuko. She used her consultations wisely, asking her friends for responses to her writing and then making her own decisions about revisions based on her developing sense of disciplinary practices.

In fact, as so often seemed the case with Yuko, she appeared to intuit which responses to her writing she should probably ignore (e.g., on final drafts or Sam's idiosyncratic rewritings) and which would most usefully lead to revisions that would facilitate the social work initiation she sought.

The Role of Reading

Yuko recognized early on that different kinds of readings and different types of courses would require different reading strategies and she used different ones, sometimes shifting from one to another when a new one seemed potentially more useful. For a few courses (e.g., group dynamics), the concepts in the lecture were so difficult for her that she had to do the readings for that class first in order to understand the lecture. In other courses (e.g., political science and anthropology), she also had to do the readings first but that was because the vocabulary used, including proper names in political science, consisted of terms she was unfamiliar with and feared not recognizing in the lecure without first anticipating that these terms would be coming up.

For most of her courses, however, the lectures served to guide her reading, indicating which sections were the most important to the instructor and therefore which ones she would have to concentrate on. Like all students, pressed for time, if she felt she could eliminate some of the reading because it merely repeated the lecture or repeated other readings, she did so, but it was also not unusual for Yuko to read texts over twice, three, as many as five times, until she felt she understood them to her satisfaction. More important, however, she relied on the lectures to orient her reading because as a newcomer to a discipline, the texts were homogenous to her, each portion on the same plane of importance as every other, not layered in terms of importance as they became with experience in the discipline. Adding to the difficulty of perceiving the information in the text as layered were certain teaching practices. Instructors in general-education courses often used quizzes to verify that students had done the readings assigned. If the quizzes focused, as they often did, on ludicrously detailed information from the readings, the appropriate degree of importance of that information within the whole text became difficult to determine. Was it important to know, for example, five different ways that suffragettes used to promote their cause? Or what the pilot who bombed Hiroshima was thinking on the flight back? The fact that such items became the focus of attention on a quiz gave them disproportionate importance.

As early as her sophomore year, as Yuko determined that factual material from one course was being repeated in another, she would then read not for content but for "perspective." That is, even though the same information was being covered, Yuko recognized that each discipline—history, political science, or social work—valued a different aspect of the information, and she read to determine which angle the particular discipline in focus was taking and how it valued or weighted the same material.

Using different strategies was essential because readings played different roles for the faculty as well. In interviews, faculty described readings variously as lecture substitutes, so that it would be possible to do only the readings, not attend lectures, and do well in the course; lecture extenders, so that what could not be covered in class would appear in the readings; and also in some cases, as irrelevant, so that it would be possible to attend the lectures and not do the readings at all and still do well in the course. In some classes, so much reading was assigned that Yuko (and her peers, she said) had no realistic hope of completing it and so they simply stopped reading altogether. In other classes (biology and anthropology), Yuko felt that she was not actually reading but rather gathering definitions. Conveniently, in the anthropology text the important terms were in bold so Yuko (and no doubt others) searched for them and skipped the rest of the actual text.

Yuko's status as a learner of English meant that her experience with the language was circumscribed and therefore caused her an additional set of challenges. She found herself needing to read texts just before exams in order to remember what she had read. Laying down and holding memories required more work of Yuko in English than in Japanese.

Second, the nature of the readings could cause problems. The first set of readings in her local studies class were folk tales. She read them with understanding and relative ease, though she found them boring, but could not determine how they fit in, what she was supposed to retain from them, what to highlight, as she said. Another set of readings in that course came from the popular press. Many of the texts are striking, sometimes moving, first-person, narrative, or journalistic accounts of mining strikes, land removals, rural poverty, bullying by the timber industry, and the hardships of daily life. What was difficult for her to understand was not, for example, how pigs were taken to market in the 1930s, but what the point was.

> Yuko: I just read, read, read. But … it doesn't say anything important.
>   (first-term senior)

Again, she could not figure out what to take note of.

The journalistic style of these articles, filled with metaphors and physical descriptions, created difficulties. She realized in addition that she had become accustomed to and could read with greater ease text-books and other digested material and that she liked the academic style of organization there.

> Yuko: The academic writing is always in some certain flow, you know, the
>   logical flow. But those articles sometimes, you know, back and for-
>   ward, kind of thing. So that was really hard to me. I need much time
>   to read those. (first-term senior)

Because these texts were journalistic and not academic, it was difficult for Yuko to use the academic reading strategies she had developed to determine what the point or the main issues were of the text she was assigned. The final reading for this local studies course was a 600-page novel. Thus, as was often the case for these bilingual students, what was intended to make fewer, and more palatable, demands on domestic students disrupted the understandings and greatly increased the burden for academically oriented students like Yuko.

THE DEVELOPMENT OF OTHER SOCIAL WORK SKILLS

The development of literacy skills was unquestionably an important aim for Yuko both as required by courses across the curriculum and even more so in the pursuit of professionalization through the social work curriculum. As noted, Yuko had more demands on her to develop a range of writing skills for a range of purposes than did any of the other focal students. However, despite all the attention to writing and reading in social work, in fact, other language and language-related skills (such as interviewing, organizing intervention programs, handling group dynam-ics) were generally assumed to eclipse the importance of literacy for BSSWs, though writing assignments were often used to promote those skills. Primary among them was listening attentively, because it under-girded several of the others. Others included speaking to clients, inter-viewing clients, handling human relations, interacting with people, and accepting diversity of all kinds.[37] The focus on skills other than strictly lit-eracy skills was manifested in the amount of course time devoted to their development. Several courses required oral presentations. Others required group work but not as a means of decreasing student or teacher workload by sharing it or conglomerating it, nor as a means of pooling individual talents and resources, but as a means of learning how to behave and work with groups of people. The social work curriculum was, in fact, the only one that, in assigning group work, actually tried to help their students learn how to do it. (See the section on Group Work.)

In the junior year, two courses were devoted to role playing. The role plays were difficult for Yuko partly because she was expected to play roles she was not familiar with in this culture—doctors, employees of the utility company who were involved in suspending services to people who had not paid bills on time, grandmothers on welfare, teenage boys in trouble with the police—and partly because of the demands it made on her English. The course instructor allowed Yuko to perform her role plays last in the class so that she could see models performed by her classmates first. Yuko talked about how nervous she was in the role-play class.

> Yuko: I sweat, my hands, kind [of] thing. But it's OK. I learn a lot. I see how I can react. ... next week we're going to start client who has problem, you know, like angry person, crying person. So maybe I will see more interest and difficulty. (second-term junior)

In fact, in this curriculum there was a lot of doing: two semesters devoted to role playing, three semesters of field practice (600 hours required to graduate), curricular requirements to volunteer at social agencies, a social work student organization devoted to creating fund raisers and other helping activities. In her final interview, Yuko noted that what promoted her education the most in social work had been her field placement work, where she had to learn to listen and reflect back what she heard, to interview using appropriate questions to bring out the information required or the emotional response she sought, to self-reflect in order to recognize where her own biases got in the way of helping a client, to use appropriate body language, and to access community resources.

This last skill was no trivial matter for BSSWs, and certainly not for Yuko. Developing an awareness of the community services available, how to access them, and who was eligible for them was not specifically addressed in the students' course work and had instead to be gleaned by word of mouth (from peers, supervisors, even clients) or from field practice. There were many students in Yuko's cohort who had had occasion during their lives to make use of social services. Obviously, for those students, information about certain community resources was a part of their unconscious knowledge about their environment; these students brought with them some awareness of the existence and sometimes the range of social services in the community. Yuko faced a fairly steep learning curve in the different town, country, and culture where she studied. But with her amazing resourcefulness, she appeared to maneuver through information gathering certainly without complaint if not without trouble, referring clients to services she thought appropriate and even compiling a pamphlet on free transportation services available locally for disabled/handicapped clients.

Volunteer work was also a required part of the students' degree program, and it was up to them to find places to volunteer, contact the organizations, and negotiate the duties. Yuko's dozens of activities included volunteering at a children's hospital, a homeless shelter, and a sexual assault center.[38]

Yuko's main focus as an undergraduate was certainly her academic work but at the same time she maintained richly varied interests and activities that allowed her to develop a range of academic, nonacademic, and professional skills that went far beyond academic literacy or English-language learning.

SOCIOACADEMIC RELATIONSHIPS

Peers

In addition to her network of Japanese, American, and other international friends, Yuko had built a vital, strong, and mutually beneficial socioacademic relationship with members of her cohort in social work, especially with Linda, Wayne, and Maggie, as mentioned earlier. This was the positive side of her socioacademic relationships. The negative side was the factionalism among her cohort.

Trained by profession to encourage self-expression, the social work faculty was unwilling to silence or to exercise heavy-handed control over disruptive students in their classes, even when they insisted on bringing up issues of strictly personal concern, why a student got such and such a grade on a paper, for example.[39]

Yuko began commenting on this behavior during the first semester of the junior year, becoming increasingly upset by it. As the students took class time with their personal agendas, other students began to ask them to stop wasting class time, which in turn led to the development of disputes taking even more class time. Yuko was exasperated to have to sit through the classes these students commandeered and witness their irritating behavior. Ever resourceful, however, one day in an interview in midsemester Yuko announced that she had solved the problem. She had decided that she would abstract herself from the situation, sit back, and try to learn something about human behavior, interaction, and intervention by observing the class scene. She started taking notes on her classmates' disruptiveness. No more frustration or irritation; instead, an opportunity to learn.

Near the end of the term in this class, perhaps the last day, the professor made a kind of speech about the behavior of the class, chiding them for their unprofessional attitude toward each other. As Yuko explained it later, as the professor talked, she saw the embarrassment and anger on the faces of her friends, Linda and Wayne, as they listened to this rebuke, students who like her had not participated in the disruptions. Realizing the injustice of this blanket blame, she resolved that she owed it to these friends to defend them. She waited until Professor O was free in his office, went in, and told him she thought his comments in class had been unfair! As is clear here, Yuko's educational experience was directly affected by the behavior of her peers and, if not for Yuko's own resourcefulness in some instances, turning disadvantage to advantage, sometimes detrimentally affected. Outside of the classroom, however, Yuko's primary socioacademic relationship was with her three study group friends, a relationship that was nearly entirely positive because it was so emotionally supportive, giving Yuko a safe place to discuss grievances, problems, or victories, and a place to be cherished and admired.

"So Sometimes I Think I Don't Need That Study Group."   Yuko's case was unusual in this research in part because her three-member study group was such a success and also in part because it was stable across her social work years, with group members taking many of the same courses together, even collateral courses. The group built a strong sense of camaraderie, defining themselves as a unity and describing themselves in the fall of their junior year as "proud" of this group. Though never meeting outside the school day, they ate lunch together fairly often and exchanged opinions on their teachers, their course work, and the results of their exams. They were all successful, if anxious, students and admirably organized in their approach to studying for exams, which was their main group function academically. At the end of her junior year, Yuko said that bonding with them was the best thing that had happened to her academically all year.

Nevertheless, despite these good social and emotional connections with Linda, Wayne, and Maggie, Yuko commented:

Yuko: Actually, I prefer to study alone. (first-term senior)

Because, as an NNES, she had to spend more time with the material in order to understand it, Yuko would prepare carefully before the study group met and would arrive already knowing the material they were meeting to study. The other members of the group could afford to wait until the actual meeting to start processing or learning the material, so they were never as well informed as Yuko. Also, as Yuko explained it, the three others were reentry students and as such experienced considerable test anxiety, which they attempted to deal with by going into great detail in their exam preparations rather than focusing primarily on main points. The youngest in the group, Yuko claimed to be able to remember the details of what the reading or the lecture covered with a simple prompt of the main point. This ability was reflected in her note-taking style in lectures, where she tended to produce lists, noting only the most important points the professor touched on. Her NES group mates, on the other hand, took, or needed to take, much more detailed notes:

> Yuko: Basically, Maggie and Linda, they took notes just like talking, I mean, you know, everything what they [the professors] said ... everything what he's talking, what he said, everything. (second-term junior)

Yuko felt that this excess of detail bogged her down in the study group meetings. Yet she continued meeting with this group partly because

> Yuko: That's a good review for me. ... I can see [if] my answer is OK or good, or if not enough, I can get some more feedback. (second-term junior)

Both structural factors and individual characteristics of the players helped to account for the development of this very supportive group, including the ice-breaking activities of the first day of the first social work class, the welcoming stance of the social work student organization, the requirement for social work students to do fieldwork outside classes, and the attitude of friendliness and acceptance promoted by the social work program as part of professional development. Also, as returning students, Linda, Maggie, and Wayne perhaps gravitated toward another somewhat marginalized or nontraditional student or they saw in Yuko someone whose seriousness of purpose matched their own. Yuko's constant references to these three, to what they said, to what they thought and did, to how they reacted, made it clear that this group played a valuable role in her undergraduate studies, and she used their behaviors as examples of possible cultural, personal, and academic bench stones.

Perhaps even without this group Yuko would have found her own way on the strength of her individual talents, values, and stamina. It is an open question what problems might have been spared Jan and Yang had the institutional structures within which they worked provided the opportunity for similar socioacademic relations.

Course-Sponsored Group Work.   Yuko had extensive spontaneous, unevaluated group-work experiences with her small social work group, Linda, Wayne, and Maggie, but only three evaluated group-work experiences. Although group projects generally do not benefit L2 students as much as might be expected (Leki, 2001), Yuko was spared the worst aspects of unsuccessful group work, in part because she had already been in classes with the same social work students for several years, she was sufficiently assertive to be clear on what she wanted and did not want, and she was respected in the program and known to do well. But she also experienced the only project in 5 years' worth of research data that began with a class-long discussion addressing some of the issues inherent in doing group projects and how to deal with problems that might arise.

The professor began this class on social policy by asking the students what they thought of the group-work requirement as stated on the syllabus. Never intimidated by their professors, the students said it was vague. He then had the students describe the kinds of problems they had experienced in previous group work and gave the class 20 minutes to formulate a better policy, focusing on four questions that reflected the problems they had noted:

- What constitutes not contributing to the group?
- How do you notify the group member of a problem?
- How should the instructor be involved and when?
- What action should be taken if a group member continues nonparticipation?

After a great deal of in-class discussion, the students came to a consensus and committed themselves to following the new policy they had developed together.

Potentially less beneficial to Yuko, however, was the project in the local studies class, which began with the same initial mistakes as so many other group-work projects. (See Leki, 2001.) Groups were assigned or chosen on the 1st or 2nd day of class when the students did not know each other. Furthermore, students were asked then and there, before getting a real feel for the content of the course or where their project might contribute to the knowledge building of the course, to decide on topics.

Yuko's group's project was a report on a town in the area with an especially interesting history. Two of the group members had grown up in the town, knew it well themselves, and had family that could inform them. Only Yuko knew nothing about the town. At first she was unsure what she could contribute to the group and seemed to want to allow them to lead her.

Yuko: So, I said, you know, if they have anything what I can do, then I'll
do anything. So tell me what we need to do … . (second-term
junior)

However, she quickly settled on an interest of her own and set to work
researching her choice, a summary of the town's more recent history, a
choice that was well received. More important, the other group members
were eager to share what they knew about this town with Yuko and spent
time at the group meetings excitedly sharing their knowledge with her.
The ultimate presentation went well, and in all, Yuko was satisfied with
the outcome, with her own contribution, and with how much she ended
up learning from the other group members, whom she considered welcoming, generous, and helpful to her.[40]
The fact that Yuko had identified an aspect of the topic that she knew
she could research by herself, one that added pertinently to the presentation, was an important factor in making the experience relatively successful for Yuko and the group. As she said:

Yuko: … [when] I couldn't know what I need to do in that group that
was really hard. But once I decided what I do and I said, I do this,
then they said, OK, you can do that. Then in that way, they are
really, I think they offer a lot of advantage. … They really understand I don't know the area, so they really help me to understand,
I think. And also, that's why I [wanted to] have the areas which I
can do by myself. I'm not dependent on [them] completely. Only
half. [Laughing] (second-term junior)

Partly because of her own committedness and self-assurance and partly
because she was lucky in her group members, Yuko was able to benefit
both socially and academically from these experiences. She did not glow
from the experience of group work as Ben had, nor did she need the academic support of a group in order to accomplish her assigned tasks as he
had. Also unlike Ben's situation where mutual support was crucial to
understanding the problem being dealt with, the formal group work Yuko
participated in did not really require a group to complete, the group
assignment being rather an administrative convenience, as were most of
the formal group assignments encountered in this research. In informal
group-work sessions, it was often her peers who benefited from Yuko's
understandings and organization rather than the other way around. Still,
her formal and informal groups were far more successful than Jan's or
Yang's had been. In the end, academically, the group-work projects were
neither a plague nor great boon, but the informal work, the socioacademic contact with her classmates, with her little clique, proved to be
socially quite vital.

Relations With Social Work Faculty

With Yuko's academic excellence, independence, self-confidence, and participation in a close, satisfying socioacademic group, she was not much affected by her relationships with the instructors of her courses in the way that both Jan and Yang were. She was generally admired by faculty, and though she did not work to make herself stand out as Jan did, Yuko also often wrote little notes of explanation, apology, or thanks on her exam papers to instructors, apologizing for bad handwriting or grammatical errors. For example, constructing herself as conscientious and concerned to do well, on an exam in political science in a starred box at the top, she wrote:

> I'm sorry!! I promise (hope?) I will cover the failure of this exam at the next one. Have a nice break.

But Yuko did spend a great deal of time consulting with faculty on writing assignments. Although she never developed any of the proverbial close mentoring relationships with faculty that have sometimes been described as changing a student's life, she did rely a great deal on her generous adviser, Sam, for direction about a variety of issues in her academic life. And she also put her social work training into practice by analyzing differences between her two closest faculty mentors, Sam and Phil:

Interviewer: So how do you feel about the difference in the approaches [of these two professors] to reacting to your writing assignments?
Yuko: Maybe personality issue. Sam is academic educator. Phil is practitioner therapist. So they look different things in different perspective. ... like Phil he want everything broad, vague, but he wants some certain core of the answer in the theme of the essay. Sam like systems, all systems, processes. ... he is kind of from bureaucratic background. (first-term senior)

It was difficult not to be continually impressed with this young woman's astute sense of her human surroundings.

SPECIAL CIRCUMSTANCES
FOR INTERNATIONAL STUDENTS

What kinds of special circumstances did Yuko have to face as an international student? What she reported mostly from general-education classes were instances of (sometimes even funny) classroom references to historical or cultural circumstances that were assumed to be shared among the class members but that she was unfamiliar with. However, even in social work, with faculty's much more careful attention to positionality issues and sensitivity not to exclude anyone, Yuko was at times called up short by the juncture between different sets of background assumptions.

General Education

Instances of cross-cultural snags occurred more persistently in Yuko's general-education courses than in the social work curriculum. An item on a political science exam, for example, looked like this:

> Question: There are eight associate justices that sit on the Supreme Court. Name two.
> [Yuko's answer] _____ & <u>Sandra</u>

Yuko was lost when the political science class turned to discussions of current political figures. She knew, as she said, "the big ones" in American politics but beyond that, as she said,

> Yuko: I was kind of out of [it]. (second-term sophomore)

Yuko's special circumstances as a university student who did not grow up with the language or in the country where she studied were often related to vocabulary items in her general-education classes. Yuko lost points on a multiple-choice biology exam because she thought a lynx was something like a rabbit, and so assumed it was prey rather than predator. But she also had difficulty capturing references in political science to such local North American cultural items as *Roe v. Wade* and creationism. The words were unfamiliar. In her notes Yuko had

> "Roby Way,"

then written over this with a marking pen:

> "Rose v. Wade,"

and finally

> "Roe v. Wade."

As Yuko explained,

> Yuko: At first I thought that was one word! [Laughing] I couldn't find what she's talking about, I couldn't find it even in textbook. (second-term sophomore)

As she prepared a writing assignment on abortion issues in her political science class, Yuko was unable to determine even who was pro- and who was antiabortion and what the supporting logic was on either side until she looked the positions up in the course textbook, which had a section laying out the issues. It was as though her course notes and general readings were encrypted and she had to turn to the course text for decoding.

Yuko's paper on evolution began:

Since my country, Japan, has very small Christian population, I had not heard the idea of creationism until I learn American history in the United States.

As she remarked in an interview:

Yuko: I didn't know even creationism existed in the world, you know. (second-term sophomore)

In her local studies class, Yuko struggled with the references to a variety of tacitly known features of cultural life, but particularly nerve wracking was the fact that the final exam was to be based on a single book, *The Dollmaker*, a book written in dialect. As Yuko described it, she eventually understood that "th" stood for "the," for example, as the author's way of capturing oral forms, but Yuko's description of her initial confusion confronted with the novel is, well, hilarious:

Yuko: It's not about like I expected. ... like for example, it start from the scene she use her mule to stop the car. And she talk to the car. And there is some description about how mule feels. Or that kind of thing. So I couldn't understand until like page 3 what this story is going on. Because I thought the first scene is this one lady who has the [a] baby. But suddenly, you know, she talk to the mule continuously. And the description is how dark outside it is, how mule [is] scared about the outside and like that thing. So, I'm thinking like, this is the story about mules couple. You know. Mules female have power over this mule. Then, finally, I could get [it]; this is a human being who is talking to the mule. So everything like that. (second-term junior)

Though it seemed amusing in the retelling, it was frustrating for her to have to spend time merely figuring out that she was not dealing with "mules couple."

In her history class, contrary to her expectation, she had a hard time understanding the material on the war with Japan, speculating that having learned the Japanese perspective made it difficult to follow the rationales presented in class. (See the section on Ideological education for an example of the rationale.) At the suggestion of a Japanese friend, to help herself see this other perspective, she read a short book in Japanese about American history, one of the many specially prepared for Japanese students studying in United States.

The history class proved problematic in other ways as well. Although Yuko was nearly always quiet in class, rarely volunteering an opinion or an answer, whenever she was called on, she always responded immediately and pertinently (making it clear that her silence was not in the least passive). In the history class, when she was specifically asked to contribute, it was often in order to get the Japanese perspective on something like the bombings of Hiroshima and Nagasaki, forcing her into the position of being the spokesperson for Japan. She recounted a particularly sensitive moment in her history discussion class:

> Yuko: [The history] TA sometimes mention to me, or sometimes joking, "Maybe you can give the other side better than I could," something like that. He was talking about George Bush and "he was fighting in World War II, and especially to Japan, so he was shooting at Japs ... er ... Japanese!" [Imitates TA's stumbling over the derogatory term, with expression of embarrassment.] ... But because I, English is not my native language, so I don't feel anything if somebody say "Jap" or anything. ... I know the meaning is not good ... but I don't feel anything. But because he tried to change the word, everybody see [looked at] me. (first-term sophomore)

Nevertheless, when this rather thoughtless TA called on Yuko for her opinion or perspective, she took the floor in a normal tone of voice, not at all intimidated, and spoke her piece.

Social Work

Social work was much more predictable, but issues arose there as well. For the first written assignment in social work, Yuko's inclination was to do as she would later do regularly, bring a first draft to the professor to learn if she was on track. But, as she explained, some of the teachers in social work thought that giving extra help to NNESs was not fair to domestic students and so she held back until the professor invited all his students to do so (although for the most part they did not).

At other times when everything seemed under control, problems would suddenly arise to remind Yuko of her extra burdens. In one of her social work classes, she had carefully prepared for one of the essay exam questions:

What was the difference between the settlement house movement and temperance society movement? But instead of asking the question straight-forwardly, the professor asked the students to imagine that Barbara Walters was interviewing someone in each of those movements. Such a frame would have made the essay exam format more informal and so easier for the domestic students but made it harder for Yuko because she had no real idea who Barbara Walters was or what she did and because she would now have to switch to a whole different approach to answering the question.

Yuko felt a disadvantage as well because of her lack of experience with the more raw sides of life that social workers might encounter.

> Yuko: ... some student did the volunteer [in] those agencies, they know how they react, how they use the word, the terms, or you know. Sometimes too teenagers will use really frank words. But [usually] we just use really polite words. I need to distinguish each of those. (first-term senior)

Yuko's contacts with U.S. society had for the most part kept her out of touch with those teenagers and their "frank words," so she was inexperienced at even distinguishing them, let alone knowing how to respond.

Not surprisingly, Yuko's deep immersion in social work English had linguistic repercussions for Yuko. She lost some of her fluency in Japanese and she realized that she was learning a great deal of specialized, professional vocabulary in English that she was unable to translate into Japanese.

The special circumstances facing Yuko, then, created both hardships and advantages for her. There was cultural catching up to do in several of her courses. Her will to assert herself as an individual was sometimes thwarted by those who fell easily into seeing her only as one of a category. In taking on facets of another culture and language, like anyone else in this situation, she faced the loss of some of the closeness to her home culture and language, despite her regular phone contacts with home. In all, however, being an international student, particularly in the social work program was not painful to Yuko. She had a strong sense of self-esteem and a considerable amount of experience that justified that sense. There is no question that Yuko worked extremely hard to bring this about but it was clear that her experiences as an international student contributed smoothly, if not effortlessly, to her personal growth and the strengthening of her identity and capacities.

Faculty Views on Having International or NNES Students in Their Classes

Among all Yuko's teachers who were interviewed, not a single faculty member felt L2 students in their classes created an extra burden or problems, although a few in general-education courses (especially those that enroll hundreds of students in large lectures) seemed to have a kind of passive, distant attitude toward them, suggesting that because they had chosen to study in the United States, whatever problems they faced were of their own making. One biology professor felt that L2 students needed to take more opportunity to practice English instead of talking together in their own language, as he heard them do in the library. Another felt that international students were at a disadvantage because domestic students, though not "actively discriminating" against them in his class, did not seem to be interested in interacting with them and left them out of the lab group work, although he did not seem to feel obligated in any way to ensure the NNESs' integration. He felt the students had trouble grasping concepts because of lack of language, but

> Biology TA: That's part of having to assimilate into another culture. I'd hate to have to go to Japan and go to a Japanese university. It would suck. I'd have to work hard.[41]

Unlike what has been reported elsewhere (Johns, 1991a), the humanities and social science faculty at this school generally felt that international students were an important addition to their classes because they added cultural diversity. Among the positive attributes mentioned: They work hard, have a strong "work ethic" (social work), are motivated, have greater "drive" than the domestic students (biology), show up more than the others (history), already have had cross-cultural experiences and so can understand them better than can the provincial domestic students from the area (anthropology), can give live testimonials for cross-cultural behavior, such as on the use of body language (social work).

What Made Life Harder for International Students?   The heavily context-embedded nature of social work practice and the way language use intersected with the practice environment were identified as creating problems for L2 students in social work.

> Professor M: A lot of what we do in social work is knowing the community, knowing the resources. I wonder if it's hard coming from another country or culture to get in, to navigate what you need to know. Especially where English isn't their primary language. ... because they really need to know the community that they're working with, they need to know the resources and not be afraid to go to the phone and call up and say, what's the eligibility to get into this shelter, what's the criteria? And I wonder if their language doesn't present a barrier for them ...

Given the closeness of the social work faculty, how well they knew their students, and the small number of internationals or L2 students in the program, the social work faculty realized Yuko was a focal student for this research and volunteered statements of their admiration of her.

Professor F: … I'm amazed that she manages with these old Alzheimer's patients, some suffering from dementia, and she has to communicate with them. One deaf patient couldn't hear what was going on so Yuko just asked her to come and sit next to her.

Professor S: … she studies hard, but probably beyond that, her involvement with other people is amazing. … people love to have Yuko in any group project; they know Yuko is really going to do her part. They love that. They really see her as a very dedicated, committed student. And people have really enjoyed her. … She brings a different perspective to class. … So it was a wonderful resource to have Yuko in the class.

Finally, commenting on international students generally, one of the social work faculty members, Professor T, remarked with regret that most domestic students could but do not seek out and benefit from their presence.

Professor T: Unfortunately, it's the case everywhere, whenever someone from another culture comes, the people who are hosting the person don't know what a treasure they have in their midst, the opportunity that they have.

Like many students studying outside their home languages and cultures, Yuko faced a range of circumstances that probably made studying more difficult for her. But she also won the admiration of many of those she interacted with and was resilient and self-confident enough to deal with the difficulties in stride.

IDEOLOGICAL EDUCATION

Nevertheless, experiences like those in her history class demonstrate the degree to which Yuko, like all the other students, was witness to, if not always the subject of, instances of ideological reinforcement, where what were presumed to be unassailable and shared values in the United States were thoughtlessly pitted against the interests or values of others. For example, in the same history class where Yuko was asked to be the spokesperson for the Japanese response to the bombing of Hiroshima and Nagasaki, she reported that at the next meeting the instructor expressed the opinion that bombing the Japanese twice had the salutary effect of having Japan surrender to the United States, rather than be invaded by the USSR, which he declared would have been worse:

> Yuko: It's more terrible [than being bombed], he said: "We saved the Japanese from communists!" (first-term sophomore)

As crude as the "better dead than red" point of view was, the longest, crudest, and most egregious example of bigotry came in social work despite the fact that the social work faculty worked hard and consciously at being sensitive to and accepting of different ways of being in the world.[42]

In this particular class, which prepared students to do social work interviews, the students role played participants in possible social work encounters. Because the instructor had lived in a Minnesota town that had received a group of Hmong refugees, she elected to devote two class periods to role playing interactions in an Asian refugee community. Unfortunately, because such a community did not exist in the location of this study, the student social workers were being asked to play out what they imagined would be the behavior of Hmong family members without knowing anything at all about them, being thus forced back on stereotypes of Asians lumped together, a few comments by Yuko, who was asked to speak for all Asians, and the "expertise" of the teacher.[43] The instructor began by invoking model-minority discourse (McKay & Wong, 1996), noting that Asian immigrants worked hard and helped others in the Asian community achieve their primary goal (from field notes):

> Teacher: ... and it doesn't matter if they're Vietnamese or Chinese, they just all help each other to assimilate.

But then came the inexplicable Hmong:

> Teacher: The Hmong haven't assimilated or integrated like the other Asian refugees did, not as well as they did. They don't buy up houses and live the American dream. They dominate the public housing in X city instead of becoming rich and moving out like the other Asians do.

They weren't the "instant achievers" that other Asian immigrants were. By way of background the instructor offered the information that the Hmong were nomadic, poor, sometimes blue-eyed because of Swedish genes (!), insular, and illiterate:

> Teacher: I don't know if they've invented a writing system yet but last I heard, they didn't have a writing system. ... It's time they get culturally acclimatized. They're nomadic anyway, so you may as well be a nomad to here and embrace the future and that's

> here. ... They are nomads; they have no language. ... But they
> seek each other out so that once one goes somewhere others
> follow; I mean, wouldn't you? That way you can keep up your
> festivals.

She expressed her puzzlement over their inability to successfully achieve
"the American dream," to get on the "American success track," involving
themselves instead with "triads," which she explained were crime-oriented
youth gangs. One of the students seemed overwhelmed by the unfath-
omable obstinacy being described and commented.

> Student: If the entire culture is in a housing project and they don't care
> what happens to their kids, I guess there's nothing I can do.

But the instructor excused this behavior by referring to the "repressive
culture" the Hmong come from.

> Teacher: ... you have to give them a lot of credit. ... It's just part of their
> culture to stay there [in the housing projects?]; they have won-
> derful festivals and good food.

In sympathy with their plight, Yuko's friend Linda offered the information
that "these people are used to being arrested in their homes." The
instructor then suggested that in situations where the Other was so inexplicable, it was important to remember that "these are traumatized people" and then turned to Yuko for agreement

> Yuko: I have no idea, my friends don't want to talk about what hap-
> pened in their country. ... but they don't want an American social
> worker in your house.

Yuko then volunteered her opinion that even if someone were a gang
member that did not necessarily mean they behaved badly to or were
regarded as bad by their parents or families; she noted that poor people
did not necessarily behave so differently from others.

> Yuko: I think it's the same thing for middle-class people; they [young
> people] do things outside the home that the parents aren't aware of.

Other students then also began to some degree to challenge the assumptions underlying the discussion. When the instructor expressed worries
about Hmong parents being able to understand what the social worker
might be trying to communicate about the danger of gangs, one student
reminded the instructor that

> Student: ... someone who can't read could also be smart enough to understand what's going on.

In spite of these mild protests, the students presumably came away from those two classes with created or confirmed stereotyped images of Asians, whose goal was assimilation and getting on the American success track and who experienced no problems doing so, a success made obvious by the fact that the instructor did not see them at her agency and that this success was achieved by most "typical" Asians. They learned that an important reason for maintaining a community was to make festivals possible and that there was something quite unusual about the Hmong. But the students learned nothing about complexities of historical or social context in the painfully trivialized experience of Asian immigrants or refugees. This perhaps well-meant but repugnant attempt to prepare the social work students for contact with immigrants was pathetically successful in inducing one student to ask where she might meet such people. The university's international house was suggested, and the student turned to Yuko with a request that Yuko accompany her there some day. Perhaps facing "such people" alone was too frightening a prospect.

CONCLUSION

The social work program defined itself as resolutely open to diverse people and cultures. It worked at training its students to accept, even seek out, experiences divergent from their own. Thus in many ways it was an ideal environment for academic study for a person like Yuko, so intelligently hard working. On the other hand, because social work deals with the public and with individuals within community contexts, one essential part of social work training, fieldwork, could potentially pose quite dramatic and even overwhelming challenges to anyone from outside the particular community they worked in, and the farther away the more difficult. Because Yuko herself was so talented, flexible, and resourceful, social work faculty was never really called on to intervene in any way in Yuko's academic experience to make it more comfortable or otherwise smooth the way for her. Nevertheless, they went out of their way generally to make students feel welcome and their contributions accepted in their classes, almost to a fault in the case of this cohort, as discussed earlier.

However, as the faculty recognized, although it has perhaps not been sufficiently recognized in the literature on the experiences of L2 students, Yuko's path was made easier by being part of a cohort and, more important, part of a small socioacademic group that worked together closely. She was able to draw considerable academic reassurance and emotional support from her collegial relationship with them that teachers, however admiring or available, were unlikely to be able to supply. At the same time, it was clear that these domestic students relied on Yuko most likely more than she relied on them for academic help. One of the most thought-provoking aspects of Yuko's approach to her education was the degree to which she took charge of it to accomplish her own goals, from choosing particular courses to choosing writing and research topics to readjusting her expectations for her classroom experiences (e.g., determining to learn from the disputing students rather than allowing them to waste her time). This also meant that she wanted to know quite exactly what the rules, directions, and guidelines were—and then she decided how, whether, and to what degree to respond to them. She carefully managed her relations with faculty, determining both what suited her best and what would work best on each of them to achieve the results she wanted. In all, her undergraduate experiences were rich, varied, and successful in great part because of the happy intersection of Yuko's own constellation of traits, the environment of the social work program, and the significant socioacademic relationships that she developed there.

6

University Literacy

The four students reported on in these case studies—Ben in engineering, Yang in nursing, Jan in marketing, and Yuko in social work—were all ultimately successful undergraduates, with Ben, Jan, and Yuko going on to graduate work in their respective fields. For Ben and Yuko, despite unpleasant disruptions in their work caused by their peers, academic life went smoothly, drawing on but not taxing their talents for evaluating their situations and responding to them positively. Academic life was a far greater struggle for Yang, partly because of the language demands of the nursing program and her inability to ever fully manage them, and for Jan, at least until he was able to develop a satisfying network of socioacademic relations and a desirable identity.

In these students' general-education courses, although their experiences varied from course to course, overall their assigned writing bore little resemblance to the kind of essays and research papers they learned to create in 1st-year writing courses. Some of the general-education writing was very formulaic (biology lab reports); in other cases, the only writing required in the course at all was on essay or short-answer exams (history); the purpose of another chunk of assigned writing was to ascertain completion of certain other activities (reading the newspaper in sociology or attending events in signing).

In their majors, their experiences varied. Because of the heavy reliance on group-work projects in engineering and in marketing, Ben and Jan participated in preparations for writing but rarely actually wrote anything themselves. Yang was plagued not only by academic writing assignments she considered off the point of her nursing education but worse by relentless, high-risk, excruciatingly time-consuming Nursing Care Plans, as she

233

picked her way through the minefield of her nursing education, working diligently to not call negative attention to her language problems. Yuko, on the other hand, came to view the kinds of writing she was assigned in social work as useful to developing a legitimate skill needed for her professionalization as a social worker. Though certainly her writing never became indistinguishable from that of her domestic peers, her intelligence, talent, intuitiveness, and ability and willingness to work hard and strategically resulted in a highly successful undergraduate career.

This chapter summarizes the findings of this study in relation to the four focal students' literacy work at the university in general-education courses and in their majors and to the role of their writing courses in preparing them for that work.

WRITING AT THE UNIVERSITY: LESS THAN EXPECTED

Before embarking on this research project, I believed what nearly all the faculty I interviewed believed, that learning to write well was a core requirement for university students, that L2 students in particular would be burdened by the extensive writing that would be required of them after they left ESL/writing classes, and that writing was central to their success at the university and in the professions they were being educated for. But the story for these students at least proved to be more complicated and made me come to question those assumptions and not only the centrality of writing to the academic experiences of these students but, along with that, the role played in those experiences by 1st-year writing, ESL, and ESL writing courses.

By writing I mean the production of text, including course or lecture notes. I recognize that many composition professionals use a broader definition of writing that includes, in some sense, all the preparation for writing or the entire process that results in text. In referring to "writing to learn" these researchers may have in mind the learning that comes as a part of that broader writing preparation and process. I prefer to maintain my more narrow definition for several reasons. First, the focal students often expressed the sense of a clear distinction between various preparations for writing and writing itself. Furthermore, even in the broader definitions of writing, it is the actual texts produced that are evaluated as evidence of growth and learning. The texts are, institutionally, the *sine qua non* of the evidence of learning whereas the preparations and processes accompanying text production may be only minimally present or may even be undetectable. Finally, the nature of L2 writing, with its greater capacity to call attention to itself as text, suggests the appropriateness of grounding the definition of writing in text.

The literacy experiences of the four students in this study spanned a range. Yuko's experiences outside English classes were probably closest to the canonical assumptions of writing professionals. Her submitted and evaluated work included academic papers, research papers, self-analyses, reports, essay exams, journals, short-response papers, book reports, and her senior-portfolio commentaries. But at the other end of the spectrum was Ben, with no research papers or academic papers, an in-class journal in one class, essay exams in one history class, and minor writing participation on engineering reports submitted as group projects. In all, the writing modes the students were assigned reflected fairly well research findings on types of writing assignments made across the curriculum, mostly informative (rather than persuasive or personal/expressive) with the professor as already-knowing audience (Melzer, 2003). Few of their assignments resembled essays or even standard research papers of the type practiced in writing classes. The students' writing tasks included nonevaluated writing like taking notes, with Yang copying many of hers from her teachers or peers and Jan (at least in the first 2 years or so) using his as a means of studying for exams by copying his notes over and over. Writing assignments were a serious burden only to Yang and mainly as a result of her fear of having her weak English skills on display. Issues of contrastive rhetoric were entirely absent from both the students' and the teachers' comments.[44]

The Impact of Writing on Student Development

The focal students generally succeeded in their writing tasks, even when they did not actually do the writing themselves. That is, they fully participated in the writing events by actively working within the groups that discussed the projects to be written up. As a result of this active participation, by the end of their undergraduate years, even Ben and Jan felt fairly confident about their ability to respond to writing demands in their majors.

But in fact the students themselves rarely on their own brought up writing assignments; other features of their educational lives were far more salient to them most of the time unless an interview date happened to fall on the same day an assignment was due and so took a more fronted position in their minds. In sum, writing was a part of these students' educational experience but not at all central.

In fact, as I worked with these students intensively for 5 years, reading their work, observing their classes, and talking to their professors, it began to seem that they had few writing experiences that promoted their intellectual or disciplinary growth in any way *particular to writing itself.* Although the students were asked at every interview session about their writing and about what they were learning from doing the writing assigned, in other words, although they were continually prompted to look for an educational benefit in their writing assignments, typically it was the work preparatory to writing—the readings, experiments, data gathering, and discussions—that the students credited with fostering their learning. What writing assignments did was to occasion prolonged focused attention on a topic. For this reason, quite a bit of learning took place incidental to writing, but the kinds of discovery of insight or meaning that writing professionals have either assumed or found with other student writing rarely showed up here, at least in the students' conscious understandings of their experiences. Also for this group of students, writing nearly always essentially recorded a preexisting reality because it was intended to display to the professor that the students had correctly manipulated the material and possibly learned it or something about it.[45] Although it would be difficult to argue from the data collected in this study that writing itself was the cause of learning, working through the individual or group assignments did help the students internalize the ways of talking and reasoning typical of the disciplines they were studying, helped them learn the jargon and the valued ways of thinking in their majors.

In sum, this research stands in relatively stark contrast to the findings of long-term L1 studies of writing in the undergraduate curriculum (Carroll, 2002; Chiseri-Strater, 1991; Curtis & Herrington, 2003; Haswell, 1991; Sternglass, 1997). There, in one study after another, the researchers find again and again how writing was crucially important in college and important to the students themselves. Several traced the growth of writing expertise, and several noted the many ways in which writing promoted personal and/or intellectual growth. Some of these L1 students experienced personal and literacy epiphanies through the writing assigned in their courses. Though it is extremely difficult to show that something did *not* happen, nevertheless, with the focal students in this study there was rarely even a hint of evidence of this kind of a role for writing.

What might account for such dramatic differences? Perhaps it is the difference between writing in a primary language and writing in a language that is not yet fully controlled or that cannot (yet) fully engage deep-seated emotional strata that are available and accessible to students writing in their L1s. Perhaps it is a difference in the majors included in those studies and this one. The writing assigned in the business and engineering curriculums (even if Ben and Jan had been the writers) would rarely have given occasion for the kinds of exploration of the writer's identity as a gay person, for example, that was possible for Curtis and Herrington's (2003) student Lawrence/Steven in his gender studies major. Or perhaps the difference lies in the assumptions of the research questions guiding the studies. Curtis and Herrington's research question asks "How do various writing tasks from courses across the curriculum foster writing development? How do various writing tasks promote or articulate personal development?" (p. 70). Because these L1 composition researchers were specifically working to uncover and explore the role and importance of writing in the undergraduate curriculum and in the lives of students, they took it as given that writing would be important. On the other hand, Carroll's (2002) study seemed to have as its central question the relationship between 1st-year composition and writing in courses across the curriculum rather than resting on the assumed importance of writing; perhaps for this reason her findings are in fact more in tune with those reported here.

WRITING FOR GENERAL EDUCATION

The general-education courses that the four focal students experienced typically did not assign writing, at least in part because of the high numbers of students enrolled in them. (See later discussion, however.) Although a few, particularly history courses, included essay questions on exams, the free-standing writing assignments that were made in these courses seemed ineffective, at least for these students, for several reasons:

- The students knew little about the subject matter and so struggled with content and sometimes with the reading required to do the assignment (e.g., biology, political science).
- The assignments were nearly always final drafts, often to be turned in on or close to the last day of class so the feedback was either ignored or the annotated paper never received.
- The writing was assigned primarily as a way of policing accomplishment of some other activity, to demonstrate that the other activity had taken place (e.g., in sign language, participating in a silent lunch and then writing a report on the activity).

When the purpose of a writing assignment was to police another activity, the students' commitment to the writing was particularly weak because having performed the activity, they saw little point in writing about it.

In some of these courses across the curriculum, attempts were made to introduce students to disciplinary kinds of writing like lab reports, perhaps merely in order to acquaint students with these genres and the style of thinking that generated them. Because a lab report is a very distinct genre, step-by-step directions and even text to include were given, so that in fact the students' main job, at least as these students performed it, became to search for a way to paraphrase an already existing text. On the other hand, in a course like ethics, guidelines for writing were quite underspecified, undetailed, leaving Jan and perhaps other students unclear about how to proceed except for obeying superficial injunctions to deliver the required number of pages and outside references, directions that were clear-cut and taken as absolutes.

But perhaps saying that the assignments were ineffective begs the question, effective for what? The main reason that faculty in these courses gave for assigning writing was simply the assertion that writing was a very important skill for college graduates. It is no secret that writing is not always used well across the curriculum but perhaps at the root of this observation is the notion that writing, in and of itself, is vitally important presumably to being an educated person or to being seen as an educated person. This view of literacy appears to arise from the traditional conception of literacy as an autonomous cognitive capacity of an individual (a view currently discredited or at least under heavy challenge; see Barton, Hamilton, & Ivanic, 1993; Lea & Street, 1998; Street, 1993) and as creating a cognitive "great divide" between literate and oral cultures or between literate and nonliterate individuals (Ong, 1983; Street, 1993). No one wants to be accused of failing to foster literate culture. So assigning writing is thought of as automatically superior to not assigning it.

One corollary to the belief in autonomous literacy that seems to underlie writing assignments in general education, the ubiquitous 1st-year writing requirement, and the exit exams that some institutions require for its graduates is that, as an autonomous skill, literacy is transferable across writing contexts. If literacy is strictly a personal, cognitive capacity and a student learns to write for a history course, or for a 1st-year composition course for that matter, that student is ready to write for a film class, a nursing course, or a social work context, barring odd, superficial genre requirements as entailed in, for example, Nursing Care Plans. This is essentially a developmental view of writing proficiency grounded in the notion that once a first stage of writing is securely in place, the next builds upon it and the next upon it in an orderly step-by-step way. But this developmental view is contradicted by the experiences of both Yang and Jan. The transferability argument inherent in the developmental, autonomous skill view seemed not to apply in Yang's case because she did well in general-education courses, including in the writing assigned there, yet in her first nursing course had her first paper returned to her as unacceptable (leading to her considerable efforts thenceforward to be sure her writing was as error free as she could get it). Jan as well was unable to draw on his growing proficiency in writing for business courses to do well on the assignments in the ethics or film courses he took in his 5th year.

Why did transfer fail to occur? Psychological views of transfer of learning make a distinction between specific, near transfer (i.e., transfer of microlearning to quite similar new contexts) and general, far transfer (i.e., of basic principles to dissimilar environments). These strongly suggest that "transfer is uncommon, but when it occurs at all it is between situations that are highly similar" (Detterman, 1993, p. 6). In his review of 100 years of experimental research in transfer, Detterman notes that "If there is a general conclusion to be drawn from the research done on transfer, it is that the lack of general transfer is pervasive and surprisingly consistent" (p. 18).[46] These conclusions seem to be borne out by the focal students' sense of what they were able to take from their early writing experiences and use in later ones. Transferability of literacy skills as general principles was much less likely to be cited than transferability of a subset of them to highly similar contexts, that is, the subset that pertained to sentence-level features, such as rule-governed grammar and mechanics, and mundane text requirements, like the use of a particular documentation style.

Only Yuko actively attempted to link the content of her general-education courses with what she was learning in her major, carefully selecting general-education courses and topics to write on to complement social work courses (e.g., women in Appalachia in her local studies course). Yang saw general-education courses, and so the work assigned in them, as annoying and unnecessary requirements for herself, a mature adult who already had an undergraduate degree; Jan saw them as hoops to jump through; Ben disregarded them as soon as they were finished.

Still the four students had fair success with the writing assignments across the curriculum that they encountered, in part because the stakes were not particularly high and evaluation of their efforts seemed relatively lenient. Because their professors were not usually attempting to verify the students' language learning, they did not seem unduly tormented by the deviations from standard English evident in the students' writing. In addition, every one of the students noted that their ability to produce more prose faster increased from their first years in college to their later years, certainly an important and helpful advance for them. Perhaps then, general-education writing assignments usefully caused the L2 students to access vocabulary and spend time pondering grammatical constructions and text organization, and in so doing, arguably reinforced appropriate neural pathways and increased access speed. They were perhaps an effective form of pushed output and syntactic encoding (Swain, 1985, 1993), essentially serving these students as language practice. If this achievement strikes general-education faculty or writing researchers as mediocre, being able to spend less time just getting required quantities of writing done was quite important to these students, as it is for most L2 students.

The institutional explanation for lack of writing in general-education courses is often based on numbers of students and lack of funding. Geisler's (1994) analysis, however, provides an additional explanation for the small quantity and generally nondisciplinary nature of the writing tasks in general-education courses. These courses are intended to build domain knowledge but not expertise. Geisler maintains that the level of domain knowledge attained must be sufficient for the recipients to consume knowledge produced elsewhere but is intentionally inadequate for either production or fundamental critique of disciplinary knowledge. Students are not supposed to develop rhetorical/strategic knowledge on general-education subject matter, but rather just enough to recognize that they are not themselves sufficiently expert to evaluate knowledge delivered to them by experts.

Such an analysis also accounts for an odd phenomenon attested in the general-education faculty interview data. Frequently, interviewed faculty maintained that the main purpose of the introduction to biology, geography, or political science course was to allow students to use the knowledge they developed in these courses in their daily lives. This purpose would certainly make sense and potentially justifies teaching nonmajors such (perhaps?) esoterica as the difference between a monocot and a dicot, the use of exogamous marriage, or the cause of eddies in flowing rivers. Yet students were never tested (the final arbiter in what is important in a school setting) on how they might or did apply information like this in their daily lives. Rather, only the information itself was tested. If there was a bridge to be made between the monocots and daily life (and here a writing task might function quite suitably), it was up to the students to build it on their own time.

Finally, although the students often got detailed guidelines for the disciplinary writing they did, typically for general-education humanities courses the instructions were most often quite generalized. Perhaps because virtually all students take 1st-year writing and the genre privileged there by the English department staff that teaches the courses tends to be essays, the liberal arts faculty that taught most general-education courses may have felt little need to provide guidelines for a genre taught in 1st-year writing courses and close enough to their discipline's own that they could assume familiarity with it. Faculty in general-education courses did not appear to recognize that requiring students to adequately structure their writing for these varying disciplines included requiring them to grasp implicit disciplinary meanings for terms like argument, structure, even narrative. But Stockton's (1995) analysis of highly successful L1 English majors' less than perfectly successful upper-division history writing exemplifies how even such closely related disciplines as history and English do not entertain the same understandings of such terms. Yet general-education faculty did appear to assume that, for example, "well organized" means the same thing across disciplines. Lea and Street (1998) call this understanding of academic literacy "the study skills approach," one that they deem politically naive and ultimately elitist in that it potentially blames the victim (i.e., the unsuccessful student writer) for not already being a disciplinary insider, that is, for not already recognizing or producing text that is "well organized." In the majors, on the other hand, such genres as NCPs, social work documentation, engineering lab reports, or market case studies had to be and were specifically taught.

WRITING IN THE MAJOR

School-Sponsored Writing and Inauthenticity

The reason faculty often gave for assigning writing in the majors referred to the writing required by professionals in that field. Yet by their own description, the writing assignments the disciplinary faculty created did not duplicate the type of writing that might take place at an actual work site. This finding that the students were being asked to write genres in their majors that did not attempt to anticipate workplace genres seemed surprising at first, especially in light of the faculty's expressed reasons for assigning this writing, that professionals in their field needed to write. But in the context of situated learning theories (Lave & Wenger, 1991), it is clear that such a duplication would most likely be impossible (see Winsor's, 1996, discussion of academic and workplace engineering writing).

The goal of writing done at a work site differs radically from the goal of academic writing assignments. In the students' majors, the goal seemed to be to open a space for pushed disciplinary output (in effect, practice), to verify that the students had learned some part of what was known to other more enculturated members of the discipline, and to ensure that the students' assumptions about information, values, reasoning, and evidence were increasingly brought in line with those of the discipline. The focus of academic writing assignments is thus not on the text but on the learner and on the learner's academic and literacy development (Dias et al., 1999). In the workplace, on the contrary, the focus of the act of writing is the production of a *text* to be used in connection with the work. In this sense, when faculty in business and engineering expressed little or no concern about which member of a group actually wrote up a group project report, they were reflecting work world values that stress product over process. Because of the importance of the document itself, a workplace text may live a long life and be read by many in a given organization and beyond. An academic text, on the other hand, has usually done its job once the text is completed and then evaluated by one reader only, which explains the short life of academic texts, sometimes so short that the student writers themselves may never bother to look at them again.

How is writing in the majors to be understood in the experiences of these L2 students since faculty did not claim that the assigned writing would anticipate professional writing? Again, certain theoretical discussions in the literature on writing in the workplace seemed helpful to me in attempting to understand the role of writing in the experiences of these students, partially by juxtaposing workplace writing to school-sponsored writing (Dias et al., 1999).[47] In particular, genre theory, activity theory, and theories of distributed cognition all give persuasive accounts of writing that is situated and socially motivated. Genre theory defines a genre as a typified response to a recurring social demand (C. Miller, 1994; Swales, 1990); activity theory analyzes human action in terms of its social embedding, homing in especially on the goals of broad-based activities (like learning) and the actions that instantiate them (like reading or writing) (Blakeslee, 1997; Dias et al., 1999; Russell, 1977); and distributed cognition explains how, in a given organization, knowledge or information is not the property or possession of individuals but rather is distributed across the human and physical resources of the organization (Winsor, 1996).

These ways of looking at workplace writing descriptively analyze it as a legitimately necessary activity within the social context in which it occurs, the workplace. School-sponsored writing deviates from workplace writing in that the "social motive" (C. Miller, 1994) for writing in school exists only as the decision of an individual teacher (and to some more distant degree, a department or institution) in great part for the purpose of evaluating the writer, not as the communal response to a social situation with the focus on the text rather than on the writer, as in workplace writing. The motivation for school-sponsored writing does not arise from within the social situation but is plastered onto it. From this point of view then, school-sponsored writing requirements may suffer from inauthenticity.

It is in fact difficult to integrate the notion of school-sponsored writing, at least as these students experienced it, with genre as a concept of study. Coe (2002) notes that "genres survive because they work, because they respond effectively to recurring situations" (p. 197). But who do these school-sponsored genres work for and to what end? He has characterized genres as "*forms* ... embodying *strategies* that have evolved for responding effectively to particular types of *situations*" (Johns et al., 2006, p. 245). But school-sponsored genres do not represent strategies developed by the writers of the genre, who have in fact been excluded from genre development by virtue of the fact that they stop contributing to genre evolution as soon as they stop being students. Thus, these school-sponsored genres do not really evolve, in the sense of responding to new environmental conditions, although those who assign the genres may well change the permissible parameters. Furthermore, K. Hyland notes that "novice writers, because they are outside a particular genre-using community, lack … familiarity [with the genre] and therefore often struggle to create appropriate texts" (Johns et al., 2006, p. 245). Yet only students appear to write school-sponsored genres, not those who assign the genres. In other words, school-sponsored writing genres are inventions of people who never write them. Thus, in many cases students are asked to produce school genres they have never seen and their teachers have never written.

The justification for writing assignments that faculty across the curriculum in this study repeatedly gave was either that the abstract ability to write well was important for a college graduate to develop or that writing would be required by postcollege professional settings. But if writing is socially embedded and viewed as a response to given social contexts, the problem becomes that the context of the workplace does not exist in the classroom and cannot be reproduced there. This unresolved contradiction accounts for the unhappiness Yang experienced as she watched real nurses perform authentic writing tasks—the NCPs at the hospital where she volunteered—and noted the difference between that writing and the NCPs, now exposed as inauthentic, that she was still being required to slave over in the nursing program. The NCPs at school were intended, at least partly, to prepare her for authentic writing but as Dias et al. (1999) point out:

> Participating in a genre means not just producing a text that looks like the ones that are usually produced in that milieu but having purposes for action, and therefore, communication, that are recognized and allowed for within that context and for which the genre has emerged adaptively as the appropriate vehicle. (p. 22)

NCPs at the hospital "emerged adaptively" for hospital settings; the ones written by the student nurses did not emerge at all but rather were constructed for their settings. Yet, like much school-sponsored writing, they were being passed off and justified as, at the very least, precursors of authentic NCPs. This argument never became convincing to Yang.

On the other hand, the trajectory of the other three students was different.[48] Each of them in different ways ended up embracing the school-sponsored writing they were doing as ways of participating in the discourse of the disciplines they were being enculturated into by taking on disciplinary styles of thinking instantiated to some degree in the writing. Yuko used the writing she did in social work as a means of transforming herself into the professional social worker she aimed to be. Ben, despite doing almost none of the actual writing in his engineering groups, participated closely in the activity in which the writing was embedded (even to the extent of sitting up all night with Cathy in the library as she wrote up their group report) and, as might be predicted by activity and distributed cognition theories, fully believed in his own active enculturation into "engineering think." Jan's trajectory was similar, participating but not writing, even if he embraced his professionalization with less conviction than did the other two. The authoritative discourse that they were each imitating became internally persuasive (Bakhtin, 1981, 1986) to each of them and as such transformed them, in their own perceptions at least, from student to budding professional. That a similar, additional transformation would be required again as they moved into their work worlds would not be relevant until it was required.

What Were the Salient Details of How These Transformations Transpired?   In the "activity" of becoming educated into their majors, writing was one of many actions the students engaged in that were set up to promote their initiation into the disciplines they studied, as was reading, listening to and taking notes on lectures, doing interviews, participating in group work, running experiments, and all the wide ranges of actions the students carried out in connection to their education. Overall writing was not a particularly privileged action but was instead embedded in others (group work, e.g.) or employed alongside others (reading or speaking or gathering information, e.g.). Even at its most onerous, writing was generally viewed within these disciplines as a tool wielded for some purpose, especially as one means of professional socialization—in nursing, for example, to allow the integration of the nursing process because the students would not have time to learn it on the job, or in engineering to allow faculty to look over the shoulders or into the minds of students as they worked through experiments.

One of the differences between the writing assigned in the general-education courses and writing assigned in the students' majors (and to some degree in nonmajor science courses) was the effort made to teach students how to respond to their assignments, to write the genre-specific reports for each of the majors, for example. Disciplinary faculty often did so by providing extensive guidelines that they fully expected to be met point by point. These detailed guidelines were a form of scaffolding. In answer to the question of what went wrong with unsuccessful student papers, by far the most common answer among faculty interviewed was that students did not follow directions. As Dias et al. (1999) note, a primary function of writing in the academy is as a means of verifying learning. To the degree that the guidelines were intended as instructions for learning disciplinary content and/or format, as steps along the path to disciplinary socialization, failure to follow them was an indication of failure to learn. Although these students (and others mentioned by the faculty) did not always in fact follow all directions for a variety of reasons, like most students, they had no illusions about the requirement to do so (Leki, 1995b).

As noted earlier, one aspect of this genre-based instruction that at first seemed peculiar was how seldom the writing assignments attempted to mimic the writing these students could expect to be doing once they graduated and began working in their fields. Instead, most of the writing assignments were clearly school genres, academic papers like a report Yang did on streptococcus B, Yuko's social work papers requiring her to integrate core concepts in a course or to self-reflect on her experiences, and even Ben's engineering reports, which resembled professional journal articles more than reports that would surface in a work setting. But as Blakeslee (1997) points out, citing a number of genre theorists, "Genres are marked less by recurring organizational patterns than by recurring purposes, such as the construction and dissemination of knowledge" (p. 135). Because classes cannot duplicate the authentically recurring purposes of work sites, students cannot produce those genres and were not asked to do so.

So the genres the students learned in their majors were academic versions of disciplinary genres and not usually the kind of writing they might be expected to produce on the job. A question that arises is just how much even of this writing the students did. Yuko certainly did a great deal of this academic version of professional writing because nearly all her social work courses required writing and each piece was individually produced. But this was not the case for the other three students. Jan rarely produced any formal writing in his business classes. Although Yang did have several individual papers to write for nursing, she concentrated her efforts on producing the NCPs, typically recopying a great deal of text from nursing books or previous NCPs. As for engineering, in the literature on writing in the professions, much has been made of the falseness of earlier assumptions that engineers do not write much. This earlier assumption has been challenged by analyses of company settings and the examination of the rhetorical moves of engineering documents (Winsor, 1996). But even Winsor's L1 engineering students in an intern program found that writing was less important than understanding the history of social relationships within the company. Ben's experience, dominated like Jan's by group work, suggests the earlier assumptions about lack of writing, at least among some engineering undergraduates, may not have been so far off the track.

What Constituted Good Writing in These Contexts?   The same themes were repeated over and over by faculty. To succeed in these academic writing tasks, the writing had to follow all directions quite closely and be clear, concise, correct (i.e., the language), and accurate (i.e., the content, mainly in engineering and nursing). Really excellent work in each of the disciplines would show signs that the students had "gone that extra step" and had actually thought about the content. This conception of good academic writing differed from what is said to be expected in professional writing contexts. The research literature on writing in the disciplines and in the professions (e.g., Bazerman, 1983, 1988; Bazerman & Paradis, 1991; Bazerman & Prior, 2004) has convincingly challenged a nonrhetorical view of professional writing even in a field like engineering. Writing in professional contexts is not, it is argued, simply a transparent medium reproducing reality in words, organizing words into a genre, and editing the words for conventional correctness. Yet, in Ben's experience—and in engineering faculty comments about writing or the program's writing manual—good writing was described quite nonrhetorically. Despite analyses of professional writing that emphasize its underlying persuasive elements, neither the faculty nor Ben ever mentioned persuasiveness as a goal of engineering writing or as emblematic of good writing, at least not in its academic form.[49] The same was true for nursing. Writing tasks were not construed rhetorically; faculty viewed language at its best as transparently mediating between activity and reader understanding. Writing that accomplished this succeeded.

In What Ways Did the Writing Contribute to the Students' Professional Development?   Given that the genres the students were writing did not duplicate professional genres, the contribution of their writing assignments to their professional development must lie somewhere other than helping the students learn professional genres. In Yang's case, the intention of the NCPs was as a tool to make automatic her mental accessing of elements of the nursing process and the issues and questions embedded there, just as Jan's early habit of writing and rewriting course notes was intended to help him memorize material. Part of Yang's frustration, however, was that she construed professionalization as related primarily to medical science and not to the nursing process; the time she spent writing was at the expense of increasing her and her classmates' medical science knowledge, and as such, writing was an obstacle to professionalization.

For the other three, however, the contribution writing made to their development as professionals was suggested by Ben's comment that doing a procedure and writing about it engaged different questions in the mind. In a sense, he intuited the concept of pushed output (Swain, 1985, 1993) as beneficial to learning. Swain suggests that pushed output such as writing in an L2 requires the learner to reanalyze semantic and propositional content syntactically in order to express it to an interlocutor. Similarly, as Ben's experiences with writing for engineering grew, he ultimately saw a positive, instructional role for writing; having to write about a lab experiment meant having to consider the rationale for the procedures described and thus permitted a deeper, more sophisticated, and more conscious, not merely intuitive, felt-sense understanding of the engineering problem and solution. In his case, whereas doing an experiment meant that he implicitly understood the procedure, having to write a report on the experiment forced him to consider issues of causation, explanation, and analysis, this despite the fact that Ben himself never actually wrote the report. Nevertheless, being in on the discussion was sufficient to produce the same effect on Ben, at least in his opinion. The pushed output effect may account as well for the sense of his own competence in marketing writing that Jan began to display as he and his group struggled with their enormous research project during his last year in school.

One feature of the writing experiences in their majors of all the students except Jan was journals. They served different functions: For Ben the journal required in one course was done in class and intended as a way for students to communicate with the professor about how their learning in that class had gone that week. For both Yuko and Yang, the journals were self-reflective, intended to throw the students back on their own thoughts and reactions so that they would become consciously aware of them and so better able to manage them. For all three students, even Yuko, who tried to learn from every experience, the journals were considered a waste of time and not useful to learning. Yuko and Yang both commented that because they already knew what they were being required to write out, the writing out constituted no new learning, a point of view shared by Jan in relation to the opinion essays in his ethics class. In addition, Yang did not believe writers were truthful in these journals in any case, and she admitted not only to holding back but also to finding it uncomfortable at her age to be required to publicly reveal to someone else her private thoughts. None of the students seemed to see these journals as opportunities for deeper reflection, but merely as extra work. The failure of journal assignments to engage these students in reflection may also come from the effort it takes to write in an L2, an effort perhaps experienced as not worth making for so little return.

The stipulations of writing assignments also sometimes focused the students' attention in unexpected directions. When an assignment included stringent page limitations (either minimum or maximum), often the focal students claimed to spend excessive amounts of time attempting to comply with the page requirements instead of concentrating on the content of the writing. Demanding high levels of grammatical accuracy had the same effect; students' attention was drawn away from the content on to more superficial features of the assignment. If there was not a strong emphasis on grammatical accuracy, however, even Yuko did not make extra efforts in this direction. So demanding grammatical accuracy might get a higher level of it but at the cost of attention to content.

Finally, a rational for making writing assignments at all, one that teachers have always known, is that demanding submission of some kind of work regulates the amount of time students spend on a given course. Work on courses that require only reading can be set aside to accommodate a deadline date for a writing assignment. In this sense, assigning writing enhanced learning in the major by causing students to spend time with the material in the course that assigned it.

WRITING, LEARNING, AND LEARNING TO WRITE

In What Ways Did These Students Find Writing Useful in Their Academic Work? Each of them was able at one point or another to articulate some benefit for writing they did, although Yang rarely saw writing as anything more than an opportunity to practice English. Because of the additional time spent with the material, the students felt that having to write about a topic allowed them to remember the content better; sometimes this was useful for upcoming exams, permitting them to skip studying for the section of the exam that would cover their paper topic. Yuko and to some degree Ben and Jan felt they understood the material better when they had written about it because writing about it called for more conscious effort. Finally, Yuko remarked that having to organize a paper on a topic caused her to also organize her thoughts on the topic, making them clearer in her own mind.

Presumably these are all examples of writing to learn: spending more time with the material, manipulating it, and becoming more consciously aware of aspects of it. At best, writing accomplished this for the students. In addition, the students learned something about disciplinary genres as well. But writing also created special problems. Having to write was an intensely negative experience for Yang because it took her enormous amounts of time, energy, and effort to get a piece into sufficiently acceptable form to submit and gave little positive back because much of the writing was repetitious. And Yang had little extra time to devote to writing in a curriculum that was acknowledged to be physically and emotionally exhausting. Furthermore, writing could betray the writer in various ways. For Yang, the betrayal was in terms of further exposing her language deficiencies before an audience already disturbed by them. For Ben, writing's betrayal was in potentially not faithfully reproducing the procedures and understandings the lab group had developed in the lab. As Ben said, it was possible to do everything correctly but fail to remember to include some procedure correctly or fully in the report and so appear to have missed something that in fact was not missed.

If writing was a betrayer, it also served as a grade booster for both Jan and Yang. For struggling students like these, writing *can* represent the possibility of exerting some control over evaluations because whatever was written outside of class could be done as slowly as necessary and could be reworked with the help of peers, tutors, partners, or teachers. Overall, writing was at times perceived as helpful and at others painful or dangerous.

If Writing Was One Factor In Promoting Disciplinary Growth, What Promoted Writing Development? The students did improve in their writing and each of them remarked on how much better their writing was by the end of their studies compared to what they were able to do in their first term. For the most part they each ascribed their improvement, logically, to time spent practicing writing by writing. This practice provided the all-important speed and document length that was the core of their concerns early on; for each of them at the beginning, the goal was very limited, simply to get texts to the required length and to get them written in a reasonable amount of time. Besides practice, increased familiarity with disciplinary content made writing easier and faster and resulted in fuller texts. Disciplinary reading increased content knowledge and exposed the students to disciplinary jargon they could then incorporate into their writing.

Perhaps the most important factor in improving these students' writing was their willingness to seek out feedback on outlines and/or early drafts and revise. Even Jan. Ironically, Jan often spent time manipulating his texts in order to circumvent some rule and yet the manipulation itself gave him significant amounts of practice, as in the case where, after directly copying information from an encyclopedia, he spent hours rephrasing the text so he would not be accused of plagiarism. Ben too claimed to have improved, at least to the extent that he could write longer and faster by the end of his undergraduate years, and yet when he brought a text in, as requested as part of this study, he always turned out to have written almost none of it. This made it difficult to corroborate his sense of improvement but it also speaks again to the possibility that writing is not so important to a successful college career as it is made out to be. Though it seems obvious that in order to improve in writing, the learner has to write, apparently a learner's writing confidence can improve without writing.

Certain forms of feedback were also extremely beneficial to the students; solicited, interdraft feedback played this role and led to multiple revisions and reworkings. Predraft and certainly postsubmission feedback had little positive effect, the first being too confusing and the second being mostly ignored, sometimes not even seen, on occasions when the paper was submitted at the end of the term.

One form of interdraft feedback available to these students was through the writing center. Faculty around campus seemed generally unaware of how the writing center might help students with writing projects beyond a vague (and incorrect) assumption that the writing center could eliminate writing errors students produced. Yang might have been able to benefit from interaction at the writing center (including oral interaction) but used its services relatively rarely for lack of time. Ben never visited the writing center, but because he almost never wrote prose, he probably did not need to. But the writing center played a crucial role in the writing development of Yuko and Jan, who both used this resource extensively and judiciously. The prevailing views on L2 students in the writing center seem to be that these students are confused about the function of the writing center and, like faculty, expect grammar correction services; they are reluctant or do not know how to own their own work and passively wait to be told what they need to change; or they are culturally programmed to obey any authority and construct the writing center tutor as such an authority. (See Harris, 1997, and Rafoth & Bruce, 2004, for a variety of explorations of L2 students and writing centers.) Neither Jan or Yuko viewed the writing center in these ways. Both used what was useful to them and left the rest.

In fact each of these students, to varying degrees and in different ways, worked hard to structure their environment to get help for themselves, including enlisting a variety of socioacademic networks to provide contextualized support for their work. None of the students was hapless, though certainly Yang and Jan had longer and more difficult struggles.

Reading and Writing

The readings assigned in these students' courses played a variety of roles, sometimes essential to understanding the lecture, sometimes repetitious of other course material, sometimes basically not required. Ben had surprisingly little reading to do in engineering, and the other three often had far more to do than was possible even in cases when they would have liked to, as sometimes happened with Yang and Yuko. When they were overloaded, Yuko and Yang read strategically, reading only what appeared to be the most important material, usually what they judged likely to appear on exams; Jan's strategy until quite late in his undergraduate years was to simply stop reading anything and hope to get what he needed from lectures.

Unfortunately, the readings were also generally rather separate from the course writing assignments. This separation had several consequences. It meant that unless the reading was covered on exams, it was likely not to get read. It also contributed to making the writing assignments seem somewhat arbitrary, work that "will be good for them" or whose main purpose, as both students and teachers acknowledged, was to account for some portion of the final grade. When the readings and the lectures were linked, this allowed discussion of readings in class and created coherence of subject matter. But then the students were left to "go beyond" the readings and the lectures in course papers, often by being required to read additional sources but not by being required to incorporate course lecture or course reading material in the paper. In theory this left students with options for new topics to explore in their papers, but in practice the lack of connection between the course readings and lectures on one hand and the required writing on the other resulted in a sense that the writing was only peripherally related to the class. The only clear exception was Yuko's political science class, which did request that students incorporate course lectures and readings in the letters to the editor they were assigned; however, the lectures and readings in this case sometimes turned out to be inappropriate to include in the writing.

ESL CLASSES

Looking back on their experiences with ESL/1st-year writing courses, the students expressed gratitude at the opportunity they had there to begin to develop a certain amount of fluency in English writing. But because the writing they did in those courses differed so widely from the writing they did across the curriculum, the students' eventual success in their cross-curricular assignments can hardly be seen as related to their work in their early writing courses (see similar conclusions in Carroll, 2002). Those early writing courses simply could never have anticipated the varied writing the students would be required to do later in college. Yet the expectation on the part of the institution, the faculty, and the students was that 1st-year writing courses would prepare students for writing later in college.

What Had ESL Classes Done for These Students? Only Jan sometimes harshly criticized his ESL classes. At other times, he concurred with the other students that the classes allowed him the time and focus on writing that increased speed and text length. The students also referred to building grammatical accuracy and text-organizing skill, and Yuko was even grateful to have learned technical grammar vocabulary and was particularly gratified to have learned an approach to writing essay exams she later put into practice in a few other courses. But she also pointed to aspects of the courses that she later found conflicted with her literacy needs across the curriculum. Some of what is taught in some ESL writing classes needs to be taught only because of the genre (and writing topics) privileged in L2 writing classes, belletristic or argumentative/persuasive essays, the hallmark of English department writing. But why are these genres privileged in the 1st-year writing classes on which L2 writing classes are usually based? If the focal students' experiences are anything close to what students in similar majors experience, it may be that they rarely have occasion to use these genres in other courses across the curriculum. For historical and political reasons, the privileging of these genres is not arbitrary; English departments typically control writing classes, enforce their genres, employ their graduate students to teach the courses, and populate their literature seminars with those same students. But logically, students in these writing classes would be no more or less disadvantaged by learning and practicing instead genres typical of other fields, reports, case studies, analyses. None of the focal students were ever asked to write argumentative essays in their majors.

Calling into question the particular genre focus of ESL writing classes allows us to understand better Yuko's surprise at finding invention techniques not very useful in her disciplinary writing. Invention techniques are intended to help writers access information they already know and bring it to consciousness for possible inclusion in a text. They permit the writer to apply the writing class advice to "write about what you know." The problem is that the point of most academic experience is to learn new material, to explore what the writer does not already know and cannot find out simply by sounding inner resources, to manage rather than generate information. The conflict that Yuko experienced in her political science class arose at precisely the juncture between what she had learned to do in her writing classes (write about what she already knew) and what she needed to do in her political science class (write about what she was learning in the class). Even trying to employ the transitional expressions she had learned in her writing class proved tricky when Yuko was required to write in her social work classes in response to preformed questions and "without the assistance of the introduction."

The point is not that L2 writing teachers need to learn and teach other genres, certainly not ones with which they are not particularly familiar, but that we L2 professionals need to perhaps interrogate the content of our courses. The same issue confronts L1 compositionists and has led to well-known and much discussed questioning of the 1st-year composition requirement (Crowley, 1993; Russell, 1991). But L2 professionals have a greater and more difficult task. As Raimes (1985) noted many years ago, L2 students need "more of everything." Yet even succeeding in making L2 writing courses credit bearing was a disciplinary struggle, and one that has not necessarily been won in every institution. Furthermore, part of the rationale for granting credit for L2 writing courses has been that these courses are the equivalent of 1st-year L1 writing courses. Being parallel to 1st-year writing has meant in essence applying 1st-year composition values, standards, and methods in L2 writing courses, including privileging English department genres. Atkinson and Ramanathan's (1995) ethnographic account of two writing programs, one L1 and one L2, demonstrates the potential injustice of requiring L2 students' literacy education to be dominated by L1 interests.

What Do These Findings Suggest for L2 Writing Classes? In light of findings based on such interpretive frames as activity theory, sociocultural approaches to learning, and situated learning, the picture does not look hopeful that L2 writing classes can have much impact on student writing proficiency beyond what the focal students remembered as useful—helping students write longer and faster in English through offering the opportunity to practice writing. The tutors and faculty interviewed in Lea and Street (1998) found themselves unable to go much beyond saying that good writing was characterized by "structure and argument"; Lea and Street ascribe this inability to the tacit nature of disciplinary knowledge that "structure and argument" index but cannot specify. If disciplinary knowledge based on manipulating language, as in writing, is tacit, it is unlikely to be a candidate for explicit teaching. Rather, as Blakeslee (1997) points out, citing Brandt, "Such knowledge accumulates through participation and through social relationships; therefore, the emphasis should be placed on talk and action in appropriate social settings, not on propositional knowledge" (p. 159) but on "interaction and engagement in domain-specific activities" (p. 160). As free-standing entities (i.e., ones not linked to other courses) that students encounter in their 1st year and then leave behind, L2 writing classes are unlikely to be able to supply those conditions. Nevertheless, for the most part the students in this study looked back on their L2 writing classes as one small stepping-stone toward the mastery of academic literacy they legitimately felt they ultimately achieved.

Expectations for Writing Instruction

Despite its diminished role for these students, and so presumably for others as well, writing nevertheless continues to hold a privileged position institutionally. Of any of the language skills these students might have needed to succeed in college, only writing was specifically "taught," either in writing courses or, in the major, through the provision of the detailed guidelines. Whereas other language skills, like speaking, were not taught even implicitly (except for interviewing skills in social work), oral communication was nevertheless extremely important for communicating with clients (Yang and Yuko) and making presentations (Jan). In the business course that resulted in Jan's 250-page report, the professor admitted that presenting the report orally rather than in written form would have been preferable, accomplishing the same learning for the students and more authentically reproducing what the business world expected. The importance of making presentations in engineering was recognized in Ben's curriculum too but because there was so much technical material to learn, very little time could afford to be devoted to having student groups make presentations. In general, certain speaking skills were expected to be already in place (e.g., understandable pronunciation) or picked up along the way, which proved a considerable handicap for Yang. Some of the reasons for writing's persistence in its privileged role have been analyzed in relation to the industry of 1st-year writing (Crowley, 1993; Leki, 2003a; Russell, 1991).

One issue that might have been expected to arise in faculty interviews in relation to these students' L2 writing, and their writing instruction, was the issue of grammatical accuracy. But the faculty, particularly in the students' majors, generally described themselves as not unduly worried about L2 errors or phrasings (although Yang's situation was a partial exception). They seemed far more able to see L2 student writing as developmental, as still improving, than they were to see L1 student writing in the same way. None of the faculty interviewed assumed that the L2 students should have already learned to write errorless English in a year of required writing classes (although the same understanding was not typically extended to L1 students). This was certainly an advantage for the focal students and an advantage that L2 students may have over L1 university students. The faculty, at least in these focal students' majors, were willing to give the L2 students some room to breathe, but this willingness also caused consternation among some faculty members who worried about the ethical dilemma of differential treatment for L2 students and L1 students who had come from weak educational backgrounds.

In both general education and the majors, faculty did expect, hope, wish that L1 students in their courses would arrive having already mastered Standard Written English and a few features of writing that they emphatically considered to be the English department's domain (e.g., grammar and mechanics, writing introductions). They expected domestic students to appear in their classes with these "basics" already firmly under control, felt it was the duty of the English department to see to it that they were well instilled during the year of 1st-year writing,[50] and seemed irritated when they perceived this not to be the case. More than once a faculty member exclaimed in effect, How can they get to this level, juniors, and not yet know "how to write"!?

WRITING AT THE UNIVERSITY AND INDIVIDUAL GOAL SETTING

Even at the undergraduate level, there is an intention to acculturate students, at least initially, into a discipline, yet Candlin and Plum (1998) dispute the idea that undergraduates have enough contact with disciplinary members to be able to view themselves as being acculturated into a discipline. Perhaps acculturation does require more contact, but the degree to which a student sees such interaction as legitimate peripheral participation is partly a question of the student's willingness or interest in making it so. In Yuko's case, for example, she interpreted nearly all her dealings with faculty, students, and literacy and volunteer work as a part of her acculturation. By the same token, the literacy, academic, and institutional context in which these four learners developed both literacy expertise and a body of academic knowledge in college was obviously not alone in influencing their struggles, failures, and eventual successes. If at least one side of the educational dialectic is context, the other is the individual. In addition to the undeniable importance of interaction with disciplinary members, these students also brought themselves to the table. That is, their own personalities, learning styles, ability to self-regulate (Purdie, Hattie, & Douglas, 1996), expectations, and sense of identity intersected with the varying contexts of learning to produce individual experiences. One factor in that personal constellation was the orientation these students displayed toward their learning. In Cumming, Busch, and Zhou (2002), the authors describe Ng and Bereiter's (1991) three types of goals that children set for algebra problems:

> (1) task completion goals (which involved just accomplishing given tasks), (2) instructional goals (aimed at determining the main points of teaching, presented either implicitly or explicitly to learners, and (3) knowledge-building goals, based on individuals' efforts to construct their personal sense of phenomena or the world. (p. 192)

Ng and Bereiter note that knowledge-building goals (Type 3) promote learning significantly better than either task-completion or instructional goals (Types 1 and 2) but tend to be less often elicited by educational tasks. In these terms, Yuko and Ben understood and set instructional goals (Type 2) for themselves quite often, but only Yuko, the most academically successful of the four students, consistently gave evidence of also engaging in knowledge-building goals (Type 3), where she intended that the work she did would serve to increase her expertise in specific areas of social work that she wanted to master. In Ben's account, he took on faculty goals more often than he created goals for himself. Yang's and especially Jan's goals, on the other hand, were more typically of the first type, knocking out assignments like ducks in a row one after the other to have them out of the way, done, behind them as soon as possible. However, as their expertise built, occasionally Yang and even Jan appeared increasingly to set the second type of goal for themselves, to try to determine what the professor's purpose was in making an assignment and to use that goal as the motivation for completing the assignment.

Other studies of the development of expertise (see Bereiter & Scardamalia, 1993) suggest that a novice approach to learning material is characterized by the effort to turn the learning process into an already known routine or to use previously routinized strategies for dealing with a new learning problem. An expert approach on the other hand is characterized by a commitment, not to the superficial features of the task (as Jan's often was), but to accomplishing the task for one's own learning purposes. It appears difficult to create educational contexts that encourage the expert approach and that work consistently with all or most learners; Ng and Bereiter's (1991) contention that educational settings encourage task-completion goals and instructional goals (Types 1 and 2) among learners seems to be borne out in many of the written tasks these four students encountered. In such settings, then, without institutional or instructional support for the development of knowledge-building goals of the kind Yuko and to some degree Ben brought with them, the burden falls on individual students to find a way to make their educations meaningful to them, to make use of their writing assignments and other classroom tasks to achieve their own purposes. Students like Yang and Jan seem less able, or less inclined, to manage this.

Also working against students' ability or inclination to set knowledge-building goals was the overstuffed curriculum that Yang complained of and that she felt led to her classmates' learned dependency. In study after study, L2 university students note the difficulty of time management. In course after course, assignments, including a great deal of reading and writing, are piled on students in an effort to get through the material, to cover the syllabus (Benesch, 2001). As seen among Yang's nursing classmates, students also press themselves beyond reason to complete their degrees as quickly as possible, and they are encouraged in this race by institutional forces (the cost of tuition, e.g.), personal and socioeconomic circumstances, and any given discipline's sense of what needs to be known by graduates in that academic domain. Operating under excessive workload and time pressures takes energy and opportunity away from the goals of knowledge building in relation to students' academic work.

CONCLUSION

As noted previously, writing researchers sometimes lament the lack of writing assignments made in courses across the curriculum. This is ironic because the primary institutional rationale for 1st-year writing courses is that they will prepare students for the many writing assignments they will encounter across the curriculum.[51] If those writing assignments are missing, should the institutional rationale for 1st-year writing be reconsidered?

But writing researchers also lament the poor quality of the writing assignments that are made across the curriculum. The focal students in this research experienced the problems associated with assigning single-draft papers and not linking course readings and lectures with writing assignments, or linking them poorly; they rarely had writing assignments that built upon previous ones; guidelines in general-education courses were minimalist; samples of successful papers were not typically available; feedback was ignored or never received. Furthermore, the programs/majors in this study also seemed to have no discernible coherent idea about which courses should assign writing (although the nursing program did at least address this question at the curricular level) or why. Writing assignments appeared to be made haphazardly, each course instructor working alone.

Often the purpose for making a writing assignment was vague, related primarily to the faculty's repeated assertion that students need to know how to write or that writing develops critical-thinking skills—or that companies complain about students' writing (and lack of group-work skills), and so writing should be assigned (and group work too). But it is difficult for students to assent to developing expertise now for a task they do not yet have to do or a skill they do not yet have to exhibit (and may believe, as Jan did, that they will never have to). Typically, general-education courses set worse, less explicit, less obviously justifiable writing assignments than did courses in the majors and in addition appeared to assume that liberal arts genres were self-evident, the standard, unmarked, and so did not have to be taught.

In these problems, compositionists may actually be witnessing the success of their own promotion of writing. Writing and making writing assignments in college classes have benefited from a great deal of positive

PR. Not one faculty member interviewed in this research said that writing was not particularly important in their course or in their discipline. Even if there was no writing assigned in a given course, the faculty invariably suggested a view of writing as an absolute good, marking a divide between the educated and uneducated. I would argue that it is this very unexamined assumption itself that led to many of the useless, poorly designed, and poorly evaluated writing assignments the focal students experienced. When writing is held to be a good under any circumstances, then any writing assignment is viewed as better than no writing assignment, "any circumstances" end up being forthcoming, and instructors in nearly every class feel compelled to make some writing assignment or other—and some group work—because these represent unfettered good for students.

How could those assignments have been made more useful, and also less difficult? A first requirement would seem to be that faculty ascertain that there is a real purpose for the writing assignments they make, not just because college students need to learn to write, and writing magically develops critical-thinking skills. It was clear that in some instances, presentations of learned material in some form other than writing would have served everyone better, either no writing at all or smaller amounts so that the students like Yuko who are conscientious have time to think about them or students like Yang get a chance to breathe.

It would seem reasonable for faculty to clarify for themselves exactly what the purpose is of particular assignments and then set them up, with explicit guidelines, sample papers, and multiple drafts to accomplish that purpose. Interdraft feedback for the students in this study was most effective; assignments split up into a series with each piece building on the last ones allow interdraft feedback that can be incorporated into the next stage of the series. Assignments linked more carefully to the lecture and readings would at least make them less arbitrary seeming.

But on the basis of this study, I would not argue for more writing but more judiciously assigned writing, especially when, for example, it is likely to get in the way of learning (as with Yang). Constructing good assignments with good guidelines and then evaluating the resulting texts is time consuming and fatiguing. Responding to those assignments is also time consuming and fatiguing, and can be threatening for L2 students especially. It would seem reasonable to expect at least that all that time and energy spent should have been put to good use. It would also seem reasonable to ask students about their perception of the usefulness of given assignments in the accomplishment of the assignments' stated purposes, even if those purposes are limited to inducing students to spend time thinking about course subject matter, organizing their thoughts in ways that might help them to learn the material, and engaging in and working through disciplinary ways of expressing ideas.

It is also important for faculty across the curriculum to realize that writing in an L2 is dramatically more time and energy consuming than in an L1. Certain forms of writing, like reflective journal, may be thought of as requiring reflection but not much effort in terms of writing. But writing is not experienced by L2 writers as simply flowing "like ink from a pen," to quote a Chinese graduate student talking about how easy it is for him to write in Chinese compared to English (Silva, 1992). Writing even a journal entry does take effort in a second language.

A study like this reveals some of the complexity in which academic literacy development is embedded for individual students. Many of the experiences of these L2 students would likely be much the same for L1 students except that the focal students also encountered university life in the United States with, among other obstacles, less experience with writing, with English, even with the library, with the typical expectations of academic writing assignments, with the content of and background for many of the courses they took at the university, especially their general-education courses in their first few years. In addition, any work mediated by language took more time and left at least Yang more vulnerable to serious criticism and even doubts about her suitability for university work. Many of their strictly academic difficulties receded with experience, particularly in their majors, but they had fewer resources to draw on in terms of family and friends and additional harassments that come with living in an alien culture, such as dealings with the Immigration and Naturalization Service.

But a central finding for me in this study was in effect the lack of importance of writing in these students' undergraduate lives relative to the rich blend of the multiple activities, learning experiences, interests, duties, and inclinations that Demanded and seduced away the students' time and attention. More centrally, the engagement in and completion of all their academic tasks took place in the context of their relationships to those around them, particularly their peers and their teachers. Ultimately their struggles, successes, and failures in their literacy work cannot be understood without reference to its social context.

7

Social and Ideological Contexts of Literacy Development

This research set out to chart the development of academic literacy among a group of L2 undergraduates but over the course of the years of interviews, observations, analyses, and reflections, it became clear that failing to attend to broader, more human and personal contexts as well as more impersonal ideological contexts that framed these students' learning distorted understanding of that development. These two factors stood out from among the many that influenced the focal students' academic growth: their socioacademic relationships and the ideological assumptions that held sway in many of their classrooms. The students' socioacademic relationships proved vital to learning; the ideological dimensions of some of their experiences are compelling, on one hand, because the professional literature rarely affords us glimpses of the kinds of assumptions made in U.S. university classrooms about shared and appropriate values and, on the other hand, because these glimpses reveal an environment where the Other, a category that implicitly included students like these, was at times constructed as unidimensional and inferior.

SOCIAL GROUP AND INDIVIDUAL IDENTITY

Socioacademic Needs

The data from this research repeatedly pointed to the dramatic importance in these students' language learning, personal satisfaction, and academic success of socioacademic relationships, those friendly relationships that students develop with peers and teachers through their academic interactions in shared classes. These relationships were not maintained out of school; nor were they deep, lasting friendships. Yet language and literacy development, academic growth, and even the ability to complete course assignments went hand in hand with the extent, stability, and success of these socioacademic relations and in some cases could not progress until such relationships were in place.

The salience of the social in individual intellectual development is not surprising. Since about the 1980s a variety of theoretical discussions of language and learning have gone beyond earlier formulations of learning as an autonomous cognitive process involving changes in individual mental reception and structuring processing and structuring of information or language input. In taking "the social turn" (Trimbur, 1994), language and writing researchers, drawing largely on Bakhtin and Vygotsky, have widely argued that language, writing, and learning cannot and do not take place primarily in the brains of isolated individual learners but are instead crucially, unavoidably, and inextricably bound up with social factors, with other humans and human activities. In some discussions, the individual seems barely more than a location where multiple strands of discourse (Gee, 1996) converge. For Bakhtin (1986), language use (and learning) becomes the appropriation, transformation, and use of the language of others, as learners "ventriloquate" others' language until that language becomes their own.

For Vygotsky (1978) too, learning is the transformation of social interaction into personal action, an act of appropriation and internalization of what exists initially as an interpersonal event. The importance to learning of help from a more capable or more savvy other highlights the interdependence of learners and their interlocutors, the individual and the social.

Building on Vygotsky and focused especially on second-language acquisition, sociocultural theory (Aljaafreh & Lantolf, 1994: Lantolf, 2000a, 2000b) emphasizes learning as a social process dependent on face-to-face, dialogic interaction between a learner and a more experienced other who scaffolds skill development in the Vygotskian Zone of Proximal Development (ZPD).

Situated learning (Lave & Wenger, 1991) also places primacy on the social dimensions of learning (see also Casanave, 2002), particularly the human contexts and interactions that move the learner from the periphery of a community of practice toward the core through a process of increasing participation in the activities of the core members, termed legitimate peripheral participation.

Each of these socially oriented theories of human learning anticipate that individuals act not alone but in concert with others, thus inevitably indexing "issues of affiliation and belonging" (Pavlenko & Lantolf, 2000,

p. 156). Social theories of learning have been particularly fruitful and influential in L2 studies, and their formulations closely mirror the processes the students in this study experienced as they became increasingly enculturated into university life in general and into their majors in particular.[52]

Identity as Group Membership. Another feature of research on language learning since the 1990s has been its attention to learner identity, and even here an individual's identity has been regarded as "fundamentally relational" (Johnston, 2003, p. 100), not as a personal experience but as membership in communities (K. Hyland, 2005). This important work demonstrates both how discourses make some identity positions available and close off others and how learners take up or resist the categories available or create alternative identity positions for themselves (Angelil-Carter, 1997; Goldstein, 1996; Harklau, 1999, 2000; Hawkins, 2005; Johnston, 2003; Norton, 2000; Norton & Toohey, 2001; Pavlenko, 2001a, 2001b, 2004; Rockhill, 1987, 1991; Thesen, 1997). The relational aspect of identity reflects the discourse of others and its intersection with the learner's own desires, including resistance to or acceptance of that discourse.[53] In educational settings, a key player in negotiations over identities is the teacher of a course, who however unconsciously can help to make institutional identity categories available to learners, for better or for worse.

Much of this relational research with its implications for identity construction has focused on children or immigrants, less so on L2 college students and their struggles to inhabit comfortable subject positions. Perhaps identity issues seem less pointed for college students because they appear to have a wider range of options open to them than might be the case for immigrants or children or perhaps institutional positionings of college students are somewhat more diffuse, less obvious or visible. But, as identity researchers have recognized, for some L2 users, learning itself may be less important than the construction and projection of a satisfying identity.[54] (See Roebuck, 2000, e.g., for a sociocultural interpretation of students' moves to position themselves advantageously even in relation to a classroom research study.) This suggests that learners may seek interaction with knowledgeable others not only with the direct purpose of learning but also, for some perhaps more so, with the purpose of being seen as a particular type of person, perhaps even simply of being seen at all. Given these groundings in the social, understanding the experiences of L2 students means attempting to understand how these undergraduates positioned themselves or were positioned in relation to others. As Lave and Wenger (1991) note, "Identity, knowing, and social membership entail one another" (p. 53).

Each of the four students in this research eventually found socioacademic groups that served to support their efforts and worked at maintaining those social nets. In some cases, institutional structures enhanced the students' ability to construct such nets. Engineering, for example, required students to work in groups on experiments, and this requirement matched Ben's predisposition to work together with others. As Ben repeatedly noted, informal group work allowed him to understand his course material better and with less effort. Even though in many cases his groups consisted of international students, particularly in the more informal study settings, the socioacademic links he was able to rely on were strong and satisfying enough to give him the support he needed. Furthermore, as was clear from Ben's emphasis on the mutuality of the help the members of his groups offered each other, the importance of these socioacademic relations was not unidirectional; Ben was not dealing exclusively with more experienced or knowledgeable others and learning from them, as in a strictly Vygotskian configuration. Rather, the existence of socioacademic relationships permitted the kinds of interactions that led Ben to exclaim "I really feel group study help each other. ... I really enjoy about it very much."

Institutional structures helped Yang and Yuko as well because they were admitted to their majors in a cohort of students with whom they then took most of their course work and who thus constituted a natural source of socioacademic relationships. Although Yuko was such a competent learner that she may have succeeded without the benefit of involvement with a group of peers, nevertheless, as early as her sophomore year, in the very first social work class she took, ice-breaking activities and the chance to meet more senior social work students allowed Yuko to begin to establish relationships that continued until she graduated and that opened a space for her to develop and display a satisfying public self. Linda, Wayne, Maggie, and Yuko were seen even by faculty as a successful and mutually supportive "clique" that Yuko was not only able to rely on but whose learning she was able to contribute to substantially. Yuko's placement within this social network, as well as the larger cohort she was a part of, thus enhanced her view of herself as a competent, strong young professional.

Being admitted in a cohort of students did not at first seem to benefit Yang. In her first semester in nursing, before she had established clear relations with her classmates, she expressed frustration at her perception that her classmates did not know how to share, how to work together. She was later especially grateful to those classmates for overcoming, as she saw it, their culturally induced competitive individuality and helping her in her struggles. As she described it, she would never have been able to do the assignments herself that the groups did and so was thankful to be working in one case even with a partner who anyone else would have considered a burden, not doing her share of the work. It was at least in part the support Yang came to feel from her classmates and teachers that encouraged her to go on working as hard as she did.

In subtle ways, however, Yang may also have resisted membership in the social group of nursing students. Yang's motivation for improving her oral English, for example, always remained extrinsic. She repeatedly spoke of needing English to stay in the nursing program and later to get a job but, perhaps significantly, she never mentioned worrying about communicating with patients. She seemed in fact reluctant to invest (Peirce, 1995) in English learning. Yang had been a doctor in China, and a published researcher; the identity roles available to her in the United States, ones she had accepted for the sake of her family, were those of a nurse and an English learner. What Yang wanted was a job, but perhaps not this imposed shift in identity.

One Complex Path Toward Belonging, Being, and Learning: Jan

Jan's situation was the most complex and best exemplified the importance of establishing satisfying socioacademic relationships and the role such relations play in identity construction. Unlike Ben or Yang, Jan never turned to peers for help with academic tasks. Rather, he turned to them first to try to create a supportive social framework that would satisfy his identity construction needs and within which his academic growth could take place. Although he wanted to survive academically, identity needs and social affiliation had to be attended to before academic growth could proceed. Thus, what Jan really struggled to achieve at first was not academic roles but satisfying relationships with peers and teachers that would allow him to occupy a subject position he perceived as desirable.

During his first 2 years of college, he established essentially no socioacademic relationships and remained socially isolated, disconnected, part of no community despite his efforts to connect especially with domestic students, the group he most wanted to join. Although he tried to strike up conversations with students in his classes, they responded politely but only perfunctorily, rarely engaging with him in the kind of interaction he craved.

With his attempts to reach out to others unsuccessful, he appeared to begin constructing a subject position from which to deal with the need for intellectual performance in the context of social isolation, and Jan began the process of making himself interesting by taking on the persona of someone too shrewd to really work at studying and who preferred instead to cut academic corners wherever he could. During this time, however, Jan also worked on establishing comfortable relationships with faculty in his courses, for example, through his personal messages to instructors on exams or papers. Jan wanted to stand out, to be personally memorable to his teachers as he waited after class in the big lectures and *counted* on his accent to prompt the professor to ask him where he was from, making him less anonymous and eliciting some interest in him and even admiration from the professor. Subject matter in courses in his first 2 years was close to irrelevant to him; what mattered was the teacher of the course.

When, in the second half of Jan's junior year, he began making tentative forays into showing intellectual commitment and a newly emerging interest in learning, in looking like an educated person,[55] this different attitude coincided with the two major changes in Jan's socioacademic situation at the time, becoming an RA and being admitted to the business curriculum, both affording him means of becoming integrated. The newfound social prestige and power, all of which he clearly relished, allowed him to invest in a new persona, the savvy elder statesman instead of the wily bad boy. In Bourdieu's (1977) terms, by virtue of his new position as an RA, Jan was now able to "impose reception" (p. 648) on his listeners.

Likewise in his business major, as he began seeing the same students over and over in business classes, engaging them in conversation became easier because they had a common history to talk about, common complaints, common concerns. He became a known quantity, again, in Bourdieu's (1977) construction, "believed, obeyed, respected, distinguished" (p. 648). He was no longer invisible or anonymous on campus but rather publicly acknowledged by his significant peer group as competent and as a desirable partner in interactions. Furthermore, his work both as an RA and in the business major confronted him with responsibilities that he was able to meet, and that were embedded in an important social context. In this way, as Wenger (1998) has argued, the critically central issues of power and belonging subtended the ongoing process of becoming a favorable self, as Jan allowed one problematic but survivalist identity to morph into another more socially acceptable one. Lave and Wenger (1991) well predicted the changes Jan experienced: "As members participate, their social relations within the community change and their understanding and knowledgeable skills develop" (p. 15).

Not all L2 students have as strong a need as Jan had to be recognized on their own terms by members of the social groups they must work next to or within. The needs of the other focal students for social affiliation and for identity construction did not appear so intense. But for students like Jan their progress may depend critically on being situated within satisfying socioacademic relations. Although he was able eventually to establish these relations, academic institutions are not particularly organized to encourage them. As Wenger (1998) notes:

Our institutions, to the extent that they address issues of learning explicitly, are largely based on the assumption that learning is an individual process, that it has a beginning and an end, that it is best separated from the rest of our activities, and that it is the result of teaching. … To assess learning we use tests with which students struggle in one-on-one combat, where knowledge must be demonstrated out of context, and where collaborating is considered cheating. … As a result, much of our institutionalized teaching and training is perceived by would-be learners as irrelevant, and most of us come out of this treatment feeling that learning is boring and arduous. (p. 3)

Institutional structures that resulted in the initial detachment of Jan's learning from any kind of personally satisfying social context may well have been central in making learning irrelevant, boring, and arduous for him. As it happened, Jan was not brought into his major in a cohort, the one institutional gesture examined so far that appeared to promote social connection and potentially help overcome the kind of social isolation Jan experienced in college. Another institutional structure conducive to the development of socioacademic relationships was reliance on group work.

Group Work

Group work, whether course sponsored or spontaneous, did in fact have an effect on the four students' socioacademic acclimatization. Three of the majors represented here placed particular emphasis on group work, and the focal students experienced frequent group projects in a wide variety of courses. Yet in this study few, if any, of the officially sponsored group-work experiences were able to attain their full positive potential.

Course-Sponsored Group Work.   The faculty named a wide variety of both pedagogical and practical benefits they felt students derived from group projects. These "learning communities" would help students learn better by having to explain and negotiate with other students their own understandings of the material; they would give quiet students more opportunities to speak; students would learn how groups function, how to allocate tasks, and how to recognize leadership traits or other group-beneficial talents in themselves or others. Group work would promote friendships. But most often the group projects, embedded as they necessarily were within disciplinary frames, institutional and social constraints, and the realities of daily life in the particular configuration they take for L2 students in a U.S. university, failed.

Membership in a group was usually determined haphazardly, often on the basis of loose proximity in the classroom, nearly always at the beginning of the semester when the students did not know each other. Rather than promoting socioacademic relationships, not being selected as a group member, as happened often to Jan in his first years, exacerbated a sense of otherness and isolation.

How to respond to variable contribution within groups was a problem. L2 students in particular may be less likely to know how to handle "freeloaders," as was the case for Yang and her unprepared and noncontributing teammate in one paired-work assignment. Faculty as well (especially engineering and at times nursing) tried to address the issue through follow-up meetings with each group, when group members were individually questioned about the content of the project. But a student who made a poor showing at this oral quizzing may in fact have made a significant contribution to the project but may have been lacking in the ability to orally display content knowledge gained from the group work. Oral questioning might pose a particular problem for L2 students because they may be less able to demonstrate their knowledge orally than to contribute to the group's knowledge construction. On the other hand, Yang was in effect barred by her well-intentioned group mates from making much of a contribution.

Because, with the exception of one social work course, students were given little to no guidance on *how* to work in teams, it is perhaps not surprising that very few course-sponsored group projects in this study could be termed fully successful in fulfilling pedagogical and socioacademic expectations. In the case of Yang's community health project, for example, she was able to develop warm relations with her group mates but with the unfortunate consequence of undermining a positive construction of her identity, making of her a sweet, smiling incompetent holding up syringes.

Spontaneous Groups.   Spontaneous groups, on the other hand, appeared to be generally more successful, both pedagogically and socioacademically. Although the spontaneous groups the students formed did have highs and lows, unlike course-sponsored group work, they enjoyed the distinct benefit of being immediately dissolvable the moment they became unbeneficial or obsolete, when, for example, the exam they prepared for was over. For the most part, the participants in this study, particularly Ben, were positive in their descriptions of these spontaneous study groups, provided that they managed to gain access to such groups (in the early years Jan could not) and that the members of the group had something to contribute (not always true for Yuko's study group because she prepared for these study meetings and the others did not).

Group Work in Academic Institutions.   Both these spontaneous and the course-sponsored groups were created for essentially pedagogical purposes. Nevertheless, as Jaques (1984) claimed, "Despite the pre-eminence of intellectual aims in learning groups it is often the emotional needs and undercurrents which are most powerful" (p. xiii). Despite their relative failure for the focal students, group work may in fact be one of the limited number of ways that institutions can potentially foster socioacademic relationships among students, which may be especially important for nonmainstream students like L2 students.

The four students in this study experienced close to 60 officially required group assignments across their undergraduate years. Considering that this comes to an average of two group projects per semester per student and considering that for the most part these group-work projects were less than fully successful, the question becomes whether more could be done institutionally to see to it that the many course-sponsored group-work projects inflicted on students yield greater benefits. Two points might be made here based on the findings of this research. First the best course-sponsored group work in the experiences of these four students took place in Ben's history class. Ironically, it was the one that was most closely overseen by the professor in the course and so in a sense the least independent. Perhaps the trade-off must be that if students are required to work together, as opposed to coming together spontaneously when they choose to, there must be closer faculty supervision of how groups work, beginning with how the members are selected and what role they are to play. Second, and following from this notion of greater supervision, it seems quite surprising that with all the group work assigned, in only one social work class were students taught how to work with others in a group. Given how few of the group work assignments met the students' expectations beyond getting the work done, it would seem that more attention might be given to helping students understand how to derive both pedagogical and socioacademic benefits from working with peers.

The Students' Institutional Presence

An exploration of the role institutions might play in promoting socioacademic relationships between, for instance, domestic and L2 students might begin with an examination of the institutional status of the nonmainstream students. Of the four majors represented in this study, responses to the presence of international and bilingual students in their respective departments were generally positive but also varied. The language constraints experienced by English learners posed the greatest problem for the nursing school along several dimensions: The students themselves experienced extra burdens; the students' language limitations potentially created risks for patients; the school itself might suffer the accreditation and rating consequences of English learners not passing the state board exams. Still there were very few English learners in the nursing program at this university and little to no hostility to them.

The engineering school enrolled greater numbers of international students and the faculty interviewed, though not hostile, might be described as being wary of or keeping their distance from these students, talking about them as though they had few interactions with them. This was a bit surprising because the engineering faculty seemed to spend a fair amount of time actually working with students in the labs on projects. Nevertheless, because the performance of the international students tended to be exceptionally high in general, no one seemed to find their presence a problem although, as in the nursing school, no one seemed to feel that their presence added particularly much to the learning atmosphere either.

The business school faculty did express appreciation of what the international and other bilingual students might be able to add to their classes and sometimes the expectation of benefits was realized with the presence of confident and vocal L2 students. However, although fair numbers of internationals and English learners enrolled in the business curriculum, the classes were generally so large and so much of the work assigned was done in groups that were not always socioacademically successful that any real effect of their presence was probably too diluted to have much of an impact.

In the social work program, with its principled commitment to diversity, more international and bilingual students would have been welcome but in fact there were very few. If the university town had had a large immigrant population, the story might have been different but most of the residents of the town and surrounding areas had not immigrated recently, but rather had lived in the vicinity for generations and could not specifically benefit from social work students from nonmainstream cultural or language backgrounds.

In sum then, although they may not have been specifically welcomed as L2 students, the general positive disposition of departmental faculty probably spared the focal students some of the difficulties that might confront English learners, immigrants, and international students in contexts where a history of conflicts or problems may have made the faculty less welcoming. (See Johns, 1991a, e.g.)

Relations With Faculty

Perhaps the most neglected of socioacademic relationships in the study of L2 students have been those with individual faculty, and yet the experiences of English learners in postsecondary education in the United States are significantly colored by their interactions in courses across the curriculum with faculty, who are largely responsible for setting the tone in their classes. The intersection between L2 students' expectations, abilities, and needs and the requirements and attitudes of their instructors may be a site of frustrating contention or of enabling accommodation on both sides. Yet nearly all the studies that have looked at the human relationships between students and teachers have taken a rather abstract approach, even though it has been argued that "the student–teacher relationship lies at the heart of education" (Johnston, 2003, p. 106). L2 undergraduates' emotional responses to their experiences are typically reported as directed either at course activities or at professors generally (Fox, 1994; Holmes & Moulton, 1995), rarely within the context of specific relationships with specific professors they encounter.

The same is true of the other side of the equation. Except in rare instances and brief glimpses, the teachers of L2 undergraduates have usually explained their expectations, plans, and opinions in relation to L2 students as a group, not as individuals (Losey, 1997; Zamel, 1995) and most of the teachers who appear in the literature are the students' writing or ESL teachers (e.g., Johnston, 2003; Schneider & Fujishima, 1995) rather than disciplinary teachers, despite the fact that L2 undergraduates ultimately have far more dealings with teachers outside writing and ESL classes. Two major exceptions to the pattern of neglecting interactions within disciplinary courses are reports by Spack (1997) and Benesch (2001).

In a few cases, research recounts faculty opinions about the performance of L2 undergraduates in courses across the curriculum. Johns (1991a), for example, reported on faculty criticism of L2 students for appearing not to know American history. Ballard and Clanchy (1991) speculated about why faculty across the curriculum did not understand L2 students' writing and behavior. Fishman and McCarthy (2001) analyzed the differing focuses that an L2 student and her philosophy professor took with regard to the work she did in his course. Zhu (2004) included information about what disciplinary faculty had to say about L2 student writing. These reports begin to get at student–faculty interactions but descriptions of the relationships between undergraduate L2 students and the faculty they encounter have remained generalized and somewhat distant.[56]

The faculty interviewed for this study were specifically asked about L2 students in their classrooms, and many professors reported going out of their way to try to make academic life easier for the L2 students. This was the case in their dealings with Yang for many of the nursing faculty, some of whom even intervened on her behalf to other faculty and to hospital staff, urging them to be more patient with her and assuring them that

Yang had a great deal to offer. Other faculty members interviewed simply expected the students to adapt to whatever conditions they found, even some that might easily be characterized as seriously and pointlessly disadvantaging them. An example might be the history professor who, fully realizing that L2 students could not follow everything he was saying, simply assumed, without troubling himself further, that they would get the pertinent information from the course textbook—although how they would know what the pertinent information was is not clear because that information was precisely what they missed in the lecture. Or the professor who conceded that "foreign students will just have to accept" the fact that they would be getting lower grades in her classes.

Nevertheless, most of the faculty expressed admiration for the L2 students they encountered, including in particular the focal students, admiring their willingness to work hard, potential contribution to the intercultural experiences of their peers, intelligence, excellent educational backgrounds, respect for education, and motivation. There were instances of cultural flattening—that is, construction of the students as two-dimensional, merely cultural representatives—where, for example, Yuko was asked to represent all Japanese (in her history class) or, worse, all Asians (in the social work class) and Jan was dubbed the "expert of the East Europe." But for the most part, these students were respected and treated well.

The Students' View of Faculty

In the meantime, of course, the focal students were also determining courses of action that would allow them to manage their relations with these all important members of their socioacademic context and forming their own opinions of the faculty they encountered. The failure of the L2 literature to record undergraduate L2 students' interactions with faculty makes it seem as though these students had no emotional stake in the interaction and went about going to classes developing no opinions, likes or dislikes, of the people they encounter. But the focal students in this study did have their own take on their experiences with the faculty and, as is to be expected, their attitudes covered a range. They were all attuned to the learning context beyond just course content and spent time interacting with their professors, at the very least mentally, and attempting to manage and understand their course work in light of their understandings of their teachers.

Ben, for example, worked hard to understand faculty motivation for assigning specific work in engineering. If he could get inside the faculty member's purpose in setting a given task, he was able to decide how to tackle it. Beyond striving to apprehend faculty purposes, he gave little sign of paying much attention to faculty as people because for him it was the subject matter that counted. But engineering faculty represented a convenient (and trusted) wedge into that subject matter.

At the opposite end of the spectrum was Jan, for whom the subject matter was close to irrelevant and what mattered most was the teacher of the course. In his first several traumatic years as an undergraduate, when Jan struggled with his academic work, he saw faculty as the enemy, bent on deceiving students, tricking them, or simply refusing to give out vital information. Rather than accepting the identity category of unsuccessful or struggling student, Jan preferred to construct himself as the victim of his professors' arbitrary and incomprehensible whims.

Jan's bid for agency also took the form of visceral responses to the faculty—some were psychopaths—and of imaginary vengeance scenarios, as when, in gleeful imagination, he consigned one to work on macros all day in a 6 × 6 room. Denied a desired subject position in his classes, Jan took advantage of the mediational power of language to reposition himself out of class as a powerful, and mocking, judge.

Despite his anger at some individual professors, Jan worked hard to bring himself to the attention of faculty, staying after class to chat, seeking faculty out in their offices, playing to stereotypes of the hard-working international student. But when the friendliness was returned, Jan was genuinely moved, as when his AfroAmerican history professor shook his hand after an exam.

Yuko took a personal, almost psychoanalytical, approach to engaging with faculty motivation and personality, sizing up Phil's background and predispositions as different from those of Sam, for example, and subtly adjusting her interactions with each of them accordingly, attempting to determine when to push a point and when to let it go, when to ask for help and when to work it out alone. Both Jan and Yuko made use of symbolic mediating systems (Lantolf, 2000b) in attempting to exert some control over their interactions with faculty, for example, in their frequent short personal messages to instructors on exams or on work they turned in, Yuko's often apologetic, Jan's funny.

Like Jan, Yang had quite emotional relationships with and opinions about the professors she encountered, especially those who she increasingly came to feel refused to understand her English. Whereas early in her nursing studies she had lamented that she did not have the language to show her knowledge, in the later years, Yang tired of having available to her primarily the subject position of incompetent English speaker and she spread responsibility for communication failures around more broadly to some of the faculty ("They just want to keep misunderstanding") and gauged her interactions "not so much according to linguistic expectations but rather by [her] chances of reception" (Bourdieu, 1991, p. 70).

Because Yang perceived her lack of power in relation to the faculty and because her relations with some of them were rocky, she became quite cautious in dealing with her instructors, managing her relationships carefully, deciding not to dispute her instructors' opinions about her, not to argue. Although she also had warm relations with many of her instructors, in evaluating her relationship to faculty, Yang perceived few options open to her to control her own destiny except to appear to accommodate to faculty wishes and in this way to pass under the radar long enough to graduate.

Clearly, despite the widespread stereotype of international students as motivated in their interactions with teachers primarily by respect for authority or learning, the actions and commentaries of the four students here make it clear that each one was also focused on and active in controlling their interactions with faculty for their own benefit.

CONCLUSION: SOCIOACADEMIC FACTORS

To varying degrees each of the students worked to restructure the contexts in which they interacted with peers and faculty, to manage the socioacademic relationships they developed, and to develop subject positions for themselves that they felt comfortable occupying given the constraints of their various communities of practice. One significant contextual constraint is the unequal power balance generally between newcomers and more experienced others. Social theories of learning view the learning space as dynamic and learning as socially mediated. Yet sociocultural theory appears to take for granted that the learner and the more experienced other share a harmonious relationship devoted to advancing the learner's development. That is, in sociocultural theory, the social relationship between learner and more experienced other who guides learning, whether students' peers or their university teachers, has tacitly been assumed to be positive.[57] Little attention has been given to the actual nature of the socioacademic relations that develop, to the power differential inherent in any learning situation, or to the consequences when relationships between learner and peer or learner and teacher are less than optimal at the personal level.[58]

In terms of faculty and students, the potentially negative impact of the power differential may in fact reach its peak in postsecondary settings, where, despite the fact that the students are all adults, their instructors have much the same kind of disproportionate power over them that teachers in K–12 have. That disproportion may be more palatable in K–12 to the degree that the subordinates are still children. University students are perhaps more likely to see themselves as autonomous and may be less inclined to accept subordination. It was apparent that the students in this study worked toward constructing themselves as more powerful and independent. Ben worked to determine faculty goals and internalize them as his own; in this way, in complying with faculty directives, he was in effect carrying out his own goals. Yang managed her relations with problematic faculty by restraining emotional responses she concluded would aggravate a negative situation. Yuko's responses to the community of practice in which she functioned were nuanced and astute, carefully fashioned to promote her academic and professional goals. Jan attempted to gain some control over his relationships partly, like Yuko, through the symbolic mediation of language and partly through his vehemently negative appraisals of some faculty members, the last resort of chafing subordinates, those in the least powerful positions; at least momentarily it was Jan who had the power to impose identity.

Perhaps for some learners such as those studied here, a part of the learning process is in fact learning to negotiate the socioacademic relationship between the participants. Not all experienced others present themselves or are viewed by the learner as a simple benevolent presence like a parent or older sibling. Nor can all learners accept the role of less experienced self without the assertion of a more powerful self as well. In the learning contexts explored here, sometimes the teachers accommodated the learners, sometimes not, but the learners each made active efforts, in their own ways, to construct a subject position from which they could comfortably interact with faculty and peers and to go beyond learning academic material or disciplinary procedures toward apprehending and/or manipulating their social environment. As recognized in descriptions of situated learning, progression from the periphery to the core of a community of practice is not inevitable (see, e.g., Lave & Wenger's, 1991, butcher apprentices or Toohey's, 1998, Surjeet). The focal students' eventual academic success was shaped by the socioacademic relationships that they were able to create and use to their advantage.

Just as theories of second language acquisition no longer view the language learner as a "lonely cactus" (Atkinson, 1999) but as a social and cultural being, in the current intellectual climate, the individual is not typically theorized as simply a separate, autonomously functioning subjectivity. Personal histories are seen as hybrid at least in part as the result of the voices, in Bakhtin's (1981) sense, that penetrate through and become entangled in an individual's experience. The experiences of these four L2 undergraduates cannot be stripped of their socioacademic contexts because the relationships that these students were able or unable to develop and sustain with others, faculty and peers, had a significant impact on their educational lives. Building reliable support networks for both academic and personal/emotional needs made their undergraduate lives easier and more satisfying. Although such is also likely the case for all students, indeed all humans in any activity, L2 students (and perhaps other nonmainstream students) may have a longer way to go before they are no longer strangers in a strange land, and they may be less linguistically and culturally equipped to anticipate and maneuver smoothly through or around obstacles or to enlist the help of others in doing so. Some features of academic institutions may promote the process of social and cultural acclimatization by, for example, admitting students in cohorts, using ice-breaking activities in classes, and preparing the right kinds of group-work projects, but many others are at best neutral in this regard, leaving students to fend for themselves. For some students, possibly L2 students, this burden may be particular difficult, while at the same time being especially important, to manage.

IDEOLOGICAL CONTEXTS:
THE UNITED STATES AND THE WORLD

If these students' language, literacy, and disciplinary development took place in the context of their socioacademic relationships, these in turn were embedded in the more abstract environment of the ideological climate of the time. Ben, Yang, Jan, and Yuko began university studies in the United States in the mid-1990s. It was the time of the "culture wars," of Newt Gingrich, Rush Limbaugh, and Dinesh D'Sousa, a group of right-wing ideologues who were successful to some fair degree in convincing the U.S. public that universities were and are overrun with radical remnants of the 1960s who indoctrinate hapless students into their favorite causes and points of view—affirmative action, multiculturalism, socialism, feminism. Radical professors were accused of expounding positions that were anti-capitalist, anti-American, anti-White male. Lamenting the imposition of such ideologically laden positionings in the name of equity, fairness, and openness to diverse views (see, e.g., Drummer, 2004, p. B4), right-wing commentators appeared innocent of the understanding that points of view that challenge hegemonic views stand out whereas those that fit the dominant ideology do not appear to be ideologically laden and in fact are scarcely noticed. As dominant ideologies occlude their ideological base and cast themselves instead as normal—the natural way of the world—points of view are seen as ideological to the degree that they deviate from the dominant. But underlying assumptions that fit the ideological schemas of listeners are absorbed as merely referencing the everyday reality that everyone experiences. Certainly, no one escapes ideological formation, nor is it possible to be ideologically neutral, but it is often easier to detect the ideology in positions we do not share than in those we do.

Some of the focal students' classroom experiences demonstrated how ideas that flowed from dominant ideological positions were reinforced in classrooms and passed unnoticed, no matter how outrageous, when they fit received ideas. These positions were revealed in comments in social work classes about the failure of the Hmong to assimilate, in engineering about communities' ability to prevent noxious plants opening in their area, in nursing about "conquering" the West, and in business about the need to educate and manipulate consumers. Points of view stemming from the dominant ideology are difficult to challenge because they only undergird commentary; they are not assertions, but taken-for-granted assumptions.

Because the focal students did not entirely share the same home cultures, histories, and discourses of their professors and classmates, the ideological components of their experiences were not quite as covert to them as they seemed to have been to their domestic classmates and teachers. To small degrees, Ben, Yang, and especially Yuko resisted these assumptions, doubting the appropriateness or even accuracy of some of what they heard, but, nearly always alone in a room full of domestic students, they were unlikely to feel comfortable disputing the professor's comments. On the other hand, Jan's embrace of capitalist business orientations and his failure, despite his many criticisms of his courses and professors, to ever express reservations about the ideological underpinnings of the business curriculum or capitalism suggest his basic agreement. Of all the ideological assumptions apparent in these students' classes, the most immediately pernicious to their well-being functioned to discursively construct an Us and a disdained Other, usually in the form of the United States in its distinctness from the rest of the world.

Issues explicitly related to an Other rarely surfaced in the data collected on Ben's experience in the engineering program, focused as it was on highly technical issues. As described in the chapter on Ben, however, the program had strong ties with industry and as such implicitly took on the assumptions of industrial players in a capitalist economy. Engineering students were required to take very few social science or humanities courses as part of their undergraduate education. Such courses might have potentially served to create a space for ethical considerations related to engineering work or for promoting an awareness of the political dimensions of engineering decisions. Instead only the technical domain was foregrounded for these students.

Ben himself tended toward a guileless willingness to take matters in his engineering education at face value, yet he also expressed a distanced skepticism of at least some of the host culture's ways. He was able to see through the propaganda of the corporate-produced videos depicting the happy and safe workers in chemical plants. More astutely, however, he questioned the reality of the "democratic" fairy tale about the willingness of industry to bow to the wishes of local communities and the power of local communities to control their environment through cooperative action with industry.

Despite the fact that the term *critical thinking* permeated the nursing school's discourse, it was difficult to tell exactly what was meant by the term because rather than disputing or making transparent received values, lectures often reinforced dominant ideological stances on U.S. culture and the relationship between the United States and U.S. practices and the vaguely existing rest of the world. In the lecture, for example, on communicable diseases where Yang's notes read "unimmunized population come from other country," the message was that the United States was immunized and would be safe if not for those "other" populations. Other lectures drew a clear line around the U.S. middle class as the presumed emotionally stable in-group ("solid America," "us") who did not experience emotional problems, which were to be expected mainly among those Others. Yang's Chinese medical degree, described by one faculty member as barely more than a chiropractor's license, was unlike medical training in the United States and conjured up the wild image of an improbable "nursing degree from Africa."

Yet Yang herself had no trouble thinking critically about the nursing program. She criticized nursing students' learned dependence rather than independent thinking about their educations and about medical issues; she saw through medical profession hype that emphasized the treatment and humanitarian benefits of good nurse–patient relations but in fact hid the real issue, the need in a capitalist economic system to competitively attract and retain customers. At least in her interviews, Yang resisted the Othering unconsciously promoted in nursing school lectures and asserted her own subjectivity, positioned to distance and critique the dominant culture. Even Yang's strategic refusal to openly object to what she deemed unfair treatment toward her manifested an assertion of her power to manipulate a situation disadvantageous to herself so that as the less powerful player she was still able to achieve her goal of graduating with her degree in nursing.

Jan and his peers appeared not to need to be convinced of capitalist values. Students in his classes found it entirely normal for an accountant's job to be to fire people, for marketers to know a great deal about the private lives of individuals, and for companies to create consumer "needs" through hammerhead product marketing. Othering of consumers and workers, however, was mild compared to depictions of international Others. Some lectures in the business school were brutal in their unquestioned assumptions about the "dumb" public in other countries, the buck-toothed Asians and the Africans too clueless to fathom that the picture of a baby on a baby food jar did not indicate ground baby inside. The consummate skeptic who prided himself on seeing self-interest behind the workings of nearly all human interactions, Jan suspended disbelief when it came to allying himself with the proclamations and embracing the underlying assumptions of the business school.

Of the four majors represented in this study, only social work overtly promoted the idea of social justice as a goal for the work they were preparing students to do but primarily in terms of equal access to social services and personal willingness and ability to accept alternative lifestyles or other kinds of diversity. The Other was recognized as deserving of sympathy and entitled to humane treatment. Nevertheless, both in social work and in other classes, Yuko too was witness to and quite conscious of egregious examples of thoughtless portrayals of the Other, not to say bigotry. In an American history class, it was the casual conclusion that the U.S. bombings in World War II were for the ultimate good of the Japanese people. In a social work class, Asians were lumped together in stereotyped images, on one hand, of the model minority and, on the other, of inscrutable Hmong communities who did not want to succeed, did not care about what happened to their children, and did not have the gumption to drag themselves out of living in project housing. They might instead have been told something about the Hmong story as Duffy (2004) relates it, something about how:

> Hmong farmers were recruited by the U.S. CIA to serve as a covert army in support of U.S. military objectives in Southeast Asia in the 1960s; how Hmong guerillas rescued U.S. pilots shot down over Laos; and how the Hmong suffered casualties so devastating that 12 year old boys were eventually sent into battle. Other stories describe the defeat of [this Hmong clandestine army] in 1975 and the exodus of thousands of Hmong to the U.S., where they arrived as economically impoverished refugees. (p. 224)

Or these students might have been told about the extensive literature on immigrant and refugee resettlement issues, some of which asserts, for example, that

> There are three features of the social contexts encountered by today's newcomers that create vulnerability to downward assimilation [i.e., the slide into poverty and perhaps crime]. The first is color, the second is location, and the third is the absence of mobility ladders (Portes, 1995, p. 73; cited in Lee, 2001, p. 507) such as access to appropriate social, educational, and economic structures.

But Yuko managed to some degree to resist the positioning that these incidents documented. She responded in several different ways. In the case of the history class, where she was the only Japanese student, she said nothing, though she recounted the incident outside the class acerbically. Perhaps the prime directive in resistance of this kind is to recognize which fights to pick. Resisting alone, without the support of a group, is difficult and in some circumstances pointless.

In the social work class, when directly asked to comment from her expertise as an Asian (and, as such, competent to speak for all Asians) on the situation of the Hmong, Yuko resisted the positioning by denying that she had any particular access to information about the Hmong, that she herself, simply because she was Japanese, was not in fact an insider: "My friends don't want to talk about what happened in their country." She next asserted the power and right of insiders to resist definition through invasion by the American social worker outsider "but they don't want an American social worker in [their] house." Her final move was to draw parallels between the purported behavior of the exotics and that of "solid America": "I think it's the same thing for middle-class people; ... [young people] do things outside the home that the parents aren't aware of." Yuko's courage in making her pointed and effective comeback statement succeeded in prompting a glimmer of resistance on the part of her classmates as well: "Someone who can't read could [still] be smart enough to understand what's going on."

CONCLUSION: IDEOLOGICAL FACTORS

As the classroom experiences of the four focal students indicate, insofar as these L2 students identified with the international Other, they were sometimes subjected to negative, if not always entirely intended, portrayals of themselves as exotics or as inferiors. Kubota (2001) challenged L2 professionals with her analysis of the conflicting discursive constructions of U.S. K–12 students as, on one hand, insufficiently literate (as evidenced by the many "Why Johnny Can't Write" laments) and, on the other hand, compared to Japanese students, as lively, imaginative, self-starting whereas Japanese school children were rote memorizers, obeyers of rules, passive. She pointed out that one useful purpose of the creation of the Other was the construction thereby of a foil, an effigy in comparison to which the observing group can find itself superior. The discursive construction of the Other was blatant in some of the classes discussed here, as it is more generally in pretertiary education where teachers often function, like the professors noted here, as cultural carriers. Olsen (1997) refers to teachers as "culture makers" whose role in schools is partially the promotion of an American identity. In Reeves's (2002) study of American high school teachers, they and their institutions also saw themselves as Americanizers of the L2 newcomers to their schools. These college courses too pressed the students into identifying with the ideologically fashioned image of savvy, healthy, law-abiding Americans.

One of the criticisms of critical pedagogy has been to insist that focusing on social justice means addressing the social issue of the day and that most L2 students, far from being interested in such topics, simply want to get on with the business of learning English or getting a degree, not with protesting a situation they may not even have to live with once they graduate. Yet stereotyping, dismissal, and mocking of the Other confronted the focal students in their classrooms. Benesch (1999) urged that L2 professionals think not only in terms of needs analysis in academic settings but also of student rights analyses. Some of the rights she maintained students have include, as Belcher (2004) described it, the right to "comprehensible lectures, clearly defined assignments, time for class discussion" (p. 175). We might also add the right not to be Othered in disciplinary classes. Rights analysis "theorizes EAP students as potentially active participants" in the framing of their academic lives and assumes that "the possibility for engagement exists" (Benesch, 1999, p. 315).

Like Benesch's (1999) students, Yuko for one did not need to be taught resistance to a misguided representation of the Hmong or to see outside the dominant ideological frame through to the rhetoric of assimilation, of festivals, and of blaming the victim. Nevertheless, in the 1990s at a time in second-language studies when researchers and scholars were worrying about the discursive construction of Otherness in our writing, teaching, and thinking (Kubota, 1999, 2001) and debating whether teaching critical thinking was hegemonically imposing Western or English cultural values on English-language learners (Atkinson, 1997), I witnessed university classes where there was no discernable critical thinking going on among the U.S. faculty or students. At a time when, in second-language studies, even the terms ESL and English as a Second Language were questioned as potentially essentializing (Spack, 1997), I was observing university classes that glibly stereotyped non-Western or non–North American people as poor, disease ridden, potentially dangerous, and uninformed. In the United States since 9/11 and the aftermath of the U.S. response, dehumanizing construction of the Other has arguably become more public and strident and, fitting snuggly within the dominant ideological frame, for some, may pass uncontested. That said, I do not wish to leave the impression that all or even most of these students' classes participated in such obvious negative representations of the Other. At the same time, as university faculty, we rarely have access to what our students experience in other classes and, D'Souza and company notwithstanding, it seems quite improbable that his school stands alone in hosting such incidents.

CONCLUSION

For Yang, Yuko, and to a lesser degree Ben, being admitted to their degree programs in cohorts of students who automatically shared classroom experiences proved to be extremely beneficial. Jan's struggle for social positioning was more painful but ultimately led to emotional satisfaction and academic success.

Four students in this study worked in varying special circumstances created for them by language and/or cultural boundaries and by power differentials that were sometimes referenced in their classes. Particularly striking in this regard was the triumphalist or self-congratulatory undercurrent evidenced in several of their classes that worked to construct the United States as superior to the rest of the world in parameters touched on by the health profession, engineering, business, and social services. Though they did not always comment on it, these students, and of course their U.S. classmates, experienced a discourse of cultural (including political and economic) indoctrination.

The social and ideological dimensions of university life framed the focal students' struggles for identity, social inclusion, and ideological resistance. These struggles took place and remained fairly completely out of the control or the purview of their literacy educators. But documenting and acknowledging these frames puts literacy education into a different perspective, perhaps one that reflects better the students' lived academic experience than one that focuses more closely on literacy development alone.

8

Conclusion

This study arose out of my desire to understand my students' writing experiences in their university lives in a second language and culture. At the same time, it was an effort to understand the role my L2 writing class could or should play for them, and to give myself a greater sense of legitimacy in teaching those classes. I had thought that what I would learn in this study would be translatable into L2 writing class/curriculum improvements. I am not satisfied that this happened in any significant way. In doing this research, I came to the opinion that writing researchers, in both L1 and L2, myself included, suffered a kind of professional deformation, exaggerating the role of writing in the lives of L2 undergraduate students and in their intellectual and academic development. (See Leki, 2003b.) The academic lives I heard about in these interviews and saw in class observations could not be reduced to issues of academic literacy.

What the study did give me was a much greater understanding of the relatively minor role that my precious writing class played in these students' lives, and that seems fine. At first what the students said about what they benefited from in the L2 classes was disappointing—some grammar, a little about organizing essays, a start on thinking about how to respond to essay exams, some increased fluency, some vocabulary, especially transition words (!). But it no longer bothers me that they did not get more because I see that they took what they could, and whatever that might have been, it helped. It seems to me now quite unlikely that what happened in their 1st year or so of writing classes would ever have been able to anticipate or really get them ready for what they were, each variously, to experience across the curriculum. The personal backgrounds, proclivities, desires, and talents of the students and the wide differences in requirements from course to course that they encountered translate expectations of making two or three L2 writing courses central in their academic lives into pure hubris.

Beaufort (2005) maintains that certain subskills are universal in successful written communication:

- Discourse community knowledge.
- Subject matter knowledge.
- Genre knowledge.
- Rhetorical knowledge.
- Writing process knowledge.

Of these five, a writing class is unlikely to have any hope of addressing the first two; serious engagement with the third is difficult without guidance from within the community that uses the genre. But rhetorical skills, like the development of audience sensitivity and inquiry techniques, and writing process exploration and expansion are certainly domains accessible to writing classes. Thus, it may be possible to discern a few directions that this study might suggest for L2 writing classes.

To avoid creating pointless work for already overburdened L2 students, it would seem reasonable to make efforts not to waste their time in our courses with filler (topics like "Read an article or two about women in the military and then write an argument for or against" come to mind) and instead to consult more with students about their agendas, including such simple hopes as writing faster so as to spend less time on writing and having more vocabulary to work with. Letting go of excessive, not to say exclusive, focus on English department genres—or at the very least acknowledging them as nonuniversal—might decrease some of the confusion that a student like Yuko faced when techniques represented to her in her writing class as universal proved not to be so. The isolation of writing classes in the 1st year of college seems problematic as well given how little writing may be assigned in other courses during those terms. As a result, students get writing instruction when they do not need it and do not have access to it when they might be able to use it, increasing the fragmentation of the curriculum and the impression that these courses are unmotivated requirements.

Because in many L2 writing classes the content for writing is relatively open, they can be used to make space and time for students to explore the world into which they have stepped by, for example, examining and making a start at responding to literacy demands across the curriculum. See, for example, Johns' (1990) suggestions for ethnographies across the curriculum. By the same token, given that moving into this world is likely to create tensions and put unusual demands on students, it should be possible at the same time to look for the opportunities that arise in Freirean "limit situations" and to use the writing class to address them. Benesch (2001) describes a limit situation as

> a personal or political obstacle perceived by humans to restrict their freedom and their ability to carry out their goals (p. 50).

Such situations confronted the focal students in a variety of ways, including finding themselves not selected for group work, given menial group-work jobs, being essentialized by professors, feeling reluctant to take the floor in class discussions, or not knowing how to defend themselves against accusations. Using their developing L2 literacy skills as tools to work toward analyzing such situations, including their hidden ideological dimensions, and developing possible solutions communally not only honors their intellect and experience but also might make L2 writing classes be remembered for more than only the use of the comma.

Finally, helping students to figure out ways of developing socioacademic relations or at the very least encouraging them to seek out such relations, though not directly related to writing, seems clearly related to their best hopes for academic success. Institutions that enroll international students, and compete for the money they bring (see discussions in Dillon, 2004; "Foreign Students," 2005; Ryan & Zuber-Skerritt, 1999; "Visa Delays," 2005) have a special obligation to see to it that the needs of these students are met. Those needs are not only for housing and English writing courses. Institutions that have recognized and attempted to accommodate these students' need for social affiliation by specifically working on community building and recognizing the cultural "treasure" they represent report increased student retention and satisfaction (Babbitt, 2001; Walqui, 2000). At the very least, a focus on socioacademic relationships might include encouraging students to make good use of writing centers, peers, partners, and professors, not only to look over drafts but to engage in the kind of "fight(ing) for your ideas" that proved so stimulating even to Jan.

In all, although generally my sense of my own position in the hierarchy of my students' academic lives and the position of L2 writing courses has deeply diminished, this is not discouraging. Instead what has been enhanced for me is my sense of the importance of attempting to understand not just the individuals seated in a given classroom but also how those individuals negotiate the complexities of the social, cultural, academic, and sociopolitical environments that surround them.

Appendix A: Interview Guides

INTERVIEW GUIDE: FOCAL STUDENTS

Beginning of Term

Activities over summer/winter break:

1. How was your summer/break? What did you do?
2. Did you spend any time on activities related to your school? Describe. Did you spend any time on activities related to your major? Describe. How will that help you in your major?
3. How much English did you speak every day and with whom?
4. How much reading in English did you do? What kind of reading? Any reading in your native language?
5. What was the best thing that happened to you all summer? What was the worst thing?

Major:

1. How are you feeling about your major now?
2. How are you feeling about being back in school again this semester? What are you looking forward to? What are you worried about?

For this part, go through the whole series of questions for each of the courses they'll be taking this term.
Work this semester:

1. What do you think _____ (whichever course) will be about? What do you expect to do or learn in _____ (whichever course)? (For Yang, ask her if she already knows any of what she expects to be learning.)

2.   (Looking over their syllabuses with them to see what kinds of writing tasks they will have:) How do you feel about the writing you will have to do this semester? Does anything concern you about it?

3.   What did you think about your first class(es) in _____? What do you think will be interesting? What worries/concerns you about the course?

INTERVIEW GUIDE: FOCAL STUDENTS

Weekly

Returned work:

1.   Was there anything that you turned in and that was returned to you since the last interview? Exams, exercises, quizzes, extra credit, papers, proposals, calculations, anything. Did any of your profs say anything you can remember about any of your assignments or exams since the last interview? What? (Get a copy of any assignments.)

2.   How well did this assignment or exam show what you know about the course material? Would there be some better way for you to be able to show what you know? What would that be?

3.   What comments did your professor make on your assignment? Do you understand the comments? Are they helpful to you? In what way?

Course work in progress this semester:
Writing assignments:

1.   What are you working on now or what will you be working on in the next 2 weeks in each of your courses?

2.   Why do you think your teacher gave you this particular kind of an assignment to do? (What is the professor's purpose in assigning it? What does the professor want you to learn from it or get out of it?)

3.   What did you learn from doing this assignment? How useful was it for you to do this assignment? (Trying to get at whether what they got out of doing it was worth the effort.)

4.   How did you do this assignment? (Did you do it at one sitting, revise a lot, get help?)

5.   What kinds of problems did you have with this assignment? How did you deal with it/solve it?

6. If you went to the writing center, what did you work on there? How many times did you go and for how long?

7. How did you figure out how to do the assignment? (Ask teacher, explicit guidelines [if so, get copy], ask classmates, follow model of some kind?)
    If there is an assignment sheet/guidelines, please note that on the work summary sheets so that we can be sure to get a copy.

8. What do you have to do to do well in this assignment? What is your teacher looking for in assigning a grade?

9. How does this assignment compare to other assignments you've done? How useful was it to you in helping you learn about the subject or about how to do something in the subject area?

Course readings:

1. What about the reading for this course? How is it related to the lectures/classes? (That is, does it overlap or does it provide additional information?) How well do you have to learn what you read? (Do you have to do all the reading, understand it, and know the information from the reading in order to do well in the course?)

2. Why do you think your teacher assigned this particular reading for you to do?

3. If you aren't reading everything that is assigned, how do you decide what is not important, what you can skip? What have the consequences been of not reading everything assigned?

Study habits:

This may overlap with reading; if so, ask these questions about the reading. If not, clarify what "studying" for this course means or entails.

1. How are you studying for this course? How much time do you spend on this course per day? What are you doing? When do you study for this course? [Probe to get a clear understanding of exactly what they're doing.]

Major and other courses:

1. How are you feeling about your major now?

2. What did you think about the last few weeks of classes? What stands out for you? What has concerned you? What concerns you about the next few weeks?

Include any of the rest of these there is time for:

Daily routine:

Describe what you did in detail today [yesterday, Saturday, Sunday, include whatever days will give us a better understanding of how their life goes].

Group work:

1. Are you involved in any group work or do you have any study partners this semester? In which classes?
2. If you have study partners, how do you help each other? (Share notes, talk about class work, edit each other's papers, divide up the reading, etc.). Can you give a specific example or show me a specific assignment you did with the help of a peer? Describe how you did this assignment.
3. If you are involved in a group project, did you get to choose the group or was it assigned?
4. What kind of project is the group working on? How do you divide up the work? Can you show me an example of an assignment you have done/ are doing in a group? Which part did you do/work on?
5. When, where, how did you meet to work on the project?
6. Do you ever have problems communicating with study partners or group project members? If so, describe.

Social life:

1. Describe your social life right now. (How much time do you spend doing things other than studying? When do you relax? With whom? What do you do? How do you feel about your social life? Do you feel you have a lot of friends?)
2. What do you do besides studying and relaxing? How much time do you spend on those other activities (family responsibilities, work, etc.) How do you feel about these other activities?

INTERVIEW GUIDE: FACULTY INTERVIEWS

Student task:

1. Of all the things you do in the course, what moves the students closest to your goals for the course? (What tasks constitute the most essential part or the core of the work in this course?)

Writing assignments:

1.   How important is the writing assigned for this course?
2.   You have [describe writing assignments]. What is your goal in making these writing assignments? (What do you want the students to get out of doing these writing assignments?)
3.   Why these particular ones as opposed to others?
4.   To what degree are these writing assignments like writing they might do as professionals?
5.   How do the students know how to do these assignments? What other resources do you expect them to draw on?
6.   What difficulties or problems do they seem to have in doing the assignments?
7.   What do you look for in evaluating this writing?
8.   What kinds of comments do you find yourself making on the papers?
9.   Describe a paper you remember that was unsuccessful.
10.   Describe a paper you remember that was really successful.
11.   Do you ever learn anything from reading Ss' writing besides learning something about the students' ability to perform the task set for them?

Group work:

1.   What is your goal in assigning group work? (Why a group assignment rather than an individual one?)
2.   What problems have you seen with group work assignments, if any?

Readings:

1.   You have [describe types of readings]. What is your goal in assigning these different types of reading? (or What is the role of this textbook in the course?)
2.   What difficulties or problems do the students say they have with the readings?
3.   How well are the students expected to know the material in the readings? (To what degree should they learn the material in the readings, rather than, for example, using the readings as background for something else?)
4.   What is the relationship between the readings and the course lectures? Is one more important than the other?
5.   How well are they expected to know the material in the lectures?

Exams:

1. What is the ideal way to study for exams in this course, apart from coming to the lecture and doing the reading? When you think of students studying for this course, what do you see them doing?

What do students find difficult in this course? Why? How important is it for them to master that difficulty? How might they go about addressing that difficulty?
What do students enjoy about the course?

International students:

1. Do you see any particular advantage or disadvantage for an international student in this course? What helps/hinders them in their work for the course? Do they ever come to talk to you about their work in your course? Have you ever felt they create an extra burden for you? Do you feel they contribute in some special way to the course?

INTERVIEW GUIDE:
DEBRIEFING RESEARCH ASSISTANTS

Courses

1. Describe what seems like a typical day in [each class you visited this term].
2. What's your impression of how [student] reacts to the course meetings? the prof? the assignments?
3. How about the other students' reactions to the same?
4. How would you describe [the student's] participation in the course?
5. What seems to be the core of the course in terms of what students need to know/learn?
6. What's your sense of the importance of writing in the class? Where do you get that sense?
7. What does it seem like the prof will look for in evaluating the writing?
8. How would you describe the goal of the course in terms of developing skills vs building knowledge?
9. What are your impressions of the group presentations you saw?
10. What else positive or negative stands out from you visits to this class?

Focal Students

1. How would you describe her/him as a student? Think of something specific that makes you think of her/him this way.
2. What's hard for her/him academically? What's easy?
3. Where does she/he seem to focus her/his attention academically? How does she/he decide where to focus her/his attention?
4. How do you think she/he is doing academically? (Somewhere between thriving and drowning.)
5. How does she/he seem to regard her/his work/progress?
6. How would you describe her/his nonacademic life, work and social? Who are her/his friends? How much in touch is she/he with her/his family?
7. How well is she/he doing in her/his nonacademic life? How satisfying is it?
8. Describe _____. What's she/he like as a person? What does she/he like? What does she/he dislike?
9. What else might be important to know about her/him?

Appendix B: Main Coding Categories for Student Interviews

References to English classes
    improving english language
    improving writing
    feedback on writing
    content of courses
Studying
    study process
    study habits
    learning by memorizing
    study guides
    definitions
    background content knowledge important
    previous knowledge
Exams
    teacher tricks us
Writing
    role of writing
    writing assignments
    purpose of writing assignments
    benefits of writing assignments
    journals
    writing process
    importance of background skill/knowledge
    teacher feedback on written work
    homework (problems/exercises)
Courses
    characterization of lectures
    course content

    class notes
    use of internet/e-mail for class
    professional training
Affect
    insecurity/uncertainty/anxiety
    upset
    anger
    learning from mistakes
    giving up/keeping trying
    frustration
    failing to understand
    pride
    personal issues/outside worries
    criticisms (teachers, teaching)
    criticisms (u.s. systems)
Teachers
    comments on teachers
    consulting with teachers
    teachers' personality
    conflict with teacher (finding t mistakes)
    teaching style
    predicting what teachers want
    interactions/relations with teachers
    how teachers feel about internationals
    teachers trick students
Reading
    vocabulary
    reading content
    reading length
    textbooks
    characterization of reading
    reading processes
    reading difficulty
Other language skills
    listening
    note taking
    speaking
    presentations
Group work
    projects
    learning from friends
    relationship with peers/classmates
    group interactions

Socioacademic relations
   cohorts
   references to domestic students
Control
   strategizing
   calculating/beating the system (how to use/buy/get books)
   time management
Student life
   work life
   social life
   money
   family (contact with home)
Special circumstances for international students
   how teachers see them
   how classmates see them
   cultural differences/comparison with home
   advantages/disadvantages
Teaching innovations
   indoctrination/propaganda

Endnotes

[1] This source of data proved to be an excessive burden on the students, resulted in relatively few entries, many of which repeated what the students told us in interviews, and was consequently dropped after the 2nd year of the study.

[2] At this institution, incoming undergraduate L2 students are placed into one of three academic English classes, the last two of which fulfill graduation requirements for 1st-year writing.

[3] This blend of gender and national background is broadly representative of the L2 student population at the study site at the time; there were, for example, very few Spanish L1 students enrolled at the time.

[4] In Wolcott's (1994) view, data "transformation" strategies may be descriptive (allowing the data to speak for itself—fully recognizing, nevertheless, that a descriptive strategy can never be simply a clear window on reality or truth), analytical (systematically identifying key features of the data, the themes or patterns the researcher discerns), or interpretive (explaining the data, attempting to specify what is to be made of it).

[5] It may be argued that the students whose experiences are examined here are not disempowered; certainly not all L2 students are (Vandrick, 1995). Yet the struggles of the students in this study would tend to index a subordinate status.

[6] The view these domestic students sometimes have absorbed of themselves as intellectually inferior is not surprising. In fact, this generally negative view of Appalachians, and perhaps other Southerners, is quite prevalent among colleagues as well both at this institution and at others across the country. When I introduce myself to colleagues at this institution as working with L2 speakers, the tiresome joke is that all the students from the area have English as second language. As for colleagues from other parts of the country, one once asked me if we "still churn butter down there," a remark cruder than most but not out of line with other prejudices expressed more diplomatically. I make a point of noting these

sentiments here partly in order to make it clear that most of the faculty interviewed for this study were not from this area originally; parochialism and bigotry seem to have few geographical boundaries.

[7]Probably 85% of the engineering student population during the years of Ben's participation in this research project was White male, with White women and African American men and women making up the other 5%.

[8]I have only general information on Ben's literacy requirements during his 1st year since he joined the study in his sophomore year. However, during his 1st year, he took five engineering courses, two chemistry courses, and two math courses, none of which would be expected to make substantial writing demands, although the reading demands, particularly in the engineering courses, may well have been heavy. He also took two of his required three-course English sequence. In these courses, although the reading requirements were relatively light, he wrote journals, essays, grammar exercises, and a short documented research paper.

[9]See Leki (2006) for similar first-term graduate students' experiences.

[10]Guidelines in Jan's business courses, described later, were provided by individual faculty rather than in the name of the whole department.

[11]It is difficult to let this division of labor pass without noting the gender roles here and later, when Ben off-handedly mentions this woman declaring that she was going through a divorce and so was easily upset and distracted from her assumed role of scribe for the group.

[12]In order to reflect this accelerated timetable, in the excerpts from the interview transcripts reproduced here, I have used junior to refer to her 2nd year and senior for 3rd/4th years, skipping the sophomore year as a time notation.

[13]TQ = teacher question, Ss = students, T = teacher.

[14]Compare this to Yuko's sense of good note taking described in chapter 5. Yuko found her domestic peers' notes overly detailed and useless because they took down every word instead of noting the main ideas, as Yuko did, to the envy of her peers.

[15]For detailed information on NCPs and how bilingual nurses learn to prepare them in their L2s, see Cameron (1998) and the work of Susan Parks (2000a, 2001; Parks & Maguire, 1999).

[16]The nursing school's version of critical thinking seemed to be in line with that of other educationists. L. Flowerdew (2000), for example, citing Gardner (1996) equates critical thinking with analysis, synthesis, and evaluation (p. 271). This version seems indistinguishable from an ordinary academic or intellectual stance and is missing any focus on power relationships. This lack differentiates these ordinary intellectual stances from critical thinking as conceived in critical theory, for example, of the Frankfurt school variety. See Sullivan and Porter (1997) for a useful discussion of the term *critical*.

[17]Although Yuko was not particularly critical of U.S. education in the way Yang was, she too characterized the note-taking goals of her classmates in Social Work as reflecting the desire to capture the lecturer's every word without any kind of critical screening, without, as Yang said, trying to "sort out what is important."

[18]His description of the leaders' response habits read like a comical parody of advice to writing teachers, especially within an expressive pedagogy paradigm, on responding as a real reader to student writers, rather than as an evaluator of writing, using the margins to encourage and challenge students.

[19]Newman, Trenchs-Parera, and Pujol (2003) refer to this form of study as learning through exposure, simple information processing. Although this approach characterized their least successful students, Newman et al. point out that students use it because they come to realize that often it is enough to succeed academically; it works fine, for example, for learning factual information such as might be tested on multiple-choice tests.

[20]He characterized multiple-choice exams in one course as including "outrageous choices and you already know that they're not right, like Mickey Mouse, or Napoleon, or dean of the university." (spring, 5th year)

[21]To enhance his chances of fitting in with his chosen world of CEOs, Jan signed up for golf during his last year as an undergraduate, figuring the well-prepared businessman would need golfing skills.

[22]Jan gave me this information via e-mail several years after he graduated. He still maintained his focus on social interaction, expressing his pleasure that his new job would allow him to "interact with people in person and make a difference instead making a million dollars a month for X Company and get pay almost nothing."

[23]Reliance on Internet research did, however, have the consequence of Jan's never learning to use the library:

Jan: I don't know how to use library yet. … It's kind of sad actually … that's my 5th year … and I'm still here and I didn't use it yet, so. (1st term, 5th year)

[24]Of course, depending on the pickiness, awareness, or knowledge of print code rules of the reader of these warnings, the sentence fragment in the guidelines themselves might arguably undermine this message for some readers.

[25]As usual in these situations with Jan, perhaps his behavior was reprehensible. Nevertheless, it cannot help but call into question what all these assignments, and all the course and curricular requirements, were about. Why did so many students refuse to take the opportunity to learn from this work? In their calculus, the benefit they might get simply did not outweigh the cost of the effort.

[26]Jan had an uncanny knack for finding errors and glitches: an incorrect answer to a geography lab exercise, an error in a management exam, an error in the times listed for the final exam in a management course syllabus, an incorrect calculation of a score on a math exam. In one of his accounting classes, the students were given problems to solve using a computer that was linked to a program that gave them their scores but did not reveal which items they had missed. Students could raise their scores by redoing the exercise blindly (i.e., without knowing which ones they had originally done wrong) but with diminishing returns: increasingly fewer additional points for correct responses. Jan found a bug in the software that allowed him to practice these exercises offline so that on what looked to the online computer like only his second attempt at the quiz he was always right.

[27]The most striking case of Jan's undergraduate years occurred in an African American studies course taught by an avowedly Afro Centrist professor. Jan tolerated, if not accepted, the Afro Centrist view of history presented in class—one that in Jan's words "basically makes you feel like shit if you're White"—because of the professor's great personal kindness. With the typical friendly openness this professor seemed to show all his students,

> Jan: After exam, he like shake my hand, spoke to me for few minutes after class. ... He likes me.

This meant a lot to Jan.

[28]In the spirit of confronting and revealing researcher bias, I have to admit that *I* did not feel comfortable with the Business School, with their uncritical acceptance of capitalism and their unabashed focus on profits. (See the section Ideological Education.)

[29]One of her short-term jobs was at a business exhibition, where she was to "go out just smiling at people. ... They just need a girl." But, she insisted, "I'm not wearing the miniskirt."

[30]This focus may also have been sustained by the fact that this question—Why is your teacher making this assignment?—was one we regularly asked in the interviews. However, we regularly asked the same question of all the participants and only Yuko and Ben appeared moved to take the teacher's purpose into their own consideration.

[31]Furthermore, the assignments were not always well thought through. In the political science class, for example, students were to write a series of letters to the editor on current topics of interest but also to use lecture/textbook material in the letter. Yuko experienced considerable difficulty here, particularly with the first letter to the editor. Up to that point in the term, the lecture material had been about the Constitution. There was little in the current news related to constitutional issues, so Yuko had a hard time finding a

topic that would have allowed her to make the required connection and ended up writing about the issue of a flat tax, a topic she knew and cared little about but that she could link to the Constitution, as required.

[32]These social work students tended to be voluble, pouring out feelings and reactions freely and extensively on the many assignments calling for such responses. This great willingness to express their feelings was the main reason for the page limitations set on assignments, which faculty struggled to get the students to respect.

[33]The following were the 10 competency areas graduating seniors in social work were to cover in their senior portfolios. In the directions, each area included a descriptor and students were supplied with a set of general directions for completion:

- Assessment and analysis.
- Planning.
- Helping interventions.
- Referrals.
- Vulnerable populations.
- Service delivery.
- Advocacy.
- Evaluation of intervention.
- Evaluation of professional growth.
- Ethical standards.

[34]Like the Nursing faculty, throughout this research social work faculty used the term *critical thinking* to mean either analytical thinking or skepticism. Never did a faculty member use the term with any connotations of power differentials.

[35]There was a certain poignancy in this activity, a young Japanese social work student interviewing an Alzheimer's patient from Appalachia who had certainly heard of Japanese people but may well have never talked or possibly even seen one in her life. Yuko used all the kinds of backchanneling, affirmation statements, and comprehension checks associated with reports in the SLA literature of native speaker/non-native speaker conversations, only the roles were reversed here as Yuko carried most of the conversational load, trying to follow, understand, and respond helpfully to the Alzheimer's patient, who drifted from topic to topic, not really answering Yuko's interview questions. Yuko gently nudged the woman back on track. Always sensitive and astute, Yuko could not but be struck by the artificiality of this exercise for both of them. As she commented:

Yuko: I mean, she start to answering my question but she end up completely different. ... it was really difficult to keep her with my interview. You know, because I am doing that for my assignment, not for her [benefit]. And that was really hard. (first-term senior)

[36] "The writer" refers to Yuko! The professor required this paper to be written in the third person.

[37] Accepting diversity in social work went far beyond encouraging students to accept racial, cultural, gender orientation diversity; rather, they were to somehow learn to swallow negative feelings about criminals and low-lifes such as child abusers.

[38] At the same time and unrelated to her social work studies, Yuko also taught Japanese and math all day at a Saturday Japanese school, in addition to, among other activities, tutoring university students taking Japanese. We never understood how she found the time.

[39] These people were rowdy; the classes were noisy, agitated. Students came and went at will in the class, walking right in front of the lecturing professor, eating and drinking freely, chattering, passing papers, making comments to neighbors apparently without a sense of the impropriety and inappropriateness of their behavior. There simply seemed to be no self-restraint. In one class, the professor twice admonished students to "stop, take a deep breath, and remember where you are." In faculty interviews in the fall semester of Yuko's junior year, two of the professors referred to this behavior as exuberance. Yuko certainly did not see it that way, and neither did her study group.

[40] An interesting feature of this town is that it participated in the research on the atomic bomb during World War II. Although this aspect of the town's history has some serious intersection with the history of Yuko's country, that aspect was apparently never brought up as an avenue of potential exploration in the group. It is not clear whether this exclusion was initially a conscious decision (Yuko's) or whether it resulted from lack of interest on the part of the domestic students in the specific contribution an international student might make to their group, a lack of interest that repeatedly appeared in this research. But in interview comments, Yuko expressly stated her reluctance, even refusal, to speak for all Japanese people on this issue or to take an emotional, non-"objective" stance in discussing it. After the presentation, the discussion did turn to the bomb and Yuko was asked to talk about its effect on the people of Hiroshima and Nagasaki. Sticking to her objectivity, she limited her comments to the radiation cancers that people currently continue to suffer from and their difficulty getting health insurance to pay for treatment.

[41] It should be noted that the TA who made this striking comment was from the Northeast and had graduated from an elite private school. Provincialism is obviously not limited to the rural Southeast.

He also remarked on how hard it was even for NESs to keep up with the fast pace of the lecture, another interesting comment that begs the question he himself never asked—Why not slow down?

[42]These sessions were, in fact, led by a nonpermanent faculty member.

[43]These 2 days were quite painful to watch, in part because of the raw stereotyping that was passing for knowledge and useful information and in part because I did not intervene and did not know how to do so. Given my commitment to principles of critical ethnography (Quantz, 1992; Sullivan & Porter, 1997), as the uncomfortable observer of a class where fairly flagrant racial and cultural stereotypes were being expressed and received as credible, I could have at least swallowed my distaste enough to talk to the instructor but I felt too emotional at the time. Not an excuse, a failing.

[44]This absence makes sense. Contrastive rhetoric has interesting insights for writing done by experienced writers in genres where there is relatively little of the kind of international cross-over that leads to more internationally homogeneous forms of writing such as in certain kinds of science writing (see, e.g., Connor & Mauranen's, 1999, analyses of funding requests written to the European Union). But the application of contrastive rhetoric analyses to student writers was always dubious and probably misplaced.

[45]Though it may be "acknowledged that writing [among professionals] does not come after the fact of research to merely record what transpired" (Canagarajah, 2002b, p. 99), these student writers did experience knowledge construction as separate from and preceding writing.

[46]Detterman's (1993) conclusions about transferability also support the practice of giving detailed work guidelines to students: "A teacher should explicitly list the exact, precise situation to which transfer is desired to occur" (p. 11) and "The lesson learned from studies of transfer is that, if you want people to learn something, teach it to them. Don't teach them something else and expect them to figure out what you really want them to do" (p. 21).

[47]See also Gollin's (1998) analysis of differences between writing in academic and professional contexts in computer science.

[48]Or, as Roebuck (2000) puts it, they each participated in different activity systems. Because the goals of the agents within an activity system form part of the system and may well differ, different agents experience the whole activity differently and in this sense participate in different systems.

[49]This is not to say that the written work Ben's groups were expected to produce was necessarily devoid of persuasive, rhetorical elements, only that such elements were never commented on in interviews.

[50]This expectation is one side of a perennial tug of war between compositionists and many other faculty. The accusation on the part of compositionists is that faculty across the curriculum fail to take on their responsibility for teaching writing. These two positions seem to reveal

noncommensurate views of what teaching writing means. Noncomposition faculty are apparently willing to teach their own genres but feel that it is the job of English departments, that is, 1st-year writing and (if they are aware of its existence) the writing center, to make sure that students write grammatically. Composition faculty chafe at this perception, typically refusing to see their role as so limited, banal, and ultimately, degrading. (See, e.g., the discussions of writing programs independent of their usual home within English departments in O'Neill, Crow, & Burton, 2002.) Their conflicting views may echo similar positions among L2 writing professionals who wanted to be seen as teaching writing, not as teaching language (e.g., Zamel, 1982).

[51]In fact, Candlin and Plum (1998) maintain that the literature on writing in technical areas at the tertiary level "clearly shows that ... extensive written assignments ... are not the norm" and cite Buell (1991) as reporting that "it is possible to survive with almost no writing skills" (p. 1). Harklau's (2001) students also reported experiencing a great deal more sustained writing in high school than in their 1st year in college.

[52]Despite high interest in the theoretical aspects of the social nature of learning and its importance for L2 learners, less published work than might be expected (except as related to peer review of writing) has shown the impact of L2 learners' social interactions with peers or colleagues. There have of course been many excellent research reports peopled with individuals, their histories, voices, and interactions with others in community settings (e.g., Cumming & Gill, 1991; Duff et al., 2000; Norton, 2000), workplaces (e.g., Goldstein, 1996; Parks, 2000b), elementary schools (e.g., Day, 2002; Toohey, 1998), high schools in English-dominant countries (Guerra, 1998; Harklau, 2000; Valdes, 2001), postcolonial contexts (Angelil-Carter, 1997; Canagarajah, 2002a; Thesen, 1997), and especially postsecondary educational settings (Canagarajah, 2002c; Carson & Nelson, 1996; Currie, 1993; Fishman & McCarthy, 2001; Fox, 1994; Harklau, 200, 2001, 2007; Hirvela & Belcher, 2001; F. Hyland, 1998; Ivanic & Camps, 2001; Johns, 1991b; Leki, 1995a, 1999, 2001, 2003b; Losey, 1997; Matsuda, 2001; Mlynarczyk, 1998; Nelson & Carson, 1998; Spack, 1997; Storch & Tapper, 1997; Thesen, 1997; Zamel, 1990, 1995). But the socioacademic relationships described in these are somewhat incidental rather than central features of the research.

We do have a picture, a relatively grim one, of L2 students' interactions with peers in North American high schools (see, e.g., Duff, 2001; Kanno & Applebaum, 1995; Lay, Carro, Tien, Niemann, & Leong, 1999; Leki, 1999; McKay & Wong, 1996; Olsen, 1997).

[53]See Norton (2000) and Peirce (1995) for studies of identity and immigrant women and Harklau (1999, 2000), Day (2002), Hawkins (2005),

and Toohey (1998) for children and high school learners of English in North American settings. Also see Parks (2000a, 2001) for work on social relations between L2 and L1 nurses and Toohey (2000) and Toohey and Day (1999) for L2 children and their L1 peers.

[54]Some researchers interpret the high dropout rates of immigrant high school students, for example, as related to issues of identity (Hawkins, 2005).

[55]That some large shift was taking place was suggested by the fact that it was in his religions course where Jan began to display a more serious stance toward his school work, despite his distinct dislike of the teacher and of the course. His new ability to distinguish his academic work as independent of its circumstances marked a departure from his previous conflation of teacher, course content, and willingness to try.

[56]The situation is quite different with graduate students (see, e.g., Belcher, 1994; Casanave, 1992; Dong, 1998; Myles & Cheng, 2003, and the Australian collection in Ryan & Zuber-Skerritt, 1999), for whom relations with faculty thesis and dissertation advisors have been shown to play important roles.

[57]See Van der Veer and Valsiner (1994) for a similar critique of Vygotsky's interpreters.

[58]This is not to say that sociocultural interpretations of learning do not include negative personal interactions, only that negative interactions between learner and more experienced other are not addressed on a theoretical level.

References

Adamson, H. D. (1993). *Academic competence: Theory and classroom practice: Preparing ESL students for content courses*. New York: Longman.

Aljaafreh, A., & Lantolf, J. (1994). Negative feedback as regulation and second language learning in the Zone of Proximal Development. *Modern Language Journal, 78,* 465–483.

Angelil-Carter, S. (1997). Second language acquisition of spoken and written English: Acquiring the skeptron. *TESOL Quarterly, 31,* 263–287.

Atkinson, D. (1997). A critical approach to critical thinking in TESOL. *TESOL Quarterly, 31,* 71–94.

Atkinson, D. (1999). TESOL and culture. *TESOL Quarterly, 33,* 625–654.

Atkinson, D., & Ramanathan, V. (1995). Cultures of writing: An ethnographic comparison of L1 and L2 university writing/language programs. *TESOL Quarterly, 29,* 539–568.

Babbitt, M. (2001). Making writing count in an ESL learning community. In I. Leki (Ed.), *Academic writing programs* (pp. 49–69). Alexandria, VA: Teachers of English to Speakers of Other Languages.

Bakhtin, M. (1981). *The dialogic imagination: Four essays by M. M. Bakhtin*. Austin: University of Texas Press.

Bakhtin, M. (1986). The problem of speech genes. In C. Emerson & M. Holquist (Eds.), *Speech genres and other late essays* (V. McGee, Trans.). Austin: University of Texas Press.

Ballard, B., & Clanchy, J. (1991). Assessment by misconception: Cultural influences and intellectual traditions. In L. Hamp-Lyons (Ed.), *Assessing second language writing in academic contexts* (pp. 19–36). Norwood, NJ: Ablex.

Barton, D., Hamilton, M., & Ivanic, R. (Eds.). (1993). *Worlds of literacy*. Clevedon, England: Multilingual Matters.

Bazerman, C. (1983). Scientific writing as a social act: A review of the literature of the sociology of science. In V. Anderson, R. Brockingham, & C. Miller (Eds.), *New essays in technical communication: Research, theory, practice* (pp. 156–184). Farmingdale, NY: Baywood.

Bazerman, C. (1988). *Shaping written knowledge: The genre and activity of the experimental article in science*. Madison: University of Wisconsin Press.

Bazerman, C., & Paradis, J. (Eds.). (1991). *Textual dynamics of the professions: Historical and contemporary studies of writing in professional communities.* Madison: University of Wisconsin Press.

Bazerman, C., & Prior, P. (Eds.). (2004). *What writing does and how it does it: An introduction to analyzing texts and textual practices.* Mahwah, NJ: Lawrence Erlbaum Associates.

Beaufort, A. (2005, June). *Do writing skills transcend cultures? A look at writing expertise.* Paper presented at the meeting of the European Association for the Teaching of Academic Writing, Athens, Greece.

Belcher, D. (1994). The apprenticeship approach to advanced academic literacy: Graduate students and their mentors. *English for Specific Purposes, 13,* 23–34.

Belcher, D. (2004). Trends in teaching English for Specific Purposes. *Annual Review of Applied Linguistics, 24,* 165–186.

Benesch, S. (1999). Rights analysis: Studying power relations in an academic setting. *English for Specific Purposes, 18,* 313–327.

Benesch, S. (2001). *Critical English for Academic Purposes: Theory, politics, and practice.* Mahwah, NJ: Lawrence Erlbaum Associates.

Bereiter, C., & Scardamalia, M. (1993). *Surpassing ourselves: An inquiry into the nature and implications of expertise.* Chicago: Open Court Press.

Berkenkotter, C., Huckin, T., & Ackerman, J. (1988). Conventions, conversations, and the writer: Case study of a student in a rhetoric PhD program. *Research in the Teaching of English, 22,* 9–44.

Berry, J. (1997). Immigration, acculturation, and adaptation. *Applied Psychology, 46,* 5–34.

Blakeslee, A. (1997). Activity, context, interactions, and authority. *Journal of Business and Technical Communication, 11,* 125–169.

Blanton, L. (2005). Student, interrupted: A tale of two would-be writers. *Journal of Second Language Writing, 14,* 105–121.

Block, D. (1995). Social constraints on interviews. *Prospect, 10,* 35–48.

Block, D. (1998). Tale of a language learner. *Language Teaching Research, 2,* 148–176.

Block, D. (2000). Problematizing interview data: Voices in the mind's machine? *TESOL Quarterly, 34*(4), 757–763.

Bourdieu, P. (1977). The economics of linguistic exchanges. *Social Science Information, 16,* 645–668.

Bourdieu, P. (1991). *Language and symbolic power.* Cambridge, MA: Harvard University Press.

Cameron, R. (1998). A language-focused needs analysis for ESL-speaking nursing students in class and clinic. *Foreign Language Annals, 31*(2), 203–218.

Canagarajah, S. (2002a). *Critical academic writing and multilingual students.* Ann Arbor: University of Michigan Press.

Canagarajah, S. (2002b). *The geopolitics of academic writing and knowledge production.* Pittsburgh, PA: University of Pittsburgh Press.

Canagarajah, S. (2002c). Multilingual writers and the academic community: Towards a critical relationship. *Journal of English for Academic Purposes, 1,* 29–44.

Candlin, C., & Plum, G. (Eds.). (1998). *Researching academic literacies.* Sydney, Australia: Macquarie University.

Carroll, L. (2002). *Rehearsing new roles: How college students develop as writers*. Carbondale: Southern Illinois University Press.

Carson, J., & Nelson, G. (1996). Chinese students' perceptions of ESL peer response group interaction. *Journal of Second Language Writing, 5,* 1–19.

Casanave, C. P. (1992). Cultural diversity and socialization: A case study of a Hispanic woman in a doctoral program in sociology. In D. Murray (Ed.), *Diversity as resource: Redefining cultural literacy* (pp. 148–180). Washington, DC: Teachers of English to Speakers of Other Languages.

Casanave, C. P. (1995). Local interactions: Constructing contexts for composing in a graduate sociology program. In D. Belcher & G. Braine (Eds.), *Academic writing in a second language* (pp. 83–110). Norwood, NJ: Ablex.

Casanave, C. P. (2002). *Writing games*. Mahwah, NJ: Lawrence Erlbaum Associates.

Chiseri-Strater, E. (1991). *Academic literacies: The public and private discourse of university students*. Portsmouth, NH: Boynton/Cook.

Coe, R. (2002). The new rhetoric of genre: Writing political briefs. In A. Johns (Ed.), *Genre in the classroom: Multiple perspectives* (pp. 197–210). Mahwah, NJ: Lawrence Erlbaum Associates.

Coffey, A., & Atkinson, P. (1996). *Making sense of qualitative data: Complementary research strategies*. Thousand Oaks, CA: Sage.

Connor, U., & Mauranen, A. (1999). Linguistic analysis of grant proposals: European Union research grants. *English for Specific Purposes, 18,* 47–62.

Cox, M. I. P., & de Assis-Peterson, A.A. (1999). Critical pedagogy in ELT: Images of Brazilian teachers of English. *TESOL Quarterly, 33,* 433–452.

Crowley, S. (1993). *Composition in the university*. Pittsburgh, PA: University of Pittsburgh Press.

Cumming, A., & Gill, J. (1991). Learning ESL literacy among Indo-Canadian women. *Language, Culture and Curriculum, 4,* 181–200.

Cumming, A., Busch, M., & Zhou, A. (2002). Investigating learners' goals in the context of adult second-language writing. In G. Rijlaarsdam, S. Ransdell, & M. Barbier (Eds.), *New directions for research in L2 writing* (pp. 189–208). Boston: Kluwer.

Currie, P. (1993). Entering a disciplinary community: Conceptual activities required to write for one introductory university course. *Journal of Second Language Writing, 2,* 101–117.

Currie, P. (1998). Staying out of trouble: Apparent plagiarism and academic survival. *Journal of Second Language Writing, 7,* 1–18.

Curtis, M., & Herrington, A. (2003). Writing development in the college years: By whose definition? *College Composition and Communication, 55,* 69–90.

Day, E. (2002). *Identity and the young English language learner*. Clevedon, England: Multilingual Matters.

Denzin, N. (1989). *The research act: A theoretical introduction to sociological methods*. Englewood Cliffs, NJ: Prentice-Hall.

Denzin, N. (1994). The art and politics of interpretation. In N. Denzin & Y. Lincoln (Ed.), *Handbook of qualitative research* (pp. 500–515). Thousand Oaks, CA: Sage.

Denzin, N., & Lincoln, Y. (1994). *Handbook of qualitative research*. Thousand Oaks, CA: Sage.

Detterman, D. (1993). The case for the prosecution: Transfer as an epiphenomenon. In D. Detterman & R. Sternberg (Eds.), *Transfer on trial: Intelligence, cognition, and instruction* (pp. 1–24). Norwood, NJ: Ablex.

Dias, P., Freedman, A., Medway, P., & Pare, A. (Eds.). (1999). *Worlds apart: Acting and writing in academic and workplace contexts*. Mahwah, NJ: Lawrence Erlbaum Associates.

Dillon, S. (2004, December 21). U.S. Slips in Attracting the World's Best Students. *The New York Times*, p. A1, column 2.

Dong, Y. (1998). Non-native graduate students' thesis/dissertation writing in science: Self-reports by students and their advisors from two U.S. institutions. *English for Specific Purposes, 17*, 369–390.

Drummer, L. (2004, August 13). [Letter to the editor]. *Chronicle of Higher Education*, p. B4.

Duff, P. (2001). Language, literacy, content, and (pop) culture: Challenges for ESL students in mainstream courses. *Canadian Modern Language Review/La Revue canadienne des langues vivantes, 58*, 103–132.

Duff, P., Wong, P., & Early, M. (2000). Learning language for work and life: The linguistic socialization of immigrant Canadians seeking careers in healthcare. *Canadian Modern Language Review/La Revue canadienne des langues vivantes, 57*(1), 9–57.

Duffy, J. (2004). Letters from the Fair City: A rhetorical conception of literacy. *College Composition and Communication, 56*, 223–250.

Dunne, E., & Bennett, N. (1990). *Talking and learning in groups*. New York: Macmillan.

Faigley, L., & Hansen, K. (1985). Learning to write in the social sciences. *College Composition and Communication, 34*, 140–149.

Faltis, C. (1993). *Joinfostering*. New York: Macmillan.

Fishman, S., & McCarthy, L. (2001). An ESL writer and her discipline-based professor: Making progress even when goals don't match. *Written Communication, 18*, 181–228.

Flower, L., Stein, V., Ackerman, J., Kantz, M., McCormick, K., & Peck, W. (Eds.). (1990). *Reading-to-write: Exploring a cognitive and social process*. New York: Oxford University Press.

Flowerdew, L. (2000). Critical thinking development and academic writing for engineering students. In M. Pally (Ed.), *Sustained content teaching in academic ESL/EFL* (pp. 96–116). Boston: Houghton Mifflin.

Foreign students at Australian colleges prefer them to British or American competitors, survey finds. (2005, October 14). *Chronicle of Higher Education/Chronicle News*. Retrieved from http:// chronicle.com/temp/email.php?id=5njh1pm26r7gvbr6tly51nepmqr6mbli/

Fox, H. (1994). *Listening to the world: Cultural issues in academic writing*. Urbana, IL: National Council of Teachers of English.

Freeman, D. (1996). "To take them at their word": Language data in the study of teachers' knowledge. *Harvard Educational Review, 66*, 732–761.

Freedman, A., Adam, C., & Smart, G. (1994). Wearing suits to class: Simulating genres and simulations as genre. *Written Communication, 11*, 193–226.

Fu, D. (1995). *My trouble is my English*. Portsmouth, NH: Boynton/Cook.

Gee, J. (1996). *Social linguistics and literacies: Ideology in discourses* (2nd ed.). London: Taylor & Francis.

Geisler, C. (1994). *Academic literacy and the nature of expertise: Reading, writing, and knowing in academic philosophy*. Mahwah, NJ: Lawrence Erlbaum Associates.

Goetz, J., & LeCompte, M. (1984). *Ethnography and qualitative design in educational research*. Orlando, FL: Academic Press.

Goldstein, T. (1996). *Two languages at work: Bilingual life on the production floor*. New York: de Gruyter.

Gollin, S. (1998). Literacy in a computer department: The invisible in search of the ill-defined. In C. Candlin & G. Plum (Eds.), *Researching academic literacies* (pp. 289–333). Sydney, Australia: Macquarie University.

Guerra, J. C. (1998). *Close to home: Oral and literate practices in a transnational Mexicano community*. New York: Teachers College Press.

Haas, C. (1994). Learning to read biology: One student's rhetorical development in college. *Written Communication, 11,* 43–84.

Harklau, L. (1994). ESL versus mainstream classes: Contrasting L2 learning environments. *TESOL Quarterly, 28,* 241–272.

Harklau, L. (1999). Representing culture in the ESL writing classroom. In E. Hinkel (Ed.), *Culture in language teaching and learning* (pp. 109–130). New York: Cambridge University Press.

Harklau, L. (2000). From the "good kids" to the "worst": Representations of English language learners across educational settings. *TESOL Quarterly, 34,* 35–67.

Harklau, L. (2001). From high school to college: Student perspectives on literacy practices. *Journal of Literacy Research, 33,* 33–70.

Harklau, L. (2007). The adolescent English language learner: Identities lost and found. In J. Cummins & C. Davison (Eds.), *International handbook of English language teaching* (pp. 559–573). New York: Springer.

Harris, M. (1997). Cultural conflicts in the writing center: Expectations and assumptions of ESL students. In C. Severino, J. Guerra, & J. Butler (Eds.), *Writing in a multicultural settings* (pp. 220–233). New York: Modern Language Association.

Haswell, R. (1991). *Gaining ground in college writing: Tales of development and interpretation*. Dallas, TX: Southern Methodist University Press.

Hawkins, M. (2005). Becoming a student: Identity work and academic literacies in early schooling. *TESOL Quarterly, 39,* 59–82.

Herrington, A. (1985). Writing in academic settings: A study of the contexts for writing in two college chemical engineering courses. *Research in the Teaching of English, 19,* 331–361.

Herrington, A., & Curtis, M. (2000). *Persons in process: Four stories of writing and personal development in college*. Urbana, IL: National Council of Teachers of English.

Herrington, A., & Moran, C. (Eds.). (1992). *Writing, teaching, and learning in the disciplines*. New York: Modern Language Association.

Hirvela, A., & Belcher, D. (2001). Coming back to voice: The multiple voices and identities of mature multilingual writers. *Journal of Second Language Writing, 10,* 83–106.

Holmes, V., & Moulton, M. (1995). A contrarian view of dialogue journals: The case of a reluctant participant. *Journal of Second Language Writing, 4,* 223–251.

Holstein, J. A., & Gubrium, J. F. (1995). *The active interview.* London: Sage.

Holt, D. (1994). Cooperative learning: A positive response to linguistic diversity. *Cooperative Learning, 14,* 4–5.

Hyland, F. (1998). The impact of teacher-written feedback on individual writers. *Journal of Second Language Writing, 7,* 255–286.

Hyland, K. (2005). Texts, transcripts, and identity: Confessions of a discourse analyst. In T. Silva & P. Matsuda (Eds.), *Second language writing: Perspectives on the process of knowledge construction* (pp. 177–189). Mahwah, NJ: Lawrence Erlbaum Associates.

Ivanic, R., & Camps, D. (2001). I am how I sound: Voice as self-representation in L2 writing. *Journal of Second Language Writing, 10,* 3–33.

Jacob, E., Rottenberg, L., Patrick, S., & Wheeler, E. (1996). Cooperative learning: Context and opportunities for acquiring academic English. *TESOL Quarterly, 30,* 253–280.

Jaques, D. (1984). *Learning in groups.* London: Croom Helm.

Johns, A. (1990). Coherence as a cultural phenomenon: Employing ethnographic principles in the academic milieu. In U. Connor & A. Johns (Eds.), *Coherence in writing: Research and pedagogical perspectives* (pp. 209–226). Alexandria, VA: Teachers of English to Speakers of Other Languages.

Johns, A. (1991a). Faculty assessment of ESL student literacy skills: Implications for writing assessment. In L. Hamp-Lyons (Ed.), *Assessing second language writing in academic contexts* (pp. 167–179). Norwood, NJ: Ablex.

Johns, A. (1991b). Interpreting an English competency examination: The frustration of an ESL science student. *Written Communication, 8,* 379–401.

Johns, A., Paltridge, B., Hyland, K., Tardy, C., Reiff, M., Barwashi, A., & Coe, R. (2006). Crossing the boundaries of genre studies: commentaries by experts. *Journal of Second Language Writing.*

Johnson, D. (1992). Interpersonal involvement in discourse: Gender variation in L2 writers' complimenting strategies. *Journal of Second Language Writing, 1,* 195–215.

Johnston, B. (2003). *Values in English language teaching.* Mahwah, NJ: Lawrence Erlbaum Associates.

Kanno, Y., & Applebaum, S. D. (1995). ESL students speak up: Their stories of how we are doing. *TESL Canada Journal/Revue TESL du Canada, 12,* 32–49.

Kubota, R. (1997). A reevaluation of the uniqueness of Japanese written discourse. *Written Communication, 14,* 460–480.

Kubota, R. (1999). Japanese culture constructed by discourses: Implications for applied linguistics research and ELT. *TESOL Quarterly, 33,* 9–35.

Kubota, R. (2001). Discursive construction of the images of U.S. classrooms. *TESOL Quarterly, 35,* 9–38.

Lantolf, J. (2000a). Second language learning as a mediated process. *Language Teaching, 33,* 79–96.

Lantolf, J. (Ed.). (2000b). *Sociocultural theory and second language learning.* New York: Oxford University Press.

Lather, P. (1991). *Getting smart: Feminist research and pedagogy with/in the postmodern.* New York: Routledge.

Lave, J., & Wenger, E. (1991). *Situated learning: Legitimate peripheral participation*. New York: Cambridge University Press.

Lay, N. D., Carro, G., Tien, S., Niemann, T., & Leong, S. (1999). Connections: High school to college. In L. Harklau, K. Losey, & M. Siegal (Eds.), *Generation 1.5 meets college composition* (pp. 175–190). Mahwah, NJ: Lawrence Erlbaum Associates.

Lea, M., & Street, B. (1998). Student writing in higher education: An academic literacies approach. *Studies in Higher Education, 23,* 157–172.

Lee, S. J. (2001). More than "model minorities" or "delinquents": A look at Hmong American high school students. *Harvard Educational Review, 71,* 505–528.

Leki, I. (1995a). Coping strategies of ESL students in writing tasks across the curriculum. *TESOL Quarterly, 29,* 235–260.

Leki, I. (1995b). Good writing: I know it when I see it: Matching student and teacher perceptions. In D. Belcher & G. Braine (Eds.), *Academic writing in a second language: Essays on research and pedagogy* (pp. 23–46). Norwood, NJ: Ablex.

Leki, I. (1999). "Pretty much I screwed up": Ill-served needs of a permanent resident. In L. Harklau, K. Losey, & M. Siegal (Eds.), *Generation 1.5 meets college composition: Issues in the teaching of writing to U.S. educated learners of ESL* (pp. 17–43). Mahwah, NJ: Lawrence Erlbaum Associates.

Leki, I. (2001). "A narrow thinking system": Nonnative-English speaking students in group projects across the curriculum. *TESOL Quarterly, 35,* 39–67.

Leki, I. (2003a). A challenge to L2 writing professionals: Is writing overrated? In B. Kroll (Ed.), *Exploring dynamics of L2 writing* (pp. 315–331). New York: Cambridge University Press.

Leki, I. (2003b). Living through college literacy: Nursing in a second language. *Written Communication, 20,* 81–98.

Leki, I. (2007). "You cannot ignore": Graduate L2 students' experience of and responses to written feedback practices. In K. Hyland & F. Hyland (Eds.), *Feedback in second language writing: Context and issues* (pp. 266–285). New York: Cambridge University Press.

Leki, I., & Carson, J. (1994). Students' perceptions of EAP writing instruction and writing needs across the disciplines. *TESOL Quarterly, 28,* 81–101.

Leki, I., & Carson, J. (1997). "Completely different worlds": EAP and the writing experiences of ESL students in university courses. *TESOL Quarterly, 31,* 39–69.

Lincoln, Y., & Guba, E. (1985). *Naturalistic inquiry*. Beverly Hills, CA: Sage.

Losey, K. (1997). *Listen to the silences: Mexican American interaction in the composition classroom and community*. Norwood, NJ: Ablex.

Matsuda, P. K. (2001). Voice in Japanese written discourse: Implications for second language writing. *Journal of Second Language Writing, 10,* 35–53.

McCarthy, L. (1987). A stranger in strange lands: A college student writing across the curriculum. *Research in the Teaching of English, 21,* 233–265.

McKay, S. L., & Wong, S. C. (1996). Multiple discourses, multiple identities: Investment and agency in second-language learning among Chinese adolescent immigrant students. *Harvard Educational Review, 66,* 577–608.

Melzer, D. (2003). Assignments across the curriculum: A survey of college writing. *Language and Learning Across the Disciplines, 6,* 86–110.

Miller, C. (1994). Genre as social action. In A. Freedman & P. Medway (Eds.), *Genre and the new rhetoric* (pp. 23–42). London: Taylor & Francis.

Miller, J. (1999). Becoming audible: Social identity and second language use. *Journal of Intercultural Studies, 20,* 149–165.

Mlynarczyk, R. (1998). *Conversations of the mind.* Mahwah, NJ: Lawrence Erlbaum Associates.

Myles, J., & Cheng, L. (2003). The social and cultural life of non-native English speaking international graduate students at a Canadian university. *Journal of English for Academic Purposes, 2,* 247–263.

Nelson, G., & Carson, J. (1998). ESL students' perceptions of effectiveness in peer response groups. *Journal of Second Language Writing, 7,* 113–131.

Nelson, J. (1990). This was an easy assignment: Examining how students interpret academic writing tasks. *Research in the Teaching of English, 24,* 362–396.

Newkirk, T. (1992). The narrative roots of the case study. In G. Kirsch & P. Sullivan (Eds.), *Methods and methodology in composition research* (pp. 130–152). Carbondale: Southern Illinois University Press.

Newman, M., Trenchs-Parera, M., & Pujol, M. (2003). Core academic literacy principles versus culture-specific practices: A multi-case study of academic achievement. *English for Specific Purposes, 22,* 45–71.

Ng, E., & Bereiter, C. (1991). Three levels of goal orientation in learning. *The Journal of the Learning Sciences, 1,* 243–271.

Norton, B. (1995). Social identity, investment, and language learning. *TESOL Quarterly, 29,* 9–31.

Norton, B. (2000). *Identity and language learning: Gender, ethnicity and educational change.* New York: Pearson Education.

Norton, B., & Toohey, K. (2001). Changing perspectives on good language learners. *TESOL Quarterly, 35,* 307–322.

Olsen, L. (1997). *Made in America: Immigrant students in our public schools.* New York: New Press.

O'Neill, P., Crow, A., & Burton, L. (Eds.). (2002). *A field of dreams: Independent writing programs and the future of composition studies.* Logan: Utah State University Press.

Ong, W. (1983). *Orality and literacy.* New York: Methuen.

Parks, S. (2000a). Professional writing and the role of incidental collaboration: Evidence from a medical setting. *Journal of Second Language Writing, 9,* 101–122.

Parks, S. (2000b). Same task, different activities: Issues of investment, identity and strategy use. *TESL Canada Journal, 17,* 64–88.

Parks, S. (2001). Moving from school to the workplace: Disciplinary innovation, border crossings, and the reshaping of a written genre. *Applied Linguistics, 22,* 405–438.

Parks, S., & Maguire, M. (1999). Coping with on-the-job writing in ESL: A constructivist-semiotic perspective. *Language Learning, 49,* 143–175.

Pavlenko, A. (2001a). "In the world of tradition, I was unimagined": Negotiation of identities in cross-cuiltural autobiographies. *The International Journal of Bilingualism, 5,* 317–344.

Pavlenko, A. (2001b). Language learning memoirs as a gendered genre. *Applied Linguistics, 22,* 213–240.

Pavlenko, A. (2004). "The making of an American": Negotiation of identities at the turn of the twentieth century. In A. Pavlenko & A. Blackledge (Eds.), *Negotiation of identities in multilingual contexts* (pp. 34–67). Clevedon, England: Multilingual Matters.

Pavlenko, A., & Blackledge, A. (Eds.). (2004). *Negotiation of identities in multilingual contexts*. Clevedon, England: Multilingual Matters.

Pavlenko, A., & Lantolf, J. (2000). Second language learning as participation and the (re)construction of selves. In J. Lantolf (Ed.), *Sociocultural theory and second language learning* (pp. 155–177). New York: Oxford University Press.

Peirce, B. N. (1995). Social identity, investment, and language learning. *TESOL Quarterly, 29*, 9–31.

Pennycook, A. (2001). *Critical applied linguistics: A critical introduction*. Mahwah, NJ: Lawrence Erlbaum Associates.

Prior, P. (1991). Contextualizing writing and response in a graduate seminar. *Written Communication, 8*, 267–310.

Prior, P. (1998). *Writing/disciplinarity: A sociohistoric account of literate activity in the academy*. Mahwah, NJ: Lawrence Erlbaum Associates.

Purdie, N., Hattie, J., & Douglas, G. (1996). Student conceptions of learning and their use of self-regulated learning strategies: A cross-cultural comparison. *Journal of Educational Psychology, 88*, 87–100.

Quantz, R. (1992). On critical ethnography (with some postmodern considerations). In M. LeCompte, W. Millroy, & J. Preissle (Eds.) *Handbook of qualitative research in education* (pp. 447–505). San Diego, CA: Academic Press.

Rafoth, B., & Bruce, S. (Eds.). (2004). *ESL writers: A guide for writing center tutors*. Portsmouth, NH: Heinemann.

Raimes, A. (1985). What unskilled writers do as they write: A classroom study of composing. *TESOL Quarterly, 19*, 229–258.

Reeves, J. (2002). *Secondary teachers' attitudes and perceptions of the inclusion of ESL students in mainstream classes*. Unpublished doctoral dissertation, University of Tennessee, Knoxville.

Riazi, A. (1997). Acquiring disciplinary literacy: A social-cognitive analysis of text production and learning among Iranian graduate students of education. *Journal of Second Language Writing, 6*, 105–137.

Rockhill, K. (1987). Gender, language and the politics of literacy. *The British Journal of Sociology of Education, 8*, 153–167.

Rockhill, K. (1991). Literacy as threat/desire: Longing to be SOMEBODY. In J. Gaskell & A. McLaren (Eds.), *Women and education* (2nd ed., pp. 333–349). Calgary, Alberta, Canada: Detselig Enterprises.

Roebuck, R. (2000). Subjects speak out: How learners position themselves in a psycholinguistic task. In J. Lantolf (Ed.), *Sociocultural theory and second language learning* (pp. 79–95). New York: Oxford University Press.

Russell, D. (1991). *Writing in the academic disciplines 1870–1990*. Carbondale: Southern Illinois University Press.

Russell, D. (1997). Rethinking genre in school and society: An activity theory analysis. *Written Communication, 14*, 504–554.

Russell, D. (2001). Where do the naturalistic studies of WAC/WID point? A research review. In S. McLeod, E. Miraglia, M. Soven, & C. Thaiss (Eds.), *WAC for the new millennium* (pp. 259–298). Urbana, IL: National Council of Teachers of English.

Ryan, Y., & Zuber-Skerritt, O. (Eds.). (1999). *Supervising postgraduates from non-English speaking backgrounds*. Buckingham, England: Society for Research into Higher Education and Open University Press.

Schneider, M., & Fujishima, N. (1995). When practice doesn't make perfect. The case of an ESL graduate student. In D. Belcher & Braine, G. (Eds.), *Academic writing in a second language: Essays on research and pedagogy* (pp. 3–22). Norwood, NJ: Ablex.

Severino, C. (1994). Inadvertently and intentionally poetic ESL writing. *Journal of Basic Writing, 13,* 18–32.

Silva, T. (1992). L1 vs. L2 writing: ESL graduate students' perceptions. *TESL Canada Journal, 10,* 27–47.

Silva, T. (1997). On the ethical treatment of ESL writers. *TESOL Quarterly, 31,* 59–363.

Spack, R. (1997). The acquisition of academic literacy in a second language. *Written Communication, 14,* 3–62.

Stake, R. (1995). *The art of case study research*. Thousand Oaks, CA: Sage.

Sternglass, M. (1997). *Time to know them*. Mahwah, NJ: Lawrence Erlbaum Associates.

Stockton, S. (1995). Writing in history: Narrating the subject of time. *Written Communication, 12,* 47–73.

Storch, N., & Tapper, J. (1997). Student annotations: What NNS and NS university students say about their own writing. *Journal of Second Language Writing, 6,* 245–264.

Street, B. (1984). *Literacy in theory and practice*. Cambridge, England: Cambridge University Press.

Street, B. (Ed.). (1993). *Cross-cultural approaches to literacy*. New York: Cambridge University Press.

Sullivan, P., & Porter, J. (1997). *Opening spaces: Writing technologies and critical research practices*. Greenwich, CT: Ablex.

Swain, M. (1985). Communicative competence: Some roles of comprehensible input and comprehensible output in its development. In S. Gass & C. Madden (Eds.), *Input in second language acquisition* (pp. 235–253). Rowley, MA: Newbury House.

Swain, M. (1993). The output hypothesis: Just speaking and writing aren't enough. *Canadian Modern Language Review/La Revue canadienne des langues vivantes, 50,* 158–164.

Swales, J. (1990). *Genre analysis: English in academic and research settings*. Cambridge, England: Cambridge University Press.

Taylor, S. J., & Bogdan, R. (1984). *Introduction to qualitative research methods: The search for meanings* (2nd ed.). New York: Wiley.

Thesen, L. (1997). Voices, discourse, and transition: In search of new categories in EAP. *TESOL Quarterly, 31,* 487–511.

Toohey, K. (1998). "Breaking them up, taking them away": ESL students in Grade 1. *TESOL Quarterly, 32,* 61–84.

Toohey, K. (2000). *Learning English in schools: Identity, social relations, and classroom practice*. Clevedon, England: Multilingual Matters.

Toohey, K., & Day, E. (1999). Language learning: The importance of access to community. *TESL Canada Journal, 17,* 40–53.

Trimbur, J. (1994). Taking the social turn: Teaching writing post-process. *College Composition and Communication, 45,* 108–118.

Valdes, G. (2000). Nonnative English speakers: Language bigotry in English mainstream classrooms. *ADE Bulletin, 124,* 12–17.

Valdes, G. (2001). *Learning and not learning English: Latino students in American schools.* New York: Teachers College Press.

van der Veer, R., & Valsiner, J. (Eds.). (1994). *The Vygotsky reader.* Cambridge, MA: Blackwell.

Vandrick, S. (1995). Privileged ESL university students. *TESOL Quarterly, 29,* 375–381.

Visa delays and fears of visa delays remain problems for colleges, officials tell Congress. (2005, September 14). *Chronicle of Higher Education/Chronicle News.* Retrieved from http://chronicle.com/temp/email.php? id=di78 rulmk0jm qijh3a3yfh4xkxgh7s36/

Vollmer, G. (2000). Praise and stigma: Teachers' constructions of the "typical ESL student." *Journal of Intercultural Studies, 21,* 53–66.

Vygotsky, L. S. (1978). *Mind in society: The development of higher psychological processes.* Cambridge, MA: Harvard University Press.

Walqui, A. (2000). *Access and engagement: Program design and instructional approaches for immigrant students in secondary school.* Washington, DC: Center for Applied Linguistics.

Walvoord, B., & McCarthy, L. (1990). *Thinking and writing in college.* Urbana, IL: National Council of Teachers of English.

Wenger, E. (1998). *Communities of practice.* New York: Cambridge University Press.

Winsor, D. (1996). *Writing like an engineer: A rhetorical education.* Mahwah, NJ: Lawrence Erlbaum Associates.

Wolcott, H. (1994). *Transforming qualitative data: Description, analysis, and interpretation.* Thousand Oaks, CA: Sage.

Zamel, V. (1982). Writing: The process of discovering meaning. *TESOL Quarterly, 16,* 195–209.

Zamel, V. (1990). Through students' eyes: The experiences of three ESL writers. *Journal of Basic Writing, 9,* 83–97.

Zamel, V. (1995). Strangers in academia. *College Composition and Communication, 46,* 506–521.

Zhu, W. (2001). Interaction and feedback in mixed peer response groups. *Journal of Second Language Writing, 10,* 251–276.

Zhu, W. (2004). Faculty views on the importance of writing, the nature of academic writing, and teaching and responding to writing in the disciplines. *Journal of Second Language Writing, 13,* 29–48.

Author Index

A

Ackerman, J., 1, 310, 312
Adam, C., 138, 165, 312
Adamson, H. D., 1, 309
Aljaafreh, A., 262, 309
Angelil-Carter, S., 263, 306, 309
Applebaum, S. D., 306, 314
Atkinson, D., 253, 275, 281, 309
Atkinson, P., 8, 10, 13, 14, 311

B

Babbitt, M., 285, 309
Bakhtin, M., 244, 262, 275, 309
Ballard, B., 271, 309
Barton, D., 238, 309
Barwashi, A., 242, 243, 314
Bazerman, C., 246, 309, 310
Beaufort, A., 284, 310
Belcher, D., 281, 306, 307, 310, 313
Benesch, S., 256, 271, 281, 285, 310
Bennett, N., 47, 312
Bereiter, C., 255, 256, 310, 316
Berkenkotter, C., 1, 310
Berry, J., 170, 310
Blackledge, A., 171, 317
Blakeslee, A., 242, 245, 253, 310
Blanton, L., 2, 310
Block, D., 10, 310
Bogdan, R., 5, 318
Bourdieu, P., 175, 266, 273, 310
Bruce, S., 250, 317
Burton, L., 306, 316
Busch, M., 255, 311

C

Cameron, R., 300, 310
Camps, D., 306, 314
Canagarajah, S., 305, 306, 310
Candlin, C., 255, 306, 310
Carro, G., 306, 315
Carroll, L., 1, 2, 144, 155, 236,
    237, 251, 311

Carson, J., 1, 5, 123, 189, 196,
    306, 311, 315, 316
Casanave, C. P., 1, 262, 307, 311
Cheng, L., 307, 316
Chiseri-Strater, E., 1, 2, 236, 311
Clanchy, J., 271, 309
Coe, R., 242, 243, 311, 314
Coffey, A., 8, 10, 13, 14, 311
Connor, U., 305, 311
Cox, M. I. P., 10, 311
Crow, A., 306, 316
Crowley, S., 253, 254, 311
Cumming, A., 255, 306, 311
Currie, P., 1, 189, 306, 311
Curtis, M., 1, 236, 311, 313

D

Day, E., 306, 307, 311, 319
de Assis-Peterson, A. A., 10, 311
Denzin, N., 5, 6, 8, 15, 311
Detterman, D., 239, 305, 311
Dias, P., 138, 241–244, 312
Dillon, S., 285, 312
Dong, Y., 307, 312
Douglas, G., 255, 317
Drummer, L., 276, 312
Duff, P., 118, 306, 312
Duffy, J., 279, 312
Dunne, E., 47, 312

E

Early, M., 118, 306, 312

F

Faigley, L., 1, 312
Faltis, C., 93, 312
Fishman, S., 271, 306, 312
Flower, L., 1, 312
Flowerdew, L., 300, 312
Fox, H., 271, 306, 312
Freedman, A., 138, 241–244, 165, 312
Freeman, D., 10, 312

Fu, D., 1, 312
Fujishima, N., 271, 318

G

Gee, J., 262, 313
Geisler, C., 240, 313
Gill, A., 306, 311
Goetz, J., 8, 313
Goldstein, T., 263, 306, 313
Gollin, S., 305, 313
Guba, E., 11, 315
Gubrium, J. F., 10, 314
Guerra, J. C., 306, 313

H

Haas, C., 1, 313
Hamilton, M., 238, 309
Hansen, K., 1, 312
Harklau, L., 1, 123, 263, 306, 307, 313
Harris, M., 250, 313
Haswell, R., 236, 313
Hattie, J., 255, 317
Hawkins, M., 263, 307, 313
Herrington, A., 1, 236, 311, 313
Hirvela, A., 306, 313
Holmes, V., 271, 314
Holstein, J. A., 10, 314
Holt, D., 47, 314
Huckin, T., 1, 310
Hyland, F., 306, 314
Hyland, K., 242, 243, 263, 314

I

Ivanic, R., 238, 306, 309, 314

J

Jacob, E., 47, 314
Jaques, D., 269, 314
Johns, A., 226, 242, 243, 270,
    271, 284, 306, 314
Johnson, D., 8, 314
Johnston, B., 263, 271, 314

K

Kanno, Y., 306, 314
Kantz, M., 1, 312
Kubota, R., 99, 201, 280, 281, 314

L

Lantolf, J., 262, 273, 309, 314, 317
Lather, P. 16, 315

Lave, J., 241, 262, 263, 266, 275, 315
Lay, N. D., 306, 315
Lea, M., 238, 241, 253, 315
LeCompte, M., 8, 313
Lee, S. J., 174, 279, 315
Leki, I., 1, 4, 5, 104, 122, 123, 174,
    189, 196, 219, 245, 254, 283,
    300, 306, 315
Leong, S., 306, 315
Lincoln, Y., 6, 8, 11, 311, 315
Losey, K., 1, 271, 306, 315

M

Maguire, M., 300, 316
Matsuda, P. K., 306, 315
Mauranen, A., 305, 311
McCarthy, L., 1, 271, 306, 312, 315, 319
McCormick, K., 1, 312
McKay, S. L., 228, 306, 315
Medway, P., 138, 241–244, 312
Melzer, D., 235, 315
Miller, C., 242, 316
Miller, J., 169, 316
Mlynarczyk, R., 306, 316
Moran, C., 1, 313
Moulton, M., 271, 314
Myles, J., 307, 316

N

Nelson, G., 306, 311, 316
Nelson, J., 1, 316
Newkirk, T., 11, 316
Newman, M., 301, 316
Ng, E., 255, 256, 316
Niemann, T., 306, 315
Norton, B., 119, 122, 175, 263,
    306, 307, 316

O

O'Neill, P., 306, 316
Olsen, L., 280, 306, 316
Ong, W., 238, 316

P

Paltridge, B., 242, 243, 314
Paradis, J., 246, 310
Pare, A., 138, 241–244, 312
Parks, S., 300, 306, 307, 316
Patrick, S., 47, 314
Pavlenko, A., 171, 262, 263, 316, 317
Peck, W., 1, 312

Peirce, B. N., 265, 307, 317
Pennycook, A., 15, 16, 317
Plum, G., 255, 306, 310
Porter, J., 16, 300, 305, 318
Prior, P., 1–3, 246, 310, 317
Pujol, M., 301, 316
Purdie, N., 255, 317

Q

Quantz, R., 15, 305, 317

R

Rafoth, B., 250, 317
Raimes, A., 253, 317
Ramanathan, V., 253, 309
Reeves, J., 280, 317
Reiff, M., 242, 243, 314
Riazi, A., 1, 317
Rockhill, K., 263, 317
Roebuck, R., 263, 305, 317
Rottenberg, L., 47, 314
Russell, D., 2, 153, 253, 254, 317, 318
Ryan, Y., 285, 307, 318

S

Scardamalia, M., 256, 310
Schneider, M., 271, 318
Severino, C., 82, 318
Silva, T., 4, 189, 259, 318
Smart, G., 138, 165, 312
Spack, R., 1, 2, 271, 281, 306, 318
Stake, R., 8, 318
Stein, V., 1, 312
Sternglass, M., 1, 2, 236, 318
Stockton, S., 240, 318
Storch, N., 306, 318
Street, B., 3, 238, 241, 253, 315, 318
Sullivan, P., 16, 300, 305, 318

Swain, M., 239, 246, 318
Swales, J., 242, 318

T

Tapper, J., 306, 318
Tardy, C., 242, 243, 314
Taylor, S. J., 5, 318
Thesen, L., 263, 306, 318
Tien, S., 306, 315
Toohey, K., 175, 263, 275, 306, 307, 316, 318, 319
Trenchs-Parera, M., 301, 316
Trimbur, J., 262, 319

V

Valdes, G., 175, 306, 319
Valsiner, J., 307, 319
van der Veer, R., 307, 319
Vandrick, S., 299, 319
Vollmer, G., 174, 319
Vygotsky, 262, 319

W

Walqui, A,. 285, 319
Walvoord, B., 1, 319
Wenger, E., 12, 121, 241, 262, 263, 266, 275, 315, 319
Wheeler, E., 47, 314
Winsor, D., 54, 241, 242, 245, 319
Wolcott, H., 1, 12, 14, 299, 319
Wong, P., 118, 306, 312
Wong, S. C., 228, 306, 315

Z

Zamel, V., 271, 306, 319
Zhou, A., 255, 311
Zhu, W., 157, 271, 319
Zuber-Skerritt, O., 285, 307, 318

Subject Index

A

academic literacy, 1, 3, 4, 8, 9, 10, 17, 198, 216, 241, 253, 259, 261, 283
accent, 16, 122, 168, 169, 171, 187, 266
accommodation, 58–60, 78, 101, 171, 172, 180, 182, 248, 271, 274, 275, 285
accounting class, 127, 130, 141, 157, 158, 173, 302
accreditation, 68, 102, 202, 270
acculturation, 7, 255
accuracy
   grammatical, 247, 258, 252, 254
   in assignment, 28, 30, 34, 36, 38, 40, 57, 68, 96, 163, 246
   in note taking, 70, 80
   of perception, 130, 277
   of pronunciation, 79
   writing reflecting understanding, 32, 191
active learner, 23, 235, 281
activism, 137
activity theory, 242, 244, 253
admissions, 20, 122, 123, 184, 192, 200, 211, 212
adult education, 79
advertising, 137, 138, 141, 173, 174
advising, 65, 100, 124, 184, 221, 307
advocacy, 16, 178, 303
affirmative action, 276
age factor, 66, 67, 95, 247
AIDS, 180, 194
American Dream, 228, 229
American Sign Language (ASL), 180, 193, 197, 233, 237
Americanization, 76, 280
analytic induction, 8
anecdote, 23, 119
anger, 149, 215, 217, 273, 296
anonymity, 14, 53, 55, 136, 161, 167, 266
anthropology, 212, 213, 226
anxiety, 67, 68, 76, 184, 185, 218, 296
APA style, 189, 211
apprentice, 35, 39, 54, 64, 72, 275

assertiveness, 51, 181, 219, 225
assimilation, 170, 175, 226, 228, 230, 277, 279, 281
assumption
   ideological, 60, 115–118, 172, 173, 201, 222, 229, chapter 7 of faculty, 35, 38, 44, 104, 214, 234, 235–237, 240, 241, 245, 250, 254, 257, 258 of students, 81, 83, 103, 162, 188, 198, 241
attendance, 60, 74, 126, 213, 233
attitude
   of faculty, 39, 55, 59, 139, 174, 186, 218, 226, 271
   of students, 53, 60, 101, 122, 139, 160, 166, 174–176, 195, 199, 217, 266, 272
   toward writing, 39, 53, 195
audience, 23, 26, 30, 35, 38, 41, 79, 142, 158, 159, 204, 235, 249, 284
authenticity, 243, 245, 254
authorial voice, 147, 155, 200, 209, see also *ownership*
authority, 34, 99, 155, 182, 244, 250, 274
autonomous literacy, 238, 262
autonomy, 64, 100, 274, 275
awareness, 105, 158, 172, 186, 187, 195, 203, 207, 215, 216, 277, 301

B

backchanneling, 78, 303
beat the system, 127, 297
believing game, 21, 48, 60
belletristic essay, 252
bias, 112–114, 118, 215, 302
bigotry, 228, 279, 300, see also *racism*
bilingualism, ix, 12, 59, 168–172, 214, 269, 270, 300
biology, 189, 193, 196, 213, 222, 226, 233, 237, 240

blame, 174, 217, 241, 281
body language, 118, 215, 226
book report, 193, 235
boredom, 20, 39, 48, 60, 213, 267
Boston Massacre, 48
Breakfast with the Head, 183
bricoleur, 6
business, 39, 137, chapter 4, 185, 199,
        200, 236, 238, 241, 254, 266, 270,
        277, 279, 282, 300–302

C

capitalism, 9, 13, 14, 16, 120, 172, 176,
        277, 278, 302
capstone course, 159
case analysis, 149–151, 153, 154
cheating, 130, 167, 267
chemistry, 27, 28, 30, 124, 300
class size, 126, 135, 137, 156, 161, 167,
        240, 266
classroom management, 186
clinicals, chapter 3, 167
coherence, 158, 248, 251, 257
cohort, 67, 68, 76, 102, 109, 175, 180,
        181, 183, 186, 216, 230, 231, 264,
        267, 276, 281, 282, 297
collaboration, 34, 44, 267
colloquial English, 78, 118, 119
commitment, 33, 34, 157, 164, 201, 220,
        227, 237, 256, 266, 270, 305
communication breakdown, 49, 113
community, 26, 121, 137, 161, 171,
        183, 197, 215, 216, 226–228,
        230, 243, chapter 7,
        284, 285, 306
community of practice, 121, 262, 274, 275
competition, 123, 264
conceptual knowledge, 27
conciseness, 36–38, 157, 158, 191, 246
confidence
    about writing, 34, 139, 140, 142, 149,
        150, 153, 235, 250
    building, 79, 150
    of faculty in students, 57, 153, 158
    of students, 66, 107, 109, 110, 137, 139,
        140, 142, 149, 235, 250, 270
    self-, 11, 135, 176, 179, 221, 227
conformity, 51, 187
confrontation, 140, 167, 182, 184, 302
confusion, 72, 82, 106, 116, 160,
        223, 250, 284

connector words, 29
constructivism, 8
consumerism, 16
contradiction, 122, 136, 165,
        166, 175, 243
contrastive rhetoric, 305
control, 120, 182, 189, 216, 225, 236,
        249, 252, 255, 273–275, 282, 297
convention, 37–39, 78, 87,
        158, 211, 246
copying, 100, 159, 170
    approved, 28, 91, 93, 94,
        104, 105, 131, 235, 245
    not approved, 29, 127, 130, 249
creationism, 222, 223
creativity, 21, 31, 33, 36, 96, 99
credibility, 34, 137, 186
critical ethnography, 305
critical pathways, 94
critical pedagogy, 281
critical theory, 300
critical thinking, 96–98, 118,
        173, 178, 202, 257, 258,
        278, 281, 300, 303
crying, 169, 181, 187, 215
cultural capital, 119
cultural differences, 49, 51, 57,
        92, 98, 100, 106, 110, 169,
        170, 172, 201, 222–229, 264, 297
culture wars, 276

D

deaf, 20, 197, 227
death, 161
delivery speed, 55, 70, 78, 107,
        109, 119, 122, 171, 172
developmental view, 238
dialect, 78, 96, 119, 223
dictionary, 80
disciplinary writing, 39, 94, 131,
        149, 203, 206, 237, 240, 252, 253
discrimination, 67, 112, 128, 226
distributed cognition, 242, 244
diversity, 17, 183, 215, 226, 230,
        270, 276, 279, 304
divorce, 182, 300
Donner Pass, 23, 24
dormitory, 17, 124, 127, 128, 161
draft, 5, 44, 139, 140, 143, 156, 159,
        196, 198, 201, 210–212, 224,
        237, 249, 250, 257, 258, 285

drinking, 128, 161
drop course, 24, 50, 72, 74,
    76, 95, 108, 113, 124, 168
dropout rate, 307

E

editing, 44, 143, 246
embarrassment, 171, 217, 224
enculturation, 70, 203, 207,
    241–244, 263
engineering, chapter 2, 64, 166, 185, 199,
    233, 235, 236, 241, 244–247, 250,
    254, 264, 268, 270, 272, 273, 277,
    282, 300
enrollment, see *class size*
epiphany, 8, 236
epistemology, 38
error, 30, 39, 44, 93, 96, 197, 238, 250,
    254, 302
ESL class, 45, 65, 122, 123, 125, 142,
    188–192, 234, 251, 252, 271, 281
essentialism, 15, 281, 285
ethics
    class, 85, 141, 149–153, 195, 238, 247
    of situation, 112, 130, 176, 185–187,
        254, 277, 303
ethnicity, 16, 88, 175, 201, 304, 305
euphemism, 111, 112
exact essay style, 191
exit exam, 238
expertise, 26, 137, 228, 236, 240, 255–257
extracurricular activity, 177, 183

F

facade, 138, 139
factionalism, 216
fairness, 96, 108, 114, 181, 217,
    224, 276, 278
fast-food job, 122
fatigue, 70, 77, 258
feedback, 9, 155, 164, 249, 258
    from peers, 41, 211, 218
    from faculty, 34, 42–44, 237, 258, 79,
        87, 89, 109, 146, 153, 156, 159,
        198, 207–211, 237, 250, 257, 295
    from writing center tutors, 142, 152,
        156, 210, 211, 250
feminism, 276
field practice, 177, 179, 187, 194, 195,
    199, 200, 207, 215, 216, 218, 230
filler, 151, 284

film class, 141, 149, 155, 176, 238
first person, 38
flattening, 272
fluency, 79, 122, 160, 225, 251
folk tales, 213
following directions, 28, 158, 195–197,
    200–202, 209, 244–246, 248
foreign language class, 126
formulaic writing, 28, 233
Fourier's Law, 35
frank words, 225
friendship, 79, 103–105, 108, 118, 119,
    123, 162, 179 ,184, 212, 218, 262,
    267, 290, 296
frustration, 24, 72, 97, 98, 101, 105, 107,
    162, 188, 200, 202, 217, 224, 246,
    264, 271, 296
funding, 240, 305

G

games, 125, 129, 131, 167, 174
gangs, 229, 230
gender, 299, 300, 304
genre knowledge, 284
genre theory, 242, 245
geography, 127, 129, 132, 171, 240, 302
grade point average (GPA), 20, 61,
    63, 65, 126, 127, 132, 136, 139
Graduate Record Exam (GRE), 29
graduate school, 33, 42, 170,
    181–183, 209, 211, 233
graduation, 76, 77, 103, 108, 109,
    113–115, 136, 149, 177, 178, 180,
    184, 192, 299
green card, 19, 24, 25
guessing, 59, 123, 126, 131, 170
guilt, 77

H

handbook (writing), 34, 39
handwriting, 74, 221
hard working, 57, 71, 73, 102,
    167, 202, 211, 225, 226,
    228, 230, 234, 250, 265,
    272, 273, see also *work ethic*
hearing impairment, 64
hedging, 203
hegemony, 16, 276, 281
helpfulness, 183, 220
heritage language, 170, 225
heteroglossia, 3

higher order thinking, 40
history, 20–24, 27, 29, 43, 45, 48,
    52, 56, 58–60, 65, 85, 103,
    193, 213, 220, 224–228, 233,
    235, 237, 238, 240, 269,
    271–273, 279, 280, 302
holistic view, 24
homesick, 20
homework, 47, 54, 58, 295
hospital, 64, 67, 68, 71, 78, 79, 92, 94,
    104, 112, 120, 216, 243, 271

I

ice-breaking activity, 184, 218, 264, 276
identity, ix, 13, 14, 23, 120, 168, 175, 225,
    233, 236, 255, chapter 7, 307
ideology, ix, x, 9, 13–15, 60, 61, 115, 118,
    119, 172, 227, chapter 7, 285
idiom, 111, 122, 211
illegibility, 131
immigrant
    population, 17, 122, 228, 230, 263, 270,
        279, 307
    students, 12, 13, 57, 101, 145, 168, 169,
        174, 175, 270
Immigration and Naturalization Service
    (INS), 24, 101, 102, 259
immigration status, 24, 168
improvement, 4, 30, 45, 74, 78–80, 87, 95,
    103, 119, 120, 156, 205, 249, 250
inauthentic writing, 241–243
independence, 54, 99, 166, 178,
    221, 275, 278
individualism, 51, 138, 264
indoctrination, 13–15, 115, 117, 118, 172,
    276, 282, 297
industry, 25, 26, 34, 39, 54, 60, 61, 277, 278
inferiority, 115, 261, 280, 299
informal English, 124, 198, 225
information gathering, 204, 205, 215,
    216, 236, 244
innovation, 40, 297
insecurity, 24, 132
insight, 31, 33, 54, 236
integration, 169, 226, 228
intellectual property, 98
intelligence, 16, 108, 120, 167, 177, 230,
    234, 236, 272, 285
internalization, 142, 187, 236, 262, 275
Internet, 147–150, 155, 296, 301
internship, 24, 25, 56, 64

intimidation, 178, 224
intuition, 31, 54, 234, 247
invention technique, 189, 252
isolation, 103, 152, 162, 175,
    178, 265, 267, 268, 284

J

"Jap", 224
jargon, 81, 119, 185, 203, 207, 209, 236, 249
jigsaw exercises, 41
job training, 65, 83, 137, 139
joking, 47, 64, 71, 122, 168, 224, 299
journal, 20, 21, 72 ,77, 84, 94, 95,
    98, 141, 179, 189, 194, 195,
    197, 202, 235, 247, 259, 295, 300

L

lab report, 22, 27, 28, 42, 193,
    196, 233, 237, 241
language card, 168
lawyers, 24
layered text, 213
leadership, 118, 135, 267
learned dependence, 256, 278
learning community, 267
learning curve, 136
learning style, 255
legal document, 68, 69, 83, 113, 199
legitimate peripheral
    participation, 255, 262
length of text
    minimum pages, 188, 247
    maximum pages, 141, 191, 204,
        205, 247, 303
    produced, 85, 141, 193,
        238, 249, 251
    to read, 97, 296
letter to the editor, 189, 193,
    198, 251, 302
library, 45, 46, 52, 55, 67, 84, 104, 125,
    127, 202, 203, 226, 244, 259, 301
licensing exam, 69, 72, 74, 112, 270
limit situation, 284
listening, 46, 55, 75, 78, 80, 169,
    171, 215, 217, 244,
    266, 276, 296
literature review, 194
logic, 45, 214, 223
logistics, 141, 162, 165
lonely cactus, 275
lounge, 68, 183

M

machine grading, 73–75
major program
  and group work, 53, 135–138, 165
  and writing, 2, 7, 67, 78, 111, 143,
      148, 155, 187, 191–193,
      195, 197, 199,
      210, chapter 6]
  culture, 59, 68, 70, 106, 109, 119, 126,
      132, 134, 145, 160, 161, 175, 182,
      183, 263, 264, 267, 287, 289
management class, 129, 167, 302
marketing, 138, 140, 141, 144, 147–151,
    153, 155, 156, 162, 163, 168, 173,
    174, 233, 247, 278
masks, 127, 139
mathematics, 20, 22, 56,
    124, 129, 300
maturity, 63, 135
MBA program, 136, 137
mechanical error, 39, 43, 53
memorization, 48, 70, 99, 131, 132,
    148, 213, 246, 280, 295
meningitis, 64
mentoring, 72, 221, 282
metacognition, 203
metaphor, 190, 214
microbiology, 27, 30
mitigation, 203
MLA style, 189
model minority, 228, 279
modeling, 186, 206, 215
motivation
  of faculty, 196, 202, 272, 273
  of students, 41, 66, 120, 144, 156,
    177, 187, 226, 242,
    256, 265, 274
movie, 110, 129, 136, 167, 176
multiculturalism, 276
multiple choice, 69, 74, 123, 125, 126,
    131, 180, 222, 301
music class, 141, 156

N

neatness, 38
needs analysis, 281
newspaper, 45, 60, 233
nonparticipation, 219
note taking, 80, 83, 131, 217,
    218, 235, 244, 296, 300, 301
novel, 214, 223

nursing, chapter 3, 167, 178, 185,
    199, 233, 238, 243–246, 256,
    257, 264, 265, 268–271, 273,
    277, 278, 300, 303, 307
Nursing Care Plan (NCP), 69, 78, 83,
    84, 87, 90–97, 101, 102, 105,
    110, 233, 238, 241, 243,
    245, 246, 300

O

organization
  and personality, 179, 217, 221, 258
  of academic program, 53, 266
  of lecture, 107
  of written work, 37, 44, 45, 84,
    86, 100, 189, 191, 211,
    214, 239, 241,
    245–248, 252, 283
  or group, 26, 61, 153, 177, 184, 199,
    215, 216, 218, 241, 242
Other, 15, 229, 261, 268, 277–281
outline, 115, 159, 196, 210, 211, 249
overload, 159
ownership, 156, 200–202, 250, see also
    authorial voice

P

page limit, see *length restrictions*
paraphrasing, 143, 189, 190, 238
pass/fail, 133
passivity, 280
paternalism, 100, 102
pathology, 66, 69, 99
pediatrics, 64, 74–76, 79,
    108, 113, 120
perception is reality, 138, 139
permanent resident, 25, 124, 168
personality, 255, 273, 296
persuasive writing, 235, 246, 252, 305
phonetic alphabet, 79
physics, 27, 28, 30
placement exam, 65, 83
plagiarism, 93, 97, 100, 130, 143, 152, 249
policing role, 128, 196–199, 237
political science, 189, 193, 210,
    212, 213, 221, 222, 223, 237,
    240, 251, 252, 302
popular culture, 138
popular literature, 2, 214
portfolio, 200–203, 207, 235, 303
poverty, 175, 214, 228, 279

power
  differential, 15, 101, 175, 274,
    282, 300, 303
  having, 175, 223, 266, 275
  lack of, 15, 16, 61, 101,
    204, 274, 299
  of community, 121, 278
  using, 166, 181, 273, 278, 280
practice, 33, 94, 95, 139, 142, 158,
  204, 205, 226, 239, 241, 248,
  249, 253, 302
pregnancy, 77, 80, 105, 108, 110
prejudice, 16, 113, 115, 133, 175, 299
presentation, 26, 36, 83, 85, 98,
  104–106, 138, 141, 159,
  195, 215, 220, 254,
  292, 296, 304
pressure, 71, 73, 95, 98, 99, 101,
  108, 120, 212, 257
problem set, 22, 27, 47, 57
procedural knowledge, 27, 28, 33
process recording, 203, 204, 206
professional training, 9, 25, 35, 66, 68,
  184–187, 197, 200, 203–207, 209,
  214, 216, 218, 234, 244, 246, 296
proficiency, ix, 12, 14, 45, 66, 80, 87, 95,
  96, 111, 113, 143, 238, 253
pronunciation, 65, 78, 79, 82, 83,
  87, 119, 122, 254
proofreading, 43, 58
proper names, 60, 212
psychology, 27, 28, 55, 124, 180, 193
pushed output, 239, 246, 247

Q

quiz, 23, 28, 60, 100, 126, 213,
  268, 288, 302

R

RA, see *resident assistant*
racism, 67, 134, see also *bigotry*
  and *ethnicity*
realistic projects, 40
reciprocity, 103, 107
reference guide, 35–37, 238
reflection, 32, 33, 60, 95, 96, 179, 182,
  194, 200, 203, 205, 206, 215, 241,
  245, 247, 259, 261
reinforcement, 33, 103, 115, 239
religion class, 130, 133–135, 140, 141,
  144–147, 156, 160, 307

repetition, 21, 66, 69, 78, 79, 91,
  93–95, 97, 109, 122, 126, 171,
  202, 246, 248, 250
reputation, 20, 50, 81
resentment, 19, 92, 104
resident assistant (RA), 127, 128,
  133, 135, 160–162, 266
resistance, 4, 119, 263, 265, 277–282
resource, 119, 170, 215, 216, 226, 227,
  242, 250, 291
respect, 175, 186, 219, 266, 272, 274, 303
responsibility, 64, 71, 96, 100, 122, 135,
  136, 164, 266, 273, 290, 306
retention, 60, 285
revision, 41, 84, 88, 95, 141–143, 156,
  197, 198, 212, 249, 287
rhetorical features of writing, 36, 37,
  90, 95, 168, 191, 203, 235, 245,
  246, 284, 305
rhetorical knowledge, 284
robot, 28
Roe v. Wade, 222
role model, 174, see also *modeling*
role play, 48, 194, 215, 228

S

safety, 68, 75, 92, 115
sarcasm, 122, 166, 176
scaffolding, 155, 191, 206, 244, 262
self-confidence, see *confidence*
self-disclosure, 185
self-esteem, 182, 225
self-reliance, 54
sensitivity, 60, 112, 171, 177,
  183, 222, 228, 284, 303
short answer, 28, 85, 125, 180, 193, 233
sign language, see *American Sign
  Language*
single parent, 77, 178, 182, 184
situated learning, 241, 242, 253, 262, 275
slang, 112, 122
slavery, 48
social justice, 16, 279, 281
social motive, 242
social services, 215, 216, 279, 282
social turn, 262
social work, chapter 5, 233, 238,
  244, 245, 252, 254, 256, 264,
  268–270, 272, 277, 279, 280,
  301, 303, 304
socialism, 276

socioacademic relationships, 13, 14,
    16, 55, 62, 67, 102, 106, 107,
    160, 175, 216–219, 231, 233, 255,
    chapter 7, 285, 297, 306
sociocultural theory, 253, 262,
    263, 274, 307
sociology, 65, 67, 85, 193, 233
solidarity, 52, 62
speech defect, 79
speech pathology clinic, 79
speed, see *delivery speed*
spelling, 53, 86, 138, 147,
    157, 158, 212
standard English, 96, 158, 239, 254
standards, 186, 253, 257
stereotype, 16, 128, 228, 230,
    273, 274, 279, 281, 305
stress, 68, 70, 71, 83, 98, 101,
    102, 185, 187, 197
subject matter knowledge,
    237, 240, 284
subtractive bilingualism, 170
Super Bowl, 138, 174
supervision, 48–50, 53, 100, 166, 269
support group, 203, 204, 210
syllabus, 5, 84, 138, 209, 219,
    256, 288, 302
symbolic mediation, 273, 275
synonyms, 29
syntactic encoding, 239

                T

TA, 28, 129, 137, 224
teamwork, 138, 164, 166
technical language, 81, 82, 93, 95,
    96, 118, 136
television, 117, 118, 160, 174, 178
Test of English as a Foreign Language
    (TOEFL), 83, 122, 124, 179
text length, see *length restrictions*
textbook, 23, 24, 47, 48, 57, 80, 81, 93,
    97, 98, 100, 101, 106, 119, 135, 159,
    160, 182, 214, 223, 272, 291, 296,
    302
theater, 48
time
    constraints, 2, 4, 49, 54, 55, 74, 79, 98,
        100, 111, 118, 147, 171, 212,
        250, 254, 256, 257
    consuming, 24, 27, 53, 57, 79, 87, 92,
        156, 233, 248, 258, 259

management, 72, 83, 84, 91,
    92, 95, 143, 146, 153,
    174, 198, 297
on, 50–52, 76, 102, 122, 186, 215
on assignment, 87–92, 97, 101,
    102, 134, 148, 156, 164,
    188, 200, 206, 210, 218,
    221, 239, 248, 249, 284
waste of, 26, 39, 83, 84, 87, 92,
    94, 98, 107, 140, 142,
    160, 184, 197, 216, 217,
    231, 246, 247, 284
tolerance, 111, 113
training camp, 26
transfer of learning, 238, 239, 305
transformation, 11–13, 15, 121,
    137, 244, 262, 299
translation, 28, 65, 80, 82, 179, 207, 225
trickery, 11, 30, 126, 129, 273, 295, 296
trivia, 60
tuition, 256
tutor, 83, 134, 140, 142, 152, 190, 207,
    211, 240, 250, 253, 304
TV, see *television*

                U

university housing, 17, 89
urban legend, 173
utilitarian, 122

                V

validity, 38, 42, 137, 158
values, 9, 14, 15, 169, 172, 173, 176, 183,
    186, 199, 213, 219, 227, 228, 236,
    241, 253, 261, 278, 281
victim, 118, 241, 273, 281
video, 26, 60, 61, 110, 119, 174, 277
visa, 24, 55, 124
vocabulary, 296
    developing, 45, 78, 87, 185, 239, 283, 284
    disciplinary, 81, 82, 95, 111, 131, 155, 184,
        185, 207, 209, 211, 212, 225, 252
    lack of, 29, 55, 170, 172, 188, 207, 222,
        225
volunteer work, 92, 215, 216, 225, 243, 255

                W

welcoming students, 104, 111,
    172, 184, 218, 220, 230, 270
welfare, 178, 215

work ethic, 172, 226, see also *hard work*
workplace writing, 241, 242
writing center, 3, 6, 9, 289, 306
   helpful, 83, 84, 89, 134, 139–142,
       144, 152, 155, 156, 175,
       190, 210, 211, 250, 285
   not helpful, 189, 207, 211, 250
   not used, 44, 147, 250

writing manual, 35–39, 44, 158, 246
writing process knowledge, 284
writing to learn, 234, 248

Z

zone of proximal development, 98, 262